In this second volume of music analyses, Ian Bent provides a further selection of newly translated writings of nineteenth-century music critics and theorists, including composers such as Wagner, Schumann and Berlioz, and critics such as A. B. Marx and E. T. A. Hoffmann. Where Volume I, on Fugue, Form and Style, presented nineteen analyses of a technical nature, all the writing here involves a metaphorical style of verbalised description, some pure examples and some hybrid forms mixed with technical analysis. The music analysed is amongst the best-known in the repertoire: Wagner writes on Beethoven's Ninth Symphony, E. T. A. Hoffmann on the Fifth, Schumann writes on Berlioz, and Berlioz on Meyerbeer. Professor Bent presents each analysis with its own detailed introduction and each is amplified by supporting information in footnotes.

CAMBRIDGE READINGS IN THE LITERATURE OF MUSIC

General Editors: John Stevens and Peter le Huray

Music Analysis in the Nineteenth Century
Volume II: Hermeneutic Approaches

CAMBRIDGE READINGS IN THE LITERATURE OF MUSIC

Cambridge Readings in the Literature of Music is a series of source materials (original documents in English translation) for students of the history of music. Many of the quotations in the volumes are substantial, and introductory material places the passages in context. The period covered will be from antiquity to the present day, with particular emphasis on the nineteenth and twentieth centuries.

Already published:

Music Analysis in the Nineteenth Century

Volume II
Hermeneutic Approaches

Edited by

Ian Bent
Columbia University, New York

CAMBRIDGE
UNIVERSITY PRESS

CAMBRIDGE UNIVERSITY PRESS
Cambridge, New York, Melbourne, Madrid, Cape Town, Singapore, São Paulo

Cambridge University Press
The Edinburgh Building, Cambridge CB2 2RU, UK

Published in the United States of America by Cambridge University Press, New York

www.cambridge.org
Information on this title: www.cambridge.org/9780521461832

First published 1994
This digitally printed first paperback version 2005

A catalogue record for this publication is available from the British Library

Library of Congress Cataloguing in Publication data

Music Analysis in the Nineteenth Century
   p.   cm. (Cambridge readings in the literature of music)
Includes bibliographical references and index.
Contents: v. 1. Fugue, form and style –
v. 2. Hermeneutic approaches.
1. Musical analysis – 19th century.   2. Music – History and criticism.
I. Bent, Ian.   II. Title: Music Analysis in the Nineteenth Century.   III. Series.
MT90.M88 1993 781'.09'034   93–12313
ISBN 0 521 46183 9 (v. 2 : hardback)

ISBN-13 978-0-521-46183-2 hardback
ISBN-10 0-521-46183-9 hardback

ISBN-13 978-0-521-67347-1 paperback
ISBN-10 0-521-67347-X paperback

In memory of Peter le Huray,
who lived to see this volume in typescript

Contents

Preface to volumes I and II

'Never confuse analysis with mere description!', Hans Keller used waggishly to say, chastising unfortunate speakers at conferences. To Keller, most so-called 'criticism' and 'analysis' was an amalgam of the descriptive and the metaphorical: 'The descriptive is senseless, the metaphorical usually nonsense.' Most analytical writings boiled down to 'mere tautological descriptions'. Not even Tovey was beyond reproach: 'his "analyses" are misnomers', Keller remarked; they were in his view 'faultless descriptions' with 'occasional flashes of profound analytical insight'; otherwise they contained 'much eminently professional tautology'.[1] More recently, V. Kofi Agawu has taken one analyst to task for failing to observe 'the distinction between description and analysis, between a critical, necessarily impressionistic commentary and a rigorous interpretative exercise . . .'[2]

With censure such as this, what justification is there for entitling the contents of these two volumes 'Music *Analysis* in the Nineteenth Century'? There are in fact two justifications, one intentional, the other actual.

First, it is upon 'analysis' that most of the authors represented in these volumes considered they were engaged. Thus, analysing is what Berlioz thought he was doing when he wrote about Beethoven's nine symphonies in 1838 ('Nous allons essayer l'analyse des symphonies de ce grand maître'), and when he reviewed the first performance of Meyerbeer's *Les Huguenots* on 6 March 1836, and later its score. 'Analysis' is what Momigny set out to do with the first movement of Mozart's D minor string quartet ('Analyse du beau Quatuor en ré mineur du célèbre Mozart') and Haydn's 'Drumroll' Symphony; it is what Reicha sought to do with harmonic, melodic and contrapuntal models in all three of his major treatises; what Fétis claimed to have done with the late string quartets of Beethoven, and what von Lenz promised his readers in his treatment of Beethoven's sonatas for piano. Basevi claimed to have 'analysed' the operas of Verdi in 1859 (he called the process 'critica analitica'), and Beethoven's string quartets Op. 18 in 1874 ('analisi dei sei quartetti'). So too did Sechter in his examination of Mozart's 'Jupiter' Finale in 1843 ('Analyse der Mozartschen Instrumentalfuge'), Dehn in his studies of three fugues from Bach's *Well-tempered Clavier* in 1858 ('zu analysiren und in Betracht ihres Baues kritisch zu beleuchten'[3]), Lobe in 1850 and Helm

---

1 Quoted from Hans Keller, 'K.503: The Unity of Contrasting Themes and Movements – I', *Music Review*, 17 (1956), 48–9; these views, always trenchantly put, are widespread in his writings.
2 *Music Analysis*, 7 (1988), 99: review of W. Frisch, *Brahms and the Principle of Developing Variation* (Berkeley: University of California Press, 1984).
3 'to analyse and illuminate critically in regard to their construction': the editor (Foreword) reporting Dehn's intentions before he died.

in 1885 in their studies of works by Beethoven, and Kretzschmar in his 'analytische Bestrebungen'.[4]

Nor was this corporate expression of purpose limited to cognate forms of the Greek word *Analysis*. A multitude of terms existed in the eighteenth and nineteenth centuries by means of which those who subjected musical fabrics, configurations, structures and styles to close scrutiny might designate what they were doing: in French, *décomposer, dégager, expliquer*; in German, *auffassen, betrachten, beurtheilen, entdecken, enträthseln, erklären, erläutern, phrasiren, zergliedern, zerlegen* – to mention only a few. Each of these terms had its own special implication, each formed part of a terminological network, each belonged to a particular array of time and space. The principal terms will be discussed at strategic points in the introductions and editorial material below.

Most of the writers represented in the present volumes characterize their work in some such terms. Surprisingly, A. B. Marx is an exception. His minutely detailed descriptions of musical formations, in his manual of composition as well as his volumes on Beethoven's works, are couched in synthetic rather than analytic terms – they are phrased constructively rather than deconstructively. (Where he used the German term *Analyse*, it was in reference to the work of others not himself, specifically that of Berlioz and Ulïbïshev.[5]) His case demonstrates that the absence of such defining terms by no means necessarily signals absence of analytical material. Nor does it for that matter imply a desire to avoid self-characterization. In the case of E. T. A. Hoffmann, for example, whose descriptions are at times highly detailed and technical, it reflects perhaps a mastery of language and a lack of self-consciousness about what he is doing.

None of this would, of course, have mollified Hans Keller, who saw the confusion as lying not in the realm of public perception, but in the mind of each deluded would-be analyst. But to return for a moment to Berlioz: when, confronted by 'bold and imposing' effects in the Act V trio of *Les Huguenots*, Berlioz pleads for 'time to reflect on my impressions', who are we to disparage his intention, which is 'to *analyze* them and *discover their causes*' (my italics)? To be sure, he was not seeking 'the latent elements of the unity of manifest contrasts' (Keller), or 'a precise formulation of norms of dimensional behaviour against which we can evaluate [the composer's] practice' (Kofi Agawu). But he *was* seeking, from an examination of Meyerbeer's complex deployment of forces in the massacre scene of this trio (three soloists and two separate on-stage choruses, with markedly conflicting gestural and emotional characters and contrasting musical styles, orchestra in the pit and brass chorus outside the auditorium) and from study of Meyerbeer's treatment of tonality here (minor key, but with the sixth degree frequently and obdurately raised), to determine precisely how the terrifying and blood-curdling effect that he

---

4   'analytical endeavours': 'Anregungen zur Förderung musikalischer Hermeneutik [I]', *Jahrbuch der Musikbibliothek Peters für 1902*, 9 (1903), 47; later issued in *Gesammelte Aufsätze aus den Jahrbüchern der Musikbibliothek Peters* (Leipzig: Peters, 1911; reprint edn ibid, 1973), p. 168. The first part of this article is translated in Bujić, 114–20.

5   Seemingly without disparagement (*Ludwig van Beethoven: Leben und Schaffen* (Berlin: Otto Janke, 1859), vol. I, p. 295 note). More likely, *Analyse* alludes to their being written in French. Marx occasionally used *zergliedern* and *Zergliederung* for what he himself did.

had observed came about. To take apart, and uncover the prime causes – is that not a type of analytical procedure?

This, then, is the second justification for the entitling of the present volumes: that, irrespective of the name given to them, there were in the nineteenth century species of activity that meet the general criteria of the present day for analysis. Dunsby and Whittall say something of this latter sort in the following statement, while qualifying it with respect to purpose:[6]

> The kind of analysis we would nowadays recognize as 'technical' has been in practice for more than two centuries. Yet it came to be regarded as a discipline apart from compositional theory only at the turn of this century. Around this time, the relationship between traditional analysis and compositional theory ceased to be significantly reflexive.

Their first sentence, however, invokes technicality, and therefore makes a slightly different point from my own. Were we still in the 1960s or 1970s, then our two statements would perhaps be saying the same thing (intentionally or not); but in the world of the 1990s I believe they no longer do this. I shall return to this in a moment.

Consider the latter two sentences of the above quotation. Taken on their own terms, the thesis that they embody is factually disprovable: the analysis of J. S. Bach's *The Art of Fugue* in vol. I, Analysis 3, dating from 1841 and as rigorous and technical as anything presented here, arose in the context not of compositional theory but of historical textuality. It formed the critical commentary to the *Art of Fugue* volume of a collected edition of Bach's keyboard works. Far from being prescriptive, it was an abstract engagement in contrapuntal process – written, as it was, by Moritz Hauptmann, one of the principal theorists of the century but a writer of 'pure' theory rather than compositionally instructional theory. Then again, the analysis of leitmotifs in *Tristan and Isolde* by Karl Mayrberger (vol. I, Analysis 13), dating from 1881 and highly technical, was a contribution not to a composition manual but to a journal intended for amateur devotees of Wagner's music dramas, a contribution that was then turned into a small monograph indicatively titled *The Harmonic Style of Richard Wagner*.

Not that the above disproof invalidates Dunsby's and Whittall's argument. The bulk of technical analysis in the nineteenth century probably did indeed reside within compositional theory. The analyses given in volume I by Reicha, Sechter, Czerny and Lobe certainly did; and those by Vogler, Dehn and Riemann in volume I and Marx in the present volume can be seen as outgrowths of composition manuals already written or edited by those authors. The effect of my disproof is perhaps no more than to set back earlier in time the moment at which the 'reflexivity' between analysis and theory began to break down. Indeed, the continuation of Dunsby's and Whittall's statement invites this very suggestion:

> Analysis became the technical or systematic study, either of the kind of familiar tonal style few composers felt to be current any longer, or of new music that the wider public found profoundly hard to understand, and the challenges of which seemed to focus on the question of whether tonal comprehensibility was present at all.

6   J. Dunsby and A. Whittall, *Music Analysis in Theory and Practice* (London: Faber, 1988), p. 62.

Hauptmann's analysis of *The Art of Fugue* perfectly exemplifies the former, itself an early manifestation of the Bach revival and its author a figure later associated with that movement; and Mayrberger's exemplifies the latter, since it was one of the earliest attempts to tackle the apparent incomprehensibility of Wagner's harmonic idiom, and its author was hailed as the seer who would unlock the technical mysteries of that idiom.

How far back might that moment of break-down then be set? Noting that Gottfried Weber's analysis of the opening of Mozart's 'Dissonance' Quartet (vol. I, Analysis 10) was probably submitted first to his own journal, *Caecilia*, and only subsequently incorporated into the third edition of his composition manual, at least as early as 1830.

But is not this chronological exercise ultimately futile? Perhaps we should address a deeper issue, namely: whether a theorist, when executing an analysis within the environment of a manual of compositional theory, might not temporarily operate as *analyst* rather than as *instructor* – might not, that is, abandon the educational mode of thought for one that is entirely analytical. Given the peculiarly absorbing, compelling, even obsessive nature of musical analysis, is it not possible that he might become drawn into the exhilarations, fascinations and frustrations of the purely analytical process, and forget the educational purpose that he was serving? Would we wish to assert that analysis became fascinating only in the twentieth century? – the question seems somehow absurd! The purpose of this long excursion is only to ask whether technical analysis might psychologically have been analysis *per se* long before it could be said to have cut any umbilical cord previously connecting it to compositional theory.

Dunsby's and Whittall's invocation of the 'technical', to which we can now at last return, was prefatory to a discussion of the work of Donald Francis Tovey (1875–1940). As they say, Tovey brought a modest technical element to his writings on music; nevertheless, he wrote for the musically untrained reader, for the music lover who hated jargon, for what he liked to think of as the 'naïve listener'. Tovey himself, though we tend to overlook the fact nowadays, was heir to a tradition – as were Schoenberg and Schenker to other traditions –: in his case, a tradition of writings for the nineteenth-century musical amateur. This is the unremarked obverse of Dunsby's and Whittall's technical tradition: a body of writings that was almost coeval with Romantic music criticism, and which was from the beginning completely independent of compositional theory. This 'elucidatory' tradition, as I have loosely styled it, sought to explain music in terms of content rather than of sonic fabric. It was Peter Kivy who in 1980 acknowledged the disesteem into which content-based music analysis has fallen in the twentieth century by virtue of its congenital subjectivity, and set himself the challenge of showing:[7]

> that a humanistic musical analysis could be reconstituted and made respectable once again in the form of the familiar emotive characterization of music – but only if two things were established: first, how it makes sense to apply expressive predicates to music (which answers the charge of unintelligibility); and, second, what the public, intersubjective criteria of application are (which answers the charge of subjectivity).

7   P. Kivy, *The Corded Shell: Reflections on Musical Expression* (Princeton: Princeton University Press, 1980), p. 132, also pp. 9–11.

Since that time, others, some of them building on, or influenced by, Joseph Kerman's appeals from the mid-1960s on for a higher form of criticism,[8] have sought to envisage such a 'humanistic' – in contrast to quasi-scientific – mode of analysis. Fred Everett Maus has propounded a type of analysis in which the distinctions between 'structural' and 'emotive', between 'technical' and 'non-technical', are lost; using a dramatic model, he interprets music in terms of 'actions' and 'agents'. The music's structure becomes a 'plot', and the analysis 'narrates' (in the fullest sense of that word) that plot.[9] Marion Guck has for some time been engaged in a systematic investigation of metaphor in analytic discourse about music with a view to locating new modes of description.[10] No longer will a statement such as the following (from Analysis 4 below) be greeted with universal scorn or discomfort:

> The movement begins with strident augmented sixths, like a sudden cry of anguish from the terrified soul. Passagework now follows, which, like some foaming mountain stream, plunges wildly into the chasm below, growls and grumbles in the depths, until at last a figure, tossing back and forth – the first principal theme – breaks away from the whirlpool, eddies up and down, then spouts up roaring in uncontrolled passion, undeterred by the wailing parallel thirds which themselves are dragged into the maelstrom.

These words, a mixture of technicality ('augmented sixths', 'passagework', and the like), simile ('like a sudden cry . . .'), metaphor ('plunges wildly into the chasm below') and partial personification ('roaring in uncontrolled passion'), map the motions of natural phenomena and the human psyche on to the motions of the music in an effort to exteriorize the interior life of that music. The words are by Ernst von Elterlein, a minor mid-nineteenth-century writer on music. Written in 1856, they depict the opening of the Finale of Beethoven's 'Appassionata' Sonata.

A significant group of thinkers is nowadays prepared to acknowledge that figurative writing containing these categories of language usage has a legitimate place in analytical discourse. Such vividly naturalistic images as the above, in such profusion, seem quintessentially Romantic, recalling (to take English examples) the paintings of John Martin or the poetry of Wordsworth and Tennyson (albeit in a debased and only semi-literary form). The 1990s have their own world of images upon which to draw for analytical purposes. The present volumes appear perhaps not inopportunely, displaying as they do a broad range of analytical types from the last century: technically theoretical, compositionally instructive, musicologically historical and metaphorically experiential.

8 J. Kerman, 'A Profile for American Musicology', *JAMS*, 18 (1965), 61–9; *Musicology* (London: Fontana/Collins, 1985), also published as *Contemplating Music* (Cambridge, MA: Harvard University Press, 1985), chap. 3 and *passim*.

9 F. E. Maus, 'Music as Drama', *Music Theory Spectrum*, 10 (1988), 56–73. Maus's approach is informed by the work of Edward T. Cone, *The Composer's Voice* (Berkeley: University of California Press, 1974), and by recent literary theory and narratology, notably by T. Todorov, *Introduction to Poetics* (Minneapolis: University of Minnesota Press, 1981). The term 'plot' was first imported into musical discourse from historian Paul Veyne by Jean-Jacques Nattiez in 'The Concepts of Plot and Seriation Process in Music Analysis', *Music Analysis*, 4 (1985), 107–18.

10 M. A. Guck, e.g. 'Rehabilitating the Incorrigible', in *'Cognitive Communication' about Music*, ed. F. E. Maus and M. A. Guck (Princeton: Princeton University Press, forthcoming); see Guck's notes 19 and 23 for a survey of recent analyses by Cone, Lewin and Treitler that use figurative language, and by Newcomb that uses emotive descriptions. Tangentially, see remarks in my own 'History of Music Theory: Margin or Center?', *Theoria*, 6 (1993), 1–21.

These two volumes differ from others already published in the series *Cambridge Readings in the Literature of Music* not only in their concern with specifically musical rather than aesthetic, social and philosophical issues (something that they share only with vol. II of *Greek Musical Writings*), but also, and most particularly, in the concern of each of the passages presented here with a single piece of music or repertory of pieces. In almost every case, the integrity of the piece or repertory under discussion demanded entire and uncut discussion. The only exceptions are Hans von Wolzogen's thematic guide to Wagner's *Parsifal* (Analysis 6 below), the sheer length of which demanded selection of an excerpt, Lobe's discussion of Beethoven's Quartet Op. 18 no. 2 (vol. I, Analysis 12), which necessitated the excision of much interwoven educational material, and one or two cases in which I have omitted an author's general introduction or a non-analytical interpolation, where these were not essential to the complete discourse.

The result is a pair of volumes with fewer and for the most part longer excerpts than in other volumes of the series. In two cases, what is presented is an entire monograph; in others, an entire chapter or section of a book. Only in the cases of the discussions of Beethoven's three periods by Fétis and Ulïbïshev (vol. I, Analyses 16b and 16d) have I excerpted brief passages in the manner of previous volumes. The two volumes in a sense serve as companions to two earlier ones: *Music and Aesthetics in the Eighteenth and Early-Nineteenth Centuries* by le Huray and Day, which was constructed around the concept of Romanticism, and *Music in European Thought 1851–1912* by Bujić, which delineated a number of themes and issues. In turn, those two volumes provide a wonderful aesthetic backdrop to the present ones that I urge the reader to explore. The four volumes can be viewed together as a subset of the series.

Every effort has been made to provide high-quality texts. Where several primary texts exist, I have usually taken the earliest, consulting first editions if possible and reporting notable differences wherever I also had access to later ones. Where two significantly divergent texts exist, I have again usually adopted the earlier, as in the case of Schumann's analysis of Berlioz's *Symphonie fantastique* (Analysis 10 below), where I have presented the original article from the *Neue Zeitschrift für Musik* of 1835 rather than Schumann's own curtailed text in his collected works of 1854, and the case of Fétis's discussion of the three periods of Beethoven's music, where preservation of the interchange between Fétis and Ulïbïshev dictated my presenting the first edition of the *Biographie universelle*. I have taken a later reading only for a good reason, as in the case of Gottfried Weber's discussion of Mozart's 'Dissonance' Quartet and Mayrberger's of Wagner's *Tristan and Isolde* (vol. I, Analyses 10 and 13), where the second version in each case significantly expands the first. Of von Elterlein I had no choice but to take a later edition, since the first was not accessible to me.

Of the analyses presented in volumes I–II, five originally incorporated the entire text of the music under discussion. In two of those cases, the music is nowadays readily available to non-specialist readers, and has not been included: the first movement of Haydn's 'Drumroll' Symphony (Analysis 8 in the present volume), and the Finale of Mozart's 'Jupiter' Symphony (vol. I, Analysis 4); information supplied by the analyst on the score has been incorporated editorially into the analytical text. In the three remaining cases, the music was supplied in the Appendix to volume I: (a) the fugue from Handel's Harpsichord Suite No. 6 in F♯ minor; (b) the Prelude No. 8 in D minor from Vogler's *Thirty-two Preludes for Organ and Fortepiano*; and (c) the Andante for Wind Quintet by Reicha (vol. I, Analyses 1, 7 and 9).

It is the translator's duty to be faithful to the original-language text throughout. A literal rendering, however, can produce a translated text that is lifeless. At worst, it can lead to a linguistic no-man's land devoid of idiom, character or rhetoric, in which the reader has to infer the original in order to understand the translation. I have sought to catch the spirit of the original as well as its narrow meaning, and at the same time to make my renderings vivid, immediate and enjoyable. I have used footnotes and square-bracketed original words to signal liberties taken, and to alert the reader to the presence of terminological problems. I have also inter-polated page numbers so as to facilitate reference to the original.

While never attempting to produce counterfeit Victorian prose, I have tried to avoid anachronistic twentieth-century terms and expressions. The volume in this series edited by Bojan Bujić was criticized by one reviewer for failing to use contemporary translations where they exist.[11] I take the contrary view. Many nineteenth-century translations of music theory were without literary merit; they were frequently guilty of excessive literalness (the use of 'clang-tone' for the German *Klangton* is a notorious example); moreover, they used technical terms that were current in their own day but now mean little or nothing. Consider the opening of John Bishop's translation of the essay by Weber (vol. I, Analysis 10):

> [Bishop:] It now remains for me to fulfil the promise made at the end of §225 . . . , of presenting an analysis of the texture of the transitions, as well as of the modulatory course and other peculiarities, in the Introduction of Mozart's violin-quartett in C . . .

> [Bent:] All that remains for me at the close of this volume is to discharge the duty that I gave myself at the end of §225 . . . of undertaking an analysis of the intricate web of passing-notes, and at the same time of the tonal scheme and other unusual features of the Introduction to the String Quartet in C by Mozart . . .

For a start, Bishop omits a phrase (*am Schlusse dieses Bandes*). Secondly, by trans-lating *modulatorisch* as 'modulatory' he shows his insensitivity to the distinction between *Ausweichung* and *Modulation*, the former being the term for what in English meant, and means, 'modulation' (for 1832, my 'tonal scheme' for *modula-torischer Gang* is admittedly a shade modern, but it conveys the sense of a difficult phrase more accurately). Thirdly, Bishop's use of 'transition' (which is nowadays a structural-tonal term) for *Durchgang* places a veil between the modern reader and the original German text, as do to a lesser degree the now antiquated term 'violin-quartett', and the archaic usage of 'peculiarities'. It is for these reasons that I also rejected the nineteenth-century translations of Reicha's main treatises, Riemann's *Katechismus der Fugen-Komposition*, Wagner's programme for the Ninth

---

11 Leon Botstein, in *19th-Century Music*, 13 (1989/90), 168–78: 'By retranslating Hanslick and Wagner, we might gain in clarity from a philosophical or revisionist historical point of view. But by abandoning Cohen and Ellis, we would lose the opportunity to use the historical surfaces of semantics and language to illuminate the nature of perceived meanings in the past and to lay bare the historical distance of texts' (p. 174).

Symphony of Beethoven, von Elterlein's *Beethoven's Clavier-Sonaten*, Spitta's Bach volume and von Wolzogen's thematic guide to *Parsifal*. Contemporaneous translations are not a satisfactory means by which to get to know nineteenth-century theoretical works; consider only how badly served has Moritz Hauptmann been with W. E. Heathcote's translation of his *Die Natur der Harmonik und Metrik*,[12] and the adverse effect that that unusable text has had on the understanding of Hauptmann's important theories in the English-speaking world.

There are only four exceptions to my rule of independent translation: the analysis by Czerny, for which the German original was unavailable to me, leaving the text by Merrick and Bishop as my only resort; that by E. T. A. Hoffmann, a translation of which by Martyn Clarke for Cambridge University Press was already underway, where to duplicate this would have been perverse (I greatly appreciate the licence he and his editor David Charlton gave me to make slight modifications to their finished text in the interests of consistency with the rest of my two volumes); and the two analyses in Italian, for which my linguistic abilities were wholly inadequate. I am grateful to Walter Grauberg and Jonathan Shiff for supplying such excellent translations of these, and also for allowing me ultimate control of the text.

My prime debt of gratitude is to the trustees of the Radcliffe Trust, who did me the honour of appointing me the first Radcliffe Fellow in Musicology, so providing me with the year's sabbatical leave, part of it spent at Harvard University, during which this project was conceived and initiated. Two Columbians and one Nottinghamian must be singled out for the special quality of help that they gave me over long periods of time: Thomas Mace, for brilliant detective work in Butler Library, and for bringing his formidable command of languages to bear on many of my translations; Robert Austerlitz, an inexhaustible fount of linguistic knowledge to me over the past five years; and Robert Pascall, my confederate on nineteenth-century matters for so many years. Numerous others have freely given advice, and have supplied me with materials and information. Such assistance is ultimately unaccountable; but where specific account is possible, I have given it in footnotes. Here, I can do no more than call an inevitably incomplete roll of generous-spirited scholars who have aided me: Milton Babbitt, David Bernstein, Julian Budden, Jennifer Day, James Day, John Deathridge, Esther Dunsby, Keith Falconer, Cynthia Gessele, Jennifer Hughes, Peter le Huray, Wulf Liebeschuetz, Lewis Lockwood, C. P. McGill, Karen Painter, Roger Parker, Leeman Perkins, Harold S. Powers, Fritz Reckow, John Reed, Jerome Roche, Janna Saslaw, Desmond Shawe-Taylor, Hinrich Siefken, Elaine Sisman, Maynard Solomon, Glenn Stanley, Richard Taruskin, Joanne Wright and James Zetzel.

Without the assistance of the librarians and staff of the following libraries, my work could not have been done: the Bibliothèque nationale, Paris; the British Library, London; Cambridge University Library (my wonderful summer work-haven!), and the Pendlebury Library, Cambridge University; Columbia University Avery, General and Music Libraries; the Eda Kuhn Loeb and Isham Memorial Libraries of Music, and Widener Library, Harvard University; the New York Public Library; The Nottingham University Arts and Music Libraries; the Österreichische

12 (Leipzig: B&H, 1853; Eng. trans., London: Sonnenschein, 1884, 2/1893).

Nationalbibliothek Musiksammlung, Vienna. I am grateful also to the National Museum of Science and Industry, London, the National Maritime Museum of Greenwich, London, and the William Herschel Society, Bath. These volumes are silent testimony to the toll that academic work is apt to take on home life; I thank my close family, all of whom have been affected in one way or another, and in particular Caroline and Jonathan, who bore the brunt, and gave nothing but love and support in return.

Abbreviations

AmZ	*Allgemeine musikalische Zeitung* (Leipzig)
B&H	Breitkopf und Härtel
Bujić	Bojan Bujić: *Music in European Thought 1851–1912* (Cambridge: CUP, 1988)
HwMT	*Handwörterbuch der musikalischen Terminologie,* ed. H. H. Eggebrecht and others (Wiesbaden: Steiner, 1972–)
JAMS	*Journal of the American Musicological Society*
JMT	*Journal of Music Theory*
le Huray/Day	Peter le Huray and James Day: *Music and Aesthetics in the Eighteenth and Early-Nineteenth Centuries* (Cambridge: CUP, 1981)
MGG	*Die Musik in Geschichte und Gegenwart,* ed. F. Blume (Kassel and Basel: Bärenreiter, 1949–69)
NGDM	*The New Grove Dictionary of Music and Musicians,* ed. S. Sadie (London: Macmillan, 1980)
NZM	*Neue Zeitschrift für Musik*
OED	*Oxford English Dictionary,* 12 vols (Oxford: Clarendon Press, 1933)
64^2	the second beat of b. 64
$^3 17$	the third beat of the bar preceding b. 17

General introduction

§1 The two opposing principles of music analysis

The General Introduction to volume I of the present work opened with Jérôme-Joseph de Momigny's self-important proclamation in 1803 of a new kind of music theory. Momigny's implementation of that theory foreshadowed to a remarkable degree the tendency of nineteenth-century theory to resort more and more to analysis. However, while that implementation typified the newly dawning one, the theory itself typified the outgoing era: the frame of mind in which Momigny wrote was explicitly that of 'the man of enlightenment', and his theory was rooted in the Enlightenment's reliance upon exact observation of natural phenomena, upon empirical sensationism – upon, in short, the *scientific* mode of viewing the world. Fairly or unfairly, we used Momigny as the paradigm for that scientific impulse toward musical phenomena which, already strong in the eighteenth century, continued through the nineteenth and on into the twentieth. To a greater or lesser extent, all the analyses presented in volume I, and especially those in Parts I and II of that volume, were imbued with the impulse to describe exactly, to measure, to quantify, the material attributes of music – its sounding phenomena (the Greek plural 'phenomena' means 'things that appear', 'appearances').

Volume II is driven by the opposite impulse. All of its analyses – again to greater or lesser extent (and ironically they include an analysis by Momigny, one of only two writers to be represented in both volumes) – are imbued with the impulse to *interpret* rather than to describe. Their concern is with the *inner life* of the music rather than with its outward, audible form. They strive to transcend that outer form and penetrate the non-material interior. Here the inscription on Sir William Herschel's telescope, *coeli munimente perrupit* ('it has pierced the walls of the heavens'), quoted by von Lenz in Analysis 16c of volume I, takes on a new aspect. Rather than bursting the barriers of the visible world to attain new scientific discoveries beyond, as Herschel intended, they penetrate the audible exterior so as to attain human discoveries within.[1] This new and opposite impulse is called the *hermeneutic principle*. While only one of the authors presented in volume II used the term 'hermeneutics' and showed an explicit awareness of the broader field of hermeneutic thought, all of them were, though to greatly varying extents, and though they themselves belonged to different traditions of music-theoretical thought, motivated by this hermeneutic impulse.

---

[1] To be fair, von Lenz was using the inscription not for new scientific discoveries but for Beethoven's reaching of his third style.

§2 General hermeneutics: the beginnings

> There are two classes of interpreters [within hermeneutics] who can be distinguished by their procedures. The one class directs its attention almost exclusively to the linguistic relations of a given text. The other pays more attention to the original psychic process of producing and combining ideas and images.

Thus declared Friedrich Schleiermacher (1768–1834), the Protestant theologian and philologist, in an address to the Berlin Academy of Sciences in 1829. The extremes of both approaches are, in Schleiermacher's view, dangerous. The interpreter who bases his interpretation of a literary work exclusively on a precise examination of language, while having no sense of the life of the author's mind, exhibits what 'we call "pedantry"'. On the other hand, he who concentrates on the author's psychological processes to the neglect of linguistic matters 'we have to call by a name that has been used . . . in the sphere of artistic productivity . . .: he is a "nebulist"'. To ensure a balanced approach, Schleiermacher advises would-be interpreters to work at both 'sides of the mountain'.[2]

Hermeneutics has its origin in *hermeneia*, Greek for interpretation, on which subject Aristotle wrote a major treatise, *Peri hermeneias*. The word derives from *hermeios*, the priest at the Delphic oracle, and is said (perhaps fancifully) to relate back to the winged messenger-god Hermes. Its earliest use in modern times may be the title of Johann Conrad Dannhauer's *Sacred Hermeneutics, or Method of Expounding Sacred Writings*, dating from 1654.[3] During the late seventeenth and eighteenth centuries hermeneutics existed as a number of separate but related fields, most significantly biblical hermeneutics, classical literary hermeneutics and juridical hermeneutics. Among the countless publications during this period, especially in Protestant north Germany, three important ones can be singled out: Johann Heinrich Ernesti's *On the Nature and Constitution of Secular Hermeneutics* of 1699, Johann August Ernesti's *Textbook for the Interpreter of the New Testament* of 1761, both in Latin and Johann Martin Chladenius's (i.e. Chladni's) *Introduction to the Correct Interpretation of Rational Discourses and Writings* of 1742, the first systematic treatise in German.[4] The last of these works introduced the notion of the unique 'point of view' (*Sehe-Punkt*), and posited that the prime cause of misunderstanding of a thing was the differences that arise between points of view of

---

2   Schleiermacher delivered two addresses in 1829: 12 August and 29 October. Together, they outlined – and were the first public declaration of – the theory of hermeneutics that he had been formulating since 1805. See *Hermeneutics: the Handwritten Manuscripts*, Eng. trans. James Duke and H. Jackson Forstman, American Academy of Religion Texts and Translation Series, vol. 1 (Missoula, MT: Scholars Press, 1977), pp. 175–214, esp. pp. 204–05. Other dates cited in notes below refer to earlier and later manuscript materials.

3   *Hermeneutica sacra sive methodus exponendarum sacrarum litterarum* (Strasbourg: Staedellius, 1654).

4   *De natura et constitutione hermeneuticae profanae* (Leipzig: n.p., 1699); *Institutio interpretis novi testamenti* (Leizpig: le Mair, 1761, 2/1762), later much cited by Schleiermacher, and of which two English translations appeared during the nineteenth century – Moses Stuart, *Elements of Interpretation* (Andover: Flagg and Gould, 1822), and Charles H. Terrot, *Principles of Biblical Interpretation* (Edinburgh: T. Clark, 1832–3); *Einleitung zur richtigen Auslegung vernünftiger Reden und Schriften* (Leipzig, 1742; reprint edn Düsseldorf: Stern, 1969), two sections of which appear in English in *The Hermeneutics Reader*, ed. and trans. Kurt Mueller-Vollmer (New York: Continuum, 1992), pp. 55–71.

that thing. Chladenius was a pioneer in seeking to recast the heterogeneous field of hermeneutics as a single general field. What he failed to do in 1742 Schleiermacher succeeded in doing between 1805 and 1833, assimilating biblical, classical and juridical hermeneutics and at the same time extending far beyond that – he imagined its being applied to oriental literature, for example, to German Romantic literature (significantly, as we will see) and ultimately to all kinds of text.[5]

In unifying the field, he drew on the work of two now largely forgotten philologists, Friedrich Ast (1778–1841) and Friedrich August Wolf (1759–1824), the latter of whom had defined hermeneutics in 1807 as 'the art of discovering with necessary insight the thoughts contained in the work of an author',[6] and had articulated the underlying notion that every text, whatever its language, and however close to or remote from our experience, is in some degree 'foreign' to us and demands to be 'understood'. This notion of 'understanding' (*Verstand*, the capacity to understand; *Verstehen*, the act of understanding) is central to hermeneutics. It is as well for us to try to distinguish here four disciplines that existed side by side in the eighteenth century: *philology* was the study of language, and focused on characteristics of discourse that were common to a culture; *criticism* was the detection of defects in a text and the restoration of damaged passages (in modern parlance, this is still precisely what distinguishes a '*critical* edition' from any other edition);[7] *exegesis* was the expounding of the possible meanings of words and phrases in a text, and centred upon the text itself rather than the author. *Hermeneutics*, by contrast, treated text as message; its concern lay with the intention of the author; its purpose was to facilitate understanding; as Chladenius declared, it was 'a discipline in itself, not in part, and can be assigned its place in accordance with the teachings of psychology'.[8] Hermeneutics started with the 'distance' (Wolf's 'foreign'-ness) that separated reader from author; it took as its premise that misunderstanding was more likely to arise than not to arise;[9] only by neutralizing this 'distance', which could be done solely by entering the mind of the author – Wolf's 'necessary insight' (*Einsicht*, literally 'seeing-into', the very power that the *hermeios* possessed) –, could one eliminate all misunderstanding.

Schleiermacher identified two distinct modes of extracting such 'insight' from a text: the *comparative* method and the *divinatory* method. To gain insight into a given passage by the former involves locating similar passages elsewhere in the work,

5 Schleiermacher, *Hermeneutics*, pp. 178–9 (1829).
6 *die Kunst, die Gedanken eines Schriftstellers aus dessen Vortrage mit nothwendiger Einsicht aufzufinden*: 'Darstellung der Alterthums-Wissenschaft nach Begriff, Umfang, Zweck und Werth', in *Museum der Altertums-Wissenschaft*, 1 (1807), 37, quoted in Schleiermacher's first address (see *Hermeneutics*, p. 180); Schleiermacher questions the necessity of insight in all cases (ibid, 183–4). The definition is embedded in a remark that hermeneutics was still searching for a widely based theoretical foundation 'in studies of the nature of the meanings of a word, the sense of a sentence, the coherence of an utterance, and many other points in *grammatical*, *rhetorical* and *historical interpretation*' (italics original).
7 Even Droysen, in lectures delivered from 1857 onwards, used to teach that 'Criticism has done away with all sorts of imperfections and impurities which the material initially had. Not only has it purified and verified them, but it has organized them so that they may lie well ordered before us.' (*The Hermeneutics Reader*, p. 127)
8 *Einleitung*, in *The Hermeneutics Reader*, p. 60.
9 Schleiermacher, *Hermeneutics*, p. 110 (1819): 'the assumption that misunderstanding occurs as a matter of course, and so understanding must be willed and sought at every point'.

in other works by the same author and in works by kindred authors, and then filling in the gaps in understanding by inferring from these similar passages. To do so by the 'divinatory' – i.e. prophetic, oracular, presentient – method involves the interpreter's standing outside himself and entering into the mind of the author, so grasping the author's personality and state of mind from within.[10] The first of these methods is at its most efficacious when dealing with an author whose works adhere to a tradition, the second method when dealing with an 'author of genius' (*genialer Autor*) – an author who coins new language and conceives novel ideas.[11] Since in reality all texts occupy a position somewhere between these two extremes, the interpreter always uses both methods.

§3 The hermeneutic circle

More than that, though. It is characteristic of hermeneutics that the interpreter *shifts constantly between one method and the other*. We can relate this notion to our opening quotation from Schleiermacher and say that the interpreter *shuttles back and forth* between the *linguistic* relations of a text and its *psychic* process – what Schleiermacher more frequently called the 'grammatical' aspect and the 'psychological' (or 'technical') aspect. The first of these aspects views a given utterance in relation to the general, impersonal language system of which it forms a part; the second views it in relation to the mental world of its author, his inner life, his personal history. These two aspects of a text, and consequently the two methods of seeking insight, complement one another, yet by their very nature the two aspects cannot be held in view simultaneously since each obscures the other; oscillation between them is the only possibility for joint consideration. Eventually such oscillation results in their fusing into a single, unified interpretation of the text. This back-and-forth exemplifies a process that is at the very heart of hermeneutics: the process, first stated by Ast, of the *hermeneutic circle*.[12]

The image conveyed by this phrase is that of an interpreter whose actions are in constant circular orbit – an orbit that intersects on one side with a particular object, and on the other with a more general and related set of objects. A good example would be the message of the New Testament, over against the sum total of messages transmitted by Greek and Hebrew texts of the time; or more narrowly one

---

10   ibid, 42 (1805: 'In interpretation it is essential that one be able to step out of one's own frame of mind into that of the author'), 150 (1819: 'By leading the interpreter to transform himself, so to speak, into the author, the divinatory method seeks to gain an immediate comprehension of the author as an individual'), 185 (1829: 'a divinatory certainty which arises when an interpreter delves as deeply as possible into an author's state of mind'), 192 ('to reconstruct the creative act that begins with the generation of thoughts which captivate the author and to understand how the requirement of the moment could draw upon the living treasure of words in the author's mind in order to produce just this way of putting it and no other'). This idea is adumbrated in Wolf, 'Darstellung' (37–8), and divination discussed (40).

11   Schleiermacher, *Hermeneutics*, pp. 192 (1829); 102–03 (1819: 'The term "absolute" is reserved for statements that achieve a maximum of both linguistic creativity and individuality: works of genius [*das Genialische*].')

12   ibid, 100, 113, 115–16 (1819), 190–96 (1829: where the idea is attributed to Ast with the classic statement: 'just as the whole is understood from the parts, so the parts can be understood only from the whole').

particular message from the New Testament, over against the totality of messages transmitted by that work. Hermeneutic writers generalize these polar opposites as *part* over against *whole*, or as *subjective* over against *objective*, either of which is easier for the music analyst to grasp. A model for the implementation of the circle is Schleiermacher's own analysis of Plato's *Republic*:[13]

> He started [writes Dilthey] with a survey of the structure, comparable to a superficial reading, tentatively grasped the whole context, illuminated the difficulties and halted thoughtfully at all those passages which afforded insight into the composition. Only then did interpretation proper begin.

None of the three writers cited so far, Ast, Wolf or Schleiermacher, investigated music interpretation; nevertheless, it is not difficult for us to translate their images into musical terms, nor is it unreasonable since Schleiermacher argued for the subjection of spoken as well as written language to the processes of hermeneutics, and did at least once allude to such processes in music and painting.[14] Thus we can translate their whole-and-parts image into that of a listener-interpreter who has expectations of a musical composition that he is about to hear – expectations of the whole that are based on his prior knowledge of the piece's declared form or genre – and who then, as he hears the moment-to-moment details of the piece in performance, repeatedly shifts back to his expectation and modifies it, this modified view of the whole in turn colouring the way he hears the subsequent particulars; and so on, back and forth, until the end is reached, when preconception of the whole and experience of the bar-by-bar details fuse into a single, fully mediated understanding of the work. (Such a process is almost perfectly exemplified by Marx's interpretation of Beethoven's Ninth Symphony (1859), given below, Analysis 12.)

Nor is it difficult to translate these three writers' objective–subjective image into music, envisaging a reviewer-interpreter or an analyst-interpreter who examines a score for what musicians might call its 'technical' features – its phrase structure, themes and motifs, harmonic syntax, modulatory plan, rhythmic scheme, etc. (quite the opposite of what Schleiermacher meant by 'technical'!) –, who equally and intermittently seeks to transport himself into the composer's mind to 'divine' the psychological motivation behind such writing, and who allows each stage of investigation to inform the succeeding, opposite stage. Successfully concluded, the product of this oscillatory process would be a psychological understanding of the work that included *but transcended* a technical understanding of the same work. (There are elements of such an interpretation in E. T. A. Hoffmann's multi-layered essay on Beethoven's Fifth Symphony (1810), Analysis 9 below; perhaps a more definitive example is the essay on Beethoven's String Quartet Op. 132 (1885), Analysis 13, below, by Helm, half of whose attention is constantly on the issue of intentionality.)

---

13 Description by Dilthey in a lecture to the Prussian Academy of Sciences in 1896/97, published as 'Die Entstehung der Hermeneutik', in *Philosophische Abhandlungen, Christoph Sigwart zu seinem 70. Geburtstag 28. März 1900 gewidmet* (Tübingen, 1900), pp. 185–202; *Gesammelte Schriften*, vol. v (Leipzig and Berlin: Teubner, 1924), pp. 317–31; Eng. trans. H. P. Rickman in W. *Dilthey: Selected Writings* (Cambridge: CUP, 1976), pp. 246–63, the quoted passage on p. 259.

14 Schleiermacher, *Hermeneutics*, p. 105 (1819); on oral language, see ibid, e.g. 109 (1819), 200 (1829).

To return now to general hermeneutics, in the following statement the two images, whole-and-parts, and objective–subjective, coexist:[15]

> The ultimate goal of technical [i.e. psychological] interpretation is nothing other than a development of the beginning [of that interpretation], that is, to consider the whole of the author's work in terms of its parts and in every part to consider the content as what moved the author, and the form as his nature moved by that content.

Here we can see hermeneutic circles spinning simultaneously in two distinct planes: between the whole and the parts, and likewise between the subjective and objective aspects of the text ('content' and 'form'). Even the allusion to goal and beginning implies that the interpretation finally 'comes full circle'. At the same time that the hermeneutic circle denotes motion ('the hermeneutical task moves constantly', remarked Schleiermacher graphically in 1828,[16] emphasizing the dynamic nature of all hermeneutic activity), it also denotes each level of the whole-and-parts scheme of things. To take our earlier examples, the Greek and Hebrew writings of the early years AD form a circle within which the New Testament message is situated ('the whole circle of literature to which a writing belongs'[17]); and the totality of New Testament messages forms a circle within which one particular message is situated; that message forms a circle within which some particular is situated, and so forth. Each circle represents the whole within which the particular is located, and provides the 'horizon' within which it has its existence. 'Circle' is no passive usage here: it is symbolic, in that whatever it denotes is seen as a 'unity', whether it be a single word, a sentence, a section, a work, an author's style, or a body of literature.

Before going further, it is important to know that Schleiermacher had from the mid-1790s been in close contact with leading members of the German Romantic movement. The occasional references in his hermeneutic writings to Friedrich and August Wilhelm von Schlegel and to Ludwig Tieck bear witness to this fact. Indeed, Friedrich von Schlegel (1772–1829) lodged with him in 1797–9, and the two men shared ideas and collaborated closely until they fell out in 1804. Schleiermacher came to know and be influenced by Schlegel's friends, and was also briefly but intensely in contact with the poet Novalis (Friedrich von Hardenberg). Schleiermacher's first book, *On Religion: Speeches to its Cultured Despisers* (1799) – one of the major works of modern Christian thought, yet a product of the very publishing house that had issued *Confessions from the Heart of an Art-Loving Friar*, Wackenroder's landmark work of Romantic aesthetic criticism that sought to elevate art to the status of religion, only two years earlier – reached out to those who felt estranged by the Enlightenment's dogmatic theology and tried to persuade them that religion was rooted first and foremost in immediate feeling and intuition. It told its Romantic contemporaries that they were not as far from religion as they believed, beckoning them with statements such as 'Recall how in religion everything strives to expand the sharply delineated outlines of our personality and gradually to lose them in the infinite in order that we, by intuiting the universe, will become one with it as much

---

15   ibid, 148 (1819).
16   ibid, 95 (1828 marginal note to the 1819 Compendium).
17   ibid, 115 (1819), also 202 (1829). Instances of the opposite sense are 113, 116 (1819); 186–7 (1829: 'This path leads us in a kind of circle').

as possible'.[18] In this work, unity is a crucial property of religion, the organic a pervasive metaphor (see volume I, General Introduction, §§ 6–7 for a discussion of the organic metaphor), and the circle a frequently used image – all of these being central to Romantic thought.

It should not surprise us, then, that the influence of Romanticism spilt over into Schleiermacher's hermeneutic writings, such that they spoke often of the unity of literary composition ('Both technical and grammatical interpretation begin with a general overview of a text designed to grasp its unity and the major features of its composition'), of unity emerging as purposive ('Discover the author's decision, i.e., the unity and actual direction of the work (psychological); then, understand the composition as the objective realization of that decision'), of interpretation 'reducing' particulars to their unity, or (most telling for our discussion of Beethoven below) of the underlying connections of a work being withheld from view so as to produce a 'hidden unity'.[19] Nor is it surprising that organic images are often found in these writings ('Organic with nature. Each plant carries out a special modification of pre-established processes'; 'there are only two types of combination, organic and mechanical, i.e., an inner fusion and an external adjoining of parts'[20]).

Moreover, in the hermeneutics of the Enlightenment period, the author was only a shadowy figure lurking behind the real focus of the interpreter, the 'text'. Schleiermacher, under the influence of Romantic thought, replaced this automaton-like impersonality of mind with the dynamic notion of 'spirit' (*Geist*): spirit as the unconscious creator at work in the individual genius.[21] With this all-important idea, hermeneutics was transformed from a set of rules for textual exegesis into an all-encompassing interpretative theory with the idea of author as creator, and of the text as the expression of creative self.[22] Thus in creating a general hermeneutics, Schleiermacher fashioned so to speak the *practical arm* of Romantic aesthetics. General hermeneutics rested on the very foundations that supported Romantic aesthetics, particularly on the notions that the artist acts in an individual capacity rather than representing a society; that he or she is 'inspired', but inspiration comes from within the self or from some transcendent reality rather than from God or some external power; that the artist functions not according to rules or norms or traditions, but according to the dictates of the creative imagination; consequently, that the artist's thoughts are original, and when that originality is absolute they manifest genius; that art is a product of the human mind and spirit rather than of nature; that art is expressive, hence message-laden, rather than imitative; and that

---

18 Anon. [Friedrich Schleiermacher], *Über die Religion: Reden an die Gebildeten unter ihren Verächtern* (Berlin: Unger, 1799), Eng. trans. Richard Crouter as *Friedrich Schleiermacher: On Religion: Speeches to its Cultured Despisers* (Cambridge: CUP, 1988), 'Second Speech: On the Essence of Religion', pp. 96–140, esp. p. 139.

19 Schleiermacher, *Hermeneutics*, pp. 147 (1819), 223 (1832–3), 51 (1805, 1809–10: 'Everything complex must be referred back to what is simple; a multiplicity of meanings must be quite consciously reduced to their unity'), 225 (1832–3).

20 ibid, 163 (1826–7), 129 (1819).

21 See Paul Ricoeur's lucid analysis of the working of this influence in 'The Task of Hermeneutics [I]', *Philosophy Today*, 17 (1973), 112–28, esp. 114–15; retranslated in *Paul Ricoeur: Hermeneutics and the Human Sciences*, ed. and trans. John B. Thompson (Cambridge: CUP; Paris: Editions de la Maison des Sciences de l'Homme, 1981), esp. p. 46.

22 See Kurt Mueller-Vollmer's discussion in *The Hermeneutics Reader*, pp. 9–12.

art moulds the prior experience that the beholder brings to it, enriching, deepening and transforming it.

Thus, having earlier distinguished hermeneutics from philology, criticism and exegesis in the eighteenth century, we can now distinguish it from *aesthetics* in the nineteenth century. As a term, 'aesthetics' was coined much later than hermeneutics – by Baumgarten in 1750 – although the concerns of both go back to antiquity. Aesthetics is a set of ideas (whether one calls it science, theory, or philosophy) about the meaning and value of art. Aesthetics addresses art and artistic activity in their own right. Hermeneutics, by contrast, addresses the interstice between a 'text' and an apprehending mind. Hermeneutics, to use Ricoeur's working definition, is 'the theory of the operation of understanding in its relations to the interpretation of texts'.[23] Even where hermeneutics is applied to a 'text' of art (which is by no means its full range of application) it moves, as it were, constantly between art and mind, its focus residing in neither, but rather in understanding. It is hermeneutics, therefore, ever active as it is, that provides the theoretical basis for the *criticism* (now in its nineteenth-century sense) and *analysis* of individual works.

I have dwelt on the work of Schleiermacher and his predecessors at greater length than might seem proportionate for two reasons. First, hermeneutics is still a relatively little known and poorly understood field among musicians. Second, such accounts of it as exist have tended to take as their sources the work of Dilthey later in the nineteenth century and of Gadamer in the twentieth, thus giving it different emphases and introducing ideas not yet present in Schleiermacher's work. At the same time, Schleiermacher's ideas are highly suggestive for music, even though the lines of influence to writers on music are admittedly tenuous.

§4 General hermeneutics after Schleiermacher

The written transmission of Schleiermacher's hermeneutic ideas was, intentionally or unintentionally, cast in a form common for its age. Like Schlegel's novel *Lucinde* of 1799 (which Schleiermacher knew and wrote about; indeed, he is the basis of one of its characters), and many of the writings of Ludwig Tieck, Sébastien-Roch Chamfort and others, it was fragmentary and aphoristic. It fell to subsequent writers to systematize the method, among them the great scholar of language, philosopher and educational reformer Wilhelm von Humboldt (1767–1835), the historian Johann Gustav Droysen (1808–84) and the philologist Philip August Boeckh (1785–1867). Boeckh was the first writer to include musical notation, and also pictures, among the types of text that might be subjected to hermeneutic enquiry.[24] He reformulated the ideas of Schleiermacher and Wolf (of both of whom he had been a pupil) systematically, and expanded their range (e.g. to include allegorical interpretation as

23 'The Task', 112.
24 'This thing communicated is either a symbol of the thing known, different from it in form, e.g., in the shape of letters, musical notation, etc.; or it is a picture agreeing in form with the object expressed in it, as in works of art or craft. [. . .] Here [in special hermeneutics] belongs the branch of artistic interpretation, which has to explain works of plastic art as one explains works of literature.' (August Boeckh, *On Interpretation and Criticism*, ed. and trans. John Paul Pritchard (Norman, OK: University of Oklahoma Press, 1968), pp. 46, 48, 55; reproduced in *The Hermeneutics Reader*, pp. 134–5, 139.)

well as literal, and to permit intuition alongside precise observation – hence 'the interpreter is born, not made'). Boeckh's *Encyclopaedia and Methodology of the Philological Sciences*, embodying the lectures that he gave many times between 1809 and his death, and published posthumously in 1877, is a lucid account of the methods of philology, hermeneutics and criticism, the latter two both being subdivided into 'grammatical', 'historical', 'individual' and 'generic' interpretation.

Droysen's perspicuous formulation 'On Interpretation', first published in 1858, was conceived around the interpretation of *historical events* rather than of a text, though it can readily be transferred to text. It articulates four stages: (1) pragmatic interpretation (of the historical 'facts' after critical reconstruction), (2) interpretation of conditions (surrounding the historical events represented by those facts), (3) psychological interpretation (of the will of those involved in events, and the moral forces driving them) and (4) interpretation of the ideas (in the minds of the individuals involved).[25] An even greater expansion of the scope of hermeneutics was accomplished by the most significant figure in the development of hermeneutics at the end of the nineteenth and beginning of the twentieth century, the philosopher and literary historian Wilhelm Dilthey (1833–1911), who himself wrote quite extensively on music. Dilthey saw hermeneutics on a vast scale as the potential foundation for what he called the *Geisteswissenschaften*, to which he published Book I of his *Introduction* in 1883. Literally 'sciences of the mind', these roughly corresponded to the humanities and social sciences (he lived at a time when psychology, sociology, economics and social anthropology were beginning to achieve independence as disciplines), conceived on a non-positivistic basis as distinct from the *Naturwissenschaften* or natural sciences, with their spirit of trenchant positivism. Whereas the natural scientist was seen as accounting for the particular *linearly* in terms of the general, the human scientist was left to account *circularly* for the relation between the part and the whole. This led to a fundamentally different mode of operation wherever the life of the human mind was an object of enquiry – a methodology in which there were no absolute starting points, no certainties, a methodology in which Schleiermacher's hermeneutic circle was the indispensable way of proceeding.[26] At the end of the day, the natural scientist could particularize, could pinpoint, could run the gamut of the phenomena that he investigated – in a word, he could *explain* it; at best, the human scientist could surmise, could conjecture, could throw light upon the phenomena concerned – in a word, he could *elucidate* it. To explain and to elucidate, *erklären* and *erläutern* – these are the crucial terms, this is the distinction that will resonate throughout the present volume, the distinction to which I have already alluded in the opening remarks of this General Introduction.

At the heart of the sciences of the mind, is 'lived experience' (*Erlebnis* or *Erleben*). As Dilthey cuttingly remarked:[27]

25 *The Hermeneutics Reader*, pp. 126–31.
26 This paragraph is in part summarized from Rickman's excellent introduction to *W. Dilthey: Selected Writings*, pp. 1–31.
27 *Introduction to the Human Sciences: [Book I] An Attempt to Lay a Foundation for the Study of Society and History*, Eng. trans. Ramon J. Betanzos (Detroit: Wayne State University Press, 1988; Ger. orig. 1883), p. 80. Book II, the core or positive part of the *Introduction*, was never written.

so long as no one maintains that he can derive and better explain the essence of the emotion, poetic creativity, and rational reflection, which we call Goethe's life, out of the design of his brain or the characteristics of his body, then no one will challenge the independent position of such a science [of experience].

The outward manifestations of this lived experience are 'expressions' (*Ausdrücke* or *Äusserungen*: 'externalizations' might be a better word), but they only indirectly manifest this inner life of the mind. It is understanding (*Verstehen*) that illuminates these 'expressions' and relates them as parts to the whole. There is thus a paradigm: *Erlebnis → Ausdruck → Verstehen*, and this paradigm 'is the specific process whereby mankind exists for us as an object of the human sciences'.[28] The hermeneutic task involves what Wolf had glimpsed with his notion of *Einsicht*, what Ernesti and Schleiermacher had adumbrated in their references to 'the psychological' and the latter with his divinatory method, and what Dilthey now formulated as *Nachfühlen* ('sympathetic feeling') or later *Hineinversetzen* ('injecting oneself into the mind of another person') – both usually translated as 'empathy'. Given 'the profound mystery . . . of how a succession of sounds and rhythms can have a significance beyond themselves', given the 'opaque, indeterminate, often unconscious' nature of what goes on in a composer's mind, *Hineinversetzen* takes on a special urgency when applied to music. Dilthey was the first hermeneuticist in a position to do more than hint at such an application.

§5 Dilthey and musical hermeneutics

Dilthey's extensive writings about music include a novella dating from 1867, reviews from the late 1870s and studies of the history of German music and music aesthetics. Above all, Dilthey left a short but incisive essay entitled 'On Musical Understanding', conveniently available in translation within the current series.[29] This essay must be understood as part of a much larger document intended as Book II of his *Introduction to the Human Sciences*, drafted between 1906 and 1910. At the same time, it is important to realize that this larger document is an editorial compilation from Dilthey's posthumously surviving papers, the sequence of which we must not regard as sacrosanct. This document, entitled 'The Construction of the Historical World within the Human Sciences',[30] and arguably his most original and exciting work, first spells out the distinction between the natural and human sciences, laying a foundation for the latter, then proceeds to 'Drafts for a *Critique of Historical Reason*', intended as the critique that Kant did not provide to an area in which instead of causality there are only 'relations of striving and suffering, action and reaction'.[31]

28   *Wilhelm Diltheys Gesammelte Schriften*, vol. VII (Leipzig and Berlin: Teubner, 1927), p. 87.
29   Bujić, 370–74. For a list of Dilthey's writings on music see *NGDM*. A number of them are assembled in *Von deutscher Dichtung und Musik: Aus den Studien zur Geschichte des deutschen Geistes*, ed. Herman Nohl and Georg Misch (Leipzig: Teubner, 1933; reprint edn Stuttgart: Teubner, 1957).
30   *Der Aufbau der geschichtlichen Welt in den Geisteswissenschaften*, ed. Bernhard Groethuysen in *Wilhelm Diltheys Gesammelte Schriften*, vol. VII; 'Das musikalische Verstehen' is on pp. 220–24. The manuscript drafts for the latter survive in an envelope labelled 'Erleben und Verstehen', within which are four inner envelopes labelled 'Nachbilden', 'Theorie der Musik', 'Musik' and 'Verstehen (Auslegung)'.
31   *W. Dilthey: Selected Writings*, p. 212. The *Critique of Historical Reason* is divided into Part I 'Experience, Expression and Understanding' and Part II 'Recognizing the Coherence of Universal

The discussion leading up to 'On Musical Understanding' takes first the genre of *autobiography* – that most intimate act of self-understanding in which creator and subject are one – as its exemplar for reflection and historical comprehension. From that, Dilthey turns to *understanding other people*, in which section there occurs perhaps the most luminous explanation to be found anywhere in his writings of the concepts of experience, expression and the various levels of understanding. The highest form of understanding is that of 're-constructing' (*nach + Bilden = Nachbilden*) or 're-experiencing' (*nach + Erleben = Nacherleben*). The poet re-experiences a succession of events in the mental life, a dramatist or historian re-experiences events in history; those events are 'filtered through the consciousness of the poet, artist or historian and lie before us in a fixed and permanent work'; in experiencing the fragments of events presented in the poem, play or historical account, we re-experience them as a continuity, which in turn widens the horizon of our own limited lives.[32]

Of particular relevance to music as a temporal art are the observations in section I on the nature of real time, especially on the 'present' moment of life, which is 'filled' by experience and is part of a 'flow', as distinct from the 'observed' moment of life, which is a moment of memory and is arrested in time. Experience has 'content', and we apprehend that content by special categories of thought not unlike our 'logical acts of distinguishing, identifying, grading, combining and dividing'.[33] The beginning of 'On Musical Understanding' reaches back to that discussion, starting with a vivid metaphor:

> It proved to be impossible to grasp the self itself in the experience [*Erleben*], either in the way it flows or in the depth of its content. It is only the small area of our conscious lives that rises, like an island, out of these unfathomable depths. But we are raised from these same depths by means of expression; for expression is a form of creation. Life itself becomes accessible to our understanding, intelligible as an imitation [i.e. a reconstructing: *Nachbilden*] of creation.

In music (interestingly he speaks of it as preserved 'in staff notation, in letters, on a gramophone record or, as it originally was, in memory'), a piece is a whole with parts (constituent phrases), each phrase a whole with its parts (pitch patterns, rhythms, harmonies), and so on down. But a piece of music is itself a part of an expanding concentric series of wholes that ultimately aggregrate to form the musical past – the historical tradition. At every level there is at work what he calls a *Tendenz* – much like a Markov chain in the parlance of the late twentieth century, such that event follows event (each event being an 'expression') in a constant flow of time, everything in principle free and undetermined except that each

---

History'. Part I further subdivides into section I, 'Experience and Autobiography', section II 'The Understanding of Other People and their Expressions', section III 'The Categories of Life', and section IV 'Biography'. The essay 'On Musical Understanding' is the first of five addenda to section II, the others being 'Experience and Understanding', 'Methods of Understanding', 'Hermeneutics' and 'The Limits of Understanding'. Sections I, II (without the addenda) and III are available in *W. Dilthey: Selected Writings*, pp. 207–45; part of section I and all of section II (without addenda) are also available in *The Hermeneutics Reader*, pp. 148–64. Kant's three critiques were, of course, those of pure reason (1781), practical reason (1788) and judgment (1790).

32 *Gesammelte Schriften*, vol. VII, pp. 214–15; *W. Dilthey: Selected Writings*, pp. 226–8; *The Hermeneutics Reader*, pp. 159–61.

33 *Gesammelte Schriften*, vol. VII, p. 197; *W. Dilthey: Selected Writings*, p. 212.

event conditions the events that follow it. We can infer from Dilthey's remarks that the interpretative task for the analyst and critic is to examine the relationships of part to whole in that constant whirl of activity known as the hermeneutic circle. We can infer, too, that such analysis may take place at any level between the single motif and the entire history of music, and that it will normally take place at several levels quasi-simultaneously. While the latter is never stated in the essay, we can see it at work in one of two examples that he gives us:

> In the first act finale of *Don Giovanni* rhythms may be heard which are different from each other not only in speed but in metre. The effect of this is a combination of quite different aspects of human life, dancing and so forth, so that the variety of the world finds expression. This is exactly what music, more generally speaking, can effect, depending as it does on the possibility of presenting simultaneously different characters or even different musical entities such as choruses etc. whereas poetry is tied to dialogue etc.

The implication of this is that differences detected at the level of the local phrase and section are transferred up to a much higher level, at which we can interpret the various levels of character and meaning that are present in the opera.

Dilthey's essay is too broad in scope to specify analytical procedures. Nor is it possible for us now to envisage precisely how an analysis conducted in accordance with his precepts would have turned out. He produced none himself.[34] 'On Musical Understanding' was not published until 1927, and few of his hermeneutic writings were made available in his lifetime, hence scope for influence on the following generation was minimal. Only Arnold Schering seems overtly to have felt that influence. Schenker, we know, had nothing but unkind things to say about hermeneutics.[35] Yet it is a curious thought that there is no music-analytic procedure more nearly capable of replicating the operation of the hermeneutic circle than that which Schenker developed in the early 1920s and used to such effect between 1925 and 1930. If we compare Schleiermacher's analysis of Plato's *Republic* (in the description quoted above) with that procedure, we see some similarities. Typically, an analysis in Schenker's *Das Meisterwerk* volumes I–II begins by displaying the

---

34   He left substantial essays on such works as the St John and St Matthew Passions and B minor Mass of J. S. Bach, Haydn's *The Creation*, and operas by Mozart, but these are historical essays that access detail by engaging text rather than music: see *Von deutscher Dichtung und Musik*.

35   Schenker in 1910:

> You need only cast a glance at the all-too-many 'concert guides', 'books of programme notes', 'analyses' – what a frightful sight they present, unbelievable! [. . .] What Kretzschmar, Riemann, Grove *e tutti quanti* write in their books and analyses about the symphonies of Beethoven, for example, is all wrongheaded and [. . .] a thousand times untrue! (*Kontrapunkt*, vol. I *Cantus Firmus und zweistimmiger Satz* (Stuttgart and Berlin: Cotta, 1910), p. XXII)

In 1916:

> What I accuse them of is [. . .] that they are quite incapable of reading music. It is out of sheer embarrassment at so elementary a shortcoming that they are obliged to draw analogies with pictures, and to prattle on about affects. (*Die letzten fünf Sonaten von Beethoven: kritische Ausgabe mit Einführung und Erläuterung* [Op. 111] (Vienna: Universal Edition, 1916), pp. 28–9 [excluded from reprint edn 1971])

And in 1922, on Kretzschmar:

> first a string of grandiloquent words, as if the hermeneuticist had picked all the fruit from the tree of authentic insight, and then a language such as was never spoken in the paradise of insight, amounting only to arid verbal-foliage on the twiggy little phrase-trees that grow in the hermeneuticist's garden. (*Der Tonwille*, 5 (1923), 23)

entire musical composition synoptically in words and graphic form (the *Ursatz*), then breaking that whole down into parts in successive stages, each stage involving a longer prose discussion and a further layer of graph, with additional subgraphs to lay bare the interiors of smaller wholes. Then the process restarts, sweeping through the piece once again with a fresh graph (the *Urlinie-Tafel*). Finally, it starts yet again, this time with the fully notated score. At each stage the discussion is repeatedly referred back to the exterior whole; and at the end, each interior whole having been shown in relation to its parts in a series of diminishing circles, the piece is reassembled so that we come full circle back to the opening graph.

This depiction of Schenker's method is oversimplified and begs many questions. Moreover, there are numerous differences of substance between Schenker and Schleiermacher. Most obvious among these is that whereas in Schleiermacher the initial presentation of the whole is heuristic and subject to constant revision in light of the parts, in Schenker the initial presentation is authoritative. This last word reminds us that while Schenker and Schleiermacher alike seek to 'get inside the mind' of the author/composer, an interpretation by Schleiermacher is genuinely investigative, starting with text and leading to a discovery of mental life, whereas in a Schenker analysis the *Hineinversetzen* takes place beforehand and the analysis starts with the benefit of that insight and proceeds to trace the process of compositional unfolding. Schleiermacher, we might say, starts from the outside and works inwards, Schenker moves in reverse. Schleiermacher's interpretation therefore lives out the exploration of the message with its reader, Schenker's analysis imparts the message to its reader. Both convey confusion and uncertainty along the way, but that of Schleiermacher is experiential, that of Schenker rhetorical. Ironically, Schenker is closer to the *hermeios*: he emerges from the Delphic temple with the message clear in his mind. Nevertheless, despite these very real differences, comparison of Schenker with hermeneutic method is not altogether unfitting. Schenker, unlike any other analyst of his time, insisted on a text-critical examination of a work before embarking on analysis, just as did all hermeneutic writers. In Schenker, the notion of organism informs all parts of his analysis just as it does that of the hermeneutic writers. Schenker's notion of the 'content' of a work is not far removed from that of the hermeneuticist. He would probably have concurred with Dilthey, whose remark in 'On Musical Understanding' is pertinent to what follows in the next section.[36]

> It is not a question of psychological relationship between emotional states and their representation in the imagination – anyone who goes after this is chasing a will-o'-the-wisp. It is rather the relationship between an objective composition, with its component parts as a creation of the imagination, and *the meaning which is to be found in each melodic strand*, that is, what the work tells the listener about a spiritual something that exists in the link between rhythm, melody, harmonic relations and impact of an emotional message. It is not psychological, but musical relationships that form the study of musical genius, composition and theory.

---

36 *Gesammelte Schriften*, vol. VII, p. 222; Bujić, 372, whose translation I have slightly adjusted.

§6 Hermeneutics and music: the beginnings

Carl Dahlhaus, in a discussion of the aesthetic divide between Rossini and Beethoven that confronted the early nineteenth century, fashions a telling comparison of two types of failure. Whereas we can speak of the failure of an opening night of a Rossini opera as a 'fiasco', the same usage would seem inappropriate of a failure at the first performance of a Beethoven late string quartet. As he says,[37]

> Even those who were disappointed felt basically that the acoustic phenomenon whose sense they were unable to grasp nevertheless harbored a meaning which, with sufficient effort, could be made intelligible. [. . .] The thought that music can be destined to be 'understood' had probably arisen a few decades earlier, around 1800; but only in connection with the reception of Beethoven did it have a significant impact on music history.

It was the interpretation of Beethoven, Dahlhaus contends, that created a divide between 'formalists' and 'content aestheticians'. And it was the need to discover behind the rugged exterior of such a work an 'idea' that imparted sense and coherence to the work, in so doing penetrating to a second level of the music beyond the sonic exterior and its technical fabric, that gave rise to a hermeneutics of music.

Dahlhaus's allusion to a kind of proto-hermeneutics beginning around 1800 probably refers more than anything else to Friedrich Rochlitz's journal, the Leipzig *Allgemeine musikalische Zeitung*, founded in 1798, where such writing found its earliest foothold. Take the following discussion of the 'Representation of Chaos' from Haydn's *The Creation* that appeared in that periodical in 1802, unsigned but apparently written by the composer and musical entrepreneur Carl Friedrich Zelter (1758–1832), close friend of Goethe, to whom A. B. Marx referred as having 'all the vulgar insolence of the Berlin philistine'. The work's best number and the 'crown atop a kingly head', the 'Representation',[38]

> harnesses as its raw materials virtually every serviceable musical instrument, assembling and deploying them to weave a tapestry of immense and incalculable proportions, replete with artistic splendours.
>
> Any objection as to the impossibility of portraying chaos through the artistic agencies of harmony, melody and rhythm visibly dissolves into a subtle affectation of understanding [*Verstandesprätension*] that would enable any composer to carry through such a commission for which he has no solution.[39] Precisely this semblance of impossibility, of contradiction – in a word, this make-believe [*Fabelhaftigkeit*] – is at the same time the poetic element, and consequently the best part of the grand conception [*ganze Intention*] that this masterly composer has laid before us in so poetic, so rich and so individual a manner. A luxuriant feast of harmonies, of melodic figures and passage work, a veritable oriental opulence abound here, with which a prince of music may

---

37   Carl Dahlhaus, *Nineteenth-century Music*, Eng. trans. J. Bradford Robinson (Berkeley, CA: University of California Press, 1989; Ger. orig. Wiesbaden: Athenaion, 1980), pp. 10–11.

38   'Recension: *Die Schöpfung* . . .', *AmZ*, 4 (1801/02), no. 24 (10 March), cols. 385–96, the translated passage on cols. 390–92. The whole review is printed in H. C. Robbins Landon, *Haydn: Chronicle and Works* (London: Thames and Hudson, 1976–80), vol. IV, pp. 592–7, and a portion translated in Nicholas Temperley, *Haydn: 'The Creation'*, Cambridge Music Handbooks (Cambridge: CUP, 1991), pp. 89–92, together with a survey of critical reception, pp. 42–6. The review refers deferentially to a short review of the piano score in *AmZ*, 3 (1800/01), no. 11 (10 December 1800), cols. 180–81, as an 'aesthetic disputation' (*Deduktion*). Attribution to Zelter is given in *MGG*, 'Zelter', and by Robbins Landon.

39   Temperley renders this passage as 'exposed as a crafty self-deception, by which a composer can if need be excuse himself for failing to solve such a problem', and *Fabelhaftigkeit* as 'marvel'.

regale the ear and taste of the most refined of his ilk, a treasure house of genius and art that he may strew before them, and that rises like a morning sun from the darkest depths. [. . .]

The writer now moves to the technical aspect of the piece, describing the visual appearance of the score in a whimsical way that uncannily foreshadows Schumann's caprice on the Liszt piano arrangement of the *Fantastic* Symphony (Analysis 10 below, p. 166), and summing up the music's total effect in words of some interest.

> Accidental dissonances[40] almost always arise in a deliberately free manner. The strangest jumble of figures and note symbols [*Notengattungen*] comprising semibreves, minims, crotchets, quavers and semiquavers, in triplets, roulades, trills and grace notes, lends the score a bizarre and mysterious appearance. It is astonishing to see the host of tiny rapid figures swarming in huge, dark masses like armies of insects on the wide horizon. But all of this, when sounded together and associated with the sombre representation of chaos, creates an infinitely splendid harmonic fabric, its tonal progressions [*Führung der Modulation*] indescribably beautiful and in many places so sublime and lofty as to inspire wonderment.

In this way, the author reconciles the Representation's function as 'representation' with its function as absolute music (by means of an elaborate pretence in which things are not what they seem), and interprets it in the language of the newly burgeoning Romantic aesthetic associated with the Schlegels, Schelling, Jean-Paul Richter, Wackenroder, Tieck and Novalis, a language that was to be fashioned into an aesthetic of musical beauty and the sublime in a series of articles by Christian Friedrich Michaelis (1770–1834) only four years later in the same periodical,[41] and that E. T. A. Hoffmann was brilliantly to formulate as a musical hermeneutic within the following three years in the selfsame journal (see Analysis 9 below).[42] The writer is not unaware that his review breaks new ground:

> It is not in the nature of things that so excellent a work should be universally recognized for what it is and will surely be, especially where certain deep-rooted theories based on earlier works come into inexorable conflict with the spirit of progress, giving rise to a critical stance that forever makes demands while conceding nothing. Such a critical stance must guard carefully against the danger of demolishing itself in the face of works such as this overture. But that is only to be expected.

It would be wrong to portray the *Allgemeine musikalische Zeitung* as a hotbed of the latest aesthetic theories. When Rochlitz assembled the 130 or more writers who were to contribute to the journal during its first decade his concern was breadth of view, his desire 'to guard against partisanship and mediocrity'.[43] He tells us that

40 *zufällige Dissonanzen*: 'Some music theorists give this name to the suspensions of notes of a preceding chord over the bass scale-step of a subsequent chord' (H. C. Koch, *Musikalisches Lexikon* (Frankfurt: Hermann, 1802; reprint edn Hildesheim: Olms, 1964)).

41 *AmZ*, 8 (1805/06), no. 43 (23 July 1806), cols. 673–83; no. 44 (30 July), 691–6; *AmZ*, 9 (1806/07), no. 46 (12 August 1807), 725–9; *AmZ*, 10 (1807/08), no. 29 (13 April 1808), 449–52. For excerpts, see le Huray/Day, 286–92, where passages from the Schlegels, Wackenroder, Franz Christoph Horn and Schelling can also be found.

42 Dahlhaus's account of the growth of this hermeneutic is compelling (*The Idea of Absolute Music*, trans. Roger Lustig (Chicago: University of Chicago Press, 1989; Ger. orig. 1978), pp. 42–6). See also the introductory material to *E. T. A. Hoffmann's Musical Writings: 'Kreisleriana', 'The Poet and the Composer', Music Criticism*, ed. David Charlton, trans. Martyn Clarke (Cambridge: CUP, 1989).

43 Letter of invitation from Rochlitz to the composer Johann Rudolf Zumsteeg, 30 May 1798, see Martha Bruckner-Bigenwald, *Die Anfänge der Leipziger Allgemeinen Musikalischen Zeitung* (Sibiu-Hermannstadt, 1938; reprint edn Hilversum: Knuf, 1965), p. 46.

he gave only a brief directive to his contributors initially, and that he published no manifesto; but that after four years he circulated privately to them, and then published, an essay by the Swiss writer and publisher Hans Georg Nägeli (1773–1836) entitled 'Attempt at Establishing a Norm for the Reviewers of the *musikalische Zeitung*'.[44] Nägeli offered four approaches to writing a review of (*kritisiren*) a piece of music: the scientific, the psychological, the historical and the architectonic. Of these, it is the psychological, in which 'one proceeds from perceived effects [*Würkungen*] to artistic essence, [. . .] from the *particular* to the special quality of its different products', that is dismissed because of lack of formal criteria. Rochlitz's original 1798 directive was more forward-looking than this, with its three cardinal steps addressing:

1   the sense and spirit [*Sinn und Geist*] of the work – At this level nothing can be demonstrated or strictly speaking proven. Throughout art, one can speak from sense only to sense;
2   the means [*Mittel*] by which the artist has striven to express this spirit – At this level not only elucidation [*Erläuterung*] is possible but also demonstration or suggestion as to how the [work's] purpose might be better achieved, etc.;
3   grammar [*Grammatik*] – to which belongs not only what is called purity of writing but also declamation of words in vocal music, all of which is pertinent to *purposive* and *correct* treatment – At this level there is actually scope to pass judgment.

It was Beethoven, as we saw from Dahlhaus a moment ago, who challenged the reviewers' criteria of judgment to the greatest degree, hence whose music prompted the most progressive critical approaches. The first critic to rise to that challenge in a significant way was the reviewer of the Third Piano Concerto score in 1805. The journal's editor had, we are told, charged this anonymous reviewer – a musician – to investigate 'the artistic and technical side' of the work.[45] What was meant by this rather ambiguous phrase (*den artistischen und technischen Theil*) came clearer when unquestionably the same anonymous writer two years later tackled the charge of excess length and undue complexity levelled by other critics against the finale of the 'Eroica' Symphony. In a fascinating discussion of 'excess' (*Nimium*) in music, he distinguished between the 'mechanical and technical side' of a work and its 'artistic and aesthetic side'.[46]

Before examining the Third Piano Concerto review, let me pursue that of the 'Eroica' of 1807 for a moment longer, for it opens with a manifesto for a new kind of criticism, and charts three stages by which such a criticism may eventually be achieved, one stage of which has already passed, a second to which the current review contributes, and a third which the reviewer anticipates as a reconciliation of the first two. The 'Eroica', it says, has:

---

44   'Versuch einer Norm für die Recensenten der *musikalischen Zeitung*', AmZ, 5 (1802/03), no. 14 (29 December 1802), cols. 225–37.
45   'Recension: *Grand Concerto . . .*', AmZ, 7 (1804/05), no. 28 (10 April 1805), cols. 445–57, esp. 446.
46   'Recension: *Sinfonia eroica . . .*', AmZ, 9 (1806/07), no. 21 (18 February 1807), cols. 319*b*–34, esp. 332.

already been talked about in these pages several times and from different points of view. First our Viennese correspondents sent news of its existence and general character, and reported the impression it made on the public at a number of performances. Since then several fellow-reporters, most recently our Mannheim correspondent and before that the reviewer of the Second Symphony piano [trio] arrangement,[47] have given similar accounts but have attempted also to probe in detail the work's purpose and character, and the causes of the impression that it makes.

At this stage the individuality [*Eigenheit*] and the rich content [*Gehalt*] of the work cry out *now* for a concentrated and serious investigation of the work's technical side that follows the composer very precisely, working step by step from this [technical] side and from the adjacent mechanical side. [. . .]

Perhaps somebody will one of these days draw all of this together and carry it to a centreground [*Mittelpunkt*]. If not, perhaps at least out of feeling, by then less imprecise and precarious, a sufficient judgment will emerge of its own accord and then gradually pass over into general meaning and so define the condition of the work, its influence on the whole, and its fate.

Consequently in this essay, while the aesthetic side will not be wholly disregarded, it will be largely the technical and mechanical side that is investigated. If the writer now presents little more than a succession of isolated observations and analyses [*Zergliederungen*], introducing little that lends itself to discourse, then this is in the nature of things, and cannot be avoided. Man cannot survive by discourse alone!

And it is indeed the case that the remainder of the review focuses mostly on the technical aspects (thematic material, mode, harmonic progression, structural ordering, contrapuntal devices) and mechanical aspects (instrumentation, clarity of texture, alternative arrangements, engraving errors). Noticeable in the prose of this review are many familiar eighteenth-century terms, including those for compositional process: *Erfindung* (invention), *Entwurf* (groundplan), *Ausführung* (execution) and *Ausarbeitung* (elaboration). Robin Wallace in his excellent survey of the critical reception of Beethoven's works during the composer's lifetime speculates that the author of these two reviews is Friedrich August Kanne (1778–1833), who later contributed articles to the Viennese journal of the same name throughout its period of publication, 1817–24, serving as that journal's editor for the last four of those years, who also wrote reviews for Viennese newspapers, and who moreover was a close friend of Beethoven in the latter's final years.[48] Kanne's later analyses of Mozart's piano works are a strange mixture of Romantic aesthetics and archaic rhetorical doctrine.[49]

From this excursion into the 'Eroica' review we can now see that reference to 'the artistic and technical side' in the Third Piano Concerto review designated *both* sides of what Schleiermacher called the hermeneutic mountain that had to be climbed. The reviewer of this concerto seems to set himself a larger task, though not yet that of his envisaged fully-fledged third stage:

---

47 The reviews referred to here are, respectively: *AmZ*, 7 (1804/05), no. 31 (1 May 1805), cols. 501–02 (Vienna report 9 April); *AmZ*, 9 (1806/07), no. 18 (28 January 1807), cols. 285–7 (Mannheim concert 3 January); ibid, no. 1 (1 October 1806), cols. 8–11 (subsection on the 'Eroica', cols. 10–11).

48 Robin Wallace, *Beethoven's Critics: Aesthetic Dilemmas and Resolutions during the Composer's Lifetime* (Cambridge: CUP, 1986), p. 17. Kanne studied medicine in Leipzig, theology in Wittenberg and composition under Christian Ehregott Weinlig in Dresden, before moving to Vienna in 1808, where he remained for the rest of his life. On friendship with Beethoven, see Maynard Solomon, *Beethoven* (New York: Schirmer, 1977), pp. 259, 261.

49 See Hartmut Krones, 'Rhetorik und rhetorische Symbolik in der Musik um 1800: Vom Weiterleben eines Prinzips', *Musiktheorie*, 3 (1988), 117–40, esp. 125–9. *Nimium* in the 'Eroica' analysis may be rhetorical in origin.

As to its spirit [*Geist*] and its impact on the listener [*Effekt*], this concerto is one of the most superb *ever* written at any time. I will try here to explicate [*erklären*], with only the work itself in mind, how this impact comes about insofar as this can be established on the basis of the musical material and its construction [*Materie . . . Konstruktion*].

That is to say, without looking outside the work itself, he set out to uncover how the features of the audible musical fabric gave rise to the effect that he detected. The reviewer showed how a 'heterogeneity' of ideas in the first movement is fused together by a short motif, how an interrupted cadence near the end 'creates an uncommonly pleasing tension of the spirit', and how the strategic use of tuttis, combined with restrained but telling use of modulation, throughout provides 'purposive *preparation* and *gradual* incitement of the listener towards the highest and most crucial moment'. This review, written 'for those who use their brains even in the enjoyment of pleasure', deals with specific details, attributing perceptible 'effects' to them. It is in the second movement that the writer went furthest in articulating the purpose behind the design, though careful to set up the diagnosis non-committally:

Of all the instrumental pieces ever written this is surely the most expressive, the most abundant in feeling. [. . .] We might call it an attempt, painted with nuances of the most refined, to portray the melancholy of a noble soul [*Seele*]. For that very reason, it only *seems* to contrast sharply [with the first movement] (as does the key: E major against C minor), whereas it is in reality a change that is perfectly rooted in the nature of the soul.

Calling for a soloist well-informed and sensitive as well as technically secure,[50] this review is remarkable in making the equation between technical stimulus and perceptual response that lies at the heart of the hermeneutic process.

It was E. T. A. Hoffmann in his writings for the *Allgemeine musikalische Zeitung* between 1809 and 1815 who contributed the aesthetic and critical high point of the journal's entire history, and established simultaneously the benchmark for all subsequent music criticism. In doing so, he drew on the theory of the sublime from Burke's *Philosophical Enquiry* (1757) and Kant's *Critique of Judgment* (1790), on the Romantic aesthetic of Wackenroder's *Confessions from the Heart of an Art-Loving Friar* (1797) and Tieck's *Imaginative Reflections on Art* (1799), and music-theoretical writings of Marpurg, Reichardt, Forkel and Gerber (to all of whom he refers) and probably others such as Johann Gottlieb Portmann and Heinrich Christoph Koch, and on the existing protocols of the journal itself.[51] The result is, in his review of Beethoven's Fifth Symphony of 1810 (see Analysis 9 below), a full-blooded example of a hermeneutic of music. The review conducts a technical examination of the musical text, no longer visually but now aurally conceived, in parallel not only with immediate moment-to-moment impressions and reactions but also with intimations of the transcendent mental-spiritual world to which the work leads its listener, and concluding with a summation of the four-movement totality. The hermeneutic circle spins between the various wholes and their parts,

50   The original puts it more tellingly, 'der [. . .] auch Kenntisse im Kopfe und ein Herz im Busen hat – sonst wird, auch bey der ausgezeichnetsten Fertigkeit und Sicherheit [. . .]', ibid, col. 457, and the above quotation 453.
51   See notes 41, 43 and 44.

and between the objective and the subjective, driven by the concepts of unity and organicism. It is hard to imagine a more sophisticated application of the principles of Schleiermacher to a piece of music – though Hoffmann cannot have had direct access to those principles.

§7 Two perspectives on musical hermeneutics: 1. Brendel

Amid the subliterature of nineteenth-century aesthetics there exist two passages now long forgotten, passages of the sort that modern aestheticians and historians pass over as ellipses, but passages of great interest to our present purpose. One was written in 1845, the other in 1903. Each provides a chronicle of what was, in its author's eyes, a new genre of writing about music. Since each serves as a preamble to a manifesto for a still newer and higher type of writing, we should treat its historical record with some caution. Nonetheless, the two accounts help us to reconstruct a genre of interpretative writing on music that has been subconsciously suppressed by twentieth-century annalists and to uncover which now needs a deliberate effort.

On 1 January 1845, Karl Franz Brendel (1811–68), later to become spokesman for the New German School or the 'musicians of the future' centred around Liszt, took over from its founding editor Robert Schumann the editorship of that long-time rival of the *Allgemeine musikalische Zeitung*, the *Neue Zeitschrift für Musik*. His first issue offered 'a critique of music criticism up to the present time', followed by a declaration of the task now to be engaged.[52] The eighteenth century, he told his readers, had seen the founding of music criticism in the scientific mould, a criticism 'limited to technical criteria', correctness of counterpoint, harmonic logic and formal elaboration, just 'lengthy descriptions of technical construction'. However, the revolution that Kant, Goethe and others wrought in science and art belatedly spread to music criticism.

> Writers emerged, schooled by those heroes, who brought to their interpretation and judgment of music a more spiritual element, men such as *Friedrich Reichardt*, the celebrated song composer and friend of Goethe, and especially *Friedrich Rochlitz*, the founder of the Leipzig *Allgemeine musikalische Zeitung*, likewise a member of Goethe's inner circle.

Johann Friedrich Reichardt (1752–1814) was editor of the *Musikalisches Kunstmagazin* (1782–91). With these two writers, music criticism was emancipated from the old laws,

> its main concern no longer verification of technical correctness but rather the capturing of content [*Inhalt*], of the feeling, indeed of the spirit expressed by the piece, i.e. [. . .] *psychological description*, or *psychological analysis*. [. . .] Objective judgment, decided by fixed rules, founded on natural laws, but devoid of spirit, was replaced by judgment that was subjective, vaguer, but spiritually richer.

Brendel singles out an evaluation by Reichardt of Mozart's *Idomeneo* in the *Berlinische musikalische Zeitung* of 1805 for special mention, and he particularly cites Rochlitz's struggle to come to terms with the works of Beethoven. Then came a younger generation of writers, with more modern ideas.

---

52   Franz Brendel, 'Zur Einleitung', *NZM*, 12 nos. 1–2 (1 January 1845), 1–12, esp. 1–4.

Pre-eminent among these were [*Gottfried Wilhelm*] *Fink* [1783–1846], primarily a teacher of music history, and an able one at that, though he left something to be desired in sharpness and precision of judgment; *Ludwig Rellstab* [1799–1860], who knew how to penetrate spiritually the music that he appreciated; *Marx* in Berlin, who implemented the new genre [*Wissenschaft*] better than anyone, a spiritually minded critic and theorist, yet the more he has recently become embroiled in controversy, the more the one-sided principle that he proclaimed may lead him astray in his own creative work; and finally, the men who founded the *Neue Zeitschrift für Musik*. . . . Most recently several noteworthy developments have occurred on the critical front, but it is early days yet to deliver a final verdict on them.

The controversy referred to over Marx blew up in Berlin in 1841: Dehn had published his *Theoretical-Practical Manual of Harmony* in 1840; Marx polemicized against this and the thoroughbass approach to harmonic theory in general, in his *The Old Music Theory in Conflict with Our Time* (1841); Fink responded the following year with what might be freely translated *The New Music's Theoretical Wailing and Gnashing of Teeth*, in which he signalled his own abandonment of advocacy for the writings of Weber, Schumann and others.[53] Marx himself proclaimed Reichardt 'the most spiritual' of the new writers, citing also 'Kirnberger, at least in isolated intuitions, F. Rochlitz, K. Stein, A. Wendt, Hotho [and] Hand, in their many striking interpretations', for transcending 'the old, oppressively narrow ideas'.[54] The founders of the *Neue Zeitschrift* were Julius Knorr, Robert Schumann, Friedrich Wieck and Ludwig Schunke, though Brendel may have had in mind more active contributors to the journal such as C. F. Becker, Karl Banck and Oswald Lorenz.[55]

At this point, Brendel did an about-face. He now rejected the new criticism on account of its many shortcomings. For the critic merely to put into words his emotional response to a piece was inherently unsatisfactory. The lack of foundation for judgment, mirrored in the absence of qualifications for the job – this was unacceptable. Moreover, faced in mid-century with the decline of opera, the materialism of the *Lied* and the superficiality of piano composition, criticism had sunk into either passivity or (as in the case of Rellstab) disgruntled antagonism. In this parlous situation, Brendel now adumbrated a three-phase development of music criticism not unlike that of the reviewer of the 'Eroica' (though with the first two stages reversed), leading to the ideal third phase.

53 S. W. Dehn, *Theoretisch-praktische Harmonielehre* (Berlin: Thome, 1840); A. B. Marx, *Die alte Musiklehre im Streit mit unserer Zeit* (Leipzig: B&H, 1841); G. W. Fink, *Der neumusikalische Lehrjammer; oder Beleuchtung der Schrift: Die alte Musiklehre im Streit mit unserer Zeit* (Leipzig: Mayer und Wigand, 1842). Marx's 'one-sided principle' was presumably the primacy of melody expounded in his four-volume composition manual of 1837–47.

54 *Die alte Musiklehre*, p. iv: 'K. Stein', pseudonym of Gustav Adolph Keferstein (1799–1861), theologian, who contributed to *NZM*, *Caecilia*, etc.; Johann Amadeus Wendt (1783–1836), philosopher and aesthetician, critic with *AmZ*, etc.; Heinrich Gustav Hotho (1802–73), aesthetician and art historian; Ferdinand Gotthelf Hand (1786–1852), aesthetician. On Wendt, see Wallace, *Beethoven's Critics*, pp. 27–35.

55 Julius Knorr (1807–61), first editor-in-chief of *NZM*; Robert Schumann, who took over months later; Friedrich Wieck (1785–1873), Schumann's piano teacher, later father-in-law, who withdrew in 1834; Ludwig Schunke (1810–34), who died too early to be an active contributor; Carl Ferdinand Becker (1804–77), reviewer of organ music; Karl Ludwig Banck (1809–89) and Oswald Lorenz (1806–89), reviewers of vocal music. For a fine study of *NZM*, see Leon Plantinga, *Schumann as Critic* (New Haven and London: Yale University Press, 1967).

The first phase of criticism dwelt on technical adjudication, the second on psychological description of the impression that it makes. [. . .] *The consolidation, the fusion, the unification of these two viewpoints could any day now be pronounced the challenge of the present age. The result – a third viewpoint – would have to preserve* the insight into content that characterized the second phase while striving to restore the objectivity that characterized the first; the first two stages would be its preconditions, but it would have to absorb these and transcend them.

It was, Brendel tells us, Beethoven's music, in which technicality and spirituality combined in ideal equilibrium, that now offered a paradigm for music criticism. Beethoven's battle with the natural laws of harmony and higher counterpoint was the obverse of the emancipation of his spirit. What resulted was a fusion of spirit and technique.

It is from this vantage point that a deeper understanding [*Begreifung*], a more professional redrawing [*wissenschaftlichere Erfassung*], of music and its history can now become a reality. As soon as with this realization our attention shifts away from the immediacy of the life of feeling, further vistas open up, and several other tasks follow logically on, tasks that can place a productive and independent criticism on a broader footing.

Wissenschaftlich in this context is extraordinarily hard to translate. It was important to Dilthey that what he was creating, while the antithesis of 'science' in our modern sense, should nonetheless be a *Wissenschaft*, and this was clearly important for Brendel, too. 'Technology' might be right for the nineteenth century, but this to modern ears has overtones of engineering. It is probably best thought of as denoting in its abstract sense 'professional discipline' or 'professional field', with all the authority and legitimacy that those phrases impart in modern parlance, and in its concrete sense 'professional genre'.

In his *History of Music in Italy, Germany and France* – his lectures at the Leipzig Conservatory in 1850 published two years later – Brendel attempted just such a genre of writing as outlined above, approached from precisely this new vantage point. As he said in his Foreword: 'The history of music conceived in this way is equally well a *practical aesthetic* and the best preparation, objective and at the same time subjective, for this professional field'.[56]

It would be irresponsible here to detach Brendel's statements from his larger, nationalistic aspirations; for he, like Marx, was deeply committed to the political unification of Germany and its identity as a single culture. There are in his writings expressions of disdain for Italian shallowness and dismissals of French superficiality that foreshadow those of Schenker sixty years later. It was Beethoven, Brendel says, who began to bring music back from its petty bourgeois state to the 'pure German lineage', with 'his stressing of the ideal, [. . .] his poetic tendency, his struggle for clarity of expression, his touch of humour'; but he was too early, and his strivings for the fatherland evaporated with the onset of the Romantic movement, as seen in the decline of post-Mozartian opera and the drift of instrumental music away from spirituality toward instrumentality (i.e. virtuoso playing, colouristic display and tone-painting), and the disintegration of its large forms into miniatures. 'Everywhere,

56   *Geschichte der Musik in Italien, Deutschland und Frankreich* . . . (Leipzig: Hinze, 1852; reprint edn Vaduz/Liechtenstein: Sändig, 1985), p. v.

content is lacking.' Music had to recover once again its *deutsche Innerlichkeit* (German profundity of feeling), its German spirit (*Geist*), German temperament (*Gemüt*).[57] The new *Wissenschaft* was needed not for itself, but in order to promote first an 'acknowledgment of [. . .] false directions taken' and 'a fresh epoch of reflection, a period of critique', second a programme of broad-based education, and finally the ushering in of a new era of artistic productivity centred on spirit.[58] But we should not write off Brendel on account of these sentiments. They were harboured to some degree by many of the great intellectuals of his age. Even within hermeneutics, we find Dilthey concerned with nationhood, and in particular with restoration of the unity of the medieval germanic tribes through great men such as Luther, Schiller and Bismarck, 'the rebuilding of our spiritual life from Lutheranism in a line to the present day', a process in which he saw an important role for music.[59] In a sense, what was *Geisteswissenschaft* if not the discovery of the essential spirituality of the German nation?

§8 Two perspectives on musical hermeneutics: 2. Kretzschmar

In 1896 or 1897 Dilthey read a paper before the Prussian Academy of Sciences – a historical survey entitled 'The Genesis of Hermeneutics' that was subsequently included in a volume of philosophical essays published in 1900.[60] Whether or not this provided the impetus for Hermann Kretzschmar we cannot tell, but he prepared something uncannily similar in the first of a pair of articles entitled 'A Stimulus to Promote a Hermeneutics of Music' in the *Yearbook* of the Peters publishing house for 1902 and 1905. The first of these articles opened by repudiating those who ridicule 'literary introductions to musical works', pronouncing the latter 'a very important theoretical discipline, in a sense the culmination – the last and most precious harvest – of all music theory: it goes by the name of "musical hermeneutics"'. His later vivid account is worth quoting in full:[61]

> Far from being a new invention, [hermeneutics] has been practised constantly, if not in so comprehensive and systematic a manner, since the dawn of modern art. [. . .] Our [nineteenth-century] instrumental music [. . .] has become more complex [than that of the eighteenth century], its public broader and more mixed, and at the same time more expert.
>   This state of affairs is cause for rejoicing, if only because it has stimulated an interest in hermeneutics. Greatest credit is due to music journalism, which from the inception of Rochlitz's *Allgemeine musikalische Zeitung* has found this to be one of its most productive areas of activity. It has persisted with this to the present time,

57   ibid, summarized from lectures 18–21, pp. 415–530, quotations from pp. 436, 509, 515, 538, 513.
58   ibid, summarized from lecture 22, pp. 500–546, quotations from 538–40.
59   e.g. *Gesammelte Schriften*, vol. VII, pp. 282–6 ('Die Nationen') and 341–2 ('Musik der Aufklärung'), and *Von deutscher Dichtung und Musik*, passim.
60   see note 13.
61   'Anregungen zur Förderung musikalischer Hermeneutik', *Jahrbuch der Musikbibliothek Peters für 1902*, 9 (1903), 45–66; later issued in *Gesammelte Aufsätze über Musik und Anderes*, vol. II, *Gesammelte Aufsätze aus den Jahrbüchern der Musikbibliothek Peters* (Leipzig: Peters, 1911; reprint edn ibid 1973), pp. 168–92, extract on pp. 177–9. For the first part of the article, excluding this extract, see Bujić, 114–20. See the introduction to Analysis 7, below, for further quotation from this article. The second article is 'Neue Anregungen zur Förderung musikalischer Hermeneutik: Satzästhetik', *Jahrbuch der Musikbibliothek Peters für 1905*, 12 (1906), 73–86; *Gesammelte Aufsätze*, vol. II, pp. 280–93.

and even in early days considerably advanced the inner development of the art of interpretation [*Auslegekunst*] by publishing significant analyses [*Analysen*] – Zelter's of works by Haydn, for example, and Hoffmann's of works by Beethoven. New character and new status have been brought to hermeneutics ever since Winterfeld and Jahn harnessed it to the purposes of music biography. Independently of music journals and of biography, Carl Maria von Weber was the first to bring musical hermeneutics to the general public in Germany through Theodor Hell's *Dresdener Abendzeitung*. Richard Wagner's programme written for the first performance in 1846 of the Ninth Symphony elevated a tradition that was already extant.

Of these, Zelter has been exemplified above (§6), Wagner and Hoffmann both below (Analyses 2 and 9). Carl Winterfeld (1784–1852) and Otto Jahn (1813–69) were pioneers of a new type of composer-biography – Winterfeld's on Palestrina (1832) and Giovanni Gabrieli (1834), Jahn's on Mozart (1856–9) – that dealt sensitively with music as well as biographical fact. (On early biographies, and especially that by Baini on Palestrina, see vol. I of the present work, Introduction to Part III, and Analysis 14, pp. 261–2, 281–3; Kretzschmar makes no mention of Spitta, a sample of whose analytical writing in the service of biography is given below, Analysis 5.) Weber's witty and stylish critical contributions to newspapers in Prague and Dresden date from 1817–21.[62]

Striking here is the absence of any mention of the critical writings of Schumann or the output of the *Neue Zeitschrift für Musik*. However, two years later Kretzschmar contributed an article to the *Yearbook* entitled 'Robert Schumann as Aesthetician', in which he cited the analytical agenda used in Schumann's *Fantastic* Symphony review – (1) form, (2) techniques of composition, (3) idea and (4) governing spirit (see Analysis 10 below) – and declared Schumann to have 'formulated with this in an eminently viable and wholly practicable way [. . .] the procedure for a rational and productive musical hermeneutics'.[63]

Kretzschmar now moves on to later generations of writers.

> The increased output [of such interpretations] will be of lasting benefit if the hermeneutic writers concerned are up to the task. That sadly cannot be said of all the writers currently thrusting analyses on to the market.
>
> What we have is first a group that, instead of proceeding soberly and objectively, approaches works in a spirit of gushing enthusiasm. Suffice it to mention the name Edmund von Hagen.[64] It is no bad thing for an explicator [*Erklärer*] to have a poetic turn of mind, but first and foremost he requires a knowledge of musical craftsmanship if he is not to sink to bogus drivel.
>
> A second group of explicators arrives at misguided aesthetic conclusions because its members lack *independent* musical insight. They operate without control of up-to-date opinions and views. They explicate Mozart's Symphony in G minor and Beethoven's in A major as works of graceful charm, they perceive Schubert's ['Unfinished'] Symphony in B minor as a sweetly romantic tone-poem, oblivious of passages that blatantly contradict such a reading. Their chief exponents are well-meaning, modish dilettantes.

---

62 See *Carl Maria von Weber: Writings on Music*, ed. John Warrack, trans. Martin Cooper (Cambridge: CUP, 1981). Theodor Hell was the *nom de plume* of Carl Gottfried Theodor Winkler (1775–1856), founder-editor of the *Dresdener Abendzeitung*, and personal friend of Weber.

63 'Robert Schumann als Ästhetiker', *Jahrbuch der Musikbibliothek Peters für 1906*, 13 (1907), 47–73; later issued in *Gesammelte Aufsätze*, vol. II, pp. 294–324, quotation from p. 310.

64 Edmund von Hagen (1850–1907): writer on music who published a study of *The Flying Dutchman* in 1880.

has been Hans-Georg Gadamer (1900–), whose *Truth and Method* (1960) took Heidegger's philosophical hermeneutics and returned it to the human sciences, and who has exemplified his method by publishing many hermeneutic analyses of literary-philosophical works. For Gadamer the interpreter's 'prejudgments' (*Vorurteile*) are not prejudices in the adverse sense, but essential products of his own historical existence, therefore not to be overcome but utilized. Moreover, interpreter and object of interpretation, far from being separated by history as Dilthey contended, form part of a historical continuum called 'effective history' (*Wirkungsgeschichte*).[74] Also important is the work of Jürgen Habermas (1929–), and the ensuing Gadamer–Habermas 'debate' has been one of the liveliest elements of the recent intellectual world.

The above two paragraphs are of course strictly extraneous to the concerns of the present volume. However, in view of the intensity of activity in hermeneutics during the twentieth century, and more particularly in view of the great interest in this field at the time of writing, it would have been perverse to disregard recent developments and procrustean to terminate the account at 1900. In music, the principally active figure was Arnold Schering (1877–1941), a pupil of Kretzschmar. Calling elucidatory analyses of instrumental music 'well intentioned games of dice with psychological explications',[75] he sought the creation of objectively researched programmes for works – programmes that constituted the 'keys' to the works concerned. Having begun with J. S. Bach, in connection with the music of whom he had developed a system of musical symbolism, he turned to Beethoven, producing two programmes in 1934, entitled 'The "Eroica", a Homer-Symphony by Beethoven?' and 'Toward interpreting the meaning of Beethoven's fourth and fifth symphonies' as Schiller-Symphony and Revolutionary Symphony respectively.[76] These were followed in the same year by a volume, entitled *Beethoven in a New Light*, presenting analyses of five string quartets and nine piano sonatas, their programmes based on Shakespeare and Schiller, with titles such as 'Piano Sonata Op. 54 in F major (*Much Ado about Nothing*)' and 'Piano Sonata Op. 106 in B♭ major according to Friedrich von Schiller's *Maid of Orleans*'.[77] In finding literary analogues for works, Schering took his clues from remarks by Schindler, Beethoven himself, and others. He claimed that within Beethoven's personal style-type there existed a 'logic of musical ideas [*Einfälle*]' in every way comparable to grammatic or mathematical logic. Drawing from his own work on Bach, he also posited a double layer of musical symbolism – an external layer being a fabric of affects, and an internal

74 Hans-Georg Gadamer, *Wahrheit und Methode: Grundzüge einer philosophischen Hermeneutik* (Tübingen: J. C. B. Mohr, 1960, 3/1972), Eng. trans. Garret Barden and William G. Doerpel as *Truth and Method* (New York: Seabury, 1975). A selection of his writings 1960–72 is *Philosophical Hermeneutics*, ed. and trans. David. E. Linge (Berkeley: University of California Press, 1976). See essays dating between 1934 and 1974 edited as *Dialogue and Dialectic: Eight Hermeneutical Studies on Plato*, Eng. trans. P. Christopher Smith (New Haven: Yale University Press, 1980).
75 *Beethoven in neuer Deutung* (see note 77 below), p. 9.
76 'Die Eroica, eine Homer-Symphonie Beethovens?', *Neues Beethoven-Jahrbuch*, 5 (1933), 159–77; 'Zur Sinndeutung der 4. und 5. Symphonie Beethovens', *Zeitschrift für Musikwissenschaft*, 16 (1934), 65–83.
77 *Beethoven in neuer Deutung*, vol. I, *Die Shakespeare-Streichquartette*, op. 74, op. 95, op. 127, op. 130, op. 131; *Die Shakespeare-Klaviersonaten*, op. 27 Nr. 1, op. 27 Nr. 2, op. 28, op. 31 Nr. 1, op. 31 Nr. 2, op. 54, op. 57, op. 111; *Die Schiller-Klaviersonate*, op. 106 (Leipzig: Kahnt, 1934).

layer being a play of mental images, states, gestures, etc. Using these two systems, and armed with a body of biographical information, Schering[78]

> constructed on a foundation of exact analysis of musical fact a certain hypothetical programme, the colours and contours of which are at first still ambivalent, but the tangibility of which at strategic points is usually so great that only a very tiny circle of relationships remains undefined. Identifying these by means of externally derived poetic or quasi-poetic material is then merely a matter of having a good nose.

Two years later there appeared *Beethoven and Poetry*, with analyses of the seventh and ninth symphonies, four more piano sonatas, seven more quartets, a piano trio and two violin sonatas. The range of literature was now much wider, and included the *Odyssey* (the 'Waldstein' Sonata), three scenes from Goethe's *Faust* (Opp. 132, 133, 135), Jean-Paul's *Flegeljahre* (Op. 59 no. 1) and Wieland's *Oberon* (the 'Archduke' Trio). These were preceded by a 100-page methodological exposition (including a potted history of Beethoven interpretations over the previous 125 years not dissimilar to that of Kretzschmar).[79]

Of the many other writers of programme notes and accessible descriptions of music, by far the most distinguished was Donald Francis Tovey (1875–1940). His six volumes of *Essays in Musical Analysis* (1935–9), very similar in organization to Kretzschmar's *Guide to the Concert Hall*, had begun life as programme notes for the Edinburgh Reid Concert Series in the mid-1910s (though some go back to 1902). In the later part of the twentieth century, scope for popular and accessible writing about music increased geometrically with documented commercial recording and broadcasting. Musical scholarship distanced itself from non-verifiable interpretation and analysis, at least until in the English-speaking world the call for a 'higher criticism' first came from Joseph Kerman in 1965, and subsequently Peter Kivy addressed the philosophical basis of subjective analysis. Since then there have occurred the exciting developments already alluded to in the Preface above, promising as they do to bring interpretative criticism and analysis back to the fold of serious cogitation about music, and to offer new modes of imaginative thinking in the musical realm.

Among the responses to Kerman's call, none has done more to re-engage the search for a musical hermeneutics than that from Lawrence Kramer. After a first book (1984) in which he brought together pairs of works, musical and literary, and by parallel analysis sought to demonstrate common 'structural rhythm', Kramer in *Music as Cultural Practice, 1800–1900* (1990) addressed frontally the issue of musical meaning, forging a new criticism that treated the musical work as embedded within culture. Kramer applied his critical method to such works as Liszt's *Faust Symphony* and Wagner's *Tristan and Isolde*. In a sophisticated introductory essay he articulated his method of locating and opening 'hermeneutic windows' in a work (usually points of discontinuity or excess), and allowing interpretation to pass through those windows out into the cultural field to find links with other music, with works of literature, visual art and philosophy, and with other cultural documents. In applying this method, he drew upon ideas from such realms as speech-act theory, psychoanalysis, feminism and deconstruction.

78 *Beethoven in neuer Deutung*, pp. 11–12.
79 *Beethoven und die Dichtung, mit einer Einleitung zur Geschichte und Ästhetik der Beethoven-deutung* (Berlin: Junker und Dünnhaupt, 1936).

PART I:

Elucidatory analysis

Introduction

As we saw in the General Introduction, there is a subtle difference between the German verbs *erklären*, 'to explain' or 'explicate', and *erläutern*, 'to elucidate' or 'cast light upon'. The natural scientist *explains* the phenomena that he observes, the human scientist (in Dilthey's terms) *elucidates* his. The first verb implies tangible data and positive methodologies, measurement and quantification, the second implies vague subject matter and imprecise methodologies, surmise and conjecture. As to the outcome of these processes, *Erklärung* implies something concrete – the interior workings of something fully accounted for –, whereas *Erläuterung* implies something less committal – an essence glimpsed, a meaning adumbrated.[1]

To present-day music-theoretical ears, the term *Erläuterung* has strong associations with Heinrich Schenker, whose *Erläuterungsausgaben*, 'elucidatory editions', of Bach's Chromatic Fantasia and Fugue in D minor and Beethoven's last five piano sonatas are familiar to theorists and historians. Significantly, those works were published in 1910 and 1913–21.[2] The similarity between a public advertisement of 1921 for the second of these and the title of a quite different volume from 1910 (my italics) – just one of many volumes published around the same time – is striking:[3]

> 1921: The Last Five Piano Sonatas of Ludwig van Beethoven: Critical Editions *with Introduction, Elucidation and Literature, together with Numerous Music Examples . . .*

> 1910: Beethoven's Symphonies *Elucidated with Music Examples . . . together with an Introduction . . .*

1 J. and W. Grimm, *Deutsches Wörterbuch*, vol. III (Leipzig: S. Hirtzel, 1862), col. 894: 'erläutern *illustrare, explanare, erhellen, klar machen. . .*'.
2 *Chromatische Fantasia und Fuge D moll von Joh. Seb. Bach: Kritische Ausgabe mit Anhang von Heinrich Schenker* (Vienna and Leipzig: Universal-Edition, 1910), Eng. trans. H. Siegel (New York: Longman, 1984); *Die letzten fünf Sonaten von Beethoven: Kritische Ausgabe mit Einführung und Erläuterung von Heinrich Schenker* (Vienna and Leipzig: Universal-Edition, 1913, 1914, 1916, 1921). The edition of Op. 106 was never issued. Schenker also wrote an aphoristic article entitled 'Erläuterungen', apparently dating from 1915–19: Eng. trans. I. Bent, *Music Analysis*, 5 (1986), 187–91; see discussion ibid, 145–7. 'Erläuterungen' will shortly be available in the new complete English translation of *Das Meisterwerk* (1925–30) currently in press in the series Cambridge Studies in Music Theory and Analysis.
3 *Der Tonwille*, 1 (1921), back page; G. Erlanger, [T.] Helm, A. Morin, [?] Radecke, [?] Sittard and [?] Witting, *Beethoven's Symphonien erläutert mit Notenbeispielen . . . nebst einer Einleitung . . .* (Frankfurt: Bechhold, [1896]). The closeness of Schenker to this tradition is seen in the title of his 1912 'Beethoven's Ninth Symphony: A Presentation of its *Musical Content* . . .'; his analysis of the Fifth Symphony (1925) has the same formulation. Particularly striking is his 1935 designation of his analytical treatment of the Fifth Symphony, Mozart's Symphony in G minor, No. 40 (1926), Chopin's Studies Op. 10 nos 5 and 6 (1925), and Schubert's Minuet in B minor (1929), as 'elucidatory presentation' (*erläuternde Darstellung*) (*Der freie Satz* (Vienna: Universal-Edition, 1935, 2/1956), p. 34 note).

The latter was a volume in a series of pocketbooks produced around that time by the distinguished Berlin publishing house of Schlesinger, the *Schlesinger Music Library*, of which it belonged to the subseries *Master Guides* – guides, that is, just like the pocketbooks supplied for tourists: *Führer*, or *Wegweiser*.[4] The series contained volumes also on the string quartets of Beethoven, the symphonies of Schumann, of Bruckner and Mahler, the orchestral works of Tchaikovsky, the symphonic poems of Liszt and Richard Strauss, and the operas of Mozart, Wagner and Strauss. A similar series of 'elucidations' was published by the firm of Philipp Reclam junior, celebrated pioneers of what we now call the 'paperback': a series under the general title *Elucidations of Great Works of Music*.[5] Eleven volumes of this were devoted to the music dramas of Wagner, from *Rienzi* to *Parsifal*; there followed further volumes, on *Carmen, Salome, Rosenkavalier, The Tales of Hoffmann*, the St Matthew Passion, the *Messiah*, d'Albert's *Tiefland*, Beethoven's *Fidelio* and the nine symphonies – thirty-six volumes in all, every one by the popular writer and editor Max Chop.[6]

Some of these guides had their origin in the late nineteenth century. Schlesinger, for example, had acquired its *Master Guides* in about 1907 from the Frankfurt-am-Main company of H. Bechhold, which had issued them initially as separate pamphlets on individual works, called *Music Guides*. Bechhold had published its first two *Music Guides*, 'elucidations' of Beethoven's Fifth and Ninth Symphonies, in 1894. Schlesinger claimed that as many as 400 of these pamphlets had ultimately been produced – and indeed an advertisement dating from c.1896 already listed *Guides* to 115 works, by thirty-one composers. Kretzschmar did not mention these *Guides* by name in the survey quoted in the General Introduction above. We can tell what he thought of them, however, from another source. In a review of Sir George Grove's *Beethoven and his Nine Symphonies* (1896), of which a German translation had appeared in 1906, he made the biting remark:[7]

> [Grove] is the father of the genre of elucidations of concert programmes that has nowadays literally run wild. His *Synoptical Analyses* for the Crystal Palace stand as the direct model for a Frankfurt factory that churns this type of material out at a great rate.

Grove had begun writing the Crystal Palace public concert notes forty years earlier, in 1856, at first sharing the work with Sir August Manns, then from 1868 entirely under his own steam.[8] (His programme note for the centenary of Mozart's birth, interestingly, recommended to the reader von Lenz's *Beethoven and his Three*

---

4   The term *Wegweiser* was used by Schlesinger in its advertisments for the series: 'Guides to the creations of individual composers . . .', and as in the title of another subseries, *Opernwegweiser*.
5   *Erläuterungen zu Meisterwerken der Tonkunst.*
6   Max Chop (1862–1929): studied law; in 1883 on Liszt's advice embarked on a writing career, notably producing books on contemporary music, Wagner, Verdi, Delius, Bungert, analyses of Liszt, Wagner and Bungert, and popular music guides. He was editor of the *Signale für die musikalische Welt* in the 1920s, and also a prolific composer.
7   H. Kretzschmar, 'Ein neues Buch über Beethoven und seine Symphonien', in *Gesammelte Aufsätze über Musik*, vol. I, *Gesammelte Aufsätze über Musik aus den Grenzboten* (Leipzig: Peters, 1910), p. 270. Sir George Grove, *Beethoven and his Nine Symphonies* (London: Novello, 1896, 2/1896, 3/1898; reprint edn 1962), Ger. trans. Max Hehemann, *Beethoven und seine neun Symphonien* (London and New York: Novello, 1906).
8   Percy M. Young, *George Grove 1820–1900: a Biography* (London: Macmillan, 1980), pp. 65–6.

Styles (1852) – see Analysis 3 below.) From the beginning these programmes comprised elegantly written amalgams of quotations from composers' letters, biography, historical information, notes on reception, technical and metaphorical description of music. A typical passage from the Eighth Symphony analysis in its 1896 form is:[9]

> We now arrive at the third portion of the *Finale*. This again begins with the initial part of the first theme in the violins, accompanied by the wonderful octaves, just quoted, in the bassoon and drum, a holding F above the tune in the flute and oboe, and with other rich support from the wind. All is hushed and mysterious, full of sly humour, which soon develops in the most telling style by the re-introduction of the terrible C sharp, after a passage gradually diminishing to ***ppp*** – like the sudden appearance of some hideous mask. The comedy here is very unmistakable and irresistible. Some passages seem to say, as plainly as possible: 'Look out!' 'I'm coming!' 'I'm dangerous!'

Grove's analyses of the Beethoven symphonies certainly deserved a place in the present volume, and would have been represented in their own right had not all original English-language analysis been excluded on grounds of space. George Bernard Shaw once referred to Grove as '"G", the rhapsodist who wrote the Crystal Palace programmes'. Shaw devised a long and learned analytical statement, only to conclude:[10]

> 'G', who was 'no musician', cultivated this style in vain. His most conscientious attempts at it never brought him any nearer than 'The lovely melody then passes, by a transition of remarkable beauty, into the key of C major, in which it seems to go straight up to heaven.' Naturally the average Englishman was profoundly impressed by the inscrutable learning of the first style (which I could teach to a poodle in two hours), and thought 'G's' obvious sentimentality idiotic.

Two years before Grove's debut as a programme-note writer, a slim anonymous volume was released in 1854 – the very year of Hanslick's *On the Musically Beautiful*, arguing the contrary belief that, while music does have spiritual substance (*geistiger Gehalt*), that substance must reside solely 'in the tone-structure itself'.[11] This anonymous volume, which contained no music examples, bore the title *Beethoven's Symphonies interpreted as to their Ideal Substance, seen in the Light of Haydn's and Mozart's Symphonies, by a Music Lover*.[12] Its author was in fact Ernst von Elterlein, whose second example of the genre, *Beethoven's Piano Sonatas, elucidated for Music Lovers* (see Analysis 4 below), emerged two years later. There was a steady stream of such popular small-format guides in the 1860s and 1870s, one of the most widely circulated being F. L. S. Dürenberg's *The Symphonies of Beethoven and Other Famous Masters, analysed and elucidated for Comprehension [zum Verständnisse erläutert]*, published by Matthes of Leipzig in 1863, and dedicated to Franz Brendel. This stream turned into a flood after 1880. An evident need for popular explanations of Wagner's music, for instance, was

---

9   *Nine Symphonies*, p. 303.
10   George Bernard Shaw, 'Beethoven's Symphonies', *Saturday Review*, 14 November 1896, reprinted in Young, *George Grove*, pp. 295–8.
11   *Vom Musikalisch-Schönen: ein Beitrag zur Revision der Ästhetik der Tonkunst* (Leipzig: Weigel, 1854), Eng. trans. Geoffrey Payzant (Indianapolis: Hackett, 1986), p. 31: Payzant at this point (chap. 3) translates *geistiger Gehalt* as 'ideal content', only later (chap. 7) rendering it 'ideal substance': see p. 114, note 9.
12   *Beethovens Symphonien nach ihrem idealen Gehalt mit Rücksicht auf Haydns und Mozarts Symphonien, von einem Kunstfreunde* (Dresden: Brauer, 1854).

supplied by August Guckeisen's *Elucidations of Wagner's 'Ring of the Nibelung'* (1879), and in particular by the only examples of the genre that are still known today, Hans von Wolzogen's *Thematic Threads through the Music of Wagner's Festspiel 'The Ring of the Nibelung'* (1876), which was later entitled *Elucidations of Wagner's Nibelung Drama* (1882), and his uniform companion volumes to *Tristan* (1880) and *Parsifal* (1882: Analysis 6 below), all of which were translated into English and widely disseminated.[13]

There is a clear and constant connection between 'elucidation' and the notion of 'content' (*Inhalt*) or 'substance' (*Gehalt*). Here lies an apparent paradox, for in Part I of vol. I we saw these very words used in a work of intensely technical description, packed with music examples, and written for the professional reader: namely, Hauptmann's *Elucidations* of Bach's *Art of Fugue*. Nothing could seem more remote from the world of Part I of the present volume; moreover, Hauptmann distanced himself at the outset from 'musical-poetic essence and value'. The solution to this paradox lies in the convergence of two senses of *Erläuterung*. On the one hand, this latter term was widely used in critical commentaries to texts, commonly found in literary editions, also in editions of music. Since Hauptmann's analyses formed the critical commentary to a volume of a collected edition, it was natural that he should use it. On the other hand Hauptmann, as a self-styled Hegelian, was indeed laying bare the *essential content*, the *wesentlicher Inhalt*, of the *Art of Fugue*. He meant by this not its human-psychological essence but its musical-contrapuntal essence – the mechanism that lies at the heart of each fugue and canon. But this was a far cry from 'verification of technical correctness' and 'technical adjudication', Brendel's slighting words of 1845 quoted in the General Introduction §7, above. On the contrary, his concern was with essence of process, not with surface manipulation of notes. Such essence fell squarely within the sphere of hermeneutics – remember Dilthey's remark, also quoted in the General Introduction §5: 'It is not psychological, but musical relationships that form the study of musical genius, composition and theory.' Thus the senses of *Erläuterung* that converge in Hauptmann's analyses (and, for that matter, in those of Schenker, too) themselves stem from the twin disciplines of exegesis and hermeneutics in the eighteenth and early nineteenth centuries, and Hauptmann's essay should be considered not only as the example of technical-fugal analysis for which it is displayed in volume I, but also as an extreme example of hermeneutic analysis in the present volume.

We can see from the above discussion, and from the latter part of the General Introduction, that a distinctive genre of elucidatory writing about music existed in the second half of the nineteenth century, its immediate ancestry traceable back to Wagner's programme notes for the works that he himself conducted, notably

---

13   *Thematischer Leitfaden durch die Musik von R. Wagners Festspiel 'Der Ring des Nibelungen'* (Leipzig: Reinboth, 1876; Eng. trans. 1882); . . . *'Tristan und Isolde'* (1880; Eng. trans. 1902); . . . *'Parsifal'* (1882; Eng. trans. 1904). All went through many editions, and underwent changes of title. *Leitfaden* is an elaborate play on words, since *Faden* ('thread') was customarily used for the melodic continuity of a piece (see vol. I, Analysis 12), *Leit-* ('lead') suggested *Leitmotiv*, the term Hans von Wolzogen applied to Wagner's symbolic themes, and yet in common parlance *Leitfaden* meant 'manual', 'textbook' or 'guidebook', synonymous with *Führer* and *Wegweiser*.

those for the Ninth Symphony (Analysis 2 below) of 1846. Resolutely aimed at the musical amateur, written in German, eschewing musical technicality and couched in descriptive, metaphorical language, initially assuming the reader's inability to follow musical notation (though music examples crept in later in the century), with a strongly educational and acculturating intention, and published in pamphlet or pocketbook format, these volumes all arise out of German idealist philosophy, many of them probably filtered at second hand from the musical aesthetics of Friedrich Theodor Vischer, whose *Aesthetics, or Science of the Beautiful* (1846–57) was enormously influential.[14] Vischer, who dealt with music in his final volume, held that music was the language of feeling, and that 'music presents the listener with a whole world wrapped in feeling and the listener unwraps it in a thousand different ways'. Instrumental music is deficient of feeling with respect to clarity and determinate content, so is 'driven by its inner deficiency to an annexation with the world and then dependent'.[15]

Not all of the examples given in Part I below are even in German, let alone belong strictly to this genre. The analyses by Wagner, von Elterlein, von Wolzogen and Kretzschmar can be directly associated with the elucidatory tradition. Spitta wrote for a more professional readership but was clearly borrowing from the elucidatory genre when writing about musical detail. Von Lenz, despite his Russian nationality and use of French, was Germanic in his musical tastes; indeed, the German edition of his *Beethoven and His Three Styles*, published in 1855–60, is completely at home in its new language, and takes its place comfortably within the elucidatory tradition. Only the earliest analysis, that by Berlioz (Analysis 1), is quite alien to this tradition, not only because it is in French but also on account of its transparency of language and ironic mode of discourse. A link does exist, albeit tenuous, between Berlioz and the world of the elucidatory interpreters, for Franz Brendel included Berlioz, with some ambivalence, among the 'musicians of the future':[16]

> The fact that he is the first Frenchman to dedicate himself predominantly to the realm of instrumental music is what elicits from us a very different attention than has hitherto generally been accorded him. This sympathy for Germany, the deep and sublime striving that lies at the heart of that sympathy, rightly claims that we meet him half way.

Moreover, the link is not exclusively via his music. No fewer than fifty-two of his writings on music, most of them from the *Journal des débats*, appeared in translation in the *Neue Zeitschrift für Musik* between 1840 and 1843, not to mention six in Marx's Berlin *Allgemeine musikalische Zeitung* in 1829.[17] His writings

---

14 Friedrich Theodor Vischer, *Aesthetik oder Wissenschaft des Schönen* (Reutlingen: Macken, 1846–57). Only the more general sections on musical aesthetics were written by Vischer, the more detailed material being provided by Karl Reinhold von Köstlin (1819–94). Sections of this work are available in Bujić, 82–9.

15 Quoted from Bujić, 85–6, and Edward Lippman, *A History of Western Musical Aesthetics* (Lincoln, NE: University of Nebraska Press, 1992), pp. 326, 327.

16 Franz Brendel, *Geschichte der Musik in Italien, Deutschland und Frankreich . . .* (Leipzig: Hinze, 1852; reprint edn Vaduz/Liechtenstein: Sändig, 1985), pp. 512–13.

17 See *Hector Berlioz: New Edition of the Complete Works*, vol. XXV, *Catalogue of the Works of Hector Berlioz* (Kassel: Bärenreiter, 1987), ed. D. Kern Holoman, pp. 452–62: forty-two items were drawn from the *Journal des débats*, ten of these being prepublication releases of the *Voyage musical en Allemagne* (Paris: Labitte, 1844), and ten items from the *Revue et gazette musicale*.

predicament into which Bruckner has put himself, the second theme of the movement – in my dilute translation – 'takes over the initiative' from the main theme,
what is actually said is that it *die geistige Führung übernimmt*, that is, 'takes over
the spiritual leadership'. This is no vacuous comment. In Hegelian terms its meaning
is very precise: the second theme exhibits greater thematic content (i.e. it has generated more motivic material); that content communicates directly with our inner
being; the greater presence that it now has within us allows it to usurp the main
theme's function. While not all writers in the elucidatory tradition could have
read Hegel directly, they did have available to them many digests and accessible
reformulations of his ideas, notably in the pages of the *Neue Zeitschrift für Musik*:
to mention but two, in 1842 ten consecutive issues were largely given over to a critique by Eduard Krüger of Hegel's ideas on music; and in 1857 eleven issues carried
abstracts by Ernst von Elterlein of the music aesthetics of Friedrich Theodor
Vischer.[20]

All in all, the analyses given in Part I exhibit a striving to do something over
which twentieth-century writers on music have in the main displayed considerable
discomfort: a striving to portray pieces of music in terms of their *sound-world* –
fragile, evanescent, infinitely variable though that world is – rather than in terms
of the fixed visual image-world in which those pieces are stored. Some of these
nineteenth-century authors were perhaps forced to do so by their own lack of
theoretical knowledge, others were doubtless impelled by the non-technical nature
of their readership. But some at least may have placed less trust than recent generations of analysts in the notational image, regarding its stability as illusory, its
semiotic resource as only a shorthand for an aural image heard and vividly retained
in the mind.

20 For Krüger's critique, see le Huray/Day, 530–38; for von Elterlein's abstracts, see below, Analysis 4,
    note 3.

Hector Berlioz (1803–1869)

'[Review of Meyerbeer: *Les Huguenots*]' (1836)

It comes as no surprise that the majority of the authors represented in these two volumes wrote, in one capacity or another, for the music journals of their day. Such journals were, after all, the primary forums for discourse about music throughout the century. Among the exceptions were some of the more pedagogically inclined authors, mostly to be found in vol. 1 – Reicha and Sechter, as conservatory professors of counterpoint, Czerny, as a private piano teacher, Momigny, music publisher, and theorist in isolation – who tended to cast their ideas in the more highly systematized form of the treatise, eschewing the literary style necessary for most journals. Other pedagogues, notably Mayrberger and Riemann, succeeded in placing serious theoretical articles with journals. Others of our authors served the periodical world from the editor's desk,[1] some being founder-editors of journals,[2] while Baini worked in the rarified world of the papal household.

A number of our authors, however, wrote music criticism outside the purely music periodicals, some of them for surprisingly long periods of time: Fétis (vol. 1, Analysis 16b) with some forty-four years of service (1827–71), not only in his own and other specialist journals, but also for the daily newspaper *Le temps* and the political and literary daily *Le national*; Wagner, with forty-three years of intermittent activity (spanning 1840–83) for such newspapers as the *Dresdener Abendzeitung* as well as for the *Revue et gazette musicale*, the *Signale für die musikalische Welt* and other music journals including that devoted to him, the *Bayreuther Blätter*; Theodor Helm, with thirty-eight years of service (1867–1905) as music critic to Viennese newspapers, the *Neues Fremdenblatt*, the *Deutsche Zeitung* and magazines, as well as contributor to music journals; Gottfried Weber (vol. 1, Analysis 10), whose journalistic career spanned thirty-six years (1803–39), his output numbering probably well over 200 articles in not only major music periodicals but also numerous non-music magazines and newspapers, including reviews of concerts and scores, and topical reports; E. T. A. Hoffmann, whose journalistic career was perforce short, and who wrote reviews and reports for theatrical magazines, literary and cultural papers and literary-musical journals, and a series of articles for the Leipzig *Allgemeine musikalische Zeitung*, over a period of seventeen years (1803–20); Schumann, whose

---

1   Hauptmann and Lobe at the Leipzig *AmZ* (1843–6, 1846–8), Dehn at *Caecilia* (1842–8), Helm at the *Kalendar für die musikalische Welt* (1875–1901).

2   Gottfried Weber of *Caecilia* (1824), A. B. Marx of the Berlin *AmZ* (1824), Fétis of the *Revue musicale* (1827), Schumann of the *NZM* (1834), Basevi of *L'Armonia* (1856), Spitta of the *Vierteljahrsschrift für Musikwissenschaft* (1885) and von Wolzogen (initial editor, though not founder) of the *Bayreuther Blätter* (January 1878–1938), to which could be added single-author journals (of which *Revue musicale* was almost one): Vogler's *Betrachtungen der Mannheimer Tonschule* (1778), and Lobe's *Fliegende Blätter für Musik* (1855).

active period as critic was even shorter, thirteen years (1831–44), the bulk of his critical writing being placed with his own *Neue Zeitschrift für Musik*;[3] and finally Lobe (vol. I, Analysis 12), who for many years was music editor of the *Illustrierte Zeitung*.

Berlioz's journalistic career outstrips all but two of these in time, and probably all of them in intensity and sheer reach. Contributing directly or indirectly to no fewer than thirty-six journals, magazines and papers, he sustained his critical writing for forty years, from 1823 to 1863, with only one fallow year in the entire time, producing an astounding output of over 900 attributed items,[4] to which may perhaps be added hundreds of smaller unidentifiable ones.[5] Although he did not receive his first true appointment as music critic until 1833, at *Le rénovateur*, he had since 1823 been making contributions to such topical publications as the popular news sheet *Le corsaire*, the Catholic *Le correspondant*, the *Revue de Paris*, the *Revue européenne* and *Revue littéraire*, including six articles at A. B. Marx's invitation to the Berlin *Allgemeine musikalische Zeitung* on the opera scene in Paris.

Berlioz wrote for two of the four main French music journals that were launched in his lifetime: Fétis's *Revue musicale* (1827–35) and its rival, Schlesinger's *Gazette musicale de Paris* (1834–5), as well as the merger of these two as *Revue et gazette musicale de Paris* (1835–80).[6] His association with the *Gazette* and the merger lasted for twenty-eight years (1834–61), yielding more than 260 articles. But it was with a non-music daily newspaper that his most prolific association occurred: the *Journal des débats*, to which Berlioz contributed close on 400 articles between 1835 and his retirement from criticism in 1863, and through the pages of which he became a commanding arbiter of Parisian musical taste.

In his busiest years, 1834–5, 1837 and 1842, he wrote an average of more than one article a week, at times serving three journals on a regular basis.[7] In 1836, he was working for the *Journal des débats* and the *Revue et gazette musicale de Paris*, and it was on 29 February of that year that Meyerbeer's second grand opera, *The Huguenots*, was given its wildly successful première at the Paris Opéra. Berlioz covered it in three instalments in the *Revue et gazette* of 6, 13 and 20 March.[8] Later that year, the score was published, and this Berlioz reviewed in two instalments for the *Journal des débats* on 10 November and 10 December.[9] It is these latter two items, constituting Berlioz's critical-analytical appraisal of Meyerbeer's score, that are reproduced below.

3   He contributed two essays to a literary journal, *Der Komet*, and a handful of articles to the Leipzig *AmZ* early in his career.
4   A catalogue of 936 is provided in *Hector Berlioz: New Edition of the Complete Works*, vol. XXV, *Catalogue of the Works of Hector Berlioz* (Kassel: Bärenreiter, 1987), ed. D. Kern Holoman, pp. 435–88, 'Feuilletons'. This total includes republications and translations in other journals, serialization of parts of the *Memoirs* (thirty-four items), and pre- and post-publication issue of parts of the *Traité d'instrumentation* in French, Italian and English (forty-two items).
5   D. Kern Holoman, *Berlioz* (Cambridge, MA: Harvard University Press, 1989), p. 160: 'Berlioz [. . .] was surely responsible for hundreds of the unsigned bits of news and gossip that appeared beneath such headings as "Nouvelles" or "Chronique Musicale".'
6   The others were Heugel's *Le ménestrel: Journal de musique* (1833–1940) and *La France musicale* (1837–70).
7   Annual attributable totals: seventy-four (1834), seventy-two (1835), sixty-six (1837), sixty-two (1842); the 1836 total was forty-six.
8   The first was reprinted in the Berlin *AmZ*. See note 12, below.
9   Both were reprinted in *Monde musical*.

It is perhaps with Berlioz that we reach the farthest remove in these two volumes from the centre of the analytical realm. Among Berlioz's hundreds of concert and opera notices, there are few if any that can be called, in their totality, 'music analyses'. This is not to say that the level of detailed technical comment is not often astonishingly high – Berlioz evidently studied scores assiduously in advance of performances, and attended rehearsals, making careful notes 'very like a modern reporter'; he also possessed an exceptional capacity to memorize entire operatic scenes, even when he had never set eyes on the score.[10] It is hardly surprising, then, that his longer reviews describe musical phenomena in exact terms. However, Berlioz was a true critic: his pivotal concern was evaluation. There were many arms to his critical apparatus, all functioning in the service of the evaluative critical act, one of these indeed being music analysis. For such analysis to come centre-stage would subvert that critical act; consequently he rarely described a whole work, or movement, or scene in continuous, precise analytical detail.

Even in his series of articles on the Beethoven symphonies,[11] where evaluation never wholly gives way to acclamation, he seldom pursued a movement through its full course. Unlike E. T. A. Hoffmann, whose concern (see Analysis 9 below) was with the listener's constant stream of experience, Berlioz strove to encapsulate each movement in a characterizing description, thereafter restricting himself to isolated musical incidents (there are exceptions: notably the link to the finale of the Fifth, and the choral finale of the Ninth). His account of the first movement of the 'Eroica' Symphony, for example, devotes two-thirds of its space, part technically, part anecdotally, to the 'extremely bizarre' horn entry at the recapitulation. That of the first movement of the Seventh Symphony cannot resist singling out the 'strange *crescendo*' in bb. 401–22:

> produced by a two-bar phrase (D–C♯–B♯–B♯–C♯) in A major, stated eleven times in succession, low in register by basses with violas, while the wind instruments sustain an E in high and lower registers and in the middle, doubled over four octaves, while the violins intone like a chime of bells the three notes E–A–E–C[♯], reiterated at an increasingly fast rate, so arranged that the dominant [E] is always sounding at the moment when the basses are playing the D or B♯, and the tonic or its third [A or C♯] when they are playing the C[♯].

The discussion of the vivace is by no means continuous: it merely touches on the character of the first theme, leaps to an unorthodox harmonic progression in bb. 154–7 and 160–63, then concludes with the above passage as an aside. The latter two, however, prove incidental to the central concern: to evaluate the propriety of using a 'rustic' theme and of allowing a single 'rhythmic formula' to saturate an entire movement.

The passage just quoted, written as if describing some particularly intricate mechanical device, shows Berlioz's love of the curious and his fascination with

---

10 Holoman, *Berlioz*, p. 237; Cohen, 'Hector Berlioz, critique musical: ses écrits sur l'Opéra de Paris de 1829 à 1849', *Revue de musicologie*, 63 (1977), 17–34.

11 *Revue et gazette musicale de Paris*, 5 (1838), 33–7, 47–50, 53–4, 64–6, 75–6, 97–101; *A travers chants* (Paris: Lévy, 1862), pp. 17–59; the passage quoted below being *Revue*, 65, *A travers*, p. 43. Berlioz had produced an earlier three-instalment article for *Le correspondant* in 1829.

how things work, not to mention his intoxication with special orchestrational effects. These proclivities explain in part his favourable response to Meyerbeer's *The Huguenots*. (His own *Treatise on Orchestration* (1843) was to begin appearing in serialized form in 1841, and many of the instrumental effects discussed in the review of the *Huguenots* score are cited in that work, as footnoted below.) Meyerbeer's experimentation with orchestral deployment, exploitation of unconventional instruments, cultivation of colouristic effect, marshalling of choruses, massing of forces, and spatial distribution of sound – all of these appealed to him, reflecting propensities of his own that are revealed in such works as the Requiem, on which he was to be working only four months later, the *Funereal and Triumphal Symphony* (1840), and ultimately the opera *The Trojans* (1858).

Berlioz's review of the first performance of *The Huguenots* in March 1836 reveals a good deal about his approach to analysis. He used *analyser* several times, once to denote merely an account of the plot, elsewhere to denote an examination of melodic and rhythmic character, orchestration and dramatic effect. Analysis was for him the product of detached thought: at the end of the first instalment of this review he pleaded 'We beg time to reflect on our impressions before analysing them and identifying their causes'; of the combination of timpani and military drum in Act IV (discussed also below) he remarked 'I have been incapable of hearing it again with a sufficiently cool head to be able to analyse as I could an Italian duet'.[12] In his review of the score, given below, where the term is never used, we find two types of what we might agree to call 'analysis'. On the one hand, there is microscopic examination of harmonic progressions, most notably of the modulation from G minor to E♭ major shown in Example 3, and of the way in which that progression strikes both the ear and the eye. On the other hand, there is one instance of what we might now call 'formal analysis' – though indicatively he uses the term *plan* rather than *forme* for what he describes there – : namely, his description of the great scene 'Conspiracy and Blessing of the Daggers' that occupies the bulk of Act IV. He portrays this mighty scene as a single, gigantic *crescendo*, with a principal theme that is deployed three times to control and ultimately end-stop its long-range intensification and with subsidiary ideas that assist in the overall contouring. He keeps careful track of tonal motion and use of forces; yet even here he takes the time to deliver an unfavourable verdict on Meyerbeer's use of the same theme for two very different emotional states, and expatiates on its implications for dramatic realism. The object of Berlioz's analysis, this reminds us, is not the music in isolation, but drama and music inseparably welded together; and the analysis remains subordinate to the act of critical judgment.

Central to this article, and to the totality of Berlioz's critical writings on opera, is the notion of musical style – not at all, as we might expect, a concern with unity or purity, but rather with appropriateness to dramatic purpose. Berlioz articulates this as a series of contrasts: external contrast between *The Huguenots* and other works, contrast between Meyerbeer and other composers, and internal contrasts within the work.

---

12   The review appears in the *Revue et gazette musicale de Paris*, 3 (1836), no. 10 (6 March), 73–7, no. 11 (13 March), 81–3, no. 12 (20 March), 89–91: see esp. 77, 81, 90.

The Huguenots is *sui generis* in that it imports the chorale by Martin Luther *A Mighty Fortress is our God* and puts it into the mouths of the Huguenot characters at several points. This lends the work a Protestant 'religious' style not present in Meyerbeer's previous opera, *Robert the Devil* (1831). Within Act IV, the juxtaposition of the 'religious' style with the 'frenetic' style, this time, however, the chanting of Catholic monks, contrasted with their intoxication with murderous intentions, creates an effect of sacrilege. Further, the 'learned' style of Meyerbeer's treatment of the chorale contrasts sharply with the 'dry scholasticism' of other composers. The 'strict' style of most of the work contrasts with the cheap theatricality into which *The Huguenots* lapses in its weakest moments, characteristic of the worst of Italian opera. Analogously, 'singers' music', cliché-ridden and lacking invention, contrasts with true dramatic music, the former, the work of ingenuity, being mere recreation, the latter, the work of genius, bringing the listener profound experience. Meyerbeer's layering and combining of resources to meet the special scenic demands of grand opera is contrasted with the layering and combining that comprises contrapuntal and fugal artifice in the work of 'church musicians'.

'[Review: Meyerbeer's] *The Huguenots*: The Score'

Source:
Hector Berlioz: [review:] 'Les Huguenots: La partition', *Journal des débats* (10 November 1836), 1–2, (10 December 1836), 1–2. *Hector Berlioz: Les musiciens et la musique*, ed. André Hallays (Paris: Calmann-Lévy, 1903), pp. 85–105. [Page numbers are those of Hallays.]

The opera *The Huguenots*, like *Robert the Devil*, indeed like most of the extended five-act works of the modern school,[13] has no overture. Perhaps it is that symphonic development on a scale fitted to the colossal dramatic subjects usually chosen for such works would exceed the bounds of what is acceptable in our theatres for [purely] instrumental music. Perhaps, too, composers are wary of overtaxing at the outset an audience whose powers of concentration are barely sufficient for what will be required of them. These two considerations may well point to a simple introduction as the most appropriate thing; but even so, especially when I see M Meyerbeer's introductions brimming with lovely ideas, I cannot help regretting that such a composer should not have written an overture. The introduction to *Robert the Devil* is a model of its kind, difficult to equal, and that of *The Huguenots*, less striking though it is by reason of its underlying religious character, {86} seems to me in its own way worthy of comparison with it in every respect. The celebrated Lutheran chorale[14] is treated in learned style, but never with the dry scholasticism that one all too often finds in such cases. Rather, it is handled in such a way that each of its transformations enhances it, each luminous harmonic effect that the composer projects on to it serves only to bathe it in even richer hues; that beneath the sumptuous fabric with which he clothes it, its sturdy forms are at all times clearly discernible. The variety of effects he has been able to draw from it, above all by the use of wind instruments, the skill with which he has gauged their *crescendo* leading up to the final outburst – these are quite marvellous.

[Act I]

The [drinking] chorus [No. 1D], 'À table, amis, à table!' [pp. 46–77][15] is remarkable for its vivacity. The melody that forms a recurring episode, 'De la Touraine versez

---

13   Of the five-act operas premièred in the previous eight years, Auber's *La muette de Portici* (1828) and *Gustave III ou Le bal masqué* (1833) had 'ouvertures' of normal length, whereas Meyerbeer's *Robert le diable* (1831) had an 'ouverture' of only sixty-four bars, and Halévy's *La juive* (1835) an 'introduction' of only 103 bars. Note Berlioz's ranking of the *Huguenots* Act III septet 'among the finest creations of modern music'.

14   Meyerbeer uses Martin Luther's chorale *Ein' feste Burg ist unser Gott* in the Introduction, and also in Act I no. 3, 'Chorale', Act II no. 12C, 'Stretta', and Act V no. 27, 'Scene', 'Murderers' Chorus', 'Vision'.

15   The page numbers in square brackets are those of the printed full score (Paris: Schlesinger, 1836), available in a facsimile edition, ed. P. Gossett and C. Rosen, in *Early Romantic Opera*, Series A, vol. xx (New York: Garland, 1980). The opening line of the chorus is in fact 'Bonheur de la table, bonheur véritable'.

Example 1

De__ la Tou - rai - ne Ver - sez les vins!_____   Le__ vin a -

p   *mf*   *p*

mè - ne Jo - yeux re - frains____   et__ dans l'i - vres - se Noy-

mf

ons sou - dain____   et__ la sa - ges - se et le cha - grin

les vins', is pleasing because of its rhythmic character [*coupe rythmique*],[16] and its
original way of modulating [see Example 1]: the piece is in C [major], and instead
of going to the dominant by the ordinary route, the composer has chosen to let it
go via E major, thereby imparting a delicious freshness to the G [major] that
immediately follows it. The only things in this number that I will criticize are a
certain laxity in text setting that makes the words extremely difficult to enunciate,
and the short 3/8 allegro [con spirito, pp. 68–72] that precedes the coda. Regrettably,
the theme of the latter, bouncy and {87} set in rapid syllables, departs totally from
the composer's style, lapsing into that of the bad Italian school; and what is more,
it destroys the scene's unity of purpose and colour, while contributing nothing to
its effect.

   The accompaniment of Raoul's recitative [No. 2: 'Non loin des vieilles tours',
pp. 81–3] is vividly suggestive: the merry cries, the provocative remarks of the
students that he has found surrounding his fair beloved, are all recognizable in it.
The romance that follows ['Plus blanche que la blanche hermine', pp. 84–95] is
more remarkable for its accompaniment than for the vocal melody itself. The viola
d'amore is prominent,[17] and the entry of the orchestra, delayed until the exclamation

16 Berlioz may be referring either to its binary metre, surrounded as it is by rapid triplet-quaver
    movement, or to its halting phrase structure.
17 This accompaniment was prompted by the availability of the viola d'amore virtuoso Chrétien
    Urhan. Berlioz quotes nineteen bars of the recitative in his *Traité d'instrumentation* (1843), p. 40,

'O reine des amours!',[18] is a happy conceit. In the couplets, 'À bas les couvents maudits!' [pp. 108–21],[19] which follow the blissful singing of the chorale by Marcel [No. 3: 'Seigneur, rempart et seul soutien', pp. 100–104], one side of the character of the elderly servant is exceptionally well portrayed: that of the puritan soldier whose joy is so lugubrious that on hearing it one cannot tell whether he is laughing or threatening. In particular, the instrumentation is most unusual, with the voice lying between the two extremes of the orchestra's timbres – double basses and piccolo –, and the rhythm is marked by muffled *pianissimo* taps on the bass drum. The trumpet fanfare in C major lends a note of ferocious triumph to the phrase 'Qu'ils pleurent, qu'ils meurent' [Example 2], and sets off to even

Example 2

better effect the fanaticism of what follows, {88} muttered *mezza voce* in the minor key, 'Mais grâce, jamais'.

Through the remainder of Marcel's role, this same quality is constantly in evidence, even in his recitatives, which the composer has accompanied with nothing

beginning at 'Ah quel spectacle enchanteur!' [p. 84: there are considerable differences between Berlioz's example and the corresponding seventeen bars of the full score and fourteen of vocal score, p. 40], commenting: 'M Meyerbeer has felicitously introduced [the viola d'amore] into Raoul's romance in Act I of the *Huguenots* [ex.]. But there it is merely a solo effect. Imagine how violas d'amore *en masse* would sound intoning, andante, a beautiful prayer in several parts [. . .]'.
18 Full and vocal score have 'bel ange, reine des amours', with the orchestra entering at 'ange'.
19 Full and vocal scores have 'Pour les couvents c'est fini'.

more than cello chords, as in early opera,[20] the harmony subdued, gothic and at the same time severe, perfectly in character with the persona.

The chorus [No. 5] 'L'aventure est singulière!' [pp. 128–55], does not seem to me at anything like the same high level. The bouncy rhythm that underlies it is undistinguished. One can tell the composer wrote these pages only with reluctance. I rather suspect they have been discreetly cut since the first performance.

By contrast, the page boy Urbain enters with an exquisite melody [No. 6B], 'Une dame noble et sage' [pp. 171–6], made still more sublime from the second period onward by a *cantabile* accompaniment with cross-accentuation on the weak beat that lends it a most piquant impression. It is gracious, with a touch of impertinence, just as every well trained page boy should be.

I must also draw attention to a not dissimilar, happy idea in the ensemble [No. 6D: Stretta] that follows, 'Les plaisirs, les honneurs!' [pp. 190–217], during which the *Te Deum* is introduced with great effect in plainsong style, sung by old Marcel in accompaniment of the other voices.

[Act II]

Act II has been criticized very harshly {89} – wrongly so, in my opinion. Its interest is nothing like as great as that of the rest of the work; but is that the fault of the composer? Could he have written anything other than graceful cantilenas, cavatinas with roulades and serene, *dolce* choruses, given lines that speak of nothing but 'laughing gardens', 'green fountains', 'melodious sounds', 'amorous waves', 'madness', 'coquetry' and 'love-refrains' that 'repeat the surrounding echoes'? We do not think so. Why, it took nothing less than a superhuman being[21] to make of it what he did. The chorus of bathers [No. 8, pp. 260–82], with its ostinato figure [*dessin continu*] in the bassoons below it[22] and the tied notes of the page boy above it, meanders amongst the harmonies with a voluptuous nonchalance.

From the dramatic point of view, the duet scene between Raoul and Queen Margaret [No. 10: 'Beauté divine, enchanteresse', pp. 299–319] is of a very high order. The composer has taken full advantage of what it offered, with all the finesse and skill that we have come to expect of him. I find fault only with the principal theme, 'Ah! si j'étais coquette!', for resembling too closely that of the chorus 'Le vin, le jeu, les belles', of *Robert the Devil*.[23] It is a type of similarity that does not normally strike the composer himself, lying as it does less in the exterior form or in the harmony than in the melodic feeling, which is never quite the same for him as it is for the listener.

20 E.g. the end of Act III no. 18 (p. 525), Marcel accompanied by solo cello in double- and triple-stopped chords and a solo double bass line that bears figurings '6', '5/3', '6♯', '4♯/3♭'. Other examples are the opening of Act I no. 3 (pp. 96–9), Tavannes–Raoul–Thoré–Nevers–Méru–Marcel, in which only Marcel's phrases are accompanied thus, the others by full string chords, sometimes with woodwind; and Act V no. 27 (pp. 831–2), Raoul–Marcel, where two of Marcel's cello chords are to be spread, harpsichord-like. These are clear allusions to the continuo of Baroque opera.

21 *un homme supérieur*: Nietzsche's *Übermensch* dates from c. 50 years later (*Also sprach Zarathustra*, 1883–92); French *surhomme*, like English 'superman', appears first in 1893.

22 *Traité d'instrumentation* (1843), pp. 131–2, quotes six bars of this passage as an 'excellent effect' in the description of rapid legato notes in the bassoon.

23 Act I no. 1B, 'Versez à tasses pleines'.

Example 3

{90} When it comes to the oath [No. 12A], 'Par l'honneur, par le nom que portaient mes ancêtres' [pp. 334–45], I find another example of the difference between musical impressions received by ear alone, and those perceived by ear reinforced by eye. The ensemble 'Devant vous nous jurons éternelle amitié' [pp. 339–40] occurs on a D major chord[24] sounded loudly by voices and orchestra for several bars [Example 3], and the solo vocal Andante quartet that follows is in E♭ [major]. The preparation for this new key is by way of the diminished triad D F♮ A♭. Its notation is crystal clear in the score, so one might imagine that the transition [*transition*] would not be too abrupt. Surprisingly, it is. Several factors conspire to render it extremely harsh: first, the violence and protractedness of the D chord, reverberating around the house with shattering effect, plants itself so firmly in the listener's mind that it would take a key [*tonalité*] still more assertive and a sound even more insistent to eliminate it; [second,] the drastic drop in volume and the extreme transience of the two notes F and A♭ of the intervening chord, whispered *pianissimo* in the low register of the orchestra, such that one can scarcely hear it, while D major rings on clamorously, at least in the mind; [third,] the similarly hushed *dolce* entry of four unaccompanied {91} voices on the E♭ chord, coming after the loud clamour of full choral and orchestral forces on the D chord; and finally the E♮ appoggiatura in the tenor, heard directly after the first notes of the new key [*ton*] and as part of a diminished [seventh] chord on the leading-note, creates confusion and undermines the E♭ tonality at the very moment when this needs to establish itself and to remove all trace of indecision on the part of the ear. In all probability, this would not strike M Meyerbeer as a fault at all. Now that I have read the score, it will be far less obtrusive for me. In the future, I shall, like the composer, hear the preparatory chord that he has placed in the orchestra, and which passes unnoticed unless one is ready for it. The tutti that follows, 'Que le ciel daigne entendre et bénir ces serments' [pp. 342–5], is enormously difficult for the voices, especially for the basses, because of the excessive number of enharmonic modulations following rapidly one upon another. The same reproach can be levelled at the composer, in my view, about the remainder of this finale. Many great harmonists such as he have been known to fall into this trap.

[Act III]

In Act III, however, we are to be amply compensated. It opens with a chorus of people out for a stroll [No. 13]: 'C'est le jour du dimanche, c'est le jour du repos' [pp. 391–99], full of happy conviviality {92} – soon to be swept away by the couplets of the Huguenot soldiers and the litanies of the Catholic women. It is a musical fabric of great magnificence. Here is a case of a difficulty overcome, turned to advantage, with wonderfully effective result. In this scene, the composer was confronted with what at first sight seemed to call for nothing but a confused jumble of sounds devoid of interest. It offered the prospect of an assemblage, laboriously

24 In the vocal score, these words are sung twice, first by four soloists in unaccompanied octaves *pianissimo*, then by soloists and male chorus together in alternating chords of G minor and D major *fortissimo*. It is to the latter that Berlioz refers. See Ex. 3.

I know of no scene in all theatre more gigantic in scale, none more skilfully judged in its growth from beginning to end. Its form [*plan*] is as follows. First comes an allegro moderato ['Des troubles renaissants', pp. 638–46] with a recurrent triplet figure in the strings, the vocal line of which is too melodic in cast for it to be called measured recitative. It is one of {97} those hybrid genres [*formes*] familiar in Meyerbeer, which exhibit features of recitative and aria equally without allying themselves to one or the other. They are excellent at times for sustaining the listener's attention; they often have the unfortunate effect of disguising the entry of an aria or ensemble piece in strict tempo, blurring, as they do, the distinction between the latter and musical *dialogue* or speech. In the present case, the use of this type of melodic declamation is all the more felicitous for being preceded by solo recitative and followed by an essentially *cantabile* andantino. It is interesting, but not particularly impressive; it prepares the ear for the major developments that are afoot: it is the inception of the *crescendo*.

The andantino to which I have just alluded, 'Pour cette cause sainte' [pp. 647–53], should be regarded as, so to speak, the principal theme of the scene as a whole. We find it in fact returning three times, relatively far apart, each time amplified by new subsidiary ideas and increasingly spirited. The two [eight-bar] periods that make up this imposing melody [*phrase*] are as felicitous as they are original in their pattern of modulation. Each, however, ventures only into keys closely related to the principal tonality of E major. The first goes via G♯ minor, reverting immediately to E [major], while the second goes via G major, {98} likewise barely touched upon, yet giving a real brilliance to the sudden and unexpected perfect cadence on to E major that brings it to a close. The tempo primo [p. 653] returns with its recurrent [triplet] figure and melodic declamation. It contains a particularly successful expressive effect, when Nevers, just as he breaks his sword [p. 662], cries:

> Tiens, la voilà, que Dieu juge entre nous.

Following a recurrence of the andantino theme ['Ma cause est juste et sainte', pp. 666–9], and a few bars of solo recitative [pp. 669–70], Saint-Bris issues orders to the conspirators in a melody [*phrase*; 'Qu'en ce riche quartier', pp. 670–79], the sombre character of which owes more to the timbre of the deep-toned singing voice and the [cellos and] basses of the orchestral accompaniment than it does to musical expressiveness as such. The sole exception to this is the final phrase, 'Tous, tous frappons à la fois' [pp. 671–2], repeated a third higher by the tenors of the chorus, then a third lower by the basses. This progression has a sinister ring to it, a menacing tone that is unmistakable.

Further on, I am prompted to make an observation that may seem pettifogging, and that I should surely have kept to myself were the subject of it not one of the greatest composers of our time. Saint-Bris bellows, allegro vivace [p. 679]:

> Le fer en main, alors levez-vous tous;
>   Que tout maudit expire sous vos coups.
> Ce Dieu qui nous entend et vous bénit d'avance,
>   Soldats chrétiens, marchera devant vous.

{99} Then Valentine says, to one side, in anguish [pp. 679–80]:

> Mon Dieu, mon Dieu, comment le secourir
> Il doit entendre, hélas! et ne peut fuir,
> Je veux et n'ose auprès de lui courir.

And yet the melody [*phrase musicale*] to which these lines, emotionally worlds apart as they are, are set, sung by two characters of whom one is intimidating, the other is in fear and trembling – that melody is, believe it or not, virtually identical.

Are dramatic propriety and expressive truth reconcilable with the double duty that this melody has to do? And does this not logically suggest either that the music itself is vague and featureless in expression, or else that it is incompatible with one or other of the two characters? [. . .]

This licence, not uncommon in light and semi-serious opera,[30] here becomes all the more grievous, it seems to me, the more crucial the scene, the loftier the approach adopted by the composer, and the more natural and faithful the [musical] language in which the composer otherwise has chosen to clothe its passionate feelings. A momentary lapse can so easily cause a great composer to stray on to a path not his own.

But with what supreme alacrity we are promptly swept back on to the right one! Three monks approach slowly: the orchestra, Poco andante, {100} sets in train a sharply accented triple rhythm, against which the three begin to chant in long-held notes their sacrilegious hymn, 'Gloire au [grand] Dieu vengeur!' [pp. 681–718]. Suddenly the menacing rhythm ceases [p. 684], and the brass intone four times a progression of two enharmonically related major chords, E and A♭,[31] while Saint-Bris and the three monks chant in unison, on just two notes (G♯, C):

> Glaives pieux, saintes épées,
> Qui dans un sang impur serez bientôt trempées,
> Vous par qui le Très-Haut frappe ses ennemis,
> Glaives pieux, par nous soyez bénis.

At this last line, the voices break unexpectedly into unaccompanied [four-part] harmony in C major, modulating gradually, and making way for the hymn tune in A♭, which is then taken up by the chorus as a whole, accompanied by the pounding rhythm of the strings[32] as heard at the opening, with the full weight of bow on string. From this chorus entry onward the ponderousness becomes so unbearable – each beat of the bar struck with such force, voices clashing in such pungent dissonances, the many different rhythmic and melodic types creating such a horrifying admixture of the religious style and the frenetic style – that a truly superhuman effort {101} is needed to put a stop to this mighty *crescendo*, some effect that transcends all that we have just enumerated.

This is how Meyerbeer solves the problem. After a few words sung *sotto voce* ['Silence, mes amis! que rien ne nous trahisse!', pp. 708–09], the monks gesture for

---

30 *dans les ouvrages légers et de demi-caractère* strictly extends beyond opera.
31 This describes the second statement, when the voices enter [pp. 685–6], rather than the first.
32 *basses et violons*: it is in fact cellos and basses in unison with three trombones and ophicleide, joined in the next bar by oboes, bassoons, horn and trumpets, and taken over in the fourth bar by violins and violas.

the assistants to kneel, then bless them, moving about slowly among the groups.[33] Then in a paroxysm of fanatical exaltation, the entire chorus takes up once again the first theme, 'Pour cette cause sainte' [p. 710]. This time, however, instead of splitting the voices into four or five separate parts as before, the composer keeps them together in unisons and octaves, achieving a massive sonority by means of which the thunderous melody is able to rise above the roar of the orchestra and ring out clearly. Furthermore, every second bar, in the rests that mark off the phrases of the melody, the orchestra swells to a *fortissimo*, and by adding an intermittent timpani roll doubled by military drum [and bass-drum stroke],[34] produces an extraordinary and unprecedented groaning sound, which strikes terror into the heart of [even] the listener least susceptible to the emotional effect of music [pp. 710–13]. This sublimely horrific effect strikes me as better than anything of the sort that has been tried in opera [*théâtre*] for many a long year; and without wishing to disparage the exceptional qualities of *Robert the Devil*, I must add that, not even excluding the celebrated trio,[35] I can think of nothing there that matches this immortal portrayal of fanaticism.

The duo that follows it ['O ciel! où courez vous?', pp. 719–85] is almost at the {102} same level. It changes key a bit too frequently for my liking, however; but the remotest modulations are handled with such deftness as to detract only slightly from the unity of the piece. One episode that stands out in my mind is the cavatina 'Tu l'as dit; oui, tu m'aimes' [pp. 744–59], the vocal line of which, tender as it is, gains fresh charm from the echoing of its phrases by the cellos, and the instrumentation of which exhibits throughout such grace and delicacy.[36] The concluding section [*péroraison*] is startling for its boldness, perfectly justifiable in its own terms [*motivée*], yet none the less realistic for that: the duet ends *solo*, virtually in *recitative*, and on the *leading-note*. Contrary to our normal expectations as it is, this musical finishing touch [*dénouement*] seems destined to lack the vehemence and fervour necessary for the conclusion of an act. In fact, quite the contrary, Raoul's final exclamation, 'Dieu, veillez sur ses jours, et moi je vais mourir',[37] is so heart-rending that the impact of the orchestral *a tempo*, though robust, is unable to surpass it.

33   'sung *sotto voce* . . . groups' is transcribed verbatim from the stage-directions.
34   *au moyen d'une attaque intermittente des timbales secondées d'un tambour*. Cf. *Traité d'instrumentation* (1843), p. 281: 'M Meyerbeer knew how to extract a strange and terrifying sonority from the combination of military drum and timpani for the famous *crescendo* roll in the Blessing of the Daggers (*The Huguenots*)'.
35   Act V no. 23, 'À tes lois je souscris d'avance'.
36   *Traité d'instrumentation* (1843), pp. 125–7, quotes the first eleven bars of this cavatina under the cor anglais, stating:

> The mixture of the low sounds of the cor anglais with the deep notes on clarinets and horns, simultaneously with a tremolo on double basses, yields a timbre as peculiar as it is novel, and just right for lending his musical ideas a menacing tinge, wherever fear and anxiety predominate. [. . .] There is a magnificent example of it in the duet in Act IV of *The Huguenots*; and I believe M Meyerbeer is the first to produce it on stage.

It also quotes the closing bars, pp. 268–70, commenting on the use of

> a bell in low F [ex.] to give the signal for the massacre of the Huguenots in Act IV. [. . .] [Meyerbeer] has, moreover, carefully located this F as a diminished fifth above B♮ in the bassoons; reinforced by the low notes of two clarinets (in A and B♭), these give a sinister tone quality that evokes the terror and alarm that pervade this sublime scene.

37   Full score has: 'Dieu veille sur ses jours! Dieu! secourable!', vocal score the same, punctuated slightly differently.

[Act V]

The *Air de danse* [pp. 787–805] that opens Act V is brief in the extreme, but remarkable for its courtly elegance. The interruptions by distantly tolling bells are artfully timed. Raoul's number, as he bursts in upon the ball, strikes me as lacking dramatic movement. The recitative [pp. 806–08] is not, for me at least, tight enough in construction; the rests punctuating the lines of verse in the vocal line cool its {103} ardour and disrupt the flood of passion just at its peak. Perhaps the composer meant these *lacunae* to simulate the sort of choking off[38] of words experienced by someone overwhelmed by horror, as Raoul must be at this moment. That would be natural enough, in all truth; but in my view such a degree of realism is inappropriate to a theatre as large as the Opéra, where the distances involved, and the level of orchestral sound, prevent the audience from registering the facial expression, the nervous trembling, the gasping for breath of the actor and the countless refinements of the art of mime, all of which can be entirely justified only if they accomplish the composer's intentions.

I am bound to say the same of the aria that follows, 'A la lueur de leurs torches funèbres' [pp. 809–25], the main fault of which is, to my mind, that it is an aria at all. Clearly the drama comes to a halt to allow the singer to describe the disasters that are bathing Paris in blood; but scarcely have the Protestants taken in the news of the massacre of their brethren, when they inevitably break in upon the bearer of these tidings with a cry, and rush from the ballroom without waiting to hear the pointless details.

The trio that follows [pp. 826–80] is quite different in conception. Although very long, occupying as it does the bulk of the final act, it is constructed so cleverly that it feels scarcely longer than any normal number. Its opening is cast in a new mould.

{104} The austere catechism by Marcel [pp. 847–9], to which the voices of the two lovers respond in piety; the deep-throated tones of the bass clarinet, full of sorrow, sole accompaniment of Marcel's vocal line;[39] even the very silence of the remainder of the orchestra: all these things conspire to bring a certain grandeur and unpredictability to the solemnity of overall musical effect in this scene.

The choirs that are now heard singing the Lutheran chorale in the nearby temple, amidst the shouts of the murderers and their raucous fanfares, set up a striking contrast [pp. 850–56]. The assassins' song and the trumpets that accompany it, even taken on their own, make an atrocious effect. The composer knew that what was required for that effect was something utterly simple; the difficulty lay in finding just the right device, and – even more – having the courage to use it. What he arrived at was the alteration of the sixth of the minor key [see Example 4]. The brutal phrase ['le ciel l'ordonne!'] into which this note is lofted [is] in A minor, the sixth degree, F, which should by rights be natural, in fact being persistently sharpened. The truly lurid effect that this produces is yet another example of the obtrusive character that this note, with or without alteration, can bring to chord structures [*combinaisons*].

---

38   *suffocation*: Meyerbeer's instruction to the singer at the beginning of the aria that follows is 'D'une voix suffoquée'.

39   *Traité d'instrumentation* (1843), pp. 148–9, quotes the first twenty-two bars (= twenty-three bars in the full score) of the 'Interrogatoires': 'M Meyerbeer has assigned an eloquent monologue to the bass clarinet in the trio of Act V of *The Huguenots*'.

Example 4

Gluck had in the past taken full advantage of it on several occasions, though by a different means. I need only cite the famous bass line of the aria from Act III of *Iphigénie en Tauride*, at the line:

Ah! ce n'est plus qu'aux sombres bords.

{105} The aria is in G minor. At this point the bass line, proceeding in conjunct motion, arrives on the E♮; unexpected, this note suddenly brings to the harmony a dark and lugubrious aura that causes a frisson. In *The Huguenots*, on the other hand, the altered sixth has a glittering effect, but glittering as of an unsheathed sword. There is a ring of exultation to it, but it is the exultation of the tiger or the cannibal, as conquerors in all holy wars emulate it. Assigned to the trumpets,[40] this note gains harshness from the penetrating instrumental tone, and rasps with a diabolical ferociousness. This [stroke of imagination] is by no means one of M Meyerbeer's lesser creations, in a work which, on top of so many beautifully expressive ideas, is resplendent with countless novel [sonorous] combinations.

Setting aside those isolated numbers of *The Huguenots* in which the style fails to live up to the exalted level of other parts of the score – such as for example Marcel's solo with harps,[41] '[Ah!] Voyez le ciel s'ouvre' [Act V no. 27C, 'Vision', pp. 857–80] – many people bowled over by the sheer force of creative power so often exhibited in this work do not hesitate to rank it higher than its precursor. Not that this preference detracts in any way from the admirable qualities of *Robert the Devil*; [but] we think it wholly justified, and the composer himself would probably not demur.

40 In fact it is given not to the trumpets but to the second horn and trombones, in a scoring for five trumpets, four horns and two bass trombones, the musicians located 'in the corridors'.
41 A solo within a trio (Valentine–Raoul–Marcel), which gives way to the chorale sung in octaves, at the end of the massacre scene; the harps continue throughout.

Richard Wagner (1813–1883)

'Bericht über die Aufführung der neunten Symphonie von Beethoven . . . nebst Programm dazu' (1846)

Wagner wrote some fourteen 'programmatic elucidations' of pieces of music. The majority of these were produced within a three-year period, 1852–4, during his exile in Zurich. Of them, the longest are the essays on Beethoven's 'Eroica' Symphony and *Coriolan* Overture, the shortest is that on the C♯ minor String Quartet Op. 131, the emotional spectrum of which is expressed in a thumbnail sketch thus: 'from the melancholic morning orisons of an oppressed soul, past visions of the charming, the winsome and the ravishing; through feelings of bliss, ecstasy, yearning, love and devotion; at last to mercurial merriment, droll delight and finally rueful resignation at the bounties of the world'.[1]

At that time, Wagner provided similar programmes for concert performances of excerpts from *The Flying Dutchman*, *Tannhäuser* and *Lohengrin*.[2] Later, in 1859 and 1863, he did likewise for excerpts from *Tristan and Isolde*,[3] in 1864 for excerpts from *The Mastersingers of Nuremberg* and *The Valkyrie*, in 1875 for excerpts from *The Twilight of the Gods* and in 1882 *Parsifal*.[4]

Most of these are written in a high-flown style that is half-prose, half-poetry. They are a literary genre in themselves, located somewhere on the spectrum between his theoretical writings and his texts for the later dramas (not to mention the fictional novella *A Pilgrimage to Beethoven*, written in 1840[5]). Throughout them, vestiges of the alliterative verse that Wagner was developing so intensely around 1850, which he used with especial power in *Tristan* and the *Ring*, keep surfacing. The most overt example occurs in his description of the 'Eroica' Symphony. In this, the *Stabreim*, with its chain of paired, alliterative, accentual syllables, followed by a

1 *Richard Wagner: Sämmtliche Schriften und Dichtungen* (Leipzig: B&H, [1911–16]). 'Eroica': vol. V, pp. 169–72; *Richard Wagner's Prose Works*, ed. and trans. W. A. Ellis (London: Routledge, 1892–9, reprint edn 1972), vol. III, pp. 221–4. *Coriolan*: vol. V, pp. 173–6/III, pp. 225–8. Op. 131: vol. XII, p. 350. Wagner wrote further on the *Coriolan* Overture in 'Beethoven' (1870), *Sämmtliche Schriften*, vol. IX, pp. 97–112; see Bujić, 65–75. In this and other notes, the German edition is cited first, the English second, separated by '/'.

2 *Dutchman*: Overture, *Sämmtliche Schriften*, vol. V, pp. 176–7/*Prose Writings*, vol. III, pp. 228–9. *Tannhäuser*: Overture, vol. V, pp. 177–9/III, pp. 229–31; Entry of the Guests (Act II) and Tannhäuser's Journey to Rome (Act III), vol. XVI, pp. 167–9. *Lohengrin*: Prelude (Act I), vol. V, pp. 179–81/III, pp. 231–3; *Männerszene* and Bridal Procession (Act II) and Wedding Music and Bride's Song (Act III), vol. XVI, p. 170.

3 *Tristan*: Prelude (with concert ending) (1859), Prelude (Love-death) and Closing Scene (Transfiguration) (1863), ibid, vol. XII, pp. 346–7; see R. Bailey, *Wagner: Prelude and Transfiguration from 'Tristan and Isolde'*, in Norton Critical Score (New York: Norton, 1985), pp. 47–8.

4 *Mastersingers*: Preludes to Acts I and III, *Sämmtliche Schriften*, vol. XII, pp. 347–9. *Valkyrie*: Siegmund's Lovesong (Act I), Ride of the Valkyries (Act II), Wotan's Farewell and the Fire Music (Act III), vol. XVI, pp. 171–2. *Twilight of the Gods*: Prelude, Hagen's Watch (Act II), Siegfried's Death and the close of Act III, vol. XVI, pp. 173–5. *Parsifal*: Prelude (Act I), ibid, vol. XII, p. 349.

5 vol. I, pp. 90–114/VII, pp. 21–45.

line of three accents, is unmistakable. Although prose, it can be laid out in verse-form – as it is below, on the left, in the German. To show how close this is to Wagner's poetic style, an example from the *Ring* (the start of Wotan's summoning of Erda, from *Siegfried*, Act III) is set out parallel with it on the right:

Wonne und Wehe,	Wache! Wache!
Lust und Leid,	Wala, erwache!
Anmut und Wehmut,	Aus langem Schlafe
Sinnen und Sehnen,	weck' ich dich schlummernde wach.
Schmachten und Schwelgen,	Ich rufe dich auf:
Kühnheit, Trotz	Herauf! herauf!
und ein unbändiges Selbstgefühl . . .	Aus nebliger Gruft,
	aus nächt'gem Grunde herauf!

The only one of these programmes to adopt an even slightly technical manner, and the only one to deal in terms of motifs, is the brief note on the Prelude to Act III of *Mastersingers*:

> The first motif in the strings has been encountered already in Act II, in the third strophe of the Cobbling Song. There it expressed the bitter sorrow of a world-weary man who outwardly preserves a cheerful and lively countenance. [. . .] Now, in the Prelude to Act III, this motif is played alone and transformed as if it were, sunk in resignation, about to give up the ghost. But at the same time, and as if from a distance, horns intone the solemn chorale with which Hans Sachs pays tribute to Luther and the Reformation. [. . .] After the first strophe, the strings, very softly and with hesitant movement, take up isolated fragments of the Cobbling Song [. . .]

The earliest of Wagner's 'elucidations' was written long before any of the above. This was the programme to Beethoven's Ninth Symphony, given below. It is the most elaborate of them all, and dates from 1846, when Wagner was still Kapellmeister at the Saxon royal court in Dresden. The occasion was the annual Palm Sunday performance by the royal court orchestra in the old opera house in Dresden. During the preceding decade, the Ninth Symphony had been performed in its entirety (performances were also given that omitted the finale) in Leipzig in 1836, 1839, 1841, 1843 and February 1846 (all by Mendelssohn) and in Berlin in 1836 and 1840 (by Möser) and 1844 (by Mendelssohn), and in Vienna in 1840 and 1843 (by Nicolai).[6] Wagner now proposed to perform the work – the score of which he had come to know first in the early 1830s, and of which he himself had heard only a rehearsal of the first three movements – on 5 April 1846. His plan encountered stiff opposition (as a later report by him on the performance tells us) on the grounds that the work 'stood in ill repute' in Dresden; but he fought an effective public campaign, and the performance – in which Wagner took many liberties of scoring, dynamics and tempo, and for which he had amassed a chorus of 300 persons who were encouraged to 'proclaim' rather than sing at certain points – was sufficiently successful for Wagner to be asked to give the work again in 1847 and 1849.[7]

---

6   See David B. Levy, 'Early Performances of Beethoven's Ninth Symphony: A Documentary Study of Five Cities' (PhD diss., Eastman School of Music, 1979).

7   Wagner's essay 'On Performing Beethoven's Ninth Symphony' was written much later, in 1873: vol. IX, pp. 231–57/V, pp. 229–51; Eng. trans. also in *Three Wagner Essays*, ed. R. L. Jacobs (London: Eulenburg, 1979), pp. 97–127.

Wagner himself says of the programme:

> The first step was to put together, in the form of a programme – modelled on the book of words customarily supplied for choral works – an introduction to the innermost comprehension [*zum gemütlichen Verständniss*] of the work: something which would operate not on the listeners' critical faculties, but purely on their feelings. Key passages from Goethe's *Faust* were a useful aid to me throughout, in drafting this programme . . .

This statement is clearly inspired by the aesthetics of Hegel, the influence of which on Wagner was strong at this stage in his life. Expression in music – alone among the arts – penetrates direct to the soul; its content is the inner life of feeling itself. Because of the vagueness of its content, it is inferior to poetry. Wagner therefore offers his listeners not technical analysis of the melodic and harmonic material (what Hegel in a non-musical context called *Verstandesanalyse*), but something which, while allowing the music to play fully on the world of the feelings, at the same time supplies comprehension (*Verständnis*) to the innermost being (*Gemüt*). This he achieves by constructing a parallel series of images in poetry (comparability of artistic worth being ensured by the choice of Goethe) – since only poetry is capable of 'unfolding the totality of an event, a successive series and the changes of the heart's movements, passions, ideas, and the complete course of an action'.[8]

In this analysis are combined two artistic personalities who were formative influences upon Wagner: Beethoven and Goethe. For Wagner, writing in *Opera and Drama* (1851), Beethoven had unlocked the inexhaustible resources of music that instrumental composers before him had been unable to release. He had done this first by breaking the mould of form and putting in its place an organic process in which melodic fragments moved constantly in and out of juxtaposition with one another, revealing unsuspected relationships; and secondly by enlisting the power of poetry to express tangible and directly intelligible 'content' (as apart from mere feeling, however potent) – though this he did in the context of symphony, namely in the Ninth Symphony, not opera.[9] In 'The Artwork of the Future' (1849), he portrayed the Ninth Symphony as a Columbus-like exploration of uncharted oceans, its anchor in the new world being 'the word':[10]

> This word was: – 'Joy!' And with these words he called out to all mankind: 'Embrace, ye millions – let this kiss, Brothers, embrace the world below!' – And this word was to become the language of the *artwork of the future*.

And that artwork was to be music drama, to which Beethoven had 'forged for the world the artistic key'. Thus, when Wagner discusses the choral sections of the Ninth Symphony's fourth movement, he quotes poetry from Schiller's 'Ode to Joy'.

---

8   Georg Wilhelm Friedrich Hegel, *Aesthetics: Lectures on Fine Art*, Eng. trans. T. M. Knox (Oxford: Clarendon, 1988), p. 960. The minor composer Hermann Hirschbach had composed three string quartets in 1838, each with a quotation from Goethe's *Faust* as a superscription – 'more as embellishment than as explication, for the music is comprehensible enough in its own terms', said Schumann, who reviewed them favourably. Curiously, of his three quotations, one couplet ('Begin once more ..') and another single line ('I take the way . . .') are also chosen here by Wagner (Robert Schumann, *Gesammelte Schriften über Musik und Musiker*, ed. Martin Kreisig (Leipzig: B&H, 5/1914), vols. I, pp. 343–4, and II, pp. 416–17).

9   *Sämmtliche Schriften*, vol. III, pp. 277–316, esp. 315–16.

10 ibid, 96.

Only when discussing the instrumental sections of that movement, and the first three movements, does he bring Goethe's poetry into play. And in a sense what he is doing for those sections of the symphony is what Beethoven himself did for the choral parts – for Wagner did not consider that Beethoven had 'set' Schiller's verses 'to music', but rather 'composed it under inspiration from their general content'.[11]

Whilst the programme contains no trace of *Stabreim* as such, it is clearly written in a heightened *Kunstprosa* that is packed with Romantic imagery. Moreover it makes liberal use of alliteration ('. . . wie in *l*etztem er*l*öschenden Wetter*l*euchten, das *z*ertheilte Gewitter ver*z*ieht'). It exploits rhetorical constructions ('So bilden Gewalt, Widerstand, Aufringen, Sehnen, Hoffen, Fast-Erreichen, neues Verschwin-den, neues Suchen, neues Kämpfen die Elemente der rastlosen Bewegung dieses wunderbaren Tonstückes . . .'), and has a pervasive sense of rhythm which at times lulls the reader, and at times disrupts the flow. The translation given below simulates some of these artifices while striving to avoid the banality into which one so easily falls in English.

The phrase 'absolute music', embodying a concept so crucial to nineteenth-century music aesthetics, arose in the writings of Wagner before its use by the writer to whom coinage is usually attributed: Eduard Hanslick. Carl Dahlhaus has identified Wagner's first use of the phrase as occurring in the Ninth Symphony programme: 'this recitative . . . almost breaking the bounds of absolute music already, turns its potent, passionate eloquence upon the other participants . . .'.[12] In context, that phrase is associated with 'pure instrumental music', which is characterized by 'an infinite and indefinite mode of expression'. Dahlhaus traces subtle changes in the phrase's meaning as used in 'The Artwork of the Future' (1849), and *Opera and Drama* (1851), where the concept is central.

---

11   ibid, 315.
12   Carl Dahlhaus, *Die Idee der absoluten Musik* (Kassel: Bärenreiter, 1978; Eng. trans. Chicago: Chicago University Press, 1989), pp. 18–19.

'Report on the Performance of the Ninth Symphony of Beethoven . . . Together with a Programme for That Work'

Source:
'Bericht über die Aufführung der neunten Symphonie von Beethoven im Jahre 1846 in Dresden . . . nebst Programm dazu', in *Sämmtliche Schriften und Dichtungen von Richard Wagner* (Leipzig: B&H, [1911–16]), vol. II, pp. 56–64.

Anyone who has not yet had the opportunity to make a close and detailed study beforehand of this extraordinarily important composition faces great difficulty in coming to grips with it now, on hearing it for the first time. A not altogether inconsiderable proportion of the audience is likely to be in that very position. Some attempt may therefore be admissible to proffer them here, if not an aid to absolute understanding of Beethoven's masterpiece – truly possible only as a product of the individual's own inner perceptions – then some intimations which may at least ease recognition of the work's technical ordering of events. For, in view of its unique character and utterly unapproached novelty, such recognition might otherwise elude the listener who is less well prepared, and who is hence more likely to become confused.

Though we may grant from the outset that in the higher realms of instrumental music what is expressed in musical sounds is by its very nature inexpressible in words, even so we believe we may be close to a solution to an insurmountable task, albeit only suggestively, in summoning to our aid the words of our great poet *Goethe*. {57} Wholly devoid as these admittedly are of any direct association with this work by Beethoven, and incapable as they are of in any way penetrating to the meaning of its purely musical creation, they nevertheless express the higher human moods of the soul that underlie that creation. So sublimely do they do this that, if the worst comes to the worst, and we can gain no deeper understanding, we might perhaps content ourselves with harbouring these moods and so at least avoid coming away from the performance entirely unmoved.

First movement

At the heart of the first movement seems to lie a struggle of titanic proportions, in which the soul, striving for joy, wrestles against the oppression of that hostile power that interposes itself between us and earthly happiness. The mighty principal theme, which steps forward at the very beginning, naked and powerful, as if from behind some unearthly veil, could perhaps without detriment to the spirit of the work as a whole be translated by *Goethe*'s words:[13]

Renunciation! – Learn, man, to *forgo*!

13   Goethe, *Faust*, Part I. *Goethes poetische Werke: vollständige Ausgabe*, vol. V *Die grossen Dramen* (Stuttgart: Cotta, 1959), p. 209 (Study Scene, Faust and Mephistopheles); Eng. trans. P. Wayne (Harmondsworth: Penguin, 1949), p. 82 (Wagner's emphasis).

Noble defiance is displayed against this powerful enemy, stout-hearted courage in a resistance which by the middle of the movement amounts to open combat with the opponent. We seem to discern two mighty wrestlers, each ultimately withdrawing from the fray, invincible. In isolated flashes of light, we glimpse the melancholy sweet smile of fortune, which appears to seek us. We strive to possess it, but our foe, with malicious force, prevents us from reaching it, concealing us under its jet-black wing. Even our vision of that far-off beneficence is blocked, and we sink back into a sombre brooding that rouses us once again to defiant resistance, to new struggles against the malevolent demon. So the elements that contribute to the restless motion of this wonderful piece of music are might, resistance, aspiration, yearning, hope, near-attainment, collapse once again, renewed questing, battle re-engaged – yet from time to time it sinks back into that prolonged state of utter joylessness conveyed by *Goethe* in the words {58}:[14]

> Yet, each new day I shudder when I wake,
> With bitter tears to look upon the sun,
> Knowing that in the journey he will make
> None of my longings will come true, not one;
> To see the tendrils of my joys that start,
> Cankered with doubts, the mind's self-conscious tares,
> To feel creation stir a generous heart,
> Only to fail before life's mocking cares,
> And when soft night has shrouded all the west,
> My anxious soul will beg her peace supreme;
> But still I lie forsaken, for my rest
> Is shattered by the wildness that I dream. etc.

At the close of the movement, this sombre, hapless mood, magnified to gigantic proportions, seems to engulf all, intending, in its fearful, imposing majesty, to take possession of this world, which God created for – *joy*.

Second movement

No sooner do we hear the pulsing rhythms of this second movement than we are swept up by a whirlwind of exhilaration. The moment we enter this new world, we are snatched away into frenzied, fevered activity. It is as if, driven by despair, in headlong flight, we are caught in constant questing for some new, unknown good fortune, since the old one that used to smile on us distantly seems to have been eclipsed and lost for ever. *Goethe* articulates a compulsion perhaps not inappropriate to this, in the words:[15]

> I do not ask for joy.
> I take the way of turmoil's bitterest gain,
> I sicken, long revolted at all learning;
> Then let us quench the pain of passion's burning
> In the soft depth of sensual delight.

14   ibid, 209; Eng. trans., 82–3.
15   ibid, 215; Eng. trans., 89 (lines 1–2 appear six lines after lines 3–12).

> Now let your muffled mysteries emerge,
> Breed magic wonders naked to our glance,
> Now plunge we headlong in time's racing surge,
> Swung on the sliding wave of circumstance.
> Bring now the fruits of pain or pleasure forth,
> Sweet triumph's lure, or disappointment's wrath,
> A man's dynamic needs this restless urge.

With the precipitous arrival of the middle section [b. 412], one of those scenes of earthly merriment and pleasant delights opens up before us suddenly. {59} There is just a hint of country-bumpkin boisterousness in the simple, often repeated theme, a naivety, a comfortable complacency that brings to mind *Goethe*'s depiction of homely happiness:[16]

> When folk make all the week a holiday.
> With scanty wit, yet wholly at their ease,
> Like kittens given their own tail to tease.

But so narrow a range of pleasures as this cannot be the goal of our ceaseless quest for fortune and the noblest joy. Our gaze drifts slowly from the scene before us; we turn away, submit anew to the restless impulse, the escape from despair, which drives us unremittingly forward to seek the state of happiness that – alas! – we are destined not to find. For at the end of the movement we come once again upon that scene of comfortable jollity that we have already encountered, and from which this time we retreat in unseemly haste upon realization.

Third movement

How differently do these tones touch our hearts! With what blissful balm do they disarm our defiance, and assuage the frenzy of the soul's despairing anguish, dissolving them into feelings of muted melancholy! It is as if a memory were awakened in our mind, a memory from earlier times of unalloyed happiness:[17]

> Time was, with sweetest touch dear heaven's kiss
> Would light upon me in the sabbath stillness.
> Then had the bells a sound of boding fulness
> And every prayer was ecstasy of bliss.

This memory in turn stirs up the sweet nostalgia that is so beautifully expressed in this movement's second theme [bb. 25ff], to which we could not unsuitably underlay *Goethe*'s words:[18]

> A strangely lovely fervency, a yearning
> Drove me to stray in fields and forests far,
> And when my heart was loosed, and tears came burning,
> I neared the threshold where no sorrows are.

---

16 ibid, 229 (Auerbach's Cellar in Leipzig, Faust and Mephistopheles); Eng. trans., 103 (Mephistopheles speaking).
17 ibid, 183 (Easter Morning, early); Eng. trans., 56.
18 ibid, 183; Eng. trans., 56. With a little ingenuity, the German lines can indeed be underlaid.

{60} It personifies love's yearning, to which the first theme, itself now made ardent by expressive embellishment, responds [bb. 43ff], inspiring hope and sweet tranquillity. Hence, when the second theme returns, it is as if love and hope were intertwined in an embrace so as to let the full force of their solace soothe our troubled spirit.[19]

> Why seek ye, heavenly sounds so mild
> And mighty, me in dust distressed?
> Go sing where tender souls are domiciled.

Thus the heart, still palpitating [bb. 61–4?], seems to want to fend them off with faint resistance. But their sweet strength is greater than our already weakened defences; conquered, we throw ourselves into the arms of these lovely harbingers of purest bliss [bb. 75–82].[20]

> Begin once more, O sweet celestial strain.
> Tears dim my eyes: earth's child I am again.

Ah yes! The wounded heart appears to recuperate, with mounting strength and mustering of courage, as the near-triumphant passage perhaps betrays toward the movement's close [bb. 120–23, 130–33, possibly 147–8, 150, 155, 157]. But recovery is not without relapse [bb. 123–4, 133–6, etc.], not without return of past upheavals. Each spasm of the old pain is soothed and suppressed by that propitious magical power, before which, as lightning dies in final flickers, the fading storm at last abates.

Fourth movement

The transition from third to fourth movement, with its shrill initial outburst, we can tellingly construe by invoking these words of *Goethe*:[21]

> Ay me, though humbly I entreat for rest,
> No more comes sweet contentment to my breast!
>   O endless pageant! – But a pageant still,
> A show, that mocks my touch or grasp or will!
> Where are the nipples, Nature's spring, ah where
> The living source that feeds the universe?
> You flow, you give to drink, mysterious nurse,
> And yet my soul is withered in despair.

The final movement having begun in this way, Beethoven's music takes on a noticeably oratorical quality. What it has maintained for {61} the first three movements it now abandons, namely the characteristic features of pure instrumental music, identifiable as an infinite and indefinite mode of expression.[22] Something

---

19   ibid, 183; Eng. trans., 56.   20   ibid, 184; Eng. trans., 56.
21   ibid, 198 (lines 1–2: Study Scene, Faust with poodle), 173 (lines 3–8: Study, Faust alone); Eng. trans., 71, 46.
22   [Wagner:] It was *Tieck* who, with this characteristic of instrumental music in mind, was moved to observe from his point of view as follows:

> We detect rising up from the deepest depths in these symphonies an insatiable yearning, undirected, turning in on itself; we discern that inexpressible longing that nowhere finds fulfilment, and that hurls itself with consuming passion into the maelstrom of madness, and then in every note struggles, sometimes overpowered, sometimes triumphant, calling out from the waves, crying for deliverance, all the time sinking ever deeper.

definite is now demanded if this work is to continue as music – a decision such as can be voiced only in human speech. We may marvel at how the master renders inevitable the advent of human speech and tongue through this vehement instrumental double-bass recitative [bb. 8ff], which, almost breaking the bounds of absolute music [*absolute Musik*] already, turns its potent, passionate eloquence upon the other participants, challenging them to decision. It slips at last [b. 92] itself into a song-like theme, the simple flow of which, as if in some joyous stately procession, draws the other instruments along with it [bb. 92–163], swelling to a mighty climax [bb. 187–202].[23] This is, it turns out, the last attempt to express in purely instrumental terms a state of happiness that is settled, serene and joyful. But the spirit of rebellion proves incapable of such restraint. It surges and subsides in foaming waves like a raging sea, and the wild, chaotic shriek of ungratified passion crowds in on our ears more clamorously than before [presto, bb. 1–8]. At that moment, a human voice rings out with the clear, confident articulateness of speech to quell the instrumental rout. We scarcely know which to marvel at the more: the bold stroke of inspiration, or the colossal naivety of the composer, in calling on the voice to defy the instruments thus:

> O friends, no more of these sounds! But let us sing
> something more cheerful, and more full of gladness!

Let there be light in the chaos! These words bring with them a {62} sure and unequivocal utterance in which we, borne thus far by the now subjugated forces of instrumental music, may at last hear expressed with ultimate clarity the vision of agelong bliss that opens before our tortured quest for joy.[24]

> Spark from the fire that Gods have fed –
>   Joy – thou Elysian Child divine,
> Fire-drunk, our airy footsteps tread,
>   O Holy One! thy holy shrine,
> Strong custom rends us from each other –
>   Thy magic all together brings;
> And man in man but hails a brother,
>   Wherever rest thy gentle wings.
>
> He who this lot from fate can grasp –
>   Of one true friend the friend to be –
> He who one faithful maid can clasp,
>   Shall hold with us his jubilee;

It is almost as if Beethoven, in conceiving this symphony, was impelled by a similar awareness of the intrinsic nature of instrumental music.

    [Bent:] Ludwig Tieck (1773–1853), profoundly influential early member of the German Romantic literary and aesthetic movement. See his *Schriften*, 28 vols (Berlin: Reimer, 1828–54). The quotation is not from *Musikalische Leiden und Freuden* (vol. XVII, pp. 281–356), or from any of his music-critical writings, to be found in Wackenroder's collected works.

23   Wagner does not suggest here that the D major theme has the character of folk melody, as he was later to imply in *Opera and Drama*, where he juxtaposed the theme with a discussion of the organic in folk melody (*Sämmtliche Schriften*, vol. III, pp. 312–16; in 'Beethoven' (1870) (ibid, vol. IX, pp. 97–112; see Bujić, 65–75) he stressed its 'childlike innocence'). A. B. Marx was to go further, and assimilate the necessity for folklike expression into the 'Idea' of the symphony as a whole (see Analysis 12, below).

24   Eng. trans. Sir Edward Bulwer Lytton, *The Poems and Ballads of Schiller* (Edinburgh and London: Blackwood, 1852), pp. 263–7.

> Yes, each who but one single heart
> > In all the earth can claim his own! –
> Let him who cannot, stand apart,
> > And weep beyond the pale, alone.
>
> All being drinks the mother-dew
> > Of joy from Nature's holy bosom;
> And Vice and Worth alike pursue
> > Her steps that strew the blossom.
> On us the grape – on us the kiss –
> > On us is faithful love bestow'd;
> And on the worm the sensual bliss;
> > And on the Cherub, room by God!

Courageous, warlike sounds now drift our way [*alla marcia*]; we seem to spy a troop of youths approaching, with boisterous heroics expressed in words [bb. 45–101]:

> Joyous as Suns careering gay
> > Along their royal paths on high,
> March, Brothers, your dauntless way,
> > March as Chiefs to Victory!

An exuberant battle ensues [bb. 101–212], depicted all by instruments. We see the youths hurl themselves valiantly into the fray – the spoils of which are *joy*. Once more we feel impelled to invoke words by *Goethe* {63}:[25]

> Only he who is driven to conquer himself each day,
> Deserves freedom as if it were life.

The victory, though never in doubt, is won. The exertions of the day give way to smiles of joy. Joy exults at the thought of happiness newly *achieved* [bb. 213–64].

> Spark from the fire that Gods have fed –
> > Joy – thou Elysian Child divine,
> Fire-drunk, our airy footsteps tread,
> > O Holy One! thy holy shrine,
> Strong custom rends us from each other –
> > Thy magic all together brings;
> And man in man but hails a brother,
> > Wherever rest thy gentle wings.

Amidst the highflown sentiment of joy, proud breasts now swear a vow of *universal brotherhood*. We turn in ardent fervour from the embrace of all humankind to the great Creator of Nature, whose beneficent being we with clear heart and mind attest; yes – whom, in a moment of supreme rapture as the blue ether seems to part for us, we fancy we espy [andante maestoso]:

> Embrace, ye millions – let this kiss,
> > Brothers, embrace the earth below!
> Yon starry worlds that shine on this,
> > Must one common Father know!
> And wherefore prostrate fall, ye millions?
> > No, starward lift adoring eyes;
> For throned above the star-pavilions
> > Dwells He who built the skies.

25 I have failed to trace these lines.

It is as if we became heirs through revelation to the seraphic belief that *every man is created for joy*. In all the force of strong conviction, we cry across to one another[26] [allegro energico, bb. 1–75]:

> Embrace, ye millions – let this kiss,
> Brothers, embrace the earth below!

and:

> Spark from the fire that Gods have fed –
> Joy – thou Elysian Child divine,
> Fire-drunk, our airy footsteps tread,
> O Holy One! thy holy shrine.

{64} For in the bond of *universal brotherhood*, consecrated by God as it is, we are free to taste the *purest* joy. Now we can respond, not *merely* in the thrall of awesome emotions but also in the knowledge of a bountiful truth revealed to us – now we can respond to the question [bb. 76–83]:

> And wherefore prostrate fall, ye millions?
> No, starward lift adoring eyes?

with the answer [bb. 84–108]:

> For throned above the star-pavilions,
> Brothers, yon starry worlds
> Must one common father know.

Our long-sought happiness achieved, our childlike love of joy regained, we now surrender ourselves to their delights. Ah! Our guilelessness of heart regained, joy folds its velvet wing o'er us in benediction [allegro ma non tanto – poco adagio].

> Joy – thou Elysian Child divine,
> Strong custom rends us from each other –
> Thy magic all together brings;
> And man in man but hails a brother,
> Wherever rest thy gentle wings.

To the gentle delights of happiness in joy now succeeds jubilation. As we clasp the world to our breast, excitement and exultation fill the air like the thundering of the heavens and the roaring of the seas, set in perpetual motion and healing vibration, which quicken the earth and preserve it for the *joy* of men, to whom God gave the world so that he might find *happiness* there.

> Embrace, ye millions – let this kiss,
> Brothers, embrace the earth below!
> Yon starry worlds that shine on this,
> Must one common Father know!
> Joy! Spark from the fire that Gods have fed!

---

26   *rufen wir uns gegenseitig zu*: cf. Wagner's 'Report':

> I succeeded in convincing the basses . . . that it was no good singing the famous passages 'Embrace, ye millions', and especially 'Brothers, Yon starry worlds that shine on this, Must one common Father know!' in the conventional fashion; that it could only be '*proclaimed* (*ausgerufen*) in highest rapture'.

Wilhelm von Lenz (1809–1883)

Beethoven et ses trois styles (1852)

'No one could enter more fully into the spirit of all those marvelous musical poems, nor better grasp the whole and the parts, nor follow with greater energy the eagle's impetuous flight and discern more clearly when he rises or when he sinks, nor say it with more frankness.'[1] Thus wrote Berlioz of Wilhelm von Lenz in a review not untinged with irony (one more of those links between Berlioz and the elucidatory tradition already discussed in the introduction to Part I, above). This comment reminds us that, in addition to articulating Fétis's tripartite stylistic classification of Beethoven (see vol. I, Analysis 16b), von Lenz made a contribution to Beethoven studies in the form of sustained analyses of the thirty-two piano sonatas, taken as exemplifying all stages of Beethoven's development. He subjected them in turn to an analytical treatment which is both enthusiastic and penetrating. We should not be deflected by the flowery verbiage. Beneath it lies a keen ear and sharp judgment. Von Lenz delivers adverse criticism when he feels it right (as here with the first and third movements); he also admits his inability to follow occasionally Beethoven's line of thought.

The middle section (167 pages) of von Lenz's tripartite book is entitled 'Analyses of the Piano Sonatas' and is itself divided into six sections or chapters, of which the present analysis falls into the first, 'Beethoven's First Manner: Sonatas 1–11'. Von Lenz's treatment is on the whole most satisfactory in the early sonatas, where the comment is wider-ranging, the handling of the material more confident, the analysis more acute. Thereafter, his perceptions gradually lose focus. For all his self-confessed inability to understand the late works, he accepted and advocated them. As Joseph Kerman has said, 'It was as much the *idea* of late Beethoven as the actual music that enraptured Lenz, and that idea was an idea of freedom, an idea of the infinite which was by definition unfathomable'.[2] Among the early sonatas, the analysis of Op. 10 no. 2 demonstrates well the flexibility with which he deploys the tripartite stylistic classification. He does not allocate works wholesale to one style or another, but discriminates stylistically between movements. Thus the first and last movements of this sonata are in the first style, whereas the second belongs to the second style. Not that this is a borderline work chronologically: he permits a work that clearly inhabits the first epoch (it dates from 1796–7) to belong in part to the second, even though the first landmark of that new epoch for him does not occur until seven years later. Von Lenz uses metaphor very richly in his analyses,

---

1   *Les soirées de l'orchestre* (Paris: Lévy, 1852; reprint edn 1968), Eng. trans. Jacques Barzun as *Evenings with the Orchestra* (New York: Knopf, 1956; reprint edn 1973), p. 317.
2   Foreword to the 1980 reprint of the 1909 edition, p. ix.

and the aesthetic comment in his concluding paragraphs is another feature of interest: his images are not intended literally; performers should take them not as gospel but as suggestive.

The powerful analysis of the second movement, with its Faustian imagery and detailed treatment of the substance and texture of the music, is the main reason for choice here. Comparison of von Lenz's analysis with those of Adolph Bernhard Marx in his *Ludwig van Beethoven: Life and Creative Output* (1859) and *Introduction to the Performance of Beethoven's Piano Works* (1863) is recommended. Whereas von Lenz treats this second movement as a 'scherzo' with 'trio', Marx regards it as a 'minuet' the peaceful trio of which has some of the attributes of an adagio. While von Lenz hears a single gigantic voice plumbing the lower regions and traversing the skies, Marx hears in the trio a dialogue between a voice of the deep [bb. 55–] and voices of the heights [bb. 74–]:[3]

> So the spirit rests here in peace, in D♭ major after the F minor, almost devoid of all external movement, in simple harmony [example: bb. 38–46]. Only softly does it stir from the depths in regular, gentle rhythmic gyration that rocks it as if on broad wings, lifts it slightly and then lets it come to rest at the close (of section I) in A♭ major [b. 54]. But it is not the peace of emptiness. The main musical idea (section I) is repeated, and our attention is drawn to the bass register in which it lies. The bass, the voice of the deep, separates itself, accented, from the mass of sound. For the first time, it now becomes a 'voice', takes on personality, and moves in melodic formation. This is, as it were, the motif [*Gedanke*] of the deep. Immediately the heights claim their right. Deep voices (middle register) in section II take up the original idea [bb. 70–79, 94–102, left hand], and the high voice, as mild and ringing as the flute in the minuet [*Hauptsatz*: bb. 16–20], sings against this [bb. 73–8, 97–103, right hand]. The whole sonorous apparition, conceived and manifested in the depths, seems to fade away into ethereality – and then to sink back once again into the depths.

Wilhelm von Lenz was born and educated in the Latvian capital city Riga, great-nephew of the Sturm und Drang poet and dramatist J. M. R. Lenz, a forerunner of the German Romantic movement. By profession he was a civil servant who lived and worked most of his life in St Petersburg. His consuming passions were the music of Beethoven and the world of pianism. He studied with Liszt in Paris in 1828 and with Moscheles in London in 1829, and claimed acquaintance with other major piano virtuosi of his day: Field, Hummel, Kalkbrenner, Chopin, Tausig and Henselt. He published a set of verbal portraits of four of these in 1872.[4] In 1850, he produced *From the Diary of a Livonian* (Livonia being a medieval name for an area of the Baltic sea coast inhabited by Baltic and Finno-Ugric tribes, controlled between the thirteenth and sixteenth centuries by the Christian Order of Teutonic Knights of Livonia), in which he recorded his European travels, and which includes a chapter on Beethoven's Violin Concerto.[5] Cosmopolitan, multi-

3   *Ludwig van Beethoven: Leben und Schaffen* (Berlin: Otto Janke, 1859), vol. I, pp. 133–4. The account of the trio in *Anleitung zum Vortrag Beethovenscher Klavierwerke* (Berlin: Otto Janke, 1863; new edn Eugen Schmitz, Regensburg: Bosse, 1912), pp. 166–7 mirrors this, with notable parallelisms.

4   *Die grossen Pianoforte-Virtuosen unserer Zeit aus persönlicher Bekanntschaft: Liszt, Chopin, Tausig, Henselt* (Berlin: Behr, 1872; Eng. trans. New York: Schirmer, 1899, reprint edn London: Regency, 1971).

5   *Aus dem Tagebuche eines Livländers*, ed. Baron Arnstein (Vienna: Gerold, 1850).

lingual, he espoused the musical culture of Germany while disparaging that of France (though like Brendel he excepted Berlioz from his censure). As described in the introduction to vol. I, Analysis 16, his *Beethoven and his Three Styles* (1852) was a vigorous rejoinder to an attack on Beethoven's symphonies by Ulïbïshev in *New Biography of Mozart* (1843).

'[Beethoven: Piano Sonata in F, Op. 10 no. 2]'

Beethoven and his Three Styles

Source:
Beethoven et ses trois styles: analyses des sonates de piano suivies d'un essai d'un cata-logue critique, chronologique et anecdotique de l'oeuvre de Beethoven (St Petersburg: Bernard, 1852; Brussels: Stapleaux, 1854; Paris: Lavinié, 1855; new edn ed. M.D. Calvocoressi, Paris: Legouix, 1909, reprint edn New York: Da Capo, 1980), [Pt II] 'Trois sonates, ut mineur, fa majeur, ré majeur, Opéra 10 (5ᵉ 6ᵉ et 7ᵉ sonates) – Dédiées à la comtesse de Browne', pp. 141–5.

As with the three sonatas Op. 2, here again three sonatas [Op. 10, nos 1–3] have been brought together to form a set – a whole world of ideas bearing a single opus number. In them our 'torrent from the high Alps' springs, surges through radiant landscapes never before revealed to human gaze, drawing near, by a thousand twists and turns, to the point which will give him his name, sweeping him towards the second metamorphosis of the genius of Beethoven. [. . .]

{143} The initial motif of the first allegro (2/4) of the Sonata [Op. 10] no. 2 in F major calls to mind the 'blue flower with heart of gold' for which the poet Novalis sought throughout his life yet never gathered.[6] However, the rich elaboration with which Beethoven is wont lavishly to adorn his themes does not arise. This allegro is thin. Its second theme [bb. 18–55] would not be out of place in some *opera buffa*; it certainly does not belong to the underlying conception [*idée*] of the movement. The passage from b. 30 suggests a duo – an argument between the Count Almaviva and the Barber. The third theme of the allegro [bb. 55–66] could well have been used by Rossini for his {144} 'Figaro qui, Figaro là' – a melodic pattern [*dessin*] of three quavers begun on the weak beat of the bar, accompanied by a rolling figure of triplet semiquavers leading to a trill in the low register. The development in the minor in section II [of the movement], [made up of] sparse, bare arpeggios, gives no hint of the genius of Beethoven. This padding modulates so far that it finishes by bringing back in D major the motif which was given out first in F. This entry has a delicious freshness to it, like a drop of dew which has fallen into the cup of a flower. The remainder is no more than a restatement developed along the lines of the first section.

Then comes the scherzo, in F minor – one of the most beautiful of its kind by the composer for the piano. It resembles the Blocksberg scene from *Faust*.[7] The nocturnal travellers who come on the scene have a strange demeanour. The dead rise from the grave, and what a wailing and moaning they set up! At last silence reigns. The majestic tones of D♭ major [bb. 38ff], in great waves of harmony, gather this assembly together, and the lord of them all gives voice [bb. 55ff]. This mighty voice

---

6   Friedrich Novalis (Friedrich von Hardenberg, 1772–1801), influential early Romantic poet, whose mythical romance *Heinrich von Osterdingen* (1802) engages its hero in a lifelong quest for the symbolic blue flower.

7   i.e. the Walpurgis Night scene in Part I of Goethe's *Faust*, in which witches and spirits gather on the Brocken (=Blocksberg, the highest peak of the Harz mountains) for their mayday-eve revels, and Faust is led to them. See Eng. trans. Philip Wayne (Harmondsworth: Penguin, 1949), pp. 167–86.

is a powerful melodic line in the low register which rapidly takes on many different guises and reaches up to high f" [bb. 73, 97], having plumbed the lower regions. These major tones, forming the trio to the scherzo, recall the grand rhythmic style of the 'Eroica' Symphony. The frequent use of syncopation, the combination of duple metre superimposed on to the [prevailing] triple metre by means of bass accents on weak beats of the bar [bb. 55–70, 79–86, 103–10] never for a moment let interest wane. This movement, which Beethoven himself scarcely surpassed in the later sonatas, bears the simple designation allegretto. We have called it a scherzo because it conforms to the mould [patron] in the proportions of its parts and in the nature of its rhythm. It is a scherzo in the manner of that so designated in the C minor Symphony [No. 5], of whose opening bars M Berlioz (*Voyage musical*, p. 303[8]) has said: 'although there is nothing particularly terrible about them, they nonetheless arouse that inexplicable feeling that one experiences under the magnetic gaze {145} of certain individuals'. The scherzo of the Sonata in F major belongs already to the second manner, the grand manner, of Beethoven.[9] Its proportions are still limited, its horizons are already immense. The sonata in which this gem is tucked away is, on the other hand, a product of Beethoven's youth, indeed one of the weakest.

The finale (presto 2/4) is a fugue devoid of interest by the side of the scherzo. This finale is to the scherzo what anyone who happened by chance to lodge for a day at the same address as Beethoven in Vienna is to Beethoven's genius. We have called the scherzo a scene of the Blocksberg. Other similes would have conveyed the mysterious meaning equally well. It is in the nature of music, we should say in order that the purport of this essay be clearly understood, not to manifest itself in concrete terms, but to awaken ideas *analogous* to those which the composer wished to express. 'Music neither can nor ought always to give a clear direction to feeling' (remark of Beethoven, Schindler, p. 291, Supplement[10]). Music has achieved its purpose so long as it has kindled a poetic idea in its performer, in its listener. The same music can quite easily arouse thoughts of sadness in one, thoughts of gaiety in another; it is a matter of secondary circumstances, external to art, and this very vagueness is one of the qualities by which music aspires to the infinite which is its soul. Its import is that an idea has presided over the work of the composer. This idea will find its echo. It may undergo a thousand metamorphoses in the public mind; it matters only that it does undergo them. *Sensit puer; salva est res!* ('The boy understood: all is well!').[11]

It will not undergo them, it will say nothing, if the composer himself says nothing.

8   *Voyage musical en Allemagne et en Italie; Etudes sur Beethoven, Gluck et Weber; Mélanges et nouvelles* (Paris: Labitte, 1844); pre-pubd in *Journal des débats* between 13 August 1843 and 9 January 1844. Berlioz's analyses of the Beethoven symphonies were first published in the *Revue et gazette musicale* between 28 January and 4 March 1838.

9   On the use of 'style' and 'manner', including 'grand manner', in the artistic context generally, see the introduction to Part III of vol. 1. On von Lenz's use of these terms, see the introduction to Analysis 16 in vol. 1.

10   Anton Schindler, *Biographie von Ludwig van Beethoven* (Münster: Aschendorff, 1840, 2/1845), p. 291, attributed to a conversation with Schindler.

11   *Salva res est* ('All is well') is a proverbial expression, probably from Roman comedy, but preserved in ancient dictionaries and commentaries. Servius's commentary on the *Aeneid* 8, 110 speaks of the proverb *salva res est, saltat senex* ('All is well, the old man is dancing'); another form has *cantat* ('is singing'); this may be von Lenz's source, with deliberate reversal of *senex* and *puer*. I am grateful to James Zetzel for this identification.

Ernst von Elterlein [Ernst Gottschald] (1826–?)

Beethoven's Clavier-Sonaten für Freunde der Tonkunst erläutert (1856)

In 1857, the year after Robert Schumann's death, Franz Brendel, editor of the *Neue Zeitschrift für Musik* since 1845, announced a new initiative for the journal: to research the means of[1]

> grasping the nature of the creative impulse, not simply by *subjective personal experience* but by the *objective* shape of a composition, *understanding the spiritual substance of a work* from its *external, technical configuration* [...], a path [...] which in fact promises to reveal a new world to musicians.

In saying 'I regard it *as one of the next tasks of this journal* to promote this advance', he invoked as the starting point a series of abstracts that were currently appearing in the journal – abstracts of Friedrich Theodor Vischer's *Aesthetics, or Science of the Beautiful* of 1846–57, the music-aesthetic material of which had just appeared in the final volume.

This series of abstracts was written by one Ernst von Elterlein, apparently a legal official in Waldheim, Saxony with amateur musical interests, of whom virtually nothing is known, and whose name is said by Riemann to be a pseudonym for Ernst Gottschald.[2] He produced, in all, seven such abstracts, in eleven instalments,[3] giving himself the task of 'presenting Vischer's aesthetics, which I have studied for years in isolation, to the musician in a series of letters'.

Von Elterlein also wrote two books of analyses of works by Beethoven. Since these were published in 1854 and 1856, it is right to see them against the background of this private study. Vischer's aesthetic system was strongly influenced by that of Hegel, and belongs to the idealist philosophical tradition. The very title of

1 'Die Aesthetik der Tonkunst', *NZM*, 46 (1857), no. 18 (1 May), 185–6; partial trans. Bujić, 130. I have reintroduced the emphasized (spaced) type of the original into Cooper's text by use of italics, here and below: 'nicht blos durch *subjective innere Erfahrung* den künstlerischen Geist zu erfassen, sondern aus der *objectiven* Gestalt des Tonstücks heraus ihn zu erkennen, aus der *äusseren technischen Gestaltung heraus das Innere, den geistigen Gehalt zu begreifen* ... auf einem Wege, dessen Verfolgung dem Musiker in der That eine neue Welt zu öffnen verspricht.'

2 H. Riemann, *Musik-Lexikon*, early editions; the name 'Ernst Gottschald' appears as the signatory of the Dedication to Vischer in the 2nd edn of his *Beethoven's Symphonien nach ihrem idealen Gehalt* (Dresden: Adolph Brauer, 2/1858), p. vi.

3 'Vischer's Aesthetik: eine Fundgrube für denkende Musiker: Briefe an einen Musiker', *NZM*, 46 (1857), no. 3 (16 January), 25–8, no. 4 (23 January), 37–41, no. 5 (30 January), 45–7, no. 6 (6 February), 53–4, no. 9 (27 February), 89–90, no. 11 (13 March), 113–16, no. 19 (8 May), 197–200, no. 24 (12 June), 249–52, no. 25 (19 June), 261–3; 47 (1857), no. 6 (7 August), 61–2, no. 7 (14 August), 69–71. A further series by von Elterlein, 'Die Aesthetik der Musik nach Vischer und Köstlin: Briefe an einen Musiker', was initiated in *NZM*, 47 (1857), no. 20 (13 November), 209–13 but not continued. (Karl Reinhold von Köstlin (1819–94) wrote all but the general material on music in Vischer's final volume.) A review (anonymous, signed 'Magdeburg') of the first two parts of Vischer's work appeared in *NZM*, 30 (1849), no. 29 (9 April), 157–9, and no. 30 (12 April), 165–8.

von Elterlein's first book proclaims its association with this tradition: *Beethoven's Symphonies Interpreted as to their Ideal Substance* [. . .] *by a Music Lover*. The book sold well, going through at least two subsequent editions, its circulation enhanced by an English translation that did likewise.[4] The second book, on the piano sonatas, was even more successful.[5]

The analysis of the *Appassionata* Sonata given here should be seen in conjunction not only with other analyses in Part I but also with that by Marx of the Ninth Symphony (Analysis 12 below). Both are essays in idealist interpretation, by men schooled in idealist philosophy. Thus von Elterlein's apocalyptic language, his jarring assembly of images – battles, maelstroms, thunderbolts, torrents, earthquake tremors, military might, and the island between two oceans – is finally 'read' for us as an allegory: the work's Idea is the artist beneath the onslaught of the forces of darkness, emerging at last tempered, resolute, but tragic rather than heroic. Each movement then takes its place in this idealist scheme: the first as a 'gruesome battle of the mind', the second as the artist's prayer, the third as grim victory.

The starkest difference between the two men is that between Marx's professionalism and von Elterlein's manifest amateurism, the latter showing through in unfortunate mismatches of music with metaphor (as when in the first movement the 'thunderbolts' of bb. 53 and 57 recur in bb. 192 and 196 and are misidentified by him as at b. 198, where they occur in diminution). Moreover, for the second movement von Elterlein drew directly from Marx's own discussion in the third volume of the latter's *Manual of Musical Composition in Theory and Practice* (1845). The two texts have quite different purposes, von Elterlein's being a narrative account of the movement, and belonging within a book of descriptive analysis, Marx's being an illustration of one specific musical form, and belonging within a book of compositional theory. Marx devoted three chapters of his volume to variation form, treating first the mechanics of theme and variation, then the genre of 'character variation' and finally variation as art form. It is under this last consideration that he described the second movement of Op. 57. Here is Marx's description, with von Elterlein's borrowings italicized:[6]

> Far more integrated in their internal unity are the variations that form the middle movement of the immortal F minor Sonata (Op. 57). Its role is none other than to communicate at a deeper level the coherence of the composition as a whole, in particular that of the preceding movement. Sufficient, then, that, *after the powerful storm, in which plangent, sweet chords, passion and joyless depths seem to drift slowly by, the theme gains a hold in the silent, dark deep, intensely self-communing, full of longing, like a prayer from out of the darkest abyss. The first variation restates it, but*

4   *Beethoven's Symphonien nach ihrem idealen Gehalt, mit Rücksicht auf Haydn's und Mozart's Symphonien, von einem Kunstfreunde* (Dresden: Adolph Brauer, [1854], 2/1858, 3/1870); Eng. trans. Francis Weber . . . *with an Account of the Facts relating to the Tenth Symphony by L. Nohl* (London: Reeves, [1893], 2/[1895]). E. Kastner, *Bibliotheca Beethoveniana: Versuch einer Beethoven-Bibliographie*, ed. T. Frimmel (Leipzig: B&H, 2/1925), gives also French titles for this and the other book, but I have been unable to verify the production of a French translation for either.

5   *Beethoven's Clavier-Sonaten für Freunde der Tonkunst erläutert* (Leipzig: Matthes, 1856, 5/1885; Eng. trans. Emily Hill (London: Reeves, 1875, 7/[1910?])).

6   Adolph Bernhard Marx, *Die Lehre von der musikalischen Komposition praktisch theoretisch*, vol. III (Leipzig: B&H, 1845, 2/1848), Book VI, chap. 8 'Die Kunstform der Variation', pp. 82–91, esp. pp. 90–91.

with hesitancy [example]. *The melody is punctuated with rests; the bass drags reluctantly but closely behind it. More consolingly in the softer* [middle] *register* and moving gently, the second variation introduces the *chorale* in more relaxed mood, and leads directly into the third, in which *the theme* is intoned in a more delicate and refined manner, *with harplike accompaniment* [example]. This passage leads, with a somewhat extended elaboration, back to the theme in the low and middle register, *in all its initial simplicity, but animated by more rapid motifs, then* however – unheard up to now – *into the* turbulent, powerfully surging *finale*. Nowhere else is a development to be found that is so tightly compact, so constant from beginning to end, nor that uses (outwardly) the simplest motifs to satisfying effect. *A devout prayer that wings its way consolingly heavenward from deepest desolation and then sinks back again.*

Around these borrowings von Elterlein constructed an account nearly twice as long as Marx's – an account that only pays lip service to Marx's perception of the movement's function as conveying the coherence of the sonata's three-movement whole. It was this notion that the unity of the variations embodied the larger unity of the whole that prompted Marx to present his description as the culminating example of variation *as art form*. Von Elterlein evidently missed the point. Instead, his account sets out to decipher the idealist code of the movement. Its aim is to specify the 'substance' (*Gehalt*) of the theme, then show how subsequent transformation (*Verwandlung* – a word that von Elterlein injected into this description[7]) is the *result* of this substance. His images and those of Marx clash and jangle – Marx's portrayal of the theme as 'like a prayer from out of the darkest abyss', and von Elterlein's immediately following it as 'a warm, soft shaft of sunlight, springing from the innermost recesses of the soul, full of infinite magic' are barely compatible. Yet, for all of its gauchenesses, von Elterlein's account is a courageous attempt to work up an idealist interpretation of this music in a tangible manner, relating effect (the dissolution of pain and suffering; the increasingly liquid consistency) with technical cause (the chromatic shift in bb. 6–7; the shift from crotchets to quavers, then semiquavers). Von Elterlein ventured what the professionals before Kretzschmar feared to do.

The principal problem for the translator of the passage below is the author's use of the word *Humor*. The term is used on no fewer than seven occasions, in reference variously to the first and third movements: once as 'thunderbolts of humour' (*Blitze des Humors*), three times as 'coruscations of humour' (*Wetterleuchten des Humors*), and three times as literally 'liberating humour' (*befreiender Humor*). This is evidently not intended as a literary mannerism, or as a Tieck-like recurring motif; rather, it relates to Vischer's theory of the comic. As Von Elterlein himself summarizes:[8]

> I shall dispense with an intensive review [of the *comic*, because Vischer's presentation is somewhat murky], all the more since the comic manifests itself in music to only a limited extent, in restricted, albeit rich, instances such as the humorous elements in Haydn and Beethoven. [. . . The principal forms of the comic] are, according to Vischer,

7 Marx does not use *Verwandlung* when discussing this movement. His normal terms for the variation process throughout his treatment of variation form are *Änderung*, *Veränderung* ('alteration') and *Variation*. He does, however, use *Verwandlung* and *Umwandlung* to denote the transformation of the theme, which in itself is an *undesignated* form, into some *designated* form such as a march, a dance, a fugue, etc., in the context of 'character variation' form (ibid, 59, 64).

8 NZM, 46 (1857), no. 6 (6 February), 54.

(a) the *objective* comic, or the *burlesque* [*Posse*]; (b) the *subjective* comic, or *wit*; (c) the *absolute* comic, or *humour*. The last of these has the degrees [i] *naive* humour, or high spirits [*Laune*] (Haydn), [ii] *broken* [humour], and finally [iii] *free* humour (elements to be found in Beethoven).

By 'broken', Vischer intended the humour of one who has a measure of self-awareness, but not the full inner consciousness of one who is master of his own fate; it is a philistine, sentimental humour. The possessor of 'free' humour is 'world-conscious' and 'manly'. *Befreiung* ('deliverance') is achieved by those who have looked evil in the face, experienced its depths and suffered pain and sorrow, and whose humour is consequently fully objective.[9] For *befreiend*, I have favoured 'redeeming' over 'liberating', 'disencumbering', 'unburdening' or other less euphonious alternatives.

---

9   Friedrich Theodor Vischer, *Aesthetik oder Wissenschaft des Schönen* (Reutlingen: Macken, 1846–57, 2/1922), vol. I, pp. 503–14. Vischer, of course, makes no reference to Beethoven in this description.

'[Beethoven: Piano Sonata] in F minor, Op. 57 (*Appassionata*)'

Beethoven's Piano Sonatas . . . Elucidated for Lovers of Music (1856)

Source:
'Op. 57, F moll, appassionata', *Beethoven's Clavier-Sonaten für Freunde der Tonkunst erläutert* (Leipzig: Heinrich Matthes, 1856, 2/1857), pp. 82–7.

If what was expressed [in the Sonata in C, Op. 53] was a state of purest unalloyed joy, of living serenity, then in this, the *Appassionata* Sonata, it is profoundest mental anguish that predominates, albeit relieved by moments of supreme rapture and punctuated by redeeming humour.

The first movement, allegro assai, in F minor, 12/8 time, begins with a short, pregnant principal motif. Convulsive spasms of pain have seized the mind, agonized tremors are heard from the depths (bb. 12–13),[10] after which the storm of passion can be heard brewing for the first time (bb. 17ff).[11] These agonized tremors start up again (b. 24),[12] but give way briefly (bb. 35ff)[13] to a second principal theme, consoling, and gently undulating in mood. We say 'briefly', for a new storm of passion is drawing near (b. 41),[14] during which thunderbolts of humour come crashing down (bb. 53, 57).[15] After the raging has ceased, {83} the convulsive spasms that we heard at the outset begin anew (b. 65),[16] summoning up renewed outbursts of passionate agitation, shot through with continuous coruscations of humour [bb. 79–92]. To the anxious heart [b. 93], a reassuring voice comes again (bb. 94ff),[17] intensified, soaring to majestic, commanding heights (bb. 114–22),[18] only to give way to a storm grown even wilder (bb. 123ff).[19] The voice of sweet consolation rings out once again (bb. 163–79),[20] but a raging storm of passion overwhelms it anew. The coruscations of humour flash once more (b. 196),[21] flickering in macabre fashion during the ***pp*** bar (bb. 204ff),[22] a comforting ray of light shines triumphantly down from the heights (bb. 210–17),[23] but in vain – at the onset of arpeggios (bb. 218ff)[24] the passion turns to veritable frenzy, broadening now to an unceasing, turbulent to-and-fro [bb. 227–34], so that after what appears to be the point of rest (b. 238),[25] from the *più allegro* on,[26] the underlying mood rises to feverish intensity, robbing even the consolatory motif of its character, and breathing passion into it. At the end, ***pp*** [b. 260], all that remains is the growling

---

10 '[p. 3,] system 3, last two bars, of the André edition'.
11 '[p. 3,] system 5'.
13 'p. 4, system 3'.
15 'p. 5, b. 1, and system 2, last bar'.
17 'p. 7, system 3' (lit. bb. 93–6).
19 '[p. 8,] system 4'.
21 'p. 11, system 2, last bar'.
23 'beginning of p. 12'.
25 'end of p. 13'.

12 '[p. 3,] penultimate bar'.
14 '[p. 4,] system 4, third bar from the end'.
16 '[p. 5,] penultimate system, last bar'.
18 'p. 8, systems 2–3'.
20 'end of p. 9, to the middle of p. 10'.
22 '[p. 11,] system 4 and onwards'.
24 '[p. 12,] system 3ff'.
26 'p. 14'.

of the thunder of passion. Such is the way that the moods unfold in this rich-hued painting. Before us is enacted a gruesome battle of the mind, dramatically {84} animated, full of sound and fury. The moods and feelings that pervade it are not general ones; they are quite specific, unique states of mind, inner experiences embodied in unique musical imagery.

The andante con moto which follows, in Ab major, 2/4 time, although more developed and elaborated than that of the Sonata Op. 54, is however less an inde-pendent movement than a transition to the final allegro. It stands in contrast to the opening and closing movements. Yet far from being unrelated to them, it exists in a most intimate relationship: it is an island situated resolutely between two tempestuous oceans. In the silent depths resounds a solemn chorale of enrap-turing peace, a fervent prayer – for such is the demeanour of this theme. It 'gains a hold', as Marx puts it of this theme, 'after the powerful storm; in it plangent, sweet chords, passion and joyless depths seem to drift slowly by, but all in the silent, dark deep, intensely self-communing, full of longing, like a prayer from out of the darkest abyss'.[27] This melody is a warm, soft shaft of sunlight, springing from the innermost recesses of the soul, full of infinite magic. The soothing lilt, the ability to dissolve pain and suffering – how uniquely is this expressed in the chro-matic shift [*Modulation*] from b. 6 to b. 7 of the first strophe. And then, in the second strophe, how serene the gaze raised toward heaven, how quietly trusting the joyousness! How wondrously, charmingly is {85} the theme now modified. It is not the formal musical construction of the theme that dictates the individual variations: the transformation [*Verwandlung*] is the result of its idealized sub-stance [*idealer Gehalt*] – it is this which determines each individual variation. In variation I [bb. 17–32], the warmth and glow that are concentrated in the theme are now released, yet the gait is still bashful. The theme, as Marx puts it, 'is restated, but with hesitancy. The melody is punctuated by rests; the bass drags reluctantly but closely behind it.' In variation II [bb. 33–48], the precious metal of the heart becomes increasingly more liquid: now we have semiquaver movement where before there was quaver movement, and before that in the theme itself crotchet movement. The chorale rings out more consolingly in the softer [middle] register. In variation III [bb. 49–80], the theme, interlaced with harplike accompa-niment, its full content thus brought out, reaches heights of ecstasy; the soul seems entirely spirited away from the world, enveloped in the infinite blue of clearest heavenly ether. Back to earth it now wends its way [b. 80]. The theme is heard again in all its initial simplicity, but animated by more rapid motifs, then leading directly into the finale. This whole andante, as Marx puts it, is 'a devout prayer that wings its way consolingly heavenward from deepest desolation and then sinks back again'. The dissonance of the final chord presages battles still to come.

In the allegro ma non troppo, in F minor, 2/4 time, these battles become reality. The movement begins with strident augmented sixths,[28] {86} like a sudden cry of

27 See the introduction and note 6, above, for the close relationship between this paragraph and that of Marx.
28 That in the right hand is enharmonically notated as a diminished seventh, while that in the left hand is a major sixth.

anguish from the terrified soul. Passagework now follows, which, like some foaming mountain stream, plunges wildly into the chasm below, growls and grumbles in the depths, until at last (b. 20)[29] a figure, tossing back and forth – the first principal theme – breaks away from the whirlpool, eddies up and down, then spouts up roaring in uncontrolled passion, undeterred by the wailing parallel thirds [b. 28] which themselves are dragged into the maelstrom (b. 64).[30] The storm continues to the end of section I in ever-mounting agitation, reaching its zenith briefly in the $f\!f$ chord (b. 112),[31] its shrill cry followed immediately by two bars of muffled growling. At the beginning of section II (b. 118)[32] a new storm of passion blows up, but soon coruscations of humour light up the sky, as in the first movement (the motif in G♭ major, bb. 130, 138),[33] against which heart-rending anguish is raised in a motif of rising and falling semitones (b. 143).[34] In bb. 158–64[35] further turbulent emotional upheavals are heard, and powerful thunderings in the deep (b. 167).[36] The struggle abates somewhat, and a wild hammering of C major octaves (bb. 168–75)[37] leads to a series of shuddering spasms which eventually lapse into exhaustion, bringing after them in evocative minims (b. 200)[38] a moment's hollow {87} silence. But only for a moment. The struggle is not yet over, hence the whole wildly feverish drama is played out anew (b. 212),[39] the imploring parallel thirds sound out again [bb. 215ff], flashes of redeeming humour (bb. 264–5)[40] illumine the pain-racked night.

Finally, in the presto [b. 308], all the militaristic might at the composer's command is arrayed in steely armour, in sturdy, virile grandeur with full-bodied chords, as if declaring to us: 'See, the storm has not sundered the oak tree; approach once more, O wild demon of passion; you will not break me!' The demon commences his wild, unceasing course once more, but the redeeming humour overcomes it decisively (the G♭ major in b. 337 and the succession of fifths in the lower voice in bb. 349–52).[41] Thereupon, although the entire work closes in grim minor-key sonorities, we can rest assured that the forces of evil have not overcome the composer: they have only tested and hardened his stalwart moral resolve through the rigours of the battle. 'The exultant glory of the major key'[42] would have undermined the work's Idea. The end had to be soberly and upliftingly tragic, for the work as a whole is tragedy played out on the stage of pure emotion. This, then, is the governing Idea of the *Appassionata* Sonata. Beethoven himself, in response to a question as to its import, is reported to have said of it: 'Read Shakespeare's *The Tempest*'.[43]

29   'p. 17, penultimate double-system, b. 3'.   30   'p. 18, system 6'.
31   'p. 19, last system'.   32   'p. 20'.
33   'p. 20, last bar of the second double-system, and b. 2 of system 4'.
34   '[p. 20,] system 5'.   35   'p. 20, last system' (lit. bb. 157–63).
36   'p. 20, system 1' (lit. bb. 164–70).   37   '[p. 21,] system 2' (lit. bb. 171–7).
38   '[p. 21,] system 5' (lit. bb. 197–211).   39   '[p. 21,] penultimate system'.
40   'p. 22, last two bars'.   41   'p. 25 . . . system 4'.
42   I have been unable to trace this quotation.
43   Reported by Schindler, *Biographie von Ludwig van Beethoven* (Münster: Aschendorff, 1840, 2/1845), p. 199: 'I asked him to let me in on the secret of the two sonatas Op. 57 (F minor) and Op. 29 [i.e. Op. 31 no. 2] (D minor). He responded, "Just go and read Shakespeare's *Tempest*".' The story is told in a slightly different context in the later edition, ed. D. W. McArdle, p. 406.

Julius August Philipp Spitta (1841–1894)

Johann Sebastian Bach, vol. I (1873)

With Spitta for the first time we encounter analysis of individual pieces in the service of historical biography. In two earlier instances we have already seen analysis at work within biographical studies: namely, those by Baini and Ulïbïshev (vol. I, Analyses 14 and 15). However, in the case of Baini, the analysis was stylistic and classificatory, as is true also of Ulïbïshev, where, moreover, biography was dispensed with after the first quarter of the book. In Spitta's case, biography is the backbone of the book, its first part devoted to 'Bach's forebears' and subsequent five parts to periods of his life. Analysis is thus set within a framework of information that embraces personal and family particulars, patronage and employment, duties of office, day-to-day events, relations with other musicians, influences from other composers and national styles, forms and genres of composition, religious and liturgical considerations, instrument design, construction, tuning and temperament, and countless other matters. As Spitta himself realized, this organization forfeited any occasion for a coherent overall view of Bach's musical output, any single perspective on his total stylistic development. Moreover, analysis was thus relegated to a relatively minor facet of a many-sided complex; and yet it was the 'window' through which the work itself was allowed indirectly to speak to us.

The analyses of the gamba sonatas fall within Part IV, 'Cöthen (1717–23)' (pp. 613–784), section I of which concerns Bach's life in service at the court of Prince Leopold, his wife's death, his journey to Hamburg, Reincken's and Mattheson's attitudes towards him, and a comparison of Handel and Bach as organists. Section III deals with Bach as a violinist, the development of suite form and of the chamber sonata, unity of musical material in the suite by analogy with north German organ fugue form, Italian dance types, the French suite composers, the concerto in Handel and Vivaldi, German orchestral music in the seventeenth and early eighteenth centuries and many other topics. These issues are clustered focally around analyses of the sonatas and suites for solo violin, two keyboard sonatas, the suites for solo cello, sonatas for violin and keyboard, for gamba and harpsichord, for flute and keyboard, and finally the Brandenburg Concertos. Taken together, these analyses occupy a mere third of section III. Spitta saw Bach as a 'node' amidst a complex play of historical forces and influences. It is clear that what he tried to do for the music itself was no less than what he sought to do for the whole Bach phenomenon: 'to separate out in the period preceding him the strands that were to form that knot, to track down the causes that resulted in their converging on a personality such as Bach'.[1]

[1] vol. I, Foreword, p. xii: I have allowed myself a linguistic play on 'node' and *Knote*.

The type of analysis engendered by this approach, when taken out of context, appears unconcentrated, intermittent, episodic, excursive. Exposing it to the light, however, has its interests, for that 'context' is a work of monumental scholarship and exacting source-critical study. Spitta was one of the founders of the modern science of musicology. Yet Hanslick, having reasoned in *On the Musically Beautiful* that the very existence of the domain of florid counterpoint was itself proof that music need not necessarily awaken feelings, and that a theory that has to ignore wholesale categories of art in order to sustain itself is false, added a footnote after publication of Spitta's first volume, saying:[2]

> Bachian devotees such as Spitta admittedly strive to turn this on its head in that, rather than contesting the theory itself in the interests of their master, they interpret his fugues and suites with emotional outpourings as eloquent and vivid as only a subtle Beethovenian [could summon up] for the sonatas of his master.

The allusion to the Beethoven literature is apposite, for Spitta adopted a mode of elucidatory analysis that (as we have already seen in Analyses 2–4) was fashioned for explaining the mysteries of Beethoven's sonatas and symphonies to an amateur readership. Spitta explains the dilemma in which he found himself (vol. I, Foreword, p. xxi):

> I have naturally placed greatest weight on the formal aspect, in proportion to the extent that this is more amenable to exact scientific measurement than is the ideal aspect. However, to neglect the latter altogether seemed to me unwarranted. [. . .] In instrumental music the writer faces the choice either of baldly confronting his reader with an anatomical exhibit, or of attempting by way of a word here and there to capture the atmosphere which alone can awaken that exhibit to burgeoning life. I have adopted the latter approach. [. . .] I can only hope I shall not be reproached for acting with undue subjectivity. [. . .]

Nowadays, we probably would so reproach him when, in a landmark work of Bach scholarship, he says of the close of the Adagio of Brandenburg Concerto No. 1 that it 'crumbles like the funeral march of the "Eroica", the insatiable plaint falling suddenly silent', or of the Andante of Brandenburg No. 2 that it 'laments in soft and maidenly fashion, [whilst] the outer movements swarm and bustle with magical vitality and youthful yearning; in truth, though Bach did not yet command the rich hues of later composers, nonetheless the entire world of German romanticism lives within his instrumental music!', or when he likens its first movement to a troop of riders with flashing eyes and rippling plumes, its musical form dramatized as a triumphal cry, a chorus of companions, and the wind intoning softly through the rustle of leaves.

In the analyses of the gamba sonatas given here, Hanslick's point is directly addressed: despite the dependence of Sonata No. 3 upon polyphony, this is a work 'of Magyar temperament'. Spitta compares the momentum of its first movement with that encountered in the overtures of Carl Maria von Weber. The image of Bach being 'carried away' by this momentum conjures up the composer at the

---

2   *Vom Musikalisch-Schönen: ein Beitrag zur Revision der Ästhetik der Tonkunst* (Leipzig: Weigel, 1854). The argument is present in the third edition (1865), pp. 25–6, and I assume it to have been so in the first; the footnote had not been added by the fifth edition (Leipzig: Barth, 1876), but is present in the seventh (1885), p. 36; 'florid counterpoint': *Figuralmusik*.

keyboard flinging himself at the gamba's theme in double octaves and fracturing his delicate two-part counterpoint with lusty three-part chords.

Instructively, Spitta creates an opposition between *motivisch* and *thematisch*. What 'we have all along [called] *motivische Gestaltung . . .* we are now accustomed to calling *thematische Arbeit*'. The former is a quintessentially mid-nineteenth-century expression, associated above all with A. B. Marx. Spitta means that historical study has taught scholars to use a more appropriately eighteenth-century term in relation to eighteenth-century music. Heinrich Christoph Koch's retrospective definition of *thematisch* in his *Lexikon* of 1802 precisely bears out Spitta's usage:[3]

> A piece of music is described as 'thematically worked out' [*thematisch gearbeitet*] if its articulation consists primarily in a variety of modifications and segmentations of the principal subject [*Hauptsatz*], unpermeated by a lot of subsidiary ideas.

There emerges in the concluding paragraph to Spitta's three analyses what may perhaps be a subtext to Spitta's musical analyses not only here but elsewhere in the book. Somewhat convoluted, it seems to say: [1] motivic working-out typifies (though not exclusively) compositional procedure in the age of Beethoven; [2] thematic working-out typifies (likewise) that in the age of Bach; [3] the former was sometimes adopted by Bach's predecessors; [4] J. S. Bach stands out by virtue of (a) having had complete mastery over both, and (b) having employed both equally and complementarily. Bach thus stands at the intersection of the old and the new, uniquely in command of both. Are we to infer from this that Bach was at least as great a master as Beethoven?

Spitta appears to share with A. B. Marx the notion that the motivic raw materials (*Stoff*) of musical composition are rudimentary life forms, not in themselves fully formed; and that they take on character only with reduplication and proliferation (Marx: 'Out of one or more of these [basic two- or three-note] formulas, the whole of a movement is constructed. Such formulas, containing the *germ seeds* and *sprouts* of the movement that grows forth from them, we call *motifs . . .*'[4]) The word *Organismus* is a favourite of Spitta, and the closing paragraph, with its reference to 'stem' and 'bloom' clearly shows how grounded his view of musical structure is in organic theory.

Julius August Spitta studied theology and classical philology at the University of Göttingen, and became a Classics teacher. While still a student, he wrote a biography of Schumann and struck up a friendship with Brahms. Becoming interested in music history, he produced the first volume of his monumental study of J. S. Bach in 1873, on the strength of which he was called in 1875 to be Professor of Music History at the University of Berlin and administrative Director at the Hochschule für Musik, gathering around him as pupils some of the greatest figures in the next generation of musicologists: Peter Wagner, Johannes Wolf,

3 'Thematisch', *Musikalisches Lexikon* (Frankfurt: A. Hermann, 1802; reprint edn Hildesheim: Olms, 1964), col. 1533. 'Thema' is cross-referred to 'Hauptsatz', cols. 745–7, where the two terms are treated synonymously, and the processes of elaboration are described by quoting directly J. G. Grohmann's *Kurzgefasstes Handwörterbuch über die schönen Künste* (Leipzig, 1794–5), the musical articles for which were written by Friedrich August Baumbach (1753–1813).

4 A. B. Marx, *Die Lehre von der musikalischen Komposition praktisch theoretisch*, vol. 1 (Leipzig: B&H, 1837), p. 27.

Max Friedlaender and many others. The second volume of his Bach study was issued in 1880, and the whole work was translated into English in 1884–5. He made major contributions to the study of Heinrich Schütz, and was the prime force behind the first complete edition of that composer's works. He was co-founder with Chrysander and Guido Adler of one of the first scholarly music journals, the *Vierteljahrsschrift für Musikwissenschaft*, and was tirelessly active as a scholar over a vast range of music history.

'[Three Sonatas for Viola da Gamba and Harpsichord, BWV1027–9]'

Johann Sebastian Bach

Source:
Philipp Spitta, *Johann Sebastian Bach*, vol. I (Leipzig: B&H, 1873), pp. 725–8.

The viola da gamba was an instrument of five or more strings, very similar to Bach's *viola pomposa*[5] in range – its lowest note being D, its highest a' – but it differed essentially from the latter by being tuned in fourths with one third, and also in being held between the knees like the cello. It therefore offered a great variety of tone colour, but was intrinsically tender and sensitive rather than robust in nature. Thus it was that Bach could arrange for gamba and obbligato harpsichord without detriment to its underlying character a trio which was originally for two flutes and continuo [BWV1029].[6] This four-movement Sonata in G major is the purest and most lovely idyll {726} that it is possible to conceive. In the high-romantic andante (E minor) alone do we hear soft and eerie whisperings, as of the faint rustling of leaves in the forest gloom, and a ghostly sound reverberates trembling through the silent thickets (the four-bar held E of the gamba [bb. 13–16] – a stroke of sheer genius). With this exception, the whole sonata is suffused with radiant, joyous sunshine under clear blue skies. In the last movement, a fugue exhibiting that sturdy gracefulness so typical of Bach, there appear between the individual groups of the development enchanting and finely spun episodes in the Corellian manner, after each of which the entry of the fugue subject, unexpected and yet so natural, has a doubly exhilarating effect. The incorporation of this sonata into a set with the other two was not the work of the composer himself, nor did he evidently intend it thus, for meticulously written individual autographs exist for two of them.

The second sonata (D major)[7] does not quite come up to the others in quality. Indeed, the opening allegro is not entirely devoid of a certain stiffness.

By contrast, the third sonata (G minor)[8] is once again a work of utmost beauty and most striking individuality. It has only three movements, as does a concerto; in fact, concerto form has had a major influence upon the construction of its fast movements. The opening allegro [*recte* vivace] begins, it is true, in the sonata style [*Sonatenmanier*]; but the long-drawn-out theme, rich in motivic raw material [*motivischer Stoff*], immediately suggests freer development. As it happens, what ensues is not a fugal-style continuation in the dominant; instead there is a more

---

5   *viola pomposa*: a five-stringed instrument in use c.1725–70, tuned in fifths, and used by Telemann, Graun and Lidarti. The association of its invention with J. S. Bach c.1724, which Spitta endorsed (vol. I, pp. 678, 824–5), is now considered erroneous.
6   [Spitta:] Bach Gesellschaft edn, vol. IX, pp. 175ff (the earlier version in the Appendix, pp. 260ff); Peters edn, S.IV, C.2, No. 1. [Bent:] Peters edn: *Oeuvres complètes de Jean Sebastian Bach publiées par C. F. Peters, Bureau de Musique* (Leipzig and Berlin, 1866–67), Série IV, Cahier 2.
7   [Spitta:] Bach Gesellschaft edn, vol. IX, pp. 189ff; Peters edn, S.IV, C.2, No. 2.
8   [Spitta:] Bach Gesellschaft edn, vol. IX, pp. 203ff; Peters edn, S.IV, C.2, No. 3.

elaborately fashioned restatement in the tonic [bb. 11–19], followed by motivic working-out [*motivische Arbeit*] that leads to the close of section I (b. 25). At first, section II is introduced by no more than a fugally answered fragment [*Partikel*] of the principal theme; but soon a new half-bar motif joins the fray (b. 30):

Example 1

If at this point we quote also the four-bar phrase that is to appear later in b. 53:

{727}

Example 2

then along with the principal theme we have the sum total of material from which the rest of the movement evolves in pure concerto fashion. There is no section III as such after this. Constantly revitalizing itself it pursues its course unremittingly to the end. If almost every new work of Bach overwhelms us with astonishment at the sheer inexhaustibility of its creative imagination, this work in particular shows us of what sharp characterization Bach's style was capable despite its dependence upon polyphony. We have here a composition of Magyar temperament. It gallops like the wind across the plains on wild, fiery steeds. The impetuous auxiliary motifs streak like lashes of the whip. Now the musical figures fall clashing into disarray with a diminished seventh chord and work their way out of the tangle beneath the piercing trill of an upper voice [bb. 66, 68];[9] now they come together again with the principal theme in a heavy unison rarely found in Bach [bb. 95–6], so that the very ground shakes with the stamping of their hooves. The irresistible momentum, for ever heightening the onward motion to the uttermost by means of new and unexpected impulses, is not unlike that which is so widely admired in the over-tures of Weber. Just how carried away by it Bach himself was is shown not only by the frequent unisons but also by b. 64, in which the underlying theme suddenly appears in the keyboard in three parts, the harmony as a whole thus becoming four-part, and then by the colossal final close (bb. 97ff), where battalions of notes plunge tumultuously from one diminished seventh chord to another. No allowance

9   The sustained note in each case is not marked with a trill in the Bach Gesellschaft edition.

is made in this movement for the tenderness so natural to the viola da gamba –
only for the instrument's wide compass and agility.

A magnificent adagio in Bb major (3/2 time) now satisfies our desire for melody
with a contemplative and spiritually uplifting strain, from the opening of which
premonitions of Beethoven emerge unmistakably.

The final allegro, too, provides an inexhaustible fund of the loveliest melodies,
and at the same time displays the most extraordinary {728} power to invent new
musical ideas out of the raw materials already presented, a technique which we are
now accustomed to calling the art of thematic working-out [*die Kunst der thematischen Arbeit*]. For this purpose, we have all along used the expression 'motivic
configuration' [*motivische Gestaltung*] as something distinct from fugal exposition
of a single unvarying subject. Apart from the opening, concerto form once again
governs the entire movement. The theme:

Example 3

is stated twice in all voices and comes to a close in Bb major [b. 19]. At this point
a soft, throbbing figure derived from b. 1 establishes itself in the bass of the harpsichord, the gamba striking up an entirely new and expressive melody over it,
the right hand [of the harpsichord] meanwhile executing broken chords in semiquavers [bb. 19–24], then exchanging roles with the gamba in F major [bb. 24–8].
After one further statement of the principal theme [in the bass, bb. 32–4], the semiquaver accompaniment figure is now motivically extended; but against this there
appears yet another new melody, every bit as enchanting as the previous one
(bb. 37–55 [harpsichord, then gamba]). Then follows thematic and motivic development of the principal theme [bb. 57–69] and the introduction of the first of the
[two previously stated] subsidiary subjects [*des ersten Seitensatzes*] in D minor;
against this yet a third idea is given out [in the harpsichord] as a countermelody,
vying with it in characteristically graceful manner (bb. 69–79). At the cadence
of this period, in C minor [b. 79], a fourth development of the principal theme
is introduced and leads back to G minor [b. 83]. Here (in b. 90), against the same
figuration that accompanied the first of the subsidiary ideas, the gamba now introduces yet a fourth [idea], which reappears in the keyboard [b. 103] after a fifth
development of the [principal] theme, and brings the movement to a final close.

Thus on the stem which constitutes the theme, one bloom springs forth after
another in a way astonishing not only for its time: even in the age of Beethoven,
when, in accordance with the altered style of instrumental music, motivic working-
out was much more the custom than thematic, it would be hard to find anything
of this kind more skilful or more inventive. Bach had just as masterly a command
over the art of motivic resources as over that of thematic resources; whereas his
predecessors often did favour the former, in him the two come together as equals,
complementing and lifting each other constantly to greater heights.

Hans von Wolzogen (1848–1938)

'Parsifal': ein thematischer Leitfaden durch Dichtung und Musik (1882)

Act I Scene 1 of *Parsifal* is an extraordinarily sophisticated dramatic construction, more than half taken up with narrative – a narrative that is highly complex. Von Wolzogen divides the scene into two unequal parts at precisely the beginning of that narrative (b. 281), perceiving the two parts as opposites: action|repose, or incident|narration, or drama|epic.

His awareness of this polarity is shown in a particularly acute way. Briefly, Gurnemanz's narration proceeds in six sequences, each one responding to remarks or questions by the squires, and each concluding in the 'now' of the narrative.[1] The time of the story is narrated non-linearly, and it is not until the beginning of the fifth sequence that we reach the earliest point of the story (Titurel; the forces of evil). The fifth therefore (and perversely von Wolzogen decrees that the 'narrative proper' does not begin until this point) traverses all the other sequences – save, that is, for one startling moment, at b. 575, when Gurnemanz introduces an ellipsis – an overt gap in the narrative:

> Amfortas strove unceasingly
> To put a stop to the sorcerous scourge;
> – You know how that worked out:

Line 3 refers listeners to their own reserves of memory, derived from previous narrative sequences. However, in the fragment of time between lines 2 and 3, the music tosses them a clue: a tiny, jerky figure, unison in strings. These strings are a token for four horns, which stated the figure earlier, at bb. 404–06:

> Armed with [the spear], Amfortas, headstrong,
> Who could restrain you
> From attacking the magician?
>
> [figure]
>
> Close by the castle, our hero is entranced,
> A woman of fiendish beauty has captivated him:
> In her arms he lies swooning,
> The sword has fallen from his hand.

---

1 For a systematic study of time in narrative, see Gérard Genette, *Narrative Discourse: an Essay in Method*, Eng. trans. J. E. Lewin (Ithaca: Cornell University Press, 1980; Fr. orig. 1972). For a discussion of narrative structure in this scene of *Parsifal*, see Carolyn Abbate, '"Parsifal": Words and Music', in *Richard Wagner: Parsifal*, ed. N. John, Opera Guide, vol. XXXIV (London: Calder, 1986), pp. 43–58, esp. 43–51. For a broader study of narrative in music, see Carolyn Abbate, *Unsung Voices: Opera and Musical Narrative in the Nineteenth Century* (Princeton: Princeton University Press, 1991).

And this in turn takes them back to near the opening of the scene (bb. 33–8), when the squires leap up from morning prayer to begin their day's work to that same figure (Example 6, bb. 1–4). On the first two occasions the figure was full of optimism; now it is a mere shadow of itself. Of this extraordinary moment, in which the music short-circuits across from the fifth to the fourth (and implicitly the third) narrative sequence, von Wolzogen offers a keen insight: it 'exerts a *dramatic* impact upon the *epic* character of this passage'.

To this figure, von Wolzogen gives the name 'drastic variation', or 'chivalric variation' of the Faith Theme. Richard Wagner, writing in 1879 of the 'unity' he had brought to his music dramas by the use of a 'web of underlying themes [*Grundthemen*] stretching the length and breadth of the artwork', remarked rather tartly that he had left a deliberate trail of information behind him in the expectation that 'others' would by then have achieved:[2]

> a critical examination of the musical forms that I have harvested from drama in my own artistic efforts. To the best of my knowledge, this path remains still untrodden. All that comes to mind is one of my younger friends, who has examined in great detail the characteristics of what he has chosen to call 'leitmotifs'. These he has examined more in terms of their dramatic significance and effect than of their relevance to musical structure (for he is far from being a musical specialist).

This 'younger friend', Hans von Wolzogen, had written his first 'thematic analysis' (his own epithet) of music by Wagner five years earlier, in 1874 – of the Prelude to *Siegfried*. He had done it 'for fun', and had turned it into an article the following year.[3] It was Franz Liszt who, he tells us, encouraged him to take his work further. He extended it to cover the whole of *Siegfried*, seeing it as a continuation of the rather different analyses of *The Rhinegold* and *The Valkyrie* already available by Gottfried (or Gottlieb) Federlein, working apparently in America.[4] At the urging of the Leipzig publisher Edwin Schloemp, he then set to work on a study of the entire *Ring* on a more compressed scale, and this appeared in book form as the first of his enormously successful volumes entitled 'thematic guide' (*thematischer Leitfaden*) – in time for the first public performance of the *Ring* as a cycle, at the newly built Bayreuth Festspielhaus between 13 and 30 August 1876. The second such guide, on *Tristan and Isolde*, came out in 1880, and the third, on *Parsifal*, in 1882.

Von Wolzogen was not the first to write in extended fashion about Wagner's mature music dramas. In 1866–7, Heinrich Porges (1837–1900), journalist and choirmaster, had written for King Ludwig a lengthy essay, 'Tristan and Isolde: An Elucidation', which remained in manuscript until von Wolzogen published it thirty-five years later.[5] In this, Porges identified motifs such as the 'Love motif',

---

2   'Über die Anwendung der Musik auf das Drama', in *Richard Wagner: Sämtliche Schriften und Dichtungen: Volks-Ausgabe*, vol. x (Leipzig: B&H, 6/n.d.), pp. 176–93, esp. 185.
3   Apparently published in *Musikalisches Wochenblatt*, for November 1875. I have been unable to consult this.
4   Allegedly in *Musikalisches Wochenblatt*, but I have been unable to verify this.
5   'Tristan und Isolde: zur Erläuterung', *Bayreuther Blätter*, 25 (1902), 186–211 [Act I]; 26 (1903), 23–48 [Act II], 241–70 [Act III]; later as Heinrich Porges, *Tristan und Isolde, nebst einem Briefe Richard Wagners*, ed. H. von Wolzogen (Leipzig: B&H, 1906). Von Wolzogen was editor of *Bayreuther Blätter* throughout its existence, 1878–1938. Wagner corresponded enthusiastically with Porges about this essay (*Richard Wagner an Freunde und Zeitgenossen*, ed. Erich Kloss (Berlin

'Death motif', 'Tristan motif', 'Sailor's cry motif', 'Motif of compassion' and so forth. But six years earlier still, the composer and conductor Wendelin Weissheimer (1838–1910) had contributed an extended review of the score of *Tristan*, in which he had cited many motifs by label: 'Love motif', 'Isolde motif', 'Tristan motif', 'Seafaring motif', 'Death motif', 'Hero motif', 'Main motif of courtly love', and provided a musical appendix indexing motifs by number and letter.[6]

Like Porges, von Wolzogen described his work as 'elucidation' (*Erläuterung*). The 'guide' was a medium intended for laymen ('they are in the same boat as myself: they too are not musicians', *Parsifal*, p. 1). It was to be read only *after* experiencing the work in performance. It was designed as an aid to memory and comprehension *post facto*, not as a handy means of self-preparation. Its purpose was to impose order on a chaos of impressions. A *Leitfaden* is a 'thread' paid out, so to speak (like Theseus's thread in the labyrinth!) through the streets and buildings of a city, to 'guide' the visitor. The city, in the present case, is the listener's memory store of a Wagnerian music drama. Through that memory store, routes are traced, circuits are drawn, connections are made. By analogy, a *Leitmotiv* is a musical entity that traces a route through a drama, to 'guide' the listener. The presence of a number of such leitmotifs constitutes a complex circuitry – or, in Wagner's own word, a 'web'.

Von Wolzogen stresses that motifs are in themselves unnameable – that attaching a name to a motif is no more than providing a device for recognition. Rather than resorting to the neutrality of numbers, he prefers to take an associated image from the drama. Such a process is hazardous in its arbitrariness (note his deference in our excerpt: 'a *Storm Figure* – it could equally well be called "Galloping motif"'). Moreover, it is essential to realize that the motif so named in no sense 'represents' its associated image: the Sword motif in the *Ring* does not 'stand for' the sword; instead, motif, image or event, and poetic word coalesce, following Wagner's own dictates, and jointly 'guide' the mind back to one of those underlying forces, such as the urge for power, which are the progenitors of all motif formations.[7]

and Leipzig: Schuster und Loeffler, 1909), pp. 461, 463–4, 484, 495). At one point, Wagner wrote (ibid, 484, letter dated 15 May 1867):

> as regards Marke and his quasi-guilt [. . .], in the postlude at the close of Act [II] you have overlooked the fact that this is derived melodically from Marke's main motif [*Hauptmotiv*] (of Well-wishing), and so contains the Motif [*Motiv*] of Self-reproach which ostensibly overwhelms Tristan.

Porges modified his description accordingly (*Bayreuther Blätter*, 26 (1903), 48 and note). Porges contributed a series of articles on the *Ring* to *Bayreuther Blätter* between 1880 and 1896. I am indebted to John Deathridge for drawing these materials to my attention.

6 NZM: 53 (1860), no. 12 (14 September), 97–8; no. 14 (28 September), 113–14; no. 15 (5 October), 121–4; no. 16 (12 October), 129–30; no. 18 (26 October), 149–52; no. 20 (9 November), 165–6 and Beilag. 54 (1861), no. 9 (22 February), 77–8; no. 10 (1 March), 87–9; no. 11 (8 March), 95–6; no. 12 (15 March), 103–05; no. 14 (29 March), 121–3; no. 15 (5 April), 129–31; no. 17 (19 April), 149–50; no. 18 (26 April), 158–60; no. 19 (3 May), 165–7. Weissheimer also wrote a book (which I have been unable to consult) entitled *Erlebnisse mit Richard Wagner, Franz Liszt und vielen anderen Zeitgenossen nebst deren Briefen* (Stuttgart: Deutsche Verlags-Anstalt, 1898).

7 e.g. from 'Dichtkunst und Tonkunst im Drama der Zukunft', in *Oper und Drama*, in *Richard Wagner: Sämtliche Schriften und Dichtungen: Volks-Ausgabe*, vol. IV (Leipzig: B&H, 6/n.d.), p. 185:

> A musical motif can create within our sensibility an impression that is specific, and that takes shape as mental activity, only if the feeling verbalized in that motif is communicated before our very eyes by a particular individual in relation to a tangible object, as something itself precise – that is, well defined.

But what of '*leit*-motif', as apart from plain 'motif'? Extraordinarily, nowhere in the sixty-four pages of his *Parsifal* analysis is 'leitmotif' used; nowhere in the thirty-four pages of his *Tristan* analysis; nowhere in the ninety-four pages of his *Ring* analysis. That is to say, throughout none of the analyses for which von Wolzogen's use of the term *Leitmotiv* is famous – if not infamous – does that term ever once appear![8] It is used only in essays of a more general nature: in an introduction, 'The Meaning of the Motifs', to the fourth edition of the *Ring* analysis (1878, which he himself claims was his first use of the term), and an extended essay entitled '"Leitmotifs"', dating from 1897.[9] Von Wolzogen is strikingly coy there about the term: 'How it was "invented" seems now beyond recall. Legend has it that I am the guilty party, but I could not with a clear conscience say that I am aware of having been so.' In particular, he makes no mention of Jähns's catalogue of Carl Maria von Weber, published only seven years earlier, in 1871, in which the term is used extensively to describe recurrent musical ideas, each denoting a person or a situation, in *Abu Hassan, Der Freischütz, Preciosa, Euryanthe* and *Oberon*.[10]

A leitmotif, as portrayed in von Wolzogen's essays of 1878 and 1897, appears to be not a single motif but a cluster of interrelated motifs. Von Wolzogen distinguishes between 'parallels' (*Parallelen*) and 'leitmotif'. An example of 'parallels' in the *Ring* would be the Rhinemaidens' motif ('Weia! Waga!'), the Ride of the Valkyries and the Woodbird's song. It would be incorrect, he says, to interpret these as related variants of one and the same leitmotivic thought: they merely have a certain kinship of rhythmic-melodic expression. Consider, on the other hand, the Sword motif, which appears first in the closing bars of *The Rhinegold*. It later splits into two: the sword itself, and its use and possession. The second of these two forms comes to life in *The Valkyrie*, Act II Scene 4 (Brünnhilde and Siegmund), when its last note is 'remodelled' as a heroic flourish that later emerges, in *Siegfried*, Act I Scene 1, as the Keeper of the sword motif (*Schwertwartmotiv*),[11] which links in turn to Siegfried's motif, the Motif of Siegfried the Wälsung, Siegfried's heroism, and eventually to Siegfried's horn call. A cluster of definable separate motifs of this sort, linked by organic mutation, is what von Wolzogen calls 'leitmotif': 'leitmotifs = music as form; parallels = music as expression'.

'Motif' is by no means the exclusive term for named musical entities in von Wolzogen's writings. In the *Parsifal* analysis alone many of them are classed by other musical terms such as 'theme', 'melody', 'song', 'chorus', 'figure', 'harmonies', 'cadence', 'variation', loosely according to their length and nature. Others are designated directly as 'covenant', 'greeting', 'call', 'prayer', 'lament', not to mention 'desolation', 'rustling of the forest', or 'flower meadow'.

8   At least, in the editions that are available to me.
9   '"Leitmotive"', *Bayreuther Blätter*, 20 (1897), 313–30.
10   F. W. Jähns: *Carl Maria von Weber in seinen Werken: chronologisch-thematisches Verzeichniss seiner sämmtlichen Compositionen* . . . (Berlin: Schlesinger, 1871), pp. 2, 129, 277, 319, 335, 366, 400–401. Consider, for example (p. 400):

> Here we have the only leitmotif to be found in *Oberon*, but one quite unique and of profound significance, for it is (as occurs in no other opera by Weber) not for a single person or situation, but for a *series of people*, for a *series of situations* and *scenes* involving particular characters.

11   This process is discussed not only in the 1897 article, but in detail (without reference to the concept of leitmotif) in the *Tristan* analysis, pp. 45, 48, 56, 67.

By Wagnerian principles, a motif stated in the orchestra alone before it has been actualized in music, word and drama together, is a 'premonition' (*Ahnung*). It stirs in the listener a desire for that actualization. Von Wolzogen treats the Prelude to *Parsifal*, which by its nature is entirely premonitory, in just that light, describing it as a foreshadowing of the Grail ceremony at the end of Act I, even underlaying words to the first motif as it will eventually be sung, and providing the words of the third motif. Likewise, in Act I Scene 1 he signals the introduction of the Fool motif, but quotes it in its stabilized form from the end of Act I, complete with text, not in the asymmetrical, compressed version that occurs at this point. While much of the analysis is thus cross-indexing of motif occurrences, mixed with pietistic exegesis, von Wolzogen attempts to highlight motivic transference and transformation, though never in more than loosely descriptive language.

A comparison of von Wolzogen's treatment of leitmotifs with that of von Wolzogen's protégé Karl Mayrberger, whom Wagner himself had called 'the so-long awaited theorist for our *Blätter*', is well worthwhile. Mayrberger produced his analysis of leitmotifs from *Tristan and Isolde* – which is translated here in its entirety as Analysis 13 in volume I – in 1881, only a year after von Wolzogen's own thematic guide. His concern was with explaining Wagner's complex harmonic language, and this he carried out with the single-mindedness of the true theorist, eschewing all reference to dramatic purpose or aesthetic effect. The two treatments could hardly have been more different. It is paradoxical, then, that in adopting von Wolzogen's labels for motifs, Mayrberger allowed von Wolzogen's non-technical segmentation of the music to form the basis for his own technical analysis.

Von Wolzogen's study of *Parsifal* went through at least twenty-one editions extending well into the twentieth century. Moreover, it underwent two independent English-language translations, one for the English market by William Ashton Ellis and the other for the American market by J. H. Cornell.[12] His approach to Wagner's music has been persistently influential; it has been heavily criticized, and in the process has itself been caricatured. Von Wolzogen wrote a number of other books, all concerning aspects of Wagner and Bayreuth.

Hans von Wolzogen was son of the intendant of the Schwerin court theatre. He studied comparative philology and philosophy in Berlin in 1868–71, and soon thereafter befriended Wagner, becoming the editor of *Bayreuther Blätter* in 1877, and continuing thus to the end of his life.

---

12   *A Key to Parsifal (with Thematic Musical Illustrations)*, Eng. trans. W. A. Ellis (London: Chappell, [Preface: 1889]); *Thematic Guide through the Music of Parsifal, with a Preface concerning the Traditional Material of the Wagnerian Drama*, Eng. trans. J. H. Cornell (New York: Schirmer, n.d.).

'Prelude', 'Act I [Scene 1]'

'Parsifal': A Thematic Guide through the Poetry and the Music (1882)

Source:
'Parsifal': ein thematischer Leitfaden durch Dichtung und Musik, Führer durch Richard Wagners Musikdramen, vol. VII (Leipzig: Senf, 1882, 20/1911), pp. 17–30.

Prelude

The Prelude ushers us into the sanctuary[13] of the Holy Grail. Solemn, ceremonious strains reach our ears – strains that will give musical portrayal at the close of Act I to the Love Feast of the Knights of the Grail. This is not the power of the Grail as revealed to the world with chivalric splendour in *Lohengrin*, bringing aid from some far-off mystic realm. Rather, this is the divine power of *love* and *belief*, imparted to human hearts by celestial proclamation, and fashioning faithful souls into a fervent fellowship of devoted servants of God. The message of eternal love, which has bestowed pity on man and shed its own blood in sacrifice for his salvation, takes voice in the empty silence, softly and musingly, its melody intoning the *Covenant of the Love Feast* (I.1. [bb. 1–6]):[14]

I The Covenant of the Love Feast

Example 1

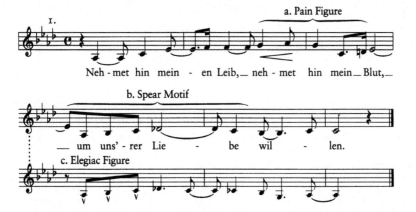

13 *Heiligthum*: this word, the medieval counterpart of the Old Testament Ark of the Covenant, is capable of denoting (1) sacredness as an abstract property, (2) sacred objects, which may be relics of the life of Christ or of a Christian saint, or the vessels and paraphernalia of the eucharist (the Grail belongs to both categories); (3) a casket or box containing such objects; (4) an architectural space in which such a casket is placed, hence in this case the Grail castle, Monsalvat (as in Act I Scene 1, bb. 495–7: 'For the sacred relic [*Heiltum*] he built a sanctuary [*Heiligtum*]'). Its uses in this passage all refer to a single concept, but have been variously translated according to the aspect that seems uppermost: 'sanctity', 'sanctuary', 'sacred relic'.

{18} With the aid of softly shimmering rapid string arpeggios [*Tremolandohar-monien*], this divine spirit of love steals swiftly into the enraptured hearts of the worshippers, who then intone the sacred covenant for a second time in hushed prayer, as if drawn up toward the celestial source of the proclamation, their inner-most souls in thrall. Then follows immediately the second part of the covenant (I.2.) [bb. 20–25]:

Example 2

The community of the faithful now assembles, and the sublime form of the sacred relic ascends, as if sprung from the musical substance of that covenant, in solemn splendour in the rising figure of the *Grail Motif* itself (II) [bb. 39–41]:[15]

II The Grail Motif

Example 3

{19} In this motif, the piece, which has up to now wafted as if on angels' wings, attains its first *forte*,[16] whereupon the third main motif [*Hauptmotiv*] associated with the Grail appears, broad and triumphantly powerful, namely the *Faith Theme*

14   *Liebesmahlspruch*: I have resisted translating *Liebesmahl* 'the Lord's supper', or 'Communion' (*heiliges Abendmahl*) in favour of the more correct 'Love Feast', i.e. the *agape* of the early Christians. Von Wolzogen identifies the melody (he calls it *Melodie*, not *Motiv*) by its *Spruch*, i.e. its formu-laic text: 'Take this my body, take this my blood, for the sake of our love' (cf. *St Matthew* 26.26–8, *St Mark* 14.22–4), which I have translated 'Covenant'. In underlaying this text to Exx. 1–2 despite the tied notes in this (purely instrumental) presentation, von Wolzogen is referring to the moment when words, music and visual image come together in the chorus of 'voices from above' in the penultimate scene of Act I, at the uncovering of the Grail, to actualize the motif. The 'elegiac figure' is a version of the Spear Motif that first appears in the Prelude in bb. 95–6, again in bb. 96–8, and in an elaborated form in bb. 98–101, as von Wolzogen later explains.

15   The 'later cadence form' occurs first in Act I Scene 1, bb. 31–2, where the top line reads: tied crotchet – dotted minim – semibreve tied.

16   This is at least notationally untrue, since the marking *forte* appears in b. 3, *poco forte* in b. 11, and *forte*, *fortissimo* and *sforzando* in b. 30.

(III) [bb. 44–50], that thrilling melody which is sung by the chorus of youths at the ceremony, with the words 'The Faith lives on! The dove hovers, sweet messenger of our Saviour.'[17]

III The Faith Theme

Example 4

Announced by wind instruments, the melody rings out like the credo of the assembled company of knights in the service of sacred love. Once its first statement has died away *diminuendo* [bb. 54–5], and the Grail Motif has answered it softly [bb. 56–9], it embarks once again, starting *piano* and gradually swelling towards *fortissimo*, on an exalted presentation of its downward-striding theme, passing through various instrumental sonorities as it descends from heights to depths. This musical image of the whole of humanity uniting in brotherhood recurs during the ceremony at the close of Act I, to the ritual embraces of the knights after the Love Feast. Lingering softly on the air, *pianissimo*, this theme re-echoes the noble universal song once more [bb. 72–9], this time from the heights, as if it were heaven's benediction on God's earthly family, and fades away finally in a low timpani roll, as if a dark bank of cloud[18] were passing over this sublime picture of religious ecstasy. With this, section I of the Prelude concludes.

{20} The sombre drumroll is transformed almost imperceptibly, with a soft subterranean rumbling, from the tonic of the Prelude, A♭, into a spine-chilling tremolo on tonic and sixth, F–A♭ [bb. 78–81].[19] At this moment, the other side of the Grail legend, its worldly aspect, is exposed to view – the suffering that sacred love incurs on earth, and in the hearts of men. With the downfall of Amfortas, the very sanctity of the Holy Grail was invaded by sin and shame. For now, however, the sounds of suffering and lament that we hear in the Prelude should be understood in more general terms. The Saviour, who forfeited his life on the cross for the expiation of a mankind sunk in mortal sin, is daily crucified anew in every sinful heart, and not even the most devout souls of the community of the faithful are free from the curse of degeneracy. So now, we hear the melody of the *Covenant of the Love Feast* rise up from the hollow depths of the bass tremolandos, only to be punctuated a moment later at the beginning of its tortured middle phrase

17 Act I, penultimate scene, bb. 68–73.
18 *Wolkenvorhang* is a theatrical term for 'sky' in scenery.
19 *wandelt sich . . . in ein schauriges Tremolo . . .* : in fact, the drumroll remains on A♭, and a tremolo F on cellos and double basses is added beneath it at b. 793.

(I.1.a) [bb. 81–2] by the sudden entry of [violin] tremolos [b. 82], pathos-laden, reaching ever higher, as if rending the music asunder, leaving it ravaged by the mortal agonies of Christ crucified. This middle phrase is repeated on its own, as if a heavy sigh.[20] The Covenant appears twice in this intensified guise, in a different key each time, as if in some new spasm of suffering.

On the third occasion [bb. 90–97], transposed a minor third higher yet again, now reaching the plaintive key of D minor, the middle phrase occurs in three overlapping statements, with an interplay of instrumental colours,[21] as if heaping pain upon pain. With this we behold the Saviour, lacerated by the spear-thrust of worldliness, a Passion of transcendent pain, the godly wound striking at the heart of the sinner, bleeding, lamenting, its lament still unuttered in words – until the final phrase (I.1.b) supplants it, in a threefold repetition, once again overlapping, giving way to an elegiac figure (I.1.c) [bb. 95–101] – a phrase of utmost simplicity, and yet deeply moving. In this plangent lament can be sensed right away a premonition of consolation mingled with resignation – consolation that breaks forth on the last occurrence in a long-drawn-out extension [bb. 99–101], calming and reverential. It {21} later forms part of what the chorus of youths sings before the ceremony: 'As once his blood was spilled with a thousand agonies for the sinful world' and so on:[22]

XIV The Saviour's Lament

Example 5

---

20   bb. 83–4: the 'sigh' is effected by the rest on b. 83[1] and *forte diminuendo* on b. 83[3] in the wind, and *sforzando diminuendo* in the tremolo divisi violins.

21   *drängt sich . . . gleich dreimalig eng aneinander* hints at the fugal device of stretto (*Engführung*): first and third statements (bb. 91–2, 93–4): two oboes, cor anglais, two clarinets and divisi violas; second statement (bb. 92–3): three flutes, oboe, clarinet and trumpet.

22   Ex. 5, merely cross-referred by von Wolzogen at this point, appears on p. 35. The music is from the purely orchestral transformation before the penultimate scene of Act I, bb. 18–21, and is related to the chorus of youths in the penultimate scene, bb. 43–8.

At this point the lamentation falls silent, save for occasional faint isolated sighs. The final phrase of the Covenant of the Love Feast, with its short rising phrase shape, fades away into the depths [bb. 105–06]. The first phrase of the Covenant now rises, just as it began the Prelude, like a redeemed soul, soaring heavenward – an image of the serene *hope* of the faithful in the inexhaustible and enduring love of God, surmounting sorrow and death; it ascends above a gradually thinning texture of pulsing [woodwind] chords [*tremolirende Begleitung*].

Act I

Act I Scene 1 falls into two large sections, broadly characterized as action and repose, or incident and narration, respectively.

[Scene 1: section] I

At the outset, section I shows Gurnemanz and the squires in silent morning prayer, while trombones sound out the waking call [bb. 1–3], restating the *Grail Motifs* from the Prelude [bb. 6–10].[23] The youths leap to their feet at Gurnemanz's bidding, their jerky movements reflected by a drastic variation [bb. 33–8] of the Faith Theme (III.1) – the theme which permeates all the actions of this knightly company of Faith, and which serves as, so to speak, its musical embodiment [*tönende Seele*]. [This variant comprises] the main figure foreshortened, then an extension brimming with chivalric verve which will later be re-used to depict Amfortas sallying forth impetuously to do battle [with Klingsor].[24] In an instant, the commotion is quelled with a firm hand: ''Tis time to await the King' – this depicted in the dragging notes of a figure that is soon to accompany Amfortas's cortège in its own right as the *Motif of Suffering* (IV) {22}.

Example 6

Here we have in close proximity the splendour and the sorrow of the Grail Knighthood. A third attribute joins them soon after: hope, in the harmonies of the Auspicious Omen of the 'Pure Fool' (V), announced [bb. 65–9] while Gurnemanz addresses the passing knights with the words 'Fools are we to hope for relief for him', and 'there is but one who can help him – but One alone'.[25]

V The Auspicious Omen (Fool Motif)

Example 7

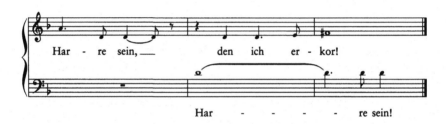

{23} Abruptly, a motif from section II, that of *Kundry*'s arrival, rings out [bb. 83–107]: a single pitch bursts forth peremptorily in scouring octaves, as the apparition draws near; a *Storm Figure* (VI) [Example 8] – it could equally well be called 'Galloping Motif' – erupts out of it, surging chromatically, leaping upward in short, powerful bounds to the heights, from whence the true *Motif of Kundry* the person (VII) [Example 8] hurtles down, *fortissimo*, over four octaves [bb. 103–07]. 'See how the wild one swooped down to earth!' What at this stage appears to denote merely 'swooping down' is in fact the musical symbol of Kundry's *curse*, a curse that clings to her unremittingly throughout the drama. It is a gesture of wild, headlong flight, as the unhappy wretch is hounded by the demon of her guilt from one world to the next. At the same time, it is the expression of her insatiable, demoniacal laughter, the curse echoing from her own breast. What confronts us

23 'Grail Motifs' signifies three themes 'associated with the Grail' (see the discussion of the Prelude): the Covenant of the Love Feast, the Grail Motif itself and the Faith Theme. Von Wolzogen's statement here does not match the stage directions of the score: Gurnemanz and the squires are asleep, not at prayer, when the first waking call – the only one played purely by trombones – sounds (bb. 1–3); and their prayers a few moments later are accompanied (by the Faith Theme) on trumpets then strings (bb. 11–25), not trombones.
24 bb. 404–06, and later at bb. 576–7.
25 In bb. 65–9 the motif is purely instrumental, on clarinets, cor anglais and bassoons. The example, with underlay and extension, shows it as sung by the chorus of youths from above in the penultimate scene of Act I just before the uncovering of the Grail.

here anew in this wonderful, mythical figure is a truly universal musical gesture, representing curser and accursed alike.

VI Kundry's Storm Figure ('Galloping Motif')

VII Kundry's Motif

Example 8

VII. Kundry's Motif

{24} Two fleeting chord progressions [bb. 107–08], and then a limpid chord at the word 'balm', and then in response to Gurnemanz's question 'Whence did you obtain this?' a succession of smoothly descending, exposed thirds [bb. 113–16] – this is the 'helpful Kundry' that we shall encounter again in Act III.[26] But a moment later, at mention of 'Arabia' [bb. 117–18], the source of her magic arts, three lingering notes hint softly but menacingly at the chromatic harmonies of the

26   Act III Scene 1, bb. 74–5, 90–91, as she comes to life and later fetches water.

Sorcery Motif (see IX), {25} later to be associated with 'Kundry in the thrall of Klingsor'.[27] Thus does the image of this enigmatic woman flit briefly but tellingly before our eyes.

At this point, Amfortas's *Motif of Suffering* reappears with its pungently syncopated accompanying chords. The sorrowful cortège approaches, its litter bearing the King, and is met by Gurnemanz's touchingly sad greeting. On the words 'as master of the gloriously triumphant race', a second variant of the Faith Theme (III.2) appears [bb. 134–6]:

Example 9

These strains, truly blissful and proud, are an echo from the unforgettable age of Titurel, before any trace of guilt had besmirched the purity of the sanctuary. But the next phrase, 'To see him as slave to his infirmity' [bb. 136–8], gently reminiscent of the Covenant of the Love Feast, immediately brings together in our mind the sufferings of the Saviour and the King's wound. A moment of peace ensues; the litter is set down. The *Motif of Suffering* accompanies Amfortas's slow-moving monologue, 'After a long night of pain' [bb. 151–6],[28] and out of it grows, at 'Now comes the morning splendour of the forest', a delightfully lilting interplay of pliant melodic strands that we shall often encounter[29] as '*The Rustling of the Forest*' [bb. 159–69]:

VIII The Rustling of the Forest

Example 10

27 Act II Scene 1 and elsewhere.
28 *langer*: score and text have *wilder*: 'After an anguished night of pain.' Von Wolzogen's text quotations diverge frequently from one or the other, or differ from both: I have not noted these variants.
29 Mostly shorn of its initial turn. Thus it recurs at bb. 260–69, 307–11, 440–44, in Act III Scene 1, bb. 295–300, and elsewhere.

{26} It is not possible for us to dwell on every single detail of the dialogue that follows (e.g. the Grail Motif and Klingsor Harmony at the reference to Gawain's quest [bb. 189–98]), but it is noteworthy that the *Auspicious Omen* (V), 'The pure fool, made wise through compassion', is now quoted in full for the first time [bb. 206–14]. It crops up like a refrain throughout this scene, throughout the whole act indeed, at the end of each section.

Just as in Kundry's first exchange with Gurnemanz, the messenger and her phial containing balm now feature in the dialogue [bb. 221–34]. But through her impetuous motif she shuns all communication [bb. 231–5, 247–50], and the King's cortège goes on its way once again down to the lake, the Motif of Suffering becoming transformed as before into the Rustling of the Forest melody, which gradually fades away into the depths [bb. 260–69]. Gurnemanz and Kundry are left alone and silent in the hushed glade.

[Scene 1: section] II

Section II of this scene might be adjudged 'epic'. Not that it is pure narration from beginning to end: Gurnemanz's first three utterances are more in the nature of brief answers to the impulsive, youthful remarks about Kundry made by the squires as they approach. Without really dropping into the narrative mode, they heighten our understanding of her personality, mysterious and yet tangibly present before our eyes, delineating its three aspects: as *messenger* for the Knights of the Grail, as *accursed* and as *slave to Klingsor's magical arts*.

Forceful, animated, the first of Gurnemanz's responses [bb. 281–313] follows a magically harmonized statement of the Grail Motif to Kundry's question 'Are animals not sacred here?' [bb. 270–71]. Her tempestuous flights hither and thither as *message-bringer* are depicted in racing upward chromatic figures [bb. 297–301], akin in character to her 'Galloping Motif'.

A pensive musing on Kundry's outlandishly enigmatic nature, Gurnemanz's second response [bb. 316–41] identifies {27} the origin of her *curse* as the sight of the reviled Saviour,[30] first by transmuting the *Covenant of the Love Feast* ('to atone for guilt from her earlier life') so as to lead directly into the demoniacal laughter of Kundry's Motif [bb. 323–8], and then by conjoining its repetition ('she practices atonement through such deeds') directly with the Auspicious Omen harmonies of the 'Fool' [bb. 330–36]. It is for redemption through the loving embraces of this fool that the accursed woman longs, yearns, even performing fool-like deeds herself out of dogged loyalty. Gurnemanz ends each of his two responses [bb. 303–07, 337–41] with a rhyming couplet of distinctly popular cast,[31] adjusting his manner in kindly paternal fashion to the level of the youths.

---

30 One of Kundry's constituent roles is that of one who mocked Christ on his way to the cross, and was condemned to wander the world seeking absolution.
31 Rhyming couplet:

> Ich wähne, ist dies Schaden,
> So tät er euch gut geraten.

and:

> Gut tut sie dann, und recht sicherlich,
> Dienet uns, und hilft auch sich.

What is more, the couplet of this second response ('So she does good', etc.) incorporates a short variant form of the Faith Theme.[32]

To portray Kundry *in the thrall of Klingsor*, the third response ('Yes – whenever she tarried long away') [bb. 345–73] weaves a picture all in the demonic threads of the *Sorcery Motif* (IX), with its sinuous chromaticism, suffusing the entire passage in an unearthly, crepuscular half-light. It borders on the narrative style, but only to convey Gurnemanz's agitated state of mind as he contemplates the harm that Klingsor has brought to the Knighthood. The Sorcery Motif, too, presses forward in an urgent *crescendo* to a stormy *forte* peak, from which the *Kundry Motif* is precipitately disgorged ('You, there! Where were you roving then?') [bb. 361–71][33], and on to an eery chordal transmutation of the Sorcery Motif ('Why did you not help us then?') [bb. 376–9].

IX The Sorcery Motif

Example 11

{28} What now follows, albeit narration of factual events, is more a grief-laden soliloquy in which Gurnemanz, in the grip of powerful emotion, surrenders himself to the recollection of the fateful events leading up to the wounding of his King: 'Oh piercing, wonderful, hallowed spear!'. The middle and final phrases of the *Covenant of the Love Feast*, convulsively wrenching free from a massive, swelling tremolando [b. 386], prompt this passionate outburst. (We should note at this point that, of the two, it is specifically the *middle phrase* of the Covenant, with its poignant semitone movement (I.1.a) that by its character comes to symbolize the Saviour's *wounds*, and by extension the wounds of sin in mankind, and the rising *final phrase* (I.1.b) that symbolizes the holy *spear* that inflicted the wound.) Next, the Faith Motif, in another variant suggesting prancing horses (III.2 + 1) [cf. Examples 9 and 6], accompanies the King as he sallies forth [bb. 404–06]; but this quickly loses its way, *ritardando* and *diminuendo*,[34] amidst the harmonies of the *Sorcery Motif*: 'A woman of fiendish beauty has captivated him' [bb. 408–13]. This devilishly sweet web of harmonies is rent asunder by the demoniacal laugh of *Kundry's Motif, fortissimo*, after 'The spear has fallen from his hand' [bb. 414–18], to be followed once again, now resignedly, by the painful [middle] phrase of the Covenant [bb. 427–9], which flows into the *elegiac figure* of the final phrase (I.1.c)

---

32   Von Wolzogen does not note that even this ends with a variant of Kundry's Motif: bb. 339–40.
33   The score has: 'Hey, you! – Listen to me. Tell me. Where were you roving then . . .?'
34   Score has only *diminuendo* (bb. 405, 407).

[bb. 430–32] to accompany the halting, plangent closing line of this dramatically powerful section, 'Tis a wound that will never heal.'

After a short exchange between Gurnemanz and the other squires as they return, as to the condition of the King, during which we hear the *Rustling of the Forest* once again [bb. 440–44], the closing line is repeated, as if it were a refrain, in silent despair.

Only now, as the squires question him about Klingsor, does narrative proper begin – the great *Narration* [bb. 452–628], 'Titurel, the pious hero' (variant 1 of the Faith Theme [cf. Example 6]), a self-enclosed musical item as skilfully constructed as it is emotionally powerful, that portrays for us first in the solemn and mysterious strains of a new variant of the *Faith Theme* (III.3 'They came to him in that so-lemn, holy night' [bb. 462–5]), hovering angelically, the 'descent of the Grail' and then the 'sacred articles of witness': the *Grail* and the *spear* [bb. 486–94]:

Example 12

In the course of this, the *Covenant of the Love Feast*, itself interleaved with state-ments of the Grail Motif, is introduced. Its middle phrase ('There on the cross his divine blood did flow' [bb. 479–82]) is rhythmically {29} adapted to that of the later sombre Good Friday Motif[35]:

---

35 The 'Good Friday Motif', in von Wolzogen's nomenclature, is a two-bar rhythmic expansion of the Covenant of the Love Feast, interpolated between bb. 2 and 3, and paralleled a fifth below by a sombre turning figure. He draws attention to it at two points: p. 57, Ex. XVIII, in Act II (full score, pp. 395–6), and p. 74 in Act III (full score, pp. 518–19). Ex. 13 shows the latter, of which von Wolzogen says: 'the *Covenant of the Love Feast* climbs out of the shuddering tremolo upwards to the *Good Friday Motif*, until this after repeated sighing . . . merges into the closing figure . . .'.

Example 13

We hear next of the 'building of the sanctuary' for the sacred relics [bb. 495–9] –
it seems to rise gleaming before us in the sound of the *Grail Motif*. The mystical
power of the Grail spreads out through the world. Tiny rising and falling figures
[bb. 499–506], each one in itself of narrow compass, and all derived from the main
motif, represent the quests of those who feel the calling of the Grail 'along paths
unknown to sinners'. Together they generate a mighty inner tumult that leads to
the proud closing words, 'strengthened by the Grail's miraculous powers', after
which the Grail Motif lights up once more, *diminuendo* as it ascends.

Starkly contrasting, the forces of darkness from the pagan magician make their
presence felt with a muffled roll in the bass [bb. 509–14]. The motifs of *Klingsor*
himself (X) [bb. 514–20] and of his *Sorcery* (IX) [bb. 521–41], closely related,
convey a distinctly malignant relish at the fostering of all that is evil and pernicious,
alloyed with seductive sounds from the Flower Maidens' scene of Act II to come
[bb. 549–61].

X The Klingsor Motif

Example 14

{30} Nor is the demoniacal laughter of *Kundry's Motif* ('gave fillip to wicked wiz-ardry', 'to lustful longing and horrors of hell' [bb. 542–3, 555–6]) absent from this satanic web of hatred, corruption and misrule. The Klingsor Motif dies away *pianissimo*, and the Grail Motif returns once more ('Titurel . . . conferred his sov-ereignty upon his son' [bb. 567–72]). The extension to the Faith Theme, with its impetuous prancing figure [bb. 576–7, cf. Example 6], takes us back to Amfortas's downfall and links the close of the Narration to Gurnemanz's earlier recollection – an inversion of the order of events which exerts a dramatic impact upon the epic character of this passage. The *Spear Motif* – as we must now call the final phrase of the Covenant of the Love Feast – falls into the sway of *Kundry's Motif* [bb. 579–80], and the *Klingsor Motif* [bb. 587–9] precipitates its repetition [bb. 589–91]. Sorcery has triumphed, the spear is in Klingsor's power: his motifs place this whole section under his spell.

However, as an epilogue to this great narration is now appended the short solemn passage, full of consolation, comprising 'Amfortas's Prayer' [bb. 597–628], in which the *Pain Figure* from the Covenant [bb. 600–603] expresses its supplicant fervour, and the *Grail* harmonies hovering and fluttering mystically above summon up the 'holy face in dream' that 'speaks clearly to him', while the melody of the *Covenant of the Love Feast* attains its full significance as it floats down *pianissimo* to yield the *Auspicious Omen* of the 'Poor Fool', quoted in full. With this, the whole section, hence Scene 1, comes to a close.

Hermann Kretzschmar (1848–1924)
Führer durch den Konzertsaal (3/1898)

Kretzschmar's *Guide to the Concert Hall* was first issued in three volumes in 1887–90, encompassing symphony and suite, sacred vocal works, oratorios and secular choral works. The work went through many editions, increasing steadily in size. In the 1930s it was further expanded by other editors, and Hans Mersmann added a fourth volume, on chamber music. Even by 1919 it comprised over 2,100 pages. By then its historical scope was vast: the first volume alone spanned music from Gabrieli (demonstrating Kretzschmar's advocacy of the Baroque) to 'the modern suite and the most recent developments in the Classical symphony'. This last category included all the symphonies of Brahms, Bruckner (except No. 8) and Mahler (except No. 9). The work was enormously popular in the German-speaking world.

Kretzschmar modestly termed what he wrote at the time 'essays' or 'articles', their task being specifically 'to elucidate works', in particular to bring out their 'ideal content' (*Ideengehalt*).[1] Later, in 1902–03, he formulated the idea behind these essays as a manifesto, entitled 'A Stimulus to Promote a Hermeneutics of Music'. In the introduction to his collected writings, he wrote of the relationship between the *Guide* and the 'Stimulus':[2]

> It was in my capacity as a conductor that I first came to hermeneutics, in response to an appeal from my concert subscribers to prepare them for unknown or difficult works. Out of such 'introductions' arose my *Guide*, and the 'Stimulus' articles in the Peters *Yearbook* give an account of the principles underlying this work.

In the article itself, he defined 'hermeneutics' thus:[3]

> In every field its aim is the same – to penetrate to the meaning and conceptual content [*Sinn und Ideenhalt*] enclosed within the forms concerned, to seek everywhere for the soul beneath the corporeal covering, to identify the irreducible core of thought [*reinen Gedankenkern*] in every sentence of a writer and in every detail of an artist's work; to explicate and interpret [*zu erklären und auszulegen*] the whole by obtaining the clearest possible understanding of every smallest detail – and all this by employing every aid that technical knowledge, general culture and personal talent can supply.

---

1 vol. I (1887), p. iii (Preface); vol. I, (3/1898), p. 657 and *passim*. For an examination of Kretzschmar's analytical strategies, and comparison with those of the Viennese annotator Robert Hirschfeld, see Leon Botstein, 'Music and Its Public: Habits of Listening and the Crisis of Musical Modernism in Vienna, 1870–1914' (PhD diss.: Harvard University, 1985), pp. 964–84.

2 *Gesammelte Aufsätze über Musik und Anderes*, vol. II, *Gesammelte Aufsätze aus den Jahrbüchern der Musikbibliothek Peters* (Leipzig: Peters, 1911; reprint edn 1973), p. v.

3 'Anregungen zur Förderung musikalischer Hermeneutik [I]', *Jahrbuch der Musikbibliothek Peters für 1902*, 9 (1903), 47–53; later issued in *Gesammelte Aufsätze*, vol. II, pp. 168–92, esp. 168–9 (Eng. trans. Martin Cooper in Bujić, 115). See the General Introduction, above, for extensive further quotation from this article.

Even in the one analysis given below we can see this aim at work. Kretzschmar constructs two parallel layers: a fabric of motifs (with music examples) and an intermittent series of images and moods. The connections between the two layers are in some cases mimetic (birdsongs), in many cases allusions to musical stock types (the hunting call, hymn, dead march, funeral chorus, dance, song of triumph, folksong), in others personification (priest, congregation), mood evocation (reverence, ceremoniousness), and depiction of active emotion (joy, terror). Technical causes are frequently attributed to effects (the flattened submediant for secretiveness, the subdominant side for Romantic warmth, rapid modulation for jubilation, chromatic scales for foreboding, sextuplet quavers for terror, not to mention the special case of ambling melody with static harmony 'denoting' the lower social classes!).

From this mass of data, Kretzschmar seeks what is particular to the Fourth Symphony from within Bruckner's symphonic output – indeed the whole symphonic tradition. He has noted already in the Seventh (for he presents it out of order) the twin traits of 'joy in Nature' and 'churchly religiosity' that he observes in the Fourth; from the First, Second and Eighth he has noted the stylistic debt to Beethoven, Wagner, and especially Schubert; and in the Third, the Christian concept of victory through faith. He now takes his cue from Bruckner's one-word title, 'Romantic', adducing repertorial evidence in parallel works by Raff, Heller, Bruch and Schumann, and cultural evidence in the early history of the German people. From the 'irreducible core' of each phrase he seeks to 'explicate and interpret' the whole, identifying the 'meaning and conceptual content', and ultimately helping us to *understand* how the work came about in Bruckner's mind. He uses the methods of the therapist, so to speak, rather than the surgeon, in reconstructing Bruckner's motivation for composing as he did.

It would be wrong to construe this as adulation. Take the issue of material and form. The fabric of motifs, which reaches across the entire four-movement structure, is presented as an organic unfolding; at the same time, it is projected against a symphonic framework, with a necessary minimum of formal terminology introduced: theme group (i.e. exposition), development, reprise (i.e. recapitulation), section, group, main theme, second theme. Motivic fabric, with its derivations and cross-references, exists in a coupled system with symphonic form. Kretzschmar is quick to criticize when the two become decoupled: when motivic process becomes disproportionately prolific for formal requirements, as it does, in his view, in the first movement, when thematic transformations go so far that they lead to formal incoherence, as in the finale, or when the motivic fabric is stretched so tightly over the framework that it becomes semi-transparent, as he hints of the scherzo. He was far harsher when writing on the Seventh Symphony in the first edition, declaring that it lacked originality and technical maturity, that the counterpoint was stiff, and that the work was deficient in logic, coherence and proportion.[4] Kretzschmar stated in his Foreword: 'Since criticism is inseparable from historical writing, the reader must excuse the fact that judgment is exercised on compositions and composers.'

4   vol. I (1887), p. 294. Even though Kretzschmar later expanded his discussion to four pages, he allowed these and other disparaging remarks to stand: vol. I (3/1898), pp. 652–6.

Kretzschmar was a professional writer, having studied composition in Dresden and Leipzig and musicology in Leipzig, graduating in 1871. He was a significant figure in historical musicology, contributing two supplementary volumes to the Bach Gesellschaft edition, two volumes to the national series *Denkmäler der deutschen Tonkunst*, and writings important in their time on Baroque Venetian opera, the German *Lied* and the history of opera. He also edited Lobe's *Lehrbuch* in the 1880s (see vol. I, Analysis 12), and we can recognize Lobe's terminology in the present analysis. Like Donald Francis Tovey some forty years after him, he combined directorship of university musical performance with an academic appointment: Tovey did so at Edinburgh from 1914, Kretzschmar at Rostock from 1877, where he was lecturer in music, then at Leipzig from 1887, where he was a professor extraordinary, then as professor of music at Berlin from 1904, combining this later with the directorship of the royal Hochschule für Musik and the Royal Academic Institute for Church Music. Like Tovey, he conducted concert series in which he gave special attention to earlier music, was concerned with enlightening the public, took special care with the programme notes that he wrote for his concerts, and (as quoted above) subsequently collected, edited and published these notes in a multi-volume work, the music categorized by genre, which was the *Guide to the Concert Hall* in its first edition.

'Anton Bruckner, Symphony No. 4 [in E♭ ("Romantic")]'[5]

Guide to the Concert Hall (3/1898)

Source:
'A. Bruckner, Vierte Sinfonie', *Führer durch den Konzertsaal*, vol. I: *Sinfonie und Suite* (Leipzig: B&H, 3/1898), pp. 665–75.

Bruckner has given his Fourth Symphony (in E♭) the name 'The Romantic'. The vein of Romanticism that he has in mind is that of the forest. The work is a 'forest symphony', but is of far greater profundity than the familiar one by Raff,[6] which displays a galant French vein of Romanticism. Bruckner's symphony is German in character through and through. It exudes a yearning for the forest, for its secrecy, for the great tranquillity of its sounds – attributes that recall the intimate 'Scenes for Pianoforte *In the Forest*' by Stephen Heller.[7] But there is more to it than this. Bruckner, like the pagans of ancient Germany, performs his religious rituals in the forest. He processes through the avenues of lofty tree trunks, in his mind the lines of the poet: 'Thou hast built up thine own pillars and founded thy temple'.[8] His thoughts have gone back to those long-gone times when we Germans were still a forest folk; and the forest was the most magnificent church, the most splendid cathedral, that the lord of all worlds had {666} built with his own hands. The forest inspires the composer with deeply religious feeling. Through the entire symphony runs an underlying spirit of ceremonious exaltation, very similar to the effect, soft and fleeting, that Bruch once achieved in his E♭ Symphony,[9] but that elsewhere he displayed only in his slow movements. The nature of its material [*geistige Haltung*], which sets it rather apart from the symphony as a prototype, is one reason for its difficulty in getting known. Another is the high quality of orchestra and precision of performance that it demands for its countless depictions of nature. A third is the undue expansiveness of some of its individual sections.

[First movement]

It is especially the first movement (*ruhig bewegt*, ₵, E♭ major) that adopts an air of deep religiosity, of reaching out into eternity. Its opening, and the group constructed

---

5 Heading in margin.
6 Joachim Raff (1822–82), Symphony No. 3 in F, Op. 153, 'In the Forest' (*Im Walde*) (1869). Kretzschmar devoted two and a half pages of the *Führer* each to discussions of that work and Symphony No. 5 in E, Op. 177, 'Leonore' (1872), vol. I, pp. 328–33, and also discussed the oratorio *Weltende, Gericht, Neue Welt*, vol. II (1890), pp. 270–71. He spoke of Raff as 'a genius of eclecticism', fusing together Beethovenian, Schumannesque and Wagnerian elements into one melodic style.
7 Stephen Heller (1813–88), *Im Walde: Charakterstücke* for solo piano, series I, Op. 86 (1854); series II, Op. 128 (1871); series III, Op. 136 (1873) – twenty pieces in all.
8 'Du hast Deine Säulen Dir aufgebaut und Deine Tempel gegründet', clearly biblical in tone, but I have been unable to identify it.
9 Max Bruch (1838–1920), Symphony No. 1 in E♭, Op. 28 (1870). Kretzschmar devoted two pages of the *Führer* to this ('in classical vein, objective in manner, heroic in content'), and half a page to the less successful Nos 2 and 3 (vol. I, pp. 609–12). Kretzschmar also discussed nine of Bruch's choral works in vol. II.

around the principal theme [*Hauptthema*], Example 1, stir thrills of prayerful devotion, wreathing the listener in incense. The orchestration [*Vortrag*] itself even

Example 1

impersonates the liturgy for us: the French horn which starts the movement [bb. 3–17] as the priest, the upper woodwind chorus which sings the melody after him [bb. 19–42] as the congregation with its responses. This first-movement principal theme is the most important ingredient for the Romantic character that Bruckner is seeking for his symphony: and the Cb with which its second phrase begins is what chiefly conveys the sense of Romantic secretiveness. After the reverent atmosphere of the ceremonious opening there soon emerges a feeling of hopeful expectation. It is conveyed by the motif shown in Example 2 [bb. 43–4], which is to

Example 2

some extent heard as an extension of the first theme. The opening, with its solemn, broad manner, expresses the composer's piety, the new motif conveys his joy in nature. So, in the two sections of the first {667} theme, we have before us the two chief constituents of the personal humanity which pervades Bruckner's works, and in which they have their origin. Bruckner fashions the next few lines of his poem out of the motif that expresses joy in nature. They soon adopt the air of an inspired hymn. The composer is swept forward in jubilation at the beauty of creation. The harmony surges on in stormy modulations [*Modulationen*], and then, as if mesmerized, suddenly comes to rest on an F major chord, all emotional strength draining away in a moment [bb. 71–3]. Bruckner loves contrasts of tone quality. The swell of the full orchestra accordingly now gives way to the hushed sound of the two horns holding a solo F for two bars. This shifts down a third as the double basses play pizzicato the Db below that, and the violas then embark upon the second theme as in Example 3 [bb. 75–9]. Bb major would have been the normal key:

Example 3

Bruckner has opted for Db. The shift [*Ausweichung*] to a more remote harmonic realm is in this instance a device to procure a special Romantic effect; but Bruckner does have a general penchant for the subdominant area, and this accounts in part for the natural warmth of his music. The opening of this second theme conveys a sense of basking in heartfelt gratitude; this feeling changes to a more cheerful mood with the recurrent motif of Example 4, which first appears as accompani-

Example 4

mental material and then comes into its own [bb. 75–87]; the music courses on through to the final phrase of the theme, Example 5 [bb. 87–96], in an expression of

Example 5

vibrant rapture. This is first proclaimed loudly, as if singing for sheer joy; and then again secretively, as if in innermost reverie. It is an uncommonly versatile motif, which can at one moment ally itself to the intimacy of the second theme and at another bring back the animated {668} strains of revelling in nature that belong to the first theme. These latter strains crowd the scene rather longer with games of various kinds, like children crying out in sheer exuberance and then performing their round-games with quiet charm. After a stormy outburst of joy, towards the end of which the full chorus of brass explodes on a D♭ major chord with the rhythm of Example 6 [bb. 165–8], Bruckner reverts unexpectedly to the more peaceful

Example 6

world of the second theme, now in the normal key of B♭ major: it dies away fragmented and *pianissimo* [bb. 169–73]. The composer closes his eyes, and images swim before his mind's eye, merging. All becomes peaceful. Feelings and forebodings glide unformed and shadowy through his breast. The music conveys this by downward-moving chromatic scales over softly rolling timpani [bb. 174–208]. The ceremonious-sounding motifs of the principal theme and the cheerful, excitable ones of the second theme become merged [bb. 193–216]. With this, the exposition [*Themengruppe*] of the first movement closes.

The development [bb. 217–364] begins in a dreamlike state with the solemn opening motif of the first principal theme, coloured with bold dissonances in strikingly Romantic fashion: Example 7. It then turns to broad elaborations upon the motif expressing joy in nature; these are distinguished from those in the exposition by a generally more serious manner. The devoutly Christian character that marks Bruckner's symphonies out from hundreds of others takes control of his imagination at this point. The section ends with chorale-like strains in which trumpets carry

Example 7

the melody [bb. 305–32]. As these fade away softly, the second theme of the movement enters (in G major), though with augmented rhythms and thus imbued with
the spirit of churchly piousness.

{669} From here onwards the transition to the recapitulation [*Reprise*] is carried
out in a completely natural and self-sufficient way. The recapitulation [bb. 365–573]
unfolds without any particular surprises, and leaves most of its listeners wishing
for some compression of material, particularly in the coda section.

[Second movement]

In order to understand the second movement (andante, **C**, C minor) one really needs
to look on to the middle section. For, at the beginning one cannot help asking in
surprise what a funeral march is doing in a forest symphony. The explanation is
to be found in the text of, among other works, Schumann's *The Pilgrimage of the
Rose*, in the lovely male-voice chorus accompanied by a quartet of French horns,
'If you have Wandered in the Woods'.[10] Bruckner is here thinking of the forest, of
nature itself, as a comforter in time of sorrow. Thus he paints for us a scene of
most poignant sadness: a funeral. The cellos sing the grief-laden melody, Example 8
[bb. 3–7]. It is simple; it seems to stem from folksong, yet is tinged slightly with

Example 8

Chopinesque atmosphere; for, after all, despite his underlying unpretentiousness
of mind, Bruckner remains always modern in everything. The accompaniment, a
Schubertian march motif, Example 9, reveals the place and the occasion of the

Example 9

10   Robert Schumann, *Der Rose Pilgerfahrt*, Op. 112 (1851), for solo voices, chorus and orchestra, on
     a text by Moritz Horn, to which Kretzschmar devoted three pages of the *Führer* (vol. II (1890),
     pp. 308–11): Part II No. 15 'Bist du im Wald gewandelt', in a brisk 6/8, bears little or no musical
     resemblance to Bruckner's second movement, but its text does indeed personify the forest as a
     comforter, e.g.:
        O Heart, when earth fails to keep its promise, when love and loyalty break oath in base
        falsity, then, then the forest calls 'Come to my tranquillity, the soft, cool rustling of my leaves
        will kiss your wounds.'

lamentation, and sets the scene for us clearly. Soon matters will be clarified even further: chorale singing, funeral choruses, giving voice as in Example 10, interrupt the march rhythm for long stretches [bb. 25–50].

Example 10

Then the march begins anew. And the grief-laden voice is heard once again, but this time much more restrainedly. It lies in the centre of the string orchestra, in the violas, almost concealed, Example 11, {670} and meanders, half-suppressed, questing

Example 11

and at the same time onward-flowing [bb. 51–83], until the march (in C major, *ppp*) falls silent again. At this moment, motifs can be heard as if from far off and from high overhead (Example 12) – motifs which first sprang up, though scarcely noticed

Example 12

then, at the very beginning of the andante. Does not this flute passage sound as if birdsongs were calling from out of the forest? In retrospect, we become aware that we have been hearing fleeting sounds of nature right from the beginning, all through the march. It was the horn, sometimes joined by the trumpet, that beckoned secretively, sometimes on a monotone, sometimes using a motif, most often with the rhythm of Example 13. Whilst the violas sang out their melody, the

Example 13

horn[11] reflected its turn of phrase as if in echo; and from time to time we heard the call of the fifth which was thematically so significant in the first movement as it is in the second.

    After this crucial passage, with which section I of the andante [bb. 1–92] closes, the character of the music changes. The [cellos and] basses muse upon the flute motif, repeating and extending it, while the violins invent new melodic ideas, full of consolation: Example 14 [bb. 92–100].

11   'the horn': *sie* incorrectly implies horn and trumpet: the reference is to bb. 63–4 and 77–8.

Example 14

Then the horn, and after that the wind, take up the grief-laden principal theme again [bb. 101–09]. But the march material, which belongs with it, is heard only for a short while in the [cellos and] basses before it disappears totally from memory; and instrument after instrument brings out the joyful and vital elements in the melody {671} more and more clearly [bb. 109–18]. It attains a mood of great exhilaration. For all that, the return to funereal tones is now inevitable. The middle section of the andante becomes fainter and fainter [bb. 119–28], then disappears like a vision, and section III, the reprise, begins.

However, the strains of the funeral chorus are now omitted, and the flute motifs return much earlier – even before the return of the viola passage [bb. 155–87]. After this, the principal theme returns once again [bb. 193–204], but this time interwoven with counterpoints that purge it of its chilling, funereal tones. The music takes on an aura of transfiguration [bb. 205–20], finally bursting forth in a triumphal song [bb. 221–30]. With all the splendour of the Brucknerian orchestra, the victory over sorrow is pronounced, and rings out over grave and funeral procession, pointing the way to heaven and eternal life. The close of this andante is its highpoint, movingly poetic in its conception, the hand of genius apparent in its musically bold execution. The transition to C major and the return to this key – from C♭ – are particularly fine.

[Third movement]

The third movement, Scherzo (*bewegt*, 2/4, B♭ major), presents the forest spirit of this symphony in a more down-to-earth, conventional manner. As early as b. 3, the horns regale us with hunting calls. The composer has given more space to them in one movement here than was ever given to them in a whole symphony before. This is as much a testimony to Bruckner's naivety as it is to his great love for capturing in music such images of external nature. But thirdly the expansive ideas that Bruckner has conjured up from simple hunting motifs bear witness to a quite prodigious talent. True, those who know and love this movement would perhaps tend to agree that his large-scale groups – particularly those of the main part [*Hauptsatz*] [bb. 1–92] – are repeated just a trifle too often. But within those large groups, taken on their own, one would be hard put to it to shorten or cut anything. They are miniature masterpieces, matchlessly vibrant, colourful and truly Romantic. What {672} fascinating interplay [*Conzertiren*] between horns and trumpets [bb. 10–34]! Where on earth did Bruckner learn to pick up such scraps of musical stock-in-trade, and then by judicious choice of harmonies, especially dissonances, imbue them with real artistic significance, turning them into images of thrilling veracity? It is an achievement on a par with comparable passages in Berlioz's Requiem and Wagner's *Tristan*.

Amidst all this music of nature, built from hunting calls, the scherzo's melodic content [*Gehalt*] diminishes to a bare minimum, amounting to the motif of Example 15 [bb. 27–36], and more rewardingly that of Example 16, which creates

Example 15

Example 16

a tenderer mood [bb. 35–42]. This is true at least for section I of the main part of the scherzo. Section II [bb. 93–255] begins by developing the motifs introduced in section I. In it, expression of deeper, more inward feelings takes precedence over the love of the chase.

The trio [bb. 256–301], as we might expect, stands in even sharper contrast to the depiction of the stirring life of the huntsman. From the outset, it sounds like a simple dance, and has a very droll, at times burlesque effect that derives from its lolloping main melody, Example 17, suggesting the lower social classes and their pleasures.

Example 17

[Fourth movement]

The finale (*mässig bewegt*, ¢, E♭ major) begins as if shrouded in mist and twilight; yet from the outset the atmosphere is one of light breaking through the cloud. Over the veiled murmuring of the strings we hear solo horn and clarinet playing solemn-sounding motifs, Example 18. {673} For a brief moment, reminiscences of the

Example 18

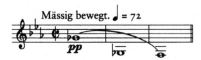

hunting music from the scherzo banish them [bb. 28–42]. Not until after a long, powerfully swelling crescendo do they unite forces to yield the principal theme of the movement, Example 19 [bb. 43–9]. It will escape no one how close this proud

Example 19

tune comes to the solemn tones of the first movement. And so it will come as no surprise if the main theme of the first movement should appear before us quite soon here in the fourth movement. It has however first, so to speak, to fight for and gain admission. It eventually makes its entrance [bb. 79–85] at a crisis in which threatening and joyful sounds mingle in terrifyingly wild scenes. There is one particular rhythmic pattern (sextuplet quavers) that creates this terrifying effect. Anyone who has doubted it up to now must recognize from this that the composer has in mind in this finale the terror of the forest, the woods at night and in storms, their sombre and ghostly character. Hard on the heels of the first-movement main theme comes a quotation, or rather a recollection of the andante and of its characteristic march-like movement in the [cellos and] basses [bb. 93–112]. The grief-laden melody has undergone a transformation: Example 20. Directly after it

Example 20

comes an engaging melody, Example 21 [bb. 105–08], which can be considered

Example 21

as the second theme of the movement. It leads to {674} a passage of graceful reverie, which sweeps us out of the present and transports us into times long past, perhaps to childhood days. This is established finally with a playful, dallying motif, Example 22 [bb. 129–38], which, once again, arose first as an accompaniment figure.

Example 22

When the second theme occurs for a second time (in the clarinet [bb. 139–42]), it quickly meets with a brusque answer: Example 23 [bb. 155–6]. This theme, built on

Example 23

the previously-mentioned sextuplet-quaver figure, now dominates the scene frighteningly for some time. Thereafter, the second theme reappears with calming influence [bb. 187–202] and brings this section of the finale, which approximates to the development, to a close.

The finale of the Romantic Symphony is among Bruckner's most difficult movements. The themes are not as simple in formation or as specific in expression as is customary elsewhere. In part they acquire their significance only through their relationship with melodies from the first movement, and this itself comes to light only after more prolonged familiarity. Thus, for example, the second theme, which is so important to the finale, is derived from the sixth-motif in the principal theme of the first movement, the secretive Example 24. But more particularly, our under-

Example 24

standing of the movement is made more difficult through the large number of themes and motifs that are generated during its course. This mass of ideas is not a sign of fecundity and abundance; rather it is the weakness of the composition, the consequence of insufficient control and mastery of its material.

All of these difficulties in the finale are only exacerbated in the recapitulation [bb. 203–507] in that the themes are transformed to the point of unrecognizability and {675} are introduced at quite different points from those which they had in the exposition of the movement. The very size of individual sections creates instability. As a result, only through exhaustive study of the movement can one come to grips with the recapitulation. One clue is the fact that the frequently stated second theme now takes over the initiative [*geistige Führung*]. There are moments when this becomes palpable, one of the most striking being the point at which the elaborately developed principal theme [bb. 295–337] quite unexpectedly disappears from sight in the wake of an interrupted cadence [b. 337]. Yet at the same time this is an example of Bruckner's skill in handling rapid change of mood. In his imaginative world, majestic images from nature give way here to wonderful, supernatural apparitions. To match them, his musical language takes on a magical and mystical flavour, the splendour of the full orchestra gives way to a void, the lush profusion of notes yields to a fumbling and stammering of disintegrated motifs [bb. 339–52]. At the same time, this passage shows very clearly the influence that Wagner's works exerted on Bruckner. We hear the transformation motif from the *Ring of the Nibelung*, and the Romantic Symphony closes with the strains of the Fire Music.

PART II

Objective–subjective analysis: the hermeneutic circle

Introduction

In Part II of volume I, we saw in the work of Johann Christian Lobe an innovative approach to the teaching of composition – an approach based on the alternation of analysis and synthesis, the discourse conducted wholly at the materialistic level using technical language and adducing rules and maxims for the student's guidance. The extract (Analysis 12), dating from 1850, dealt with first-movement form in the string quartet. For seventy-five pages, Lobe discussed formal plan, melodic construction, the invention of musical ideas, and the scoring and final polishing of a movement – a purely technical treatment of form based on what little was known in that pre-Nottebohm era of Beethoven's sketching habits.

This particular extract, however, continues for a further fifteen pages with a chapter entitled 'Spiritual Content in Pieces of Music'.[1] It is not sufficient, this chapter tells us, for a piece to sound well and exhibit order and symmetry (its 'external manifestations'): it must also have effective content and perceptible expression (its 'internal manifestations'). Accordingly, Lobe now instructs the student in the communication of feeling through instrumental music, using analysis. He takes instances first of fear (in *The Magic Flute*), then of grief (the third movement of Beethoven's String Quartet Op. 59 no. 1), of conflicting emotions (there and in Weber's *Der Freischütz*), then of cheerfulness (quoting a celebrated analysis by Gerber of the main theme from the first movement of Haydn's Symphony No. 104),[2] and finally fateful questioning (Beethoven's String Quartet Op. 135).

Coming after 365 pages of technical rules, this chapter is little more than a piece of aesthetic tokenism. We should admittedly give Lobe credit for what must have been a break-through in the teaching of composition for its time. Marx had offered only three cursory, unsubstantiated pages on 'content' in his *Manual of Musical Composition in Theory and Practice*, tucked away in the middle of the third volume,[3] whereas Lobe at least addressed the issue frontally and gave it illustrated treatment, albeit it in a rather inhibited manner.

However, the significance of all of this for present purposes is the distance that Lobe placed between technical and aesthetic analysis. He kept them separate in two senses. First, he conducted his aesthetic analyses on a completely different set of pieces. For a book that makes a virtue of cumulative effect, and recycles its music

1   'Geistiger Inhalt der Tonstücke', *Lehrbuch der musikalischen Komposition* (Leipzig: B&H, 1850), chap. 30, pp. 366–81.
2   Ernst Ludwig Gerber (1746–1819), 'Eine freundliche Vorstellung über gearbeitete Instrumentalmusik, besonders über Symphonien', *AmZ*, 15 (1812/13), no. 28 (14 July 1813), cols. 457–63.
3   *Die Lehre von der musikalischen Komposition praktisch theoretisch*, vol. III (Leipzig: B&H, 1845, 2/1848), pp. 326–9.

examples again and again so as to view them from constantly different angles, this was a departure. Moreover, after dozens of examples drawn from the chamber music repertory, only two of his five examples now come from that literature. Of those two, one is a special case, since it rests on Beethoven's own inscription of the question and answer 'Must it be? . . . It must be!' in the last movement of his Op. 135. Of the others, one relies on Gerber's setting of words ('Glad am I now! all my cares have bade farewell; joy smiles on me: what more could I want?') to Haydn's theme; and two are drawn from the totally different world of opera. The second sense is that technical and aesthetic analysis are kept in permanently separate compartments: having at last addressed the matter of content, Lobe failed to capitalize on it: he neither revisited from an aesthetic standpoint works already analysed technically, nor allowed aesthetics to inform his future analyses.

Of the six analyses that comprise Part II of the present volume, and that conclude our two-volume conspectus of the nineteenth century's engagement with the analytic process, each to some degree does what Lobe in his analytical mode failed to do: namely, to bring both *objective* and *subjective* (or, to use the language of hermeneutics: *grammatical* and *psychological*) criteria to bear on a single piece of music. It would be improper to suggest that all six therefore exemplify the hermeneutic model, let alone to imply that any of their writers were consciously following hermeneutic prescriptions, or for that matter were even cognizant of hermeneutics. Nevertheless, we can gain some insight by looking at these analyses through the hermeneutic glass.

Take, for example, Schumann's review of Berlioz's *Fantastic* Symphony (1835: Analysis 10). It begins with an idiosyncratic essay by Florestan that Schumann himself later disowned (or rather, chose not to include in his collected edition). But consider with what verve and *élan* it sets the hermeneutic circle turning! It succeeds – glance back once again at the description of Schleiermacher's analysis of Plato's *Republic* on p. 5 above – in grasping the content of the whole synoptically ('roughing it out in rapid brush strokes'), thus in putting us in touch with the totality before we encounter the parts. At the same time, it locates Berlioz succinctly in his historical place, addresses the aesthetic problem of Berlioz's music, and 'sets up' the creativity/dissection polarity that is to run through the entire analysis. And all of this it does with a passion and outrageous extravagance that whets our appetite. Indeed, the very interplay of personas (latent throughout this analysis, though not formally present after the second instalment) is an enactment of Schleiermacher's *shuttling back and forth*, the whole/parts and subjective/objective oscillation that constitutes the hermeneutic circle. (Schumann terms Florestan's approach 'psychological', and contrasts its 'poetic' mentality to his own professionally musical one.)

Moreover, within his own technical discussion Schumann oscillates between whole and parts: on form, for example, he first places the *Fantastic* Symphony in the context of the Beethoven symphonies and those of Berlioz's contemporaries, then views the work as a five-movement whole before infiltrating the movements individually; likewise, on phrase periodicity he switches from detail to the general nature of rhythm and the possibility of rhythmless music; and from the text of the Symphony's programme he switches to a polemic on the utility of programmes in general. Again and again, Schumann does what is typical of true hermeneutic analysis (for example, Gadamer's studies on Plato[4]) – namely, he steps outside the arena of discussion and broadens the frame of reference before returning to the detail of the argument, bringing back fresh insight as he does so. It is not *digression* or *excursion* with which we are dealing, but a *temporary expansion of the horizon of reference*. Moreover, the basic oscillation between psychological and technical is ironized by Schumann's affected distaste for 'dismembering critique'. In the end, the hermeneutic circle stops spinning, and the analysis fuses in the quotation from Odillon de Barrot (also later excised by Schumann!) that 'crime has a certain poetry about it'.

Hoffmann's analysis of Beethoven's Fifth Symphony (1810: Analysis 9) begins by describing three concentric contextual circles for the symphony. The outermost circle (presented ahistorically) delineates instrumental music as an independent and purely abstract art with the power to transport its listeners out of the world of the senses and into the world of transcendent spirit. Within that circle, the second encapsulates the triumvirate Haydn–Mozart–Beethoven as a historical succession that enacts that transcendentality: Haydn purely and ultimately human, his music exuding optimism and melancholic longing, Mozart for the first time penetrating the transcendental realm, and evoking infinite yearning and a sense of magic, Beethoven fully inhabiting the transcendental world, and evoking awe and fear. The innermost circle, lastly, focuses on Beethoven, embodying two special qualities: a peculiarly lucid *self-knowledge* (which he possessed in common with Haydn and Mozart) and *genius* (in which he surpassed them). These two are inseparably coupled, the former (the rational spirit of the Enlightenment) controlling the latter (the spirit of Romanticism).

These three contextual circles arm us with a 'sense' of the whole. It is like a reverse drawing of the symphony, and creates a vacuum that cries out to be filled. Our attention now shifts to the other extreme, the most specific level, shuttling freely between technical detail and local psychological impression. At the end of the first movement Hoffmann shifts level to a summary of the movement as a whole; at the end of the second movement he does so twice, first to summarize the movement and then to survey in retrospect the two movements so far experienced (thus rounding out the first instalment of the review in its original form). At the end of the scherzo he draws together the thematic development of the movement in a synoptic example; and at the end of the finale he surveys the entire work as a single sequence, identifying the unifying thematic forces and linking the entire discussion back to the contextual circles of the opening. Even in the course of a movement he occasionally draws connections between the local level and highest contextual levels. In short, Hoffmann oscillates constantly between whole and parts and between objectivity and subjectivity in the manner of a hermeneutic interpreter.

The hermeneutic status of Hoffmann's analysis is admittedly debatable. The review can be seen as a true example of hermeneutic writing. Alternatively, it can

---

4   Hans-Georg Gadamer, *Dialogue and Dialectic: Eight Hermeneutical Studies on Plato*, Eng. trans. P. Christopher Smith (New Haven: Yale University Press, 1980).

be said to possess only the appearance of the hermeneutic – an appearance that results from Hoffmann's having exploited the review as a platform for his larger aesthetic ideas, having consequently prefaced the review-proper with an extended essay, and then having alluded to that essay during the main body of the review. To decide the matter would take further study of Hoffmann. We can, however, impose some order on what is in some respects a disorderly review to read by viewing this analysis as a practical example of hermeneutic writing.

Marx's analysis of the Ninth Symphony (1859: Analysis 12) also starts with an extended essay, this time not aesthetic or historical, but psycho-biographical. (It is, of course, preceded in the larger sense by the totality of the biography up to that point.) This essay concerns the symphony's 'Idea', first as the imperative rounding-out of the composer's life work, second as a necessary expansion of the realm of instrumental music (which involves the work's relationship to Schiller's *Ode to Joy*). Marx's detailed analysis constantly oscillates between subordinate detail and superordinate structure, and at the same time between objective technicality and subjective response. This oscillation is heightened by the way in which the opening essay sets the work up as itself a process of slowly dawning realization (the concept is discussed more fully in the introduction to Analysis 12). At each moment of actual realization in the progress of the work the analysis accordingly reaches back to the opening essay: at each of these crucial moments in the score the technical working-out demands that a larger decision be made by the composer, and this automatically switches the analysis to a higher structural level. In this way, the analysis incessantly connects us back to the inner biographical life of the composer, like an electrical current returning to ground. So great is the scale of the analysis, and so immense the work being analysed, that one has a sense, as one reads, of cogwheels turning at differing and related rates, like some huge mechanism.

Helm's analysis of the String Quartet Op. 132 (1885: Analysis 13) also begins with an essay, but this time a shorter and very different essay that chides Marx for the liberties he has taken in interpreting instrumental music. Helm takes issue with the existing hermeneutic interpretation of Op. 132 by Marx, from the latter's Beethoven biography (1859). His is thus both a hermeneutic analysis in its own right and a critique of another such analysis. Moreover, portions of that other analysis are embedded within his, the latter often commenting directly upon the former. The discourse thus shifts from 1885 text to 1859 text, from 1885 analysis of Op. 132 to 1885 commentary on 1859 analysis, and from 1885 analysis back to introductory essay. Marx had taken the superscription on the third movement as ground for treating the entire quartet as a psychological portrayal of the experience of chronic illness and eventual recuperation. Helm considered this untenable, hence his analytical discourse works the distance between the technical and the psychological with particular intensity.

It would be improper to suggest that Momigny's analysis of Haydn's 'Drumroll' Symphony (1805: Analysis 8) and Basevi's of Verdi's *Simon Boccanegra* (1859: Analysis 11) belong to the peculiarly Germanic lineage of hermeneutic interpretation – they are, after all, products of their own French and Italian intellectual worlds, and are expressed in languages of Romance culture. Nevertheless, to view them through the hermeneutic glass, as we did Marx and Helm, can help us understand something about their structure and motivation. Ultimately, though, their inclusion here rests on their treatment of the subjective as well as the objective aspects of their subject, and also of their sheer length. To be sure, Momigny imputes character to the individual periods of Haydn's structure, using the three labels 'period of verve', 'melodious period' and 'launching period'; but these are only stock types, and communicate structural function rather than expressive value. True, Momigny does expand the horizon of reference at times, but he does so on technical matters such as irregular phrase structure, the notation of the diminished sevenths and orchestration, rather than on broad historical or aesthetic issues. But Momigny's technical-structural and subjective analyses are separate and parallel, with virtually no cross-reference between the two and no concluding confluence. The fact remains, however, that Momigny made a sustained attempt, unprecedented for the dawn of the nineteenth century, to *exposer le sujet* of this symphonic movement – i.e. to uncover its subject matter, or perhaps to bring out its subjective element. This analysis is far more elaborate than his several earlier attempts in the *Complete Course* (see an example in volume I of the present work, Analysis 1). It amounts to a full-scale dramatization of the music, complete with choruses and scenery. The result is for its day an extraordinarily well balanced and rounded portrayal of the Haydn piece, and a major monument in the history of analysis.

Basevi's analysis, while not unlike Berlioz's of *The Huguenots* in its general manner (Analysis 1 above), does expand and contract its horizon of reference in order to address three broader historical issues: the nature of recitative in seventeenth- and eighteenth-century opera, music's power of suggestion in the aria, and the principles of Wagnerian music drama as the music of the present and future. These are presented in three miniature essays supplied shortly after the beginning of the analysis. Once stated, they feed the detailed analysis and furnish criteria for the judgment of individual numbers. Basevi raises other issues too: notably the dramatic inappropriateness of duet cadenzas and the superfluousness of word painting. The analysis concludes with a drawing together of threads that places *Simon Boccanegra* in the history of Italian operatic reform.

We might recall Brendel's words, quoted in the General Introduction §7 above, prefiguring a new mode of writing about music that would be 'the consolidation, the fusion, the unification' of two phases already encountered, a mode that would 'preserve the insight into content that characterized the second era while striving to restore the objectivity that characterized the first; the first two stages would be its preconditions, but it would have to absorb these and transcend them'.[5] Brendel then continued:

> Art [. . .] is the most intimate union of spirit and matter, of Idea and raw material. Neither side can exist in isolation, the two cannot be torn apart. Spirit is nothing without the perceptible material to embody it, and perceptible material is nothing without spirit.

Of the analyses given below in Part II, half of which precede Brendel's manifesto (1845), and two of which belong to worlds utterly different from his, all give their

5   *NZM*, 12 (1845), nos 1–2 (1 January), 10.

attention to both the material and the spiritual dimensions of music. If any of them go further than that, and go some way toward effecting the fusion of subjective and objective for which Brendel called, let alone achieving the transcendency that he envisaged, then they do so not through literal 'absorption' but through that *oscillation* which is the underlying methodology of the hermeneutic principle.

Jérôme-Joseph de Momigny (1762–1842)
Cours complet d'harmonie et de composition (1805)

The theorist who 'abandons his readers to their own analyses of good models without demonstrating [how to conduct] such analysis' neglects his duty.[1] As we saw in vol. I of the present work (see the General Introduction, §§1–2, and the Introduction to Part I), Momigny's *Complete Course in Harmony and Composition* of 1803–05 resorts frequently to analysis of 'musical masterpieces'. The analytical content of the central chapters is astonishingly high. Thus, of the twenty pages comprising the chapter on counterpoint, eighteen contain microscopic analyses of seven two-part passages by Handel, C. P. E. Bach and Haydn; of the seven pages on canon, six give operation-by-operation analyses of canons by Clementi and Haydn; of the twenty-seven pages comprising Momigny's chapter on fugue (see vol. I, Analysis 1), twenty-five are devoted to analysing two whole examples, one by Bach, one by Handel.[2]

Above all, of the 103 pages making up the two chapters on free composition in four parts, sixty-five are devoted to an analysis of the first movement of Mozart's String Quartet in D minor, K 421/417*b* – an analysis of unprecedented length and detail that moves through four stages.[3] The first performs a segmentation into primary phrase-units (*vers*) and sub-units (*hémistiches*), down to the atomic upbeat-downbeat unit of music (*cadence*), and then up again to the level of period and key structure. The second stage performs a chordal analysis, harmony by harmony. The fourth stage revisits the movement's twenty-five periods, this time to categorize them functionally, yielding a high-level syntactic structure that is rhetoric- and affect-based.

The third stage of this Mozart analysis is quite different, and concerns what Momigny called 'the musical style' of the piece. 'I took the view that the best way of conveying the true expression [of the movement] to my readers was to set words to it.' He perceived two primary sentiments in the piece: nobility and pathos. What better way of extrapolating those sentiments than to take Virgil's

---

1   *Cours complet d'harmonie et de composition*, vol. II, p. 405.
2   Chap. 28, 'De la manière de former un Contre-point', vol. I, pp. 270–90; chap. 29, 'Du Canon à deux Parties, ou du Duo en écho', vol. I, pp. 291–7; chap. 39, 'De la composition asservie <à un ou à plusieurs Desseins>, ou <du> Contre-point obligé: de la Fugue <et de ce qui y a rapport>', vol. II, pp. 517–43. Each chapter has its own series of engraved music examples, with identical plate- and chapter-number, providing analytical musical examples. (Angle brackets contain additions found in the Table of Contents only.)
3   Chap. 30, 'De la Composition, libre ou obligée, à quatre Parties', vol. I, pp. 297–382 (analysis: 307–39, 363–79); chap. 31, 'Analyse de la seconde Reprise de l'Allegro moderato du Quatuor de Mozart <en ré mineur>', vol. II, pp. 387–403. Reprise I: stage 1 = pp. 307–39, stage 2 = pp. 363–71, stage 3 = pp. 371–9; Reprise II/1: stage 2 = pp. 387–92, stage 3 = pp. 392–7; Reprise II/2, p. 397; Whole movement: stage 4 = pp. 398–403.

monologue of Dido addressing her departing lover Aeneas, and harnessing it to his purposes? Adapting it into French verse, he underlaid it to Mozart's first violin part, and incorporated it into a remarkable ten-stave score that illustrates the stages of the analysis in parallel, and that itself belongs to an analytic lineage going back to Rameau in 1722 (see vol. I, Analysis 2; also the introduction to Part I).[4] This harnessing of words to abstract music belongs to a tradition known as *parodie* (which in the late eighteenth century signified the translating of foreign vocal music into the home tongue, especially Italian opera into French, not necessarily with humorous or satirical intent[5]). A celebrated north German precedent was Gerstenberg's setting from 1767 of C. P. E. Bach's C minor Keyboard Fantasy to Hamlet's monologue 'To be, or not to be' ('Seyn oder Nichtseyn'), with Socrates' hemlock monologue as an alternative.[6] Other early instances exist of the application of poems to specific pieces of music.[7] A later and more modest example of the process has already been referred to above in the Introduction to Part II, namely Gerber's analysis (1813) of the spirit of Haydn's Symphony No. 104 through the setting of words to the first theme of its first movement.

The analysis of the first movement of Haydn's 'Drumroll' Symphony, given below, is somewhat shorter than that of the Mozart quartet; but it contains seemingly similar elements. Of the twenty-four pages comprising Momigny's chapter on 'The Symphony for Full Orchestra', twenty-one are given over wholly to this analysis.[8] Less 'pure', so to speak, than that of the Mozart quartet, it dwells on what he calls *les distributions*, namely the marshalling of orchestral forces in conjunction with motivic materials and dynamic levels. The bases of scoring, and the principles of instrumental doubling, are set forth in the preamble. The analysis falls into two clear stages, each treating the entire structure (the final section getting shorter shrift). Momigny's range of analytical approach here is remarkable. See how he delights to set up tension between himself and his reader ('After finishing section I [. . .] with such a furore, how can Haydn recapture interest at the outset of section II? [. . .] How will he go about it?'). At one moment he will animate the orchestra ('the second violin seizes the first six notes of the theme and sets up a mournful undulation . . .'), at another he will take us behind the scenes and reveal Haydn as the master-puppeteer ('see how skilfully he handles the motif . . .'). At times he pauses to underline some technical point. What we have is a sort of *analyse raisonnée*, in which he digresses as issues arise (on orchestral instruments as 'actors', or his pontifications on modulatory restraint, on avoiding banality,

4   Plate 30, ibid, vol. III, pp. 109–56. See Bent/Drabkin, *Analysis*, pp. 20–22. Reprise II/1–2 are given on only six staves. Momigny even offers guidance on how to apply verse to music: vol. I, pp. 379–82.

5   J. J. O. Meude-Monpas, *Dictionnaire de musique* (Paris: Knapen, 1787), 'Parodie'. Momigny acknowledges *les parodistes*, notably André-Joseph Grétry, nephew of the composer, blind from youth, who wrote comedies, novels and libretti, and could add words to music 'aptly and effortlessly' – a tradition not unrelated to the *contrafactum* in the Middle Ages, to satirical adaptation in the seventeenth and eighteenth centuries, or to the eighteenth-century melodrama.

6   See E. Helm, 'The "Hamlet" Fantasy and the Literary Element in C. P. E. Bach's Music', *The Musical Quarterly*, 58 (1972), 277–96.

7   Mark Evan Bonds quotes examples by Johann Friedrich Reichardt (1782), Carl Friedrich Cramer (1783) and August Apel (1806) (Bonds, *Wordless Rhetoric: Musical Form and the Metaphor of the Oration* (Cambridge, MA: Harvard University Press, 1991), pp. 169–71, where further bibliography is given).

8   Chap. 46, 'De la symphonie à grand Orchestre', vol. II, pp. 583–606 (Haydn: pp. 586–606).

and notating diminished seventh chords). He observes thematic development but interprets it through eighteenth-century eyes as melodic fragmentation, governed by taste and the rule of diversity in unity, and as variation and embellishment, lacking Reicha's sense of thematic 'development'. Although he recognized the principal character of a symphony as deriving from the first of its three or four movements, the modern concept of sonata form, born in the nineteenth century, was non-existent for him. In formal terminology, however, he exhibits a major inconsistency. The Mozart Quartet movement he treats as a large binary form, with 'Reprise I' (in modern terms, Exposition), 'Reprise II, Part I' (Development) and 'Reprise II, Part II' (Recapitulation). In the Haydn Symphony allegro, on the other hand, after beginning with 'Reprise I' he then switches to the pervasive use of 'section I', 'section II' and 'section III', as if it were a ternary form. He thus has in common with Reicha an ambivalent view of what came later to be known as sonata form.

His 'Picturesque and Poetic Analysis' is quite different from his Dido-monologue rendering of Mozart. Only the principal thematic materials are set to words. It has the trappings of operatic performance: there are stage directions ('The scene takes place in the countryside'; 'The rustic dance is struck up again'); instruments are treated as for theatrical effect (timpani-roll as thunder, tutti diminished seventh chord as thunderbolt, deep horn octaves as a sepulchral voice), there are choruses of maidens, boys, shepherds, women and elders, which interact much as in the revolutionary operas of Momigny's time such as Cherubini's *Medea* (1797), which featured a temple, prayers by the people (Act II), and a great storm scene with vivid thunder and lightening (Act III: prophetic of the storm in *The Valkyrie*), and *Anacreon* (1803), which also had a storm scene.

Momigny was the first to provide cogent analyses of extended musical structures. He left three in all, the third being his treatment of Haydn's Piano Trio in C major, Hob. XV/27, published in 1821, which concentrates on phrase structure and modulatory scheme.[9]

Belgian by birth, Momigny worked for a time as teacher and organist in Lyon before establishing a music publishing and printing house in Paris in 1800, by which means he published not only his own theoretical and didactic works and many compositions, but also an extensive list of music by other composers. He wrote the *Complete Course* over a period of at least two years, issuing it in the meantime by instalments. Essentially in accord with Rameau that the laws of harmony derived from the harmonic spectrum of a sonorous body, and that harmony precedes melody, he laid emphasis on his own theoretical innovations, seeking to distance himself from his illustrious predecessor.[10] After issuing the *Complete Course* three times (1803–05, 1806, 1808), he published a summary of his theory, *Succint Exposé of the Only Musical System*, in 1808 and one further treatise, *The Only True Theory of Music*, in 1821. Momigny formally submitted the *Complete Course* to the Institut National. At the end of his life, deeply embittered, he had still failed to win the official approval for which he had so long petitioned.

9   *La seule vraie théorie de la musique* . . . (Paris: Momigny, 1821), chap. 9, 'De la contexture d'un morceau', pp. 100–112.
10   Ian Bent, 'Momigny's "Type de la Musique" and a Treatise in the Making', in *Music Theory and the Exploration of the Past*, ed. C. Hatch and D. Bernstein (Chicago: Chicago University Press, 1993), 309–40.

'Analysis of Haydn's Symphony [No. 103 in E♭ ("Drumroll")]'

Complete Course in Harmony and Composition

Source:
'Analyse musicale de la symphonie d'Haydn, qui est fig. A, pl. 46', *Cours complet d'harmonie et de composition, d'après une théorie nouvelle et générale de la musique*, vol. II (Paris: Momigny, 1805), pp. 586–606; vol. III (Paris: Momigny, 1803–05), pp. 245–92 (Plate 46).

[Analysis I]

Intrada, Adagio

339. *First period* [bb. 1–13]. In this Introduction, with its delightful simplicity – a simplicity imposed by the theme [*sujet*], intended as it is to resemble plainchant – Haydn has taken care to shape these first twelve bars [bb. 2–13] into two six-bar units, interpolating two bars of [wood]wind. His 'prayer' would have been all the more monotonous for the fact that it is played in the lowest strings. He felt the need for an antithesis [*opposition*]; so, in order to justify that, he has suggested the voices of assistants responding to the officiants with an 'Amen', or some similar short response.

340. *Second period* [bb. 14–25]. Always faithful to variety without ever detracting from unity, Haydn does not at this point introduce another motif. He repeats the same one, but with other instruments, and with modifications that give the effect of something new.

What magic there is in those three notes on the French horns: B♭ B♭ B♭ [bb. 19–20]!

341. *Third period* [bb. 25–39]. What plaintive and religious strains this third period conveys! How devout the bassoon sounds, as it doubles the second violin and {587} viola [bb. 25–7]! How eloquent the flute, as it doubles the first violin [bb. 25–9]. He had deliberately kept the flute silent during the preceding period. How effectively it now takes over from the horns and oboes, which have just been heard at the conclusion of the second period! How effectively the oboes in their turn respond to this [bb. 28–32]!

How well-judged is the unison which concludes this period, both as a succession to the prayer in plainchant, and as a momentary respite from harmony!

342. Had the second period not been a repetition of the first, the Introduction would have been too long, which would have been a serious fault since it would have bored the listeners. This is one of those faults into which I see composers falling every day.

Haydn needed his third period in order to accomplish the modulation from the tonic E♭ major on to the dominant of C minor. It is with this dominant that he concludes the Introduction, in order that the key of the Allegro, E♭ major, may be thrown into sharper relief than it would have been after the dominant of E♭.

Allegro con spirito

[Reprise I (= Section I)]

343. *First period* [*bb.* 40–47]. So that his period *de verve*[11] shall make a stronger effect, Haydn presents his theme [*sujet*] here *piano*. Had he been obliged to begin *forte*, he would have had to repeat his theme *piano* to avoid two loud periods in succession, since one destroys (or at least weakens) the effect of the other.

344. *Second period* [*bb.* 48–60]. {588} I identify this general *forte* as the period *de verve*, because it is normally full of warmth and vitality.

345. *Third period* [*bb.* 60–64]. The first period was *piano*, the second was *forte*. This one is a mixture of *piano* and *forte*. Horns, trumpets and timpani are silent throughout it.

346. *Fourth period* [*bb.* 64–79]. This period, although *forte* from the very beginning, undergoes an intensification from *forte* to *fortissimo*. The *fortissimo* begins its growth in the third and fourth bars [mid-b. 66 to mid-b. 68,[12] actually marked *sf*]. On the consequent [*conséquent*] or downbeat of the seventh bar [i.e. first half of b. 71] there is a searing *fortissimo* which is prolonged for two bars in order that the wind instruments should have time to make their effect. This *fortissimo* is a masterstroke which is worthy of note. The phrase ends with a perfect cadence, after which there occurs a complement to the period,[13] which could be regarded as a short period in its own right. This becomes a general *forte* after two bars, and one expects it to end with a second perfect cadence. But Haydn, the great master, makes use of a pull-back [*reticence*: b. 80][14] – just what is needed at this point – to avoid a strong cadence [*chûte*], which would feel a little pedestrian. Instead of giving the first violin the notes F, A♮, B♭,[15] he gives it F, A♮, and then immediately begins the pastoral and rustic melody to which I have suggested in my second[16] analysis that shepherds and shepherdesses dance.

11 *période de verve*: one of the four main periods [*périodes capitales*]: 'that which normally occurs after the [period *de*] *début* and a gentle intermediate period. [. . . It] is full of vigour, and quite often concludes the first large section of the first reprise' (vol. II, pp. 397–8).

12 Momigny here counts his bars from upbeat to downbeat, hence from half-bar to half-bar, in accordance with his general theory of rhythm – a theory anticipated by Koch and ultimately formulated by Riemann.

13 *complément de la période*: a *période complémentaire*, one of the three lesser periods [*périodes inférieures*], is 'used to render the sense [of a passage] more complete. [. . . It] functions as a sort of "cornice" or "frame" for the period that precedes it' (vol. II, pp. 397–8).

14 A combination of *subito piano* and the telescoping of the final bar of one period with the first of another – a device described by Reicha (1814) under *supposition* (i.e. 'suppression': see vol. I of the present work, Analysis 8), and by Koch as *Tacterstickung*. Momigny later (§351) observes the difference between the process at b. 80 and that at b. 74.

15 Momigny punctuates his music examples with commas according to the upbeat–downbeat patterns of the *motifs* that are the basis of his theoretical system – *not* to indicate barlines. Thus the opening theme of the allegro con spirito of this movement is represented as G, G A♭ G, G F E♭, E♭ D E♭ G B♭, B♭, whereas the barlines fall G G A♭ | G G F E♭ E♭ D E♭ G | B♭ B♭. I have occasionally added commas for consistency where Momigny has not supplied them.

16 *première*: this is one of two pieces of evidence suggesting that the 'Picturesque and Poetic Analysis', now Analysis II, may originally have been placed at the beginning: the heading before §349 reads *Troisième coup-d'œil sur la première Reprise* [. . .] , where it is in fact the second discussion of Reprise I. Moreover, there are points in what is now the first analysis that seem to refer back to what is now the second (e.g. §§339, 356). The *Cours complet* bears many signs of Momigny's having revised his intentions.

347. *Fifth period* [*bb. 80–86*]. This is the period to which I give the name 'melodious period',[17] because it normally contains a really pretty tune, and also because there is no counterpoint to obscure it. Instead, there is a simple accompaniment in the Italian manner, or one might say in pianistic style.

{589} The pretty tune on the oboe is doubled on first violins.[18] At the end of this period, Haydn had still one other danger point to overcome in the form of a third perfect cadence – a danger which would have been fatal for him, and which many people would have failed to avoid. Supreme composer as he is, Haydn knew just how to guard against this by cutting off the oboe in mid-sentence, as it were, at the eighth bar [b. 87]. Instead of letting the oboe play B♭ C B♭, with great skill he repeats the seventh bar of his phrase *forte*, accompanied by full orchestra, and in this way embarks on his sixth period, thereby avoiding the pitfall and increasing the vitality of his writing.

348. *Sixth period* [*bb. 87–94*]. This concluding period is a sort of refrain, or perhaps a 'Gloria Patri', and is thus a conventional device. Nevertheless, a clever man will always stand out in a crowd, and just so Haydn leaves his imprint on such common passages in the following way: (1) he distributes the parts more skilfully – with his instruments thus playing in comfortable registers, the total effect is much stronger; (2) he generates greater vitality in the phrase; (3) he derives his idea [*dessein*] from the preceding material rather than finishing the section with something banal or foreign.

Second[19] consideration of Reprise I of this Allegro con spirito

349. Nowhere are forced modulations to be found, or remote [tonal] excursions. Haydn does not resort to such false {590} means: he leaves them to children trying to make an impression. He is too much in command of his art, he has a vitality too abundant, a logic too sure, ever to stoop to such things. He belongs among the company of those who do not need strangeness for strangeness' sake. Let me explain myself.

The man who lacks genius is forced, if he is not to fall by the wayside, to have recourse to incongruous transitions. Finding precious little to say to his listeners, he parades them out of the first salon into which he has taken them, through room after room, house after house, often using a wrong key or a faulty transition. He often lifts a trapdoor instead of opening a door, sending his listeners tumbling from the top of the building to the basement or even worse. No doubt this inspires great surprise. But what is a surprise in an art such as music, when all it does is to dislocate things, and moreover in a harsh and barbarous manner? The only surprises that can be condoned are those flashes of genius, those sudden and unexpected shafts of light that illuminate rather than lead astray. Nothing is so easy to learn as how to make transitions *ex abrupto*,[20] equally there is nothing so puerile as to abuse it.

17   *période mélodieuse*, one of the four main periods: it has 'a supremely singing quality' (vol. II, pp. 397–8).
18   [Momigny:] In this case it may be expedient for the first violin of the orchestra [i.e. the leader, concertmaster] to accompany the oboe alone.
19   *Troisième*: see note 16.
20   *transition* signifies movement from key to key (whether diatonic, chromatic or enharmonic), thus

In Haydn all appears simple, for his art is infinite. Not a single note is lost in his mighty orchestra, for not one note is out of place, whether it be of primary importance, secondary, or merely accessory. No instrument ever destroys the effect of another; instruments when they sound together conspire, each according to its nature, towards a common end.[21]

350. In the opening four bars of the big {591} *forte* [bb. 48–51] which make up the second period of Reprise I, what is the double bass playing?: E♭, E♭, E♭ E♭ E♭. And this is precisely what the bassoons, the horns, the trumpets and the timpani are playing as well.

What are the clarinets, the flute[22] and the violas playing?: the same as the first violin. What are the second violins doing?: doubling the cellos. The cellos and second violins in this passage are playing two parts at once, namely the bass and the second violin: the bass with E♭, E♭, E♭ E♭ E♭, the second violin with E♭, G A♭, B♭ C B♭. The latter part alone is doubled by the oboes. There are only three distinct parts in this passage, so that the first violin and cello between them encompass the entire texture. But what gives these two parts their power, their fullness and their brilliance, is the way in which the various instruments double each other and colour the design.

351. Note that this big general *forte* is followed by a *piano*, which supplies a much-needed element of contrast. However, this *piano* would never be heard if something did not draw attention to it; that something is the piercing tone of the oboe [b. 80].

The phrase that it plays has been fragmented, since a long phrase after what has just been heard would throw cold water on the musical argument. For the course of this period, the orchestra could best be described as intermittent. Significantly, the orchestra responds with unanimous voice to the plaintive tones of the oboe – an effective touch, the more so since its line gives some relief from harmony.

The first big *forte* takes place partly over a {592} tonic pedal on E♭ [bb. 48–51]; the second occurs over a tonic [pedal] on B♭ [bb. 64–8], and the loudest instruments fall silent after this pedal, to reappear with greater impact three bars later, when a perfect cadence in C minor is interrupted devastatingly by the chord of the diminished seventh on the augmented fourth of B♭ major [b. 71]. Only in appearance, however, is the chord a diminished seventh on E♮. In reality it is such a chord on C♯: C♯ E G B♭. I cannot understand why members of the German school always commit this fault of placing two sevenths in succession in the same cadence: D♮/C – E♮/D♭.[23] The D♭ in this context serves less as the antecedent of D♮ than as the consequent of C, for what is the D♭ at this point? It is the chromatic flattened third of the key B♭; hence it cannot be raised to D♮ without committing a fault in logic, without perpetrating a solecism.

equates with the modern English 'modulation' (which has a different and particular meaning in Momigny's theory); *transition ex abrupto* is therefore a sudden, unmediated modulation.

21 'It is intrinsic to a symphony that all the instruments that make up the full orchestra be used each according to its character and its importance': vol. II, p. 584. Momigny gives a guide to orchestral doublings: vol. II, p. 585.

22 In Momigny's score, only one flute is called for throughout the entire movement, whereas Haydn in his autograph calls for 'Flauti' in movements 1–3 (though actually dividing the flutes only in movement 2) and only 'Flauto' in movement 4. Modern editions all call for two flutes.

Why is this passage so appealing? Why? Because it is indeed very beautiful, and because this note which our eyes tell us is D♭ our ears tell us is C♯. By notating it as he has, Haydn treats his orchestra as if it were a keyboard, on which the same key serves for C♯ and D♭, a fact which does not for a moment prevent the true musician from discerning perfectly well when that key is C♯ and when it is D♭. The fault here thus lies in musical orthography.[24]

{593} Note the skill with which at the end of this phrase [b. 74] Haydn makes the final B♭ of the phrase appear less the culmination of a perfect cadence than the first note of the phrase which follows: B♭, A♮ B♭ G etc.

There is however a difference between this cadence and the one with which the period ends [bb. 79–80]. In the first there is no hint of a pull-back [*reticence*].[25] Such is the artistry with which the great composer makes the connections between his ideas.

Reprise [II] of the allégro con spirito

Section II of the Movement

352. *First period* [bb. 94–104].[26] After finishing section I of the movement with such a furore, how can Haydn recapture interest at the outset of section II? By increasing the noise still further? But that is beyond his powers, since he has already used all the resources at his command. How will he go about it? See how he fragments his opening theme, [taking the portion] G, G A♭ G, G F E♭ and making out of it successively Г, F G F, F E♭ D, E♭ [bb. 94–5: second violins] and B♭, B♭ C B♭, B♭ A♭ G, G F E♭ [bb. 95–6: violas] etc., etc.

Now, what is that called in technical terms [*termes de l'art*]?

It is called imitation at the fifth below, since the second violin plays F, F G, the viola B♭, B♭ C. Then as the viola continues with [B♭,] B[♭] A♭ G, G F E♭, as if {594} playing G A♭ G, G F E♭, and as the bass responds with C, C D♭ C, C B[♭] A♭, this again is imitation at the fifth below. What makes this set of entries so very fine is that not only does one entry occur while the other is still continuing, but also an entry is made at the octave which imbues the imitation at the fifth with much richer harmony and brings to the answering entries a greater vivacity. Thus, when the viola has been imitating the second violin at the fifth below for three notes, the first violin repeats what the viola has just played an octave higher [bb. 95–6]. Then in turn it repeats what the bass plays, C, C D♭ C, C B♭ A♭. At that point the second violin seizes the first six notes of the theme and sets up a mournful undulation, [C,] C D♭ C, C B♮ C, and by this device Haydn relieves his listeners, on whose minds all this counterpoint has put a great strain, and recalls, unexpectedly yet naturally, his subject [first violins: bb. 104–05]: C, C D♭ C, C B♭ A♭, A[♭] G A♭ C E♭, E♭.

23 'Г' indicates a simultaneity, the lower note preceding and the upper note following the 'Г'. The original has the upper note above the lower.
24 [Momigny:] It may be felt that I am making light here of the difference that exists between a tempered sound and a natural sound and that I regard C♯ and D♭ as equal.
25 Regarding bb. 79–80, see §346 and note 14 above.
26 From here on, Momigny centres his headings. This edition continues the style of heading used up to this point.

353. *Second period* [*bb.* 104–12]. If, with this first set of entries, he has flummoxed those musicians who know nothing of counterpoint, he dumfounds them now with the second set, in which he treats two subjects simultaneously, namely the theme that I have just quoted (i.e. the opening theme) and that of E♭ A♭ G F G which is announced by the flute and imitated by the oboe at the fourth below. Note that these two instruments are doubled at the octave below, the one by second violin, the other by viola, whether to give support and direction to the {595} wind instruments, or to make the entries clearer and more harmonious.

354. Note how skilfully the gradation of this period is controlled. The music seems at first to converse quite peacefully, but with each recurrence it stirs, rekindles and in the end flares up in most violent fashion.

Third period [*bb.* 112–21]. Always judicious in what he does, Haydn now leaves aside the technical prowess [*science*] of the contrapuntist for fear of wearying his audience. But in its place he does not give us some mere irrelevance, some digression which bears no relation to the subject of the music.

355. Haydn always has something to say which is appropriate to his opening theme [*sujet*]. Here, he recalls in the basses the prayer with which he began, but without changing the tempo of his allegro.

Over this bass, the first violin adopts two roles: it simulates a deep voice praying or murmuring and a high voice lamenting.

NB In a symphony, where the facility exists for having a large number of interlocutors, there is no need for an actor to play several characters except when he is telling a story, whether he be impersonating someone or playing the impostor. But when the actor is expressing only his own feelings, if he is not playing the role of deceiver, he needs only one language. {596}

356. *Fourth period* [*bb.* 121–9]. A conversation begins, using imitation at the third below. The first violin plays D♭ C C [b. 119]; at three quavers' distance the second [violin] replies B♭ A♭ A♭. The first violin rejoins with C♭ B♭ B♭,[27] and the second [violin] retorts with A♭ G G. They continue with voices rising until soon they are both talking at once, whereupon the spectators' join in the quarrel, and the air is full of threats and cries.

357. At the *forte* in the sixth bar of this period [b. 126], Haydn reintroduces the beginning of this period *de verve* [from bb. 48–9] (the second period of Reprise I), inverted and in the relative minor – it is by such means that he preserves the unity [of the movement]. It is after these two bars and from there to the end of the period that the air is full of threats and cries.

358. *Fifth period* [*bb.* 130–43]. Haydn fragments his opening theme [*sujet*] for the second time, this time taking only five notes, A♭, A♭ B♭ A♭, A♭, accompanying this at the sixth [in the second violins], and imitating it at the tenth by contrary motion in the viola: F, F E♮ F, F.

The bass line echoes the viola, at the same time bridging the gap between the first and second sets of imitative entries.

27 C♭ B♭ A♭.

Next an overlapping imitation at the fifth is set up between first violin and bass: G♭, G♭ A♭ G♭, G♭, [answered by] C, C D♭ C, C. To this he adds parallel thirds below the first violin and above[28] {597} the bass, so making this set of imitations very harmonious; and for fear that these [latter] parallel thirds might not be audible enough he doubles the viola with bassoons.

359. The voices at this point [bb. 135–7] seem to draw apart from each other discontentedly, and mutter at each other from afar.

The cellos play A♭, A♭ B♭♭ A♭, the flute plays C, C D♭ C.

The oboes enter with an exclamation [b. 136: E♭/G♭, tied dotted minims] and then play E♭/G♮, E♭/G♮–F/A♭–E♭/G♮.[29] The G♭ [b. 136] in the oboe is an F♯, at least [in the second half of b. 137] over the A♮ in the bass. It forms the chord of the diminished fifth plus the major sixth, A♮ C E♭ F♯, which resolves on to a 6/4 chord, B♭ E♭ G – not the chord of the diminished seventh A♮ C E♭ G♭. However, since this note arises first as a G♭ over an A♭, forming a dominant seventh, Haydn preferred not to change it to an F♯ so as to be surer of his oboes, and perhaps to bring about a bigger surprise, or perhaps once again because this is the German usage.[30] After this exclamation, they take their turn in imitating the fragment of the opening theme [*premier thème*] which is being passed from mouth to mouth. From the oboes it passes to the French horns [b. 139], from there to the first clarinet, at the same time returning to the violins and viola, then passing back to the flute and the oboes, then to the clarinets, finally to the violins [and viola], at which point one expects the first subject [*premier sujet*] to return in its entirety.

360. *Sixth period* [*bb. 144–9*]. Precisely because one expects the first subject, Haydn instead presents the melodious period {598} A♭, F D♭, D♭ C, B♭ A♭ G♭ G♭. But this time, the first violin is no longer blended with the tone colour of the oboe. Instead, the flute imitates it very closely at the third above: C, B♭ G♭ F. Furthermore, Haydn is not content this time with the simple accompaniment in the Italian manner. He assigns the bassoons to play sustained the notes that the second violins and viola are playing repeated and detached, and the oboes to re-inforce the principal notes of the violin.

361. *Seventh period* [*bb. 150–59*]. See how he avoids here the sort of heavy-footed, commonplace cadence that fills the shabby works of ordinary composers; see how skilfully he handles the motif [*portion de phrase*] F F G♭ A♭ [b. 150], which passes through a variety of pitches on its way from the key of D♭ major to a point of repose on the dominant of E♭ major! It will be remembered that he used this same motif [*motif*] to conclude Reprise I on a cadence in B♭ major [bb. 47–51], and it should come as no surprise that he has avoided using it in exactly the same way here. This would have been an affront to his inexhaustible resourcefulness. Note that he has contrived a big general *fortissimo*[31] here in order that his motif [i.e. his first subject], which he is about to re-introduce *piano*, shall form a contrast.

28 *au-dessous* ('below').
29 Momigny gives G♭s throughout this passage of text, yet has G♮s in his score.
30 Cf. §351 above.
31 *forte*.

Section III of this Allegro

362. I have nothing to say about the first seventeen bars of section III, since they are a literal repetition of the first seventeen bars of section I of the allegro. {599}

I will note only that Haydn, who always knows how to be great when required and avoid being long-winded, has deemed it necessary to abbreviate section III by proceeding straight from the end of the second period of section I[32] [b. 57] to the end of the fourth [b. 77]. How different he is, in this as in everything else, from composers who write sonatas on the pattern of those of Steibelt[33] without having either the genius, the charm or the effectiveness that excuses the latter his eternal repetitions and his many other faults.

363. *Third period [bb. 180–86]*. This time, his melodious period is sustained and enriched by horns instead of by bassoons, and the oboe replaces the flute in the little imitation at the third which we described in the sixth period of section II of the allegro [b. 145].[34]

No mere caprice guides him in deployment of forces: rather it is a knowledge of the true resources of the various instruments – a knowledge that he has amassed through long and thoughtful experience – a knowledge that could be acquired in very little time from the fine examples that he gives, by anyone capable of appreciating them.

364. *Fourth period [bb. 187–201]*. What use he makes here of that same little motif that he exploited in so astonishing a way in the seventh period of section II of this allegro [bb. 150–55]![35]

The trumpets often join the horns, but {600} the most glorious outbursts are allotted particularly to the trumpets, because the instrument has a more trenchant sound quality.

The timpani, which play only the tonic and the dominant below that, are scarcely heard except in those general *forte* passages where one or other of these notes, or both in alternation, can be sounded.[36]

Analysis II
Elucidation of the Subject Matter of this Symphony:
Picturesque and Poetic Analysis

[Intrada, Adagio]

365. *[First period, bb. 1–13]*. In order to catch the attention of his audience, Haydn often begins his symphonies with a general *forte* accompanied by a timpani roll.

32 *douzième partie*: 'section XII', presumably misprint for *deuxième*, itself an error for *première*.
33 Daniel Steibelt (1765–1823), pianist, composer of operas, concertos, string quartets, and many works for solo piano. Cf. 'Discours Préliminaire', vol. I, p. 19: 'Among the most pleasant composers who have written for the piano – one of the most difficult areas of music to handle in a manner worthy of respect – must be distinguished particularly Steibelt, full of effectiveness and charm . . .'.
34 Cf. §360 above.
35 Cf. §361 above.
36 Perhaps this aside is prompted by b. 188, in which the rest of the orchestra plays chords of C minor and first-inversion E♭ dominant seventh, with bass C G, forcing the timpani to play notes from the inner parts, E♭ B♭.

But to begin this one, the timpani play a roll entirely solo. Why is that? – because this time he wishes to depict the sound of thunder.

The scene takes place in the countryside.

We must imagine that a fearful storm has been raging for so long that the inhabitants of the village have betaken themselves to the Temple of God. After the clap of thunder, conveyed by the timpani, we hear the prayer begin.

In order more strongly to suggest ecclesiastical chant and the serpent[37] that accompanies it, Haydn begins this prayer with the bassoon and cellos in their lowest octave, playing in unison with the double bass.

Anyone not seized with holy respect {601} right from the outset of these first twelve bars lacks a sensitive spirit, and has never tasted the religious and emotional pleasure of joining in prayer with his fellow men beneath the echoing vaults of a vast, sacred temple in the face of a common peril.

In the sixth and seventh bars[38] the flute and oboes give voice to an exclamation which seems to well up from the heart of the chorus of young maidens. They utter only two words: 'Great God!' So imbued are these words, however, with the emotion that fills them that they bring tears to the eyes. This same interjection is repeated five bars later at a higher pitch and accompanied by French horns, thus pointing up the gradual increase in the passage.

366. *Second period of the Introduction* [bb. 14–25]. The first and second violins repeat the prayer which has just been played in the first period by the bassoons, cellos and basses.[39] The latter represent the elders and grown men, the violins represent the women, the girls and the young boys.

367. The second violin, moving in syncopation [*contre-tems*], expresses the agitation and fear of the tender-hearted mothers, {602} trembling not so much for themselves as for their children.

The exclamation from the first period is repeated here, but modified so as to add a little variety.

368. The three deep notes on horns, Bb/Bb–Bb/Bb–Bb/Bb, resemble a hollow and sinister voice issuing from the tombs; and this only increases the emotion and terror with which the younger souls are stricken.

The Cb in the first violins and the quaver rests in the seconds and viola, which [now] begin, show that fear is spreading and taking hold bit by bit.

369. *Third period of the Introduction* [bb. 25–39]. With the third period, the flute adds its imploring supplications to those of the first violin. The strains of the second[40] violin and viola are reinforced by those of the bassoons [bb. 25–7],

---

37   Serpent: wind instrument with cup mouthpiece but finger holes, made of wood, and serpentine in shape. It was invented in France c.1590, and was used extensively to accompany plainchant throughout the seventeenth and eighteenth centuries, gradually dying out in the nineteenth. Momigny implies only that the tone colour suggests this, and not also the serpentine shape of the melodic line. One wonders whether the resemblance of the opening four notes, Eb D Eb C, to the opening of the *Dies irae* chant had struck Momigny when he suggested that the line recalled plainchant.

38   *cinquième et sixième*, i.e. bb. 5–6 of the structural unit bb. 2–13.

39   [Momigny:] Whenever the 'bass' is referred to after the cellos, the double basses are always meant, unless it be in an incomplete orchestra, in which the lower cellos take the part of the double bass, the remainder that of the cellos.

40   *premier*.

G/Bb–Ab/C–Bb/Db–Ab/C, and then by those of the oboes. The double basses fall silent for a moment [bb. 29–33], in order to let the plaintive sounds of the cellos come through. Finally, all the strings complete the prayer at the octave or in unison.

370. The moment the thunder has ceased its rumbling, everyone emerges from the church, and the allegro con spirito begins.

[*Allegro con spirito*]

First period of the Allegro [*bb. 40–47*]. The less frightened [among them] find their voices, saying to the others: 'My, oh my! My, oh my! That had you really scared!'⁴¹ {603}

Second period [*bb. 48–60*]. At this point, all give vent to the joy that they feel at seeing the danger abate.

371. *Third period* [*bb. 60–64*]. The oboes say: 'They're laughing at us.' The majority reply forcibly: 'Stop it, stop it, poking fun at them'.

Fourth period [*bb. 64–79*]. Each group says: 'Stop poking fun at them'. 'Remember Lycas,⁴² struck down by thunder a year ago': F#, G, Eb, D, F#, G [bb. 68–71]. On this [last] G falls the image 'struck by thunder', where it is depicted by the diminished seventh chord on the augmented fourth degree E♮ G Bb Db.

'Lycas was poking fun, as are you, when struck down': F, A♮ [b. 79]. It is this staccato A♮ which depicts the blow.

372. *Fifth period* [*bb. 80–86*]. The oboes, in unison with the first violins, break into a rustic dance, which the young shepherds and shepherdesses instantly take up.

Sixth period [*bb. 87–94*]. Now joy is rife, and everyone dances.

{604}

Point II or Section II of the Symphony

373. *First period* [*bb. 94–104*]. Each says to the other: 'I saw you: you were afraid'.

From the fourth bar to the end of the period, the second violin repeats: 'Yes, how you cried and bewailed': C, C Db C, C B♮ C [bb. 98⁴–104³].

Second period [*bb. 104–12*]. The first violin reiterates mockingly: 'My, oh my! My, oh my! That had you really scared!' [bb. 104–06].

The flute, doubling the second violin at the octave, replies: 'I was not afraid'; then the oboe, doubling the viola at the octave, replies likewise [bb. 106–08].

The horns and trumpets dissent: 'It is not true, it is not true, no, no, no, no' [bb. 108–12].

The clarinets [comment]: 'Oh my, oh my. Oh what a fright, yes, yes' [bb. 108–12].

---

41   Although Momigny's avoidance of music examples masks the fact, he has clearly devised dramatic tags that fit the melodic material. Thus 'Ah mon dieu! ah mon dieu! que vous avez eu peur!' can be sung to the first violin theme of bb. 40–42. My English translations of these tags are designed to do the same.

42   Lycas: perhaps Lycaon, King of Arcadia, who had fifty sons, and who murdered a child and offered the flesh to Zeus to eat, for which Zeus struck him and his sons down with thunderbolts. I am indebted to Cynthia Gessele and Elaine Sisman for help in this identification.

The timpani [declare]: 'No, no' [bb. 108–09].

The basses [mock]: 'How terrified you were! Yes, you were scared, you were scared, yes, yes!' [bb. 108–12].

374. *Third period [bb. 112–21].* The violas and basses [assert]: 'I'm still convinced that I heard you at prayer': E♭, D E♭ C, A♭ F D, [F B♭ E♭] [bb. 112–14]. These, the very notes which began the prayer itself, are re-used {605} here in a faster tempo – an ironic use of them to hurl ridicule at those who were praying.

The violins [concur]: 'Yes, how you prayed!': A♭, A♭ A♭ G; 'How you bewailed!': B♭, A♮ A♭ G [bb. 113–15] and so on right to the end of the period.

375. *Fourth period [bb. 121–9].* The strings persist in poking fun at the others with increasing spite for the dismay and consternation that they showed while praying.

At the fifth bar the exasperated victims retort with some vehemence: 'It is not true. It is not true. No no, no no, no no!' [bb. 125–9, oboes].

376. *Fifth period [bb. 130–43].* The argument continues, but with less heat.

Sixth period [bb. 144–9]. The rustic dance is struck up again, lasting for the entire period.

Seventh period [bb. 150–59]. The seventh period rises to a great tumult.

Section III of the Symphony

The first and second periods are those of section I of the symphony. At the third period the rustic dance strikes up again.[43] {606}

377. *Fourth period [bb. 187–201].* At this point, the crisis boils over. The argument flares up again, everyone taking part. So full of venom does it become that the vituperation loses all restraint. Fury is written on every face, and the gathering rage rises to its highest pitch.

In Haydn's portrayal of this scene, all these feelings of hatred can be heard boiling up, and the agitation that they produce infects·the minds of the listeners.

What more eloquent contrast could Haydn interpose at this point than that of a prayer which has already been woven as an essential element into his plan? Is there anything, indeed, more remote and at the same time more immediate than the frenzied delirium of passions that seems to give man the belief in his own all-powerfulness, and [yet] the sense of his insignificance which brings him to prostrate himself before the divinity?

What is there that will silence these passions, the din of which is so appalling? *A clap of thunder* – and that is what we hear.

Seized anew with terror, everyone returns to the Temple. The prayer begins again.

However, the clouds disperse, and with them the fear. The hymn which has been begun gives way to a return of the dance. But this time, amid the furore, occasioned by joy, no longer are strains of discord to be heard. Peace has entered once more into the hearts [of the people]; the cries of fury are replaced by the intoxication of contentment. All are happy and Haydn's tableau is complete.

---

43   There is no full-point at the foot of this page, hence it is not certain that this paragraph is complete.

Ernst Theodor Amadeus Hoffmann (1776–1822)
'[Review: Beethoven's Symphony No. 5 in C minor]' (1810)

Arguably the most celebrated document in the history of music criticism, this review, astonishing in its length and cogency, harbours beneath its richly Romantic imagery a formidable array of technicalities. Robin Wallace has suggested, indeed, that it 'belongs in a textbook on theory'.[1] Hoffmann's terminology, moreover, was modern for its day. When speaking of transition from key to key, for example, rather than the time-honoured *Ausweichung* he used *Modulation* and *moduliren*, German usages admittedly going back to Marpurg in 1760, but still unstable in 1810 and only to be established independently in the mid or late nineteenth century.[2] He coupled it with *chromatisch* ('chromatic modulation'), and used it alongside the perhaps even more modern *Übergang* ('transition'), which twice happens by 'enharmonic exchange'.

He also sports a battery of formal-structural designators: not only the all-purpose *Satz* ('movement', 'phrase', 'subject'), but also *Anfangssatz* ('opening phrase'), *Hauptsatz* ('main subject'), *Nebensatz* ('secondary phrase'), *Schlußsatz* ('closing passage'), and also the fugally derived *Gegensatz* ('countersubject') and *Zwischensatz* ('episode'); not only *Thema* ('theme'), but also *Hauptthema* ('main theme'), *erstes Thema* ('opening theme') and *zweites Thema* ('second theme'). On the sub-thematic level, he uses *Figur* ('figure'), *Schlußfigur* ('closing figure'), *Gedanke* ('idea'), *Hauptgedanke* ('main idea') and *Nebengedanke* ('secondary idea'). On the other hand, *Motiv*, as an irreducible germinal unit in the nineteenth-century sense, is not used. He also has many terms for musical processes: the Baroque *Ausführung* and the later *Durchführung* (both 'development'), *Fortführung* ('continuation'), *Erweiterung* ('extension'), *Nachahmung* and *Imitation* ('imitation'); and specific technical devices such as *Grundton* ('root', avoiding ambiguity by reserving *Tonika* for 'tonic', its other meaning), *Sexten-Akkord* ('first inversion'), *verminderter Septimen-Akkord* ('diminished seventh chord'), *Orgelpunkt* ('pedal'), *Restriktion* ('stretto') and others.

The base layer of analysis does something new for its time: it records the moment-to-moment responses of the listener, the expectations, the gratifications and surprises, it registers the recognition of already-heard ideas, it narrates the listener's perceptual experience. At the beginning of the first movement Hoffmann withholds verbs so as to convey a sense of breathless disorientation ('In the second bar a fermata,

---

1 R. Wallace, *Beethoven's Critics: Aesthetic Dilemmas and Resolutions during the Composer's Lifetime* (Cambridge: CUP, 1986), p. 143, also 26: 'As a critic [. . . Hoffmann] was not a technician, but a theorist, in the boldest sense of the word'.

2 Sulzer, Kirnberger and Koch used *Modulation* as a synonym for *Ausweichung*; Gottfried Weber in 1818, Dehn in 1840 and Lobe in 1850 still qualified it as *ausweichende Modulation*. In French, *modulation* in this sense existed by the early eighteenth century. See *HwMT*, 'Modulation'.

then the idea repeated a tone lower, then another fermata; both times strings and clarinets only'), concluding: 'Not even the key is yet certain; the listener assumes E♭ major' – a remarkable anticipation of the heuristic, cognitive approach of the contemporaneous theorist Gottfried Weber (see vol. I, Analysis 10).[3] Thus: 'After the first inversion [mvt I, b. 214 . . .] the reviewer would have expected G♭ minor as the next chord . . .', when what actually follows surprises and puzzles him; the fermatas of the first movement create a special effect of expectation; newly encountered elements replicate the opening idea by imitation, copying, transposition, reordering and re-orchestration; or are stretched and compressed; or 'recall' some earlier phrase, even from movement to movement. Although reviewing from the score and parts, possibly without ever having heard the work,[4] Hoffmann reconstitutes the listener's conscious stream of thought, almost conveying the turn of the head from violins to clarinets, to cellos and basses, the bewilderment at the fading *pianissimo*, the jolt at the sudden *fortissimo*. Particularly gripping is his portrayal of the listener's disorientation in the final thirteen bars of the finale (here again he withholds verbs), with its powerful concluding descriptive simile: 'like a fire that is thought to have been put out but repeatedly bursts forth again in bright tongues of flame'.

Over this base layer is a second layer: the retrospective analyses of the first and third movements that immediately follow the stream-of-consciousness analysis in each case. That of the third movement sets out in a music example five versions of the main theme, thus displaying the processes of melodic extension and the intensification that they can generate. That of the first movement posits a deeper level at which all the secondary material is imbued with the 'rhythmic content' of the opening two-bar figure. A third layer is provided by the concluding survey of the symphony as a whole, suggesting that the 'close relationship of the individual themes' provides a unity at a still deeper level, not susceptible to surface demonstration. (See our hermeneutic reading of these layers in the Introduction to Part II.)

The review is prefaced by an aesthetic statement of great importance, which concerns the supreme status of instrumental music, ascribes to Beethoven both 'genius' (*Genie*) and 'rational awareness' (*Besonnenheit*), and alludes to the organic image of 'the splendid tree, buds and leaves, blossom and fruit [. . .] springing from the same seed' as a metaphor for musical process.[5] (Hoffmann later recast this section and what has been described above as the second and third layers of

---

3 See Janna Saslaw, 'Gottfried Weber and Multiple Meaning', *Theoria*, 5 (1990–91), 74–103; and 'Gottfried Weber and the Concept of "Mehrdeutigkeit"' (PhD diss., Columbia University, 1992).

4 One isolated use of past tense seems to recall a moment of performance no longer available for reconsideration: 'This may strike people as amusing, but in the reviewer it *produced* [*erweckte*] an uneasy feeling'; but reference, which is to bb. 161–70 of the third movement, could be to inner hearing rather than live performance. Hoffmann's failure to comment on the vivid effect of the *pizzicato* in bb. 244–54 of that movement (see note 19 below), his painstakingly literal description of the notation at this point and his quotation of the cello line in Ex. 18 without *pizz.* marking, may suggest that he had not heard a live *pizzicato* performance of the passage.

5 On Hoffmann's language, and *Genie* and *Besonnenheit* in particular, see Peter Schnaus, *E. T. A. Hoffmann als Beethoven-Rezensent der Allgemeinen musikalischen Zeitung* (Munich-Salzburg: Katzbichler, 1977); and on organicism and rhetoric see Mark Evan Bonds, *Wordless Rhetoric: Musical Form and the Metaphor of the Oration* (Cambridge, MA: Harvard University Press, 1991), pp. 177–80. The organic imagery quoted here is actually attributed to the works of Shakespeare, not Beethoven, and is thus at best an oblique reference to musical process.

analysis, with material from his review of Beethoven's Piano Trios Op. 70, for his cycle of musical writings entitled *Kreisleriana*, published in 1814–15.)[6]

The duality of Hoffmann's review lies precisely in the marriage of this aesthetic essay with the technical base layer – a duality quite different from Momigny's of 1805, which comprised two separate, complementary analyses. Here, the two facets are tightly coupled: they are interwoven threads, their common purpose springing from certain crucial statements in the initial essay. On the one hand, the insistence on technicality arises from the remark:

> it is usual to regard [Beethoven's] works merely as products of a genius who ignores form and discrimination of thought and surrenders to his creative fervour and the passing dictates of his imagination. [. . .] only the most penetrating study of the inner structure of Beethoven's music can reveal its high level of rational awareness . . .

On the other hand, the frequent reference to emotional response, and to regions beyond human consciousness, derive from his attribution to Beethoven of special romantic status (emphasis added):

> [Whereas] Mozart [. . .] takes as his province the superhuman, magical quality residing *in the inner self* [. . . Beethoven's Fifth Symphony . . .] sweeps the listener *into the wonderful spirit realm of the infinite.*

Repeatedly, Hoffmann shows how this symphony transcends its physical, acoustical world and transports the listener to that spirit realm, imbuing the transported mind with a 'haunted yearning'. Thus it is that the pounding tutti chords at bb. 168–79 of the first movement 'are sounds at which the breast, constricted and affrighted by presentiments of enormity, struggles for air'. This is no mere programmaticism; this is not something *portrayed* by the music; this is the music *acting upon the listener's mind.* In isolating the musical phenomena that give rise to a pervasive anxiety and presentiment – the dominant fermatas, the rising sequences with their increasing tension, the constant repetition of short phrases and single chords – Hoffmann links the rational and irrational as cause and effect, encapsulated in his final proclamation of 'the composer's rational genius [*besonnene Genialität*]'.

The attention to detail of Hoffmann's musical commentary and the particularity of his observation are quite extraordinary for his time, and like nothing else before the twentieth century. The text given below perhaps errs on the generous side in keying in bar numbers, and correcting references to instruments. At the risk of irritating some readers, it was felt worthwhile to offer the opportunity to savour Hoffmann's love of minutiae, to revel in his fascination with the inner workings of the music. Surprisingly, in some respects one could say that Hoffmann's response to Beethoven's structures is that of the true theorist.

Unlike any other author in this volume, Ernst Theodor Amadeus Hoffmann was a major literary figure of his time – one of the foremost representatives of Romanticism in the early nineteenth century. In childhood, he studied both painting and music, including violin, piano, figured bass and counterpoint. After completing law studies

---

6   Published as part of his *Fantasiestücke in Callot's Manier. Kreisleriana* is translated in *E. T. A. Hoffmann's Musical Writings: 'Kreisleriana', 'The Poet and the Composer', Music Criticism*, ed. David Charlton, trans. Martyn Clarke (Cambridge: CUP, 1989), pp. 236–51.

at Königsberg University (1792–5), he began to compose, taking lessons from J. F. Reichardt. Between 1808 and 1814, he held various positions with theatre companies as music director and conductor, in Bamberg, Dresden and Leipzig, and taught singing and piano privately. Over the period from 1799 to 1817, he wrote five singspiels, three melodramas and four operas, of which *Undine* (1816) is best known, and music for many plays; also a symphony, chamber music, piano sonatas and vocal music sacred and secular. He wrote anonymously for the *Allgemeine musikalische Zeitung* of Leipzig from 1809 to 1815. His career as a writer progressively took over. His tales of the supernatural and fantastic, and other writings, later to inspire Schumann's *Kreisleriana* (1838), Offenbach's *The Tales of Hoffmann* (1881) and Tchaikovsky's *The Nutcracker* (1892), were collected as *Fantasy Pictures in the Style of Callot* (1814–15), *The Separion Brethren* (1819–21) and *Tomcat Murr's Views on Life* (1820–22). In 1815 he returned to his legal career; like Gottfried Weber, who became a fiscal procurator in 1819, Hoffmann achieved high judicial rank as a supreme court judge in 1816.

'[Review: Beethoven's Symphony No. 5 in C minor]'

Source:
E. T. A. Hoffmann: [Unsigned review:] 'Sinfonie pour 2 Violons, 2 Violes, Violoncelle et Contre-Violon, 2 Flûtes, petite Flûte, 2 Hautbois, 2 Clarinettes, 2 Bassons, Contre-basson, 2 Cors, 2 Trompettes, Timbales et 3 Trompes, composée et dediée etc. par Louis van Beethoven. à Leipsic, chez Breitkopf et Härtel, Œuvre 67. No. 5. des Sinfonies. (Pr. 4 Rthlr. 12 Gr.)', *AmZ*, 12 (1809/10), No. 40 (4 July 1810), cols. 630–42, No. 41 (11 July 1810), cols. 652–9.

translated by Martyn Clarke
with David Charlton and Ian Bent[7]

{630} The reviewer has before him one of the most important works by the master whose pre-eminence as an instrumental composer it is doubtful that anybody {631} would now dispute; he is utterly permeated by the subject of the present review, and may nobody take it amiss if he exceeds the limits of conventional appraisals and strives to put into words all the profound sensations that this composition has given rise to within him.

When music is spoken of as an independent art the term can properly apply only to instrumental music, which scorns all aid, all admixture of other arts, and gives pure expression to its own peculiar artistic nature. It is the most romantic of all arts – one might almost say the only one that is *purely* romantic. Orpheus's lyre opened the gates of Orcus. Music reveals to man an unknown realm, a world quite separate from the outer sensual world surrounding him, a world in which he leaves behind all feelings circumscribed by intellect in order to embrace the inexpressible. How dimly was this peculiar nature of music perceived by those instrumental composers who tried to represent such circumscribed sensations or even events, and thus to treat sculpturally the art most utterly opposed to sculpture! Dittersdorf's symphonies of this type,[8] as well as all the newer *Batailles des Trois Empereurs* etc.,[9] should be condemned to total oblivion as ridiculous aberrations. In singing, where the juxtaposed poetry suggests precise moods [*Affekte*] through words, the magical power of music acts like the philosopher's miracle elixir, a few drops of which make any drink wonderfully delicious. Any passion – love, hate, anger, despair, etc. – presented to us in an opera is clothed by music in the purple shimmer of romanticism, so that even our mundane sensations take us out of the everyday into the realm of the infinite. Such is the power of music's spell that, growing ever stronger, it can only burst the fetters of any other art.

---

7   The translation given here is essentially that given in *E. T. A. Hoffmann's Musical Writings* (see note 6 above), pp. 96–103, by prior agreement modified to the conventions of the present volume.

8   [Charlton:] e.g. *Trois simphonies, exprimant trois métamorphoses d'Ovide* published in 1785 from a total of twelve that included the stories of Phaeton's fall, Actaeon's transformation into a stag and the peasants transformed into frogs.

9   [Charlton:] Probably Jacques-Marie Beauvarlet-Charpentier, *La Bataille d'Austerlitz surnommé la Journée des trois Empereurs, symphonie militaire et historique à grand orchestre* (Paris, 1806) and Louis-Emmanuel Jadin's symphony of the same name also issued in 1806, or the piano arrangement of the latter, published in Leipzig.

It is certainly {632} not merely an improvement in the means of expression (perfection of instruments, greater virtuosity of players), but also a deeper awareness of the peculiar nature of music, that has enabled great composers to raise instrumental music to its present level. Haydn and Mozart, the creators of modern instrumental music, first showed us the art in its full glory; but the one who regarded it with total devotion and penetrated to its innermost nature is Beethoven. The instrumental compositions of all three masters breathe the same romantic spirit for the very reason that they all intimately grasp the essential nature of the art; yet the character of their compositions is markedly different.

Haydn's compositions are dominated by a feeling of childlike optimism. His symphonies lead us through endless green forest glades, through a motley throng of happy people. Youths and girls sweep past dancing the round; laughing children behind trees, lying in wait behind rose bushes, teasingly throw flowers at each other. A world of love, of bliss, of eternal youth, as though before the Fall; no suffering, no pain; only sweet, melancholy longing for the beloved vision floating far off in the red glow of evening, neither approaching nor receding; and as long as it is there the night will not draw on, for the vision is the evening glow itself illuminating hill and glade.

Mozart leads us deep into the realm of spirits. Dread lies all about us, but withholds its torments and becomes more an intimation of infinity. We hear the gentle voices of love and melancholy, the nocturnal spirit world dissolves into a purple shimmer, and with inexpressible yearning we follow the flying figures kindly beckoning to us from the clouds to join their eternal dance of the spheres (as, for example, in Mozart's Symphony [No. 39] in E♭ major, known as the 'Swan Song').[10]

In a similar way {633} Beethoven's instrumental music unveils before us the realm of the mighty and the immeasurable. Here shining rays of light shoot through the darkness of night, and we become aware of giant shadows swaying back and forth, moving ever closer around us and destroying within us all feeling but the pain of infinite yearning, in which every desire, leaping up in sounds of exultation, sinks back and disappears. Only in this pain, in which love, hope and joy are consumed without being destroyed, which threatens to burst our hearts with a full-chorused cry of all the passions, do we live on as ecstatic visionaries.

Romantic sensibility is rare, and romantic talent even rarer, which is probably why so few are able to strike the lyre that unlocks the wonderful realm of the infinite. Haydn romantically apprehends the humanity in human life; he is more congenial to the majority. Mozart takes as his province the superhuman, magical quality residing in the inner self. Beethoven's music sets in motion the machinery of awe, of fear, of terror, of pain, and awakens that infinite yearning which is the essence of romanticism. Beethoven is a purely romantic, and therefore truly musical, composer. This may well explain why his vocal music is less successful since it [does not permit] vague yearning but can only depict from the realm of the infinite

10   [Charlton:] Mozart, Symphony No. 39 in E♭ major, K543 (1788). The nickname 'Swan Song' was of unknown provenance, according to Hermann Abert, W. A. Mozart (Leipzig: B&H, 6/1923–4), vol. II, p. 578, note 3. For a different interpretation, see the poem by A. Apel in AmZ 8, nos 29–30 (16, 23 April 1805).

those feelings capable of being described in words, and why his instrumental music rarely appeals to the multitude. But even the multitude oblivious of Beethoven's depths will not deny him a high degree of invention; on the contrary it is usual to regard his works merely as products of a genius [*Genie*] who ignores form and discrimination of thought and surrenders to his creative fervour and the passing dictates of his imagination. He is nevertheless fully the equal of Haydn and Mozart in rational awareness [*Besonnenheit*], his controlling self detached from the inner realm of {634} sounds and ruling it in absolute authority. Just as our aesthetic overseers have often complained of a total lack of real unity and inner coherence in Shakespeare, when only profounder contemplation shows the splendid tree, buds and leaves, blossom and fruit as springing from the same seed, so only the most penetrating study of the inner structure of Beethoven's music can reveal its high level of rational awareness, which is inseparable from true genius and nourished by continuing study of the art. Beethoven bears the romanticism of music, which he expresses with such originality and authority in his works, in the depths of his spirit. The reviewer has never felt this more acutely than in the present symphony. It unfolds Beethoven's romanticism, rising in a climax right to the end, more than any other of his works, and irresistibly sweeps the listener into the wonderful spirit realm of the infinite.

[First movement]

The first allegro [con brio], C minor in 2/4 time, begins with the main idea [*Hauptgedanke*] consisting of only two bars, which subsequently appears again and again in a variety of forms. In the second bar a fermata, then the idea repeated a tone lower, then another fermata; both times strings and clarinets only. Not even the key is yet certain; the listener assumes E♭ major. The second violins begin again with the main idea, then the key note C played by cellos and bassoons in the second bar [b. 7] establishes the tonality of C minor; violas and first violins enter in imitation until the latter finally add two bars to the main idea, play them three times [bb. 14–19] (the last time joined by the whole orchestra) and end with a fermata on the dominant [b. 21], giving the listener presentiments of unknown mysteries. The beginning of the allegro up to this pause [*Ruhepunkt*] determines the character of the whole piece, and the reviewer therefore inserts it here for the reader's inspection [bb. 1–21]:[11]

---

11 Ex. 1 occupies cols 635–6.

Example 1

{637} After this fermata, violins and violas remain in the tonic and imitate the main idea, while the bass here and there adds a figure [*Figur*] that also copies it [bb. 28–9, 32–3 etc.], until an ever rising episode [*Zwischensatz*; bb. 33–44] brings back earlier presentiments, this time more strongly and urgently. It leads to a tutti [bb. 44–56], the theme of which again follows the rhythmic pattern of the main idea and is closely related to it [bb. 44–8]:

Example 2

The first inversion [*Sexten-Akkord*] above a D in the bass [b. 58] prepares the relative major Eb, in which the horns again imitate the main idea [bb. 59–62]. The first violins now take up a second theme [*zweites Thema*; bb. 63ff], which is melodious but preserves the mood of anxious, restless yearning expressed by the movement as a whole. This theme is played by the violins alternating with the clarinet, while every three bars the cellos and basses interject the imitating figure previously referred to, so that the new theme is artfully woven into the overall texture. As a continuation [*Fortführung*] of this theme [bb. 83–94] the first [and second] violins and cellos play a two-bar figure five times in the key of Eb minor while the [violas and] double basses [*Bässe*] ascend chromatically.[12] A new episode [bb. 95–109] leads to the closing passage [*Schluss*: bb. 110–17] in which the wind instruments repeat the first tutti in E♭ major [bb. 44–56], and finally the whole of the orchestra ends in E♭ major with the frequently mentioned imitation of the main theme in the bass.

Section II begins with the main theme [*Hauptthema*] again, in its original form, but transposed up a third and played by clarinets and horns [bb. 125–8]. The various elements [*Sätze*] of section I follow in F minor [bb. 129–43], C minor [bb. 144–51] and G minor [bb. 153–8], but are differently arranged and orchestrated. Finally, after an episode [bb. 158–68] again built only on a two-bar phrase {638} taken up alternately by the violins and wind instruments, while the cellos play a figure in contrary motion and the double basses rise, the following chords are heard from the whole orchestra [bb. 168–79]:

Example 3

They are sounds at which the breast, constricted and affrighted by presentiments of enormity, struggles for air. But like a friendly figure moving through the clouds and shining through the darkness of night, a theme now enters that was touched on by the horns in E♭ major in the fifty-ninth bar of section I.[13] First in G major [bb. 179–87], then in C major [bb. 187–95] the violins play this theme in octaves while the [violas, cellos and] basses have a descending figure that to some extent recalls the tutti phrase at the forty-fourth bar of section I:

Example 4

12   [Charlton:] It is interesting that Beethoven altered the phrasing of this passage in order to counteract the symmetry implied by Hoffmann: see Norton Critical Score, ed. Elliot Forbes (New York: Norton, 1971), p. 130.
13   'the fifty-eighth bar'.

The wind instruments take up this theme *fortissimo* in F minor [b. 195], but after three bars the strings seize upon the previous two bars and alternate with the winds in playing them five more times [bb. 198–209], followed by further alternation of single chords in a gradual diminuendo [bb. 210–27]. {639} After the first inversion [b. 214]:

Example 5

the reviewer would have expected Gb minor as the next chord in the sequence, which could then be changed enharmonically to F# minor if a modulation of the type used here [*moduliert werden*] was required to G major. The wind instruments that play the chord following this first inversion, however, are written thus [b. 215]:

Example 6

The strings then play this F# minor chord [b. 216]:

Example 7

which is repeated four times by them and the winds alternating every bar [bb. 217–20]. The chords for the wind instruments continue to be written as shown above, for which the reviewer can find no reason. Now the first inversion chord [b. 221]:

Example 8

is treated in the same way, gradually getting softer and softer. This again has an ominous, eerie effect. The full orchestra now bursts out with a theme in G major [bb. 228–32] almost identical to that heard forty-one bars previously, in unison except for the flute and trumpet holding out the dominant D. After only four bars, however, this theme is interrupted by seven *pianissimo* diminished seventh chords [bb. 233–9]:

Example 9

exchanged between strings with horns and the remaining winds. Then the [cellos,] basses [bassoons and horns] take up the main idea followed in the next bar by the other instruments in unison; the bass and upper parts imitate each other in this way for five bars [bb. 240–45], combine for three bars, and then in the next bar [b. 248] the whole orchestra with timpani and trumpets comes in with the main theme in its original form.

Section I is now repeated [bb. 253–74] with a few slight differences. {640} The theme that earlier began in E♭ major now enters in C major [b. 303], and leads to a jubilant close in C major with timpani and trumpets. But with this close the music turns towards F minor [bb. 375–81]. After five bars of the first inversion from the full orchestra [bb. 382–6]:

Example 10

clarinets, bassoons and horns softly play an imitation of the main idea [bb. 387–8]. One bar's general pause is followed by six bars of [bb. 390–95]:

Example 11

All the wind instruments repeat the imitation and now violas, cellos and bassoons [bb. 398ff] take up a theme that was heard earlier in section II in G major [bb. 228–32], while two bars later the violins enter in unison with a new counter-subject [Gegensatz; bb. 400ff]. The music now remains in C minor, and with slight changes the theme that began in b. 71 of section I[14] is repeated by the violins, first alone [bb. 423–38] then alternating with the wind instruments [bb. 439–55]. The alternating phrases get shorter and shorter, first one bar, then half a bar [bb. 456–60]. It becomes an irresistible surge – a swelling torrent whose waves break higher and higher – until the beginning of the allegro is heard once more twenty-four bars from the end [b. 478]. There follows a pedal point [bb. 484–91], above which the main theme is imitated, and finally the movement is brought to a strong and powerful close.

14   [Charlton:] Hoffmann refers to b. 423, a free extension of music originally heard at bb. 63 and 71. His observation also implies that the rising quaver fourths in bb. 418–22 are connected with the same interval in bb. 63 and 71.

There is no simpler idea than that on which Beethoven has based his entire allegro:

Example 12

and one perceives with admiration how he was able to relate all the secondary ideas [*Nebengedanken*] and episodes by their rhythmic content [*rhythmischer Verhalt*] to this simple theme, so that they serve to reveal more and more facets of the movement's overall character, which the theme by itself could only hint at. All the phrases [*Sätze*] are short, consisting merely of two or three bars, and are also constantly exchanged between {641} strings and winds. One would think that such ingredients could result only in something disjointed and hard to follow, but on the contrary it is precisely this overall pattern, and the constant repetition of short phrases and single chords, that maintains the spirit in a state of ineffable yearning. Quite apart from the fact that the contrapuntal treatment betokens profound study of the art, the episodes and constant allusions [*Anspielungen*] to the main theme demonstrate how the whole movement with all its distinctive features was not merely conceived in the imagination but also clearly thought through.

[Second movement]

Like the voices of a propitious spirit that fills our breast with comfort and hope, we now hear the lovely (and yet content-laden [*gehaltvoll*]) theme of the andante [con moto], Ab major in 3/8 time, played by the violas and cellos. The further development [*Ausführung*] of the andante recalls several middle movements in Haydn symphonies, in that the main theme is varied in diverse ways between intervening episodes.[15] It cannot be compared with the opening allegro in originality, although the idea of repeatedly interrupting the Ab major with a stately passage in C major for timpani and trumpets has a striking effect. The transition [*Übergang*] into C is twice achieved by enharmonic change [*enharmonische Verwechslung*] [bb. 28–30, 77–9]:

Example 13

---

15 [Charlton:] e.g. Haydn Symphonies Nos. 70, 90, 101, 103. Other similarities exist in the essentially ternary movement of No. 100.

whereupon the stately theme enters and then the modulation [*Modulation*] back to the dominant chord of A♭ major takes place in the following way [bb. 41–8, 90–97]:

Example 14

{642} The third time, flutes, oboes and clarinets prepare the transition to the C major theme more simply, though with great effect [bb. 144–7]:

Example 15

All the material in this andante is very melodious, and the main subject [*Hauptsatz*] is almost ingratiating. The very course of this theme, however, passing through A♭ major, B♭ minor, F minor, B♭ minor and then back to A♭, the repeated juxtaposition of the major keys A♭ and C, the chromatic modulations – all these again express the character of the whole work and make this andante a part of it. It is as though the awful phantom that seized our hearts in the allegro threatens at every moment to emerge from the storm cloud into which it disappeared, so that the comforting figures around us rapidly flee from its sight.

[Third movement]

{652} The minuet[16] following the andante is again as original and as captivating to the soul as one would expect from this composer in the movement that, according to the Haydn pattern which he followed, should be the most piquant and witty of all. The distinctive modulations; the closes on the dominant major, its root [*Grundton*] becoming the tonic of the following bass theme in the minor mode [bb. 45–6, 96–7]; this theme itself, repeatedly extended by a few bars at a time [see Example 16]: it is particularly these features that express so strongly the

16   [Schnapp:] This description of the third movement, headed only allegro by Beethoven, seems strange and is doubtless merely a term of expedience. <A concert report in the *Vossische Zeitung*, 70 (12 June 1819), for example, mentions 'the very difficult minuet of Beethoven's *Sinfonia Eroica*'.>. It is quite clear from his analysis that Hoffmann was not thinking of a minuet in the proper sense. [*E. T. A. Hoffmann: Schriften zur Musik: Nachlese* (Munich: Winkler, 1963, 2/1978), p. 39. <> = not in 1st edn]

character of Beethoven's music described above, and arouse once more those disquieting presentiments of a magical spirit world with which the subject materials [*Sätze*] of the allegro assailed the listener's heart. The theme in C minor, played by cellos and basses alone, turns in the third bar towards G minor; the horns then sustain the G while violins and violas, together with bassoons in the second bar and clarinets in the third, have a four-bar phrase cadencing on G [bb. 5–8]. Cellos and basses repeat the theme but after the third bar in G minor it turns towards D minor, then C minor, and the violin phrase is repeated [bb. 15–18]. Now, while the strings provide chords on the first crotchet of each bar, the horns play a subject that leads into Eb major [b. 19]. The orchestra takes it into Eb minor and closes on the dominant Bb major [bb. 27–45]; in the same bar the {653} cellos and basses take up the main theme again just as in the opening in C minor, but now in Bb minor. The violins etc. also repeat their phrase [bb. 49–52], and there follows a pause on F major. Cellos and basses repeat the theme [b. 52] but extend it by passing though F minor, C minor, G minor and then returning to C minor [bb. 52–71], whereupon the tutti that first occurred in Eb minor takes the music through F minor to a chord of C major [bb. 71–97]. Just as they previously moved from Bb major to Bb minor, the cellos and basses now take up the root C as the tonic of the C minor theme. Flutes and oboes [bb. 101ff], imitated in the second bar by clarinets, now have the phrase previously played by the strings, while the latter repeat a bar from the above-mentioned tutti. The horns have a sustained G, and the cellos begin a new theme [bb. 101ff] to which is added first a further elaboration [*Ausführung*] of the opening violin phrase [*Anfangssatz der Violinen*; bb. 109–14] and then a new subject in quavers [bb. 114–30] (which have not been heard up to this point). Even the new cello theme contains allusions to the main subject and is thereby closely related to it, as well as by having the same rhythm. After a short repetition of the earlier tutti the minuet section closes in C minor *fortissimo* with timpani and trumpets [bb. 133–40].

Cellos and basses begin section II (the trio) with a theme in C major [b. 140] that is imitated by the violas [and bassoons] fugally at the dominant [b. 146], then by the second violins in an abbreviated form [b. 152], and then by the first violins [b. 154], similarly in stretto [*Restriktion*]. The first half of this section closes in G major. In the second half cellos and basses start the theme twice [bb. 161, 163] but stop again, and only at the third attempt do they keep going [bb. 165ff]. This may strike many people as amusing, but in the reviewer it produced an uneasy feeling. After several imitations of the main theme it is taken up by the flutes [b. 181], supported by oboes, clarinets, and bassoons above a pedal [*Grundton*] G from the horns.[17] It dies away in single notes, first from clarinet and bassoon [bb. 228–30],[18] then from cellos and basses [bb. 231–5]. {654} The theme of section I is repeated by cellos and basses [b. 235] but instead of violins, wind instruments now have the phrase in short notes [bb. 241–4], ending with a pause. After this, as in section I, comes the extended main subject [bb. 244–54], but with crotchets and crotchet

17 [Charlton:] bb. 217ff: Hoffmann's description omits the second statement of the trio material in bb. 197ff.
18 'clarinets and bassoons'.

rests in place of the minims.[19] The other elements of section I, mostly abbreviated, also return in this form [bb. 255–323].

The restless yearning inherent in the theme now reaches a level of unease that so constricts the breast that only odd fragmented sounds escape it. A G major chord [b. 323] seems to be leading to a close, but cellos and basses sustain a *pianissimo* A♭ pedal for fifteen bars [bb. 324–38], the violins and violas likewise the C a third above, while the kettledrum plays the C first in the rhythm of the often-mentioned tutti, then once a bar for four bars, then twice for four bars, then on every beat. The first violins finally take up the opening theme and continue for twenty-eight bars [bb. 339–66] with repeated allusions to it, ending on the dominant seventh of the home key. In the meantime the second violins and violas have been sustaining the C, the kettledrum its C in crotchets, and cellos and basses their pedal G likewise, after moving down the scale from A♭ to F♯ and back to A♭ [bb. 341–8]. Now the bassoons come in [b. 366], then one bar later the oboes, then three bars later flutes, horns and trumpets, while the kettledrum plays its C in continuous quavers. This leads straight into the C major chord with which the final allegro begins. Why Beethoven continued the kettledrum C to the end despite its dissonance with the chord is explained by the character he was striving to give the whole work. These heavy, dissonant blows, sounding like a strange and dreadful voice, arouse a horror of the extraordinary, of ghostly fear. The reviewer has previously mentioned the intensifying effect {655} extending a theme by a few bars, and in order to make this clearer he illustrates these extensions together [bb. 1–4, 8–18, 44–8, 52–63]:

Example 16

When section I is repeated this phrase appears in the following form [bb. 244–52]:

---

19   [Charlton:] It is noteworthy that Hoffmann omits mention of *pizzicato* in the strings at bb. 231 and 244; he does not comment on the awkward extra two bars originally printed in error after b. 237, and pointed out by Beethoven to the publisher in 1810.

Example 17

Just as simple and yet, when it is glimpsed behind later passages, just as potent as the theme of the opening allegro is the idea of the minuet's first tutti [bb. 27–8]:

Example 18

[Fourth movement]

With the splendid, exultant theme of the final movement in C major we hear the full orchestra, with piccolo,[20] trombones and contrabassoon now added, like a brilliant shaft of blinding sunlight suddenly penetrating the darkness of night. The subjects of this allegro are more broadly treated than the preceding ones, being not so much melodious as forceful and susceptible to contrapuntal imitation. The modulations are unaffected and clear. Section I particularly has almost the energy of an overture. It continues for thirty-four bars in C major as a tutti for the full orchestra. Then against a strong, rising figure in the bass a new theme [bb. 28–41] in the leading voice modulates to G major and leads to the dominant chord {656} of this key. Now another theme enters [b. 44] consisting of crotchets and triplets; in rhythm and character it is quite different from the previous ones, pressing urgently forward like the subjects of the first allegro and the minuet [bb. 44–9]:

Example 19

With this theme and its further development through A minor to C major, the spirit returns to the mood of foreboding which temporarily receded amid the joy and jubilation. A short, furious tutti [bb. 58–63] again takes the music towards G major and violas, bassoons and clarinets begin a theme in sixths [bb. 64ff] that is subsequently played by the whole orchestra [bb. 72ff]. After a brief modulation into F minor with an energetic figure in [contrabassoon, cellos and] basses [bb. 80–81], taken up by the violins in C major and then by the bass again *al rovescio* [b. 84],[21] section I closes in C major.

This figure is retained at the beginning of section II in A minor [bb. 86–9],[22] and the earlier characteristic theme consisting of crotchets and triplets is heard again

20 'piccolos'.   21 Contrabassoon, cellos and double basses play the figure in inversion.
22 [Charlton:] i.e. on a chord of E major, its dominant.

[bb. 90–99]. This theme is now developed [*durchgeführt*] for thirty-four bars [bb. 99–132], in abbreviated and stretto configurations, and during this development the character already apparent in its original guise fully emerges [*entwickelt*], owing in no small measure to the interspersed secondary phrases, the sustained notes from the trombones, and the off-beat triplets from the timpani, trumpets and horns. It finally comes to rest on a pedal [*Orgelpunkt*] G played first by [cellos and] basses [with contrabassoon] [bb. 132–44] and then, when they join the violins in a closing unison figure, by the bass trombone, trumpets, horns and timpani [bb. 144–53]. The simple theme of the minuet

Example 20

now returns for fifty-four bars [bb. 153–206], in the last two of which {657} the transition from the minuet to the allegro is repeated in a condensed form.

With a few minor differences and remaining in the principal key [*Haupttonart*], the material of section I is recapitulated [bb. 207–94], and a furious tutti seems to be leading to a close [bb. 302–17]. After the dominant chord, however, bassoons, horns, first flute, first clarinet, first bassoon, first oboe and piccolo[23] successively take up a theme that has previously only been touched upon [bb. 317–27]:

Example 21

There follows another closing passage [*Schlußsatz*; bb. 327–34], but this time the phrase is taken up by the strings, then by piccolo, oboe and horns,[24] then by violins [bb. 334–43]. Again the music moves towards a close [bb. 344–62], but with the final chord on the tonic the violins (after a *più stretto* a few bars earlier) launch *presto* into the phrase heard in the sixty-fourth bar of the allegro, while the bass figure is the same as that in b. 28 of the first movement allegro, which vividly recalls the main theme, as has been noted above, by virtue of its close rhythmic relationship to it. With the opening theme of the final allegro [bb. 390ff] (the [contrabassoon, cellos and] basses enter one bar later canonically imitating the upper parts) the whole orchestra approaches the close, which is drawn out by a series of brilliant figures and comes forty-one bars later [bb. 405–44]. The final chords themselves are oddly placed. The chord that the listener takes as the last is followed by one bar's rest, then the same chord, one bar's rest, the same chord again, one bar's rest, then the chord again for three bars with one crotchet in each, one bar's rest, the chord, one bar's rest, and a C played in unison by the whole orchestra. The perfect composure of spirit engendered by the succession of closing figures is

23 'bassoons, horns, flutes, oboes, and clarinets'.   24 'oboes, clarinets and horns'.

destroyed again by these detached chords and rests, which recall the separate strokes in the symphony's Allegro and place {658} the listener once more in a state of tension.[25] They act like a fire that is thought to have been put out but repeatedly bursts forth again in bright tongues of flame.

Beethoven has preserved the conventional order of movements in this symphony. They seem to follow a continuous fantastic sequence, and the whole work will sweep past many like an inspired rhapsody. The heart of every sensitive listener, however, is certain to be deeply stirred and held until the very last chord by *one* lasting emotion, that of nameless, haunted yearning. Indeed for many moments after it he will be unable to emerge from the magical spirit realm where he has been surrounded by pain and pleasure in the form of sounds. As well as the internal disposition of orchestration, etc., it is particularly the close relationship of the individual themes to each other which provides the unity that is able to sustain *one* feeling in the listener's heart. In the music of Haydn and Mozart this unity prevails everywhere. It becomes clearer to the musician when he discovers the bass pattern that is common to two different passages,[26] or when the similarity between two passages makes it apparent. But often a deeper relationship that is not demonstrable in this way speaks only from the heart to the heart,[27] and it is this relationship that exists between the subjects of the two allegros and the minuet, and that brilliantly proclaims the composer's rational genius. The reviewer believes he can summarize his judgment of this composer's splendid work in a few words, by saying that it is conceived of genius and executed with profound awareness, and that it expresses the romanticism of music to a very high degree.

No instrument has difficult music to perform, but only an extremely reliable, {659} well-trained orchestra animated by a *single* spirit can attempt this symphony; the least lapse in any detail would irredeemably spoil the whole work. The constant alternation, the interlocking of string and wind instruments, the single chords separated by rests, and suchlike, demand the utmost precision. It is therefore also advisable for the conductor not so much to play with the first violins more strongly than is desirable, which often happens, as to keep the orchestra constantly under his eye and hand. The way the first violin part is printed, showing the entries of the obbligato instruments, is useful for this purpose.

The engraving is correct and clear. From the same publisher this symphony has appeared for piano duet under the title: *Cinquième Sinfonie de Louis van Beethoven, arrangée pour le Pianoforte à quatre mains. Chez Breitkopf et Härtel à Leipsic (Pr. 2Rthlr. 12 Gr.).*[28] Normally the reviewer is not especially in favour

25 [Charlton:] Here Hoffmann appears to recall the first movement progression at bb. 196ff, which had an 'ominous, eerie effect'; also his summing-up of the first movement refers to the 'constant repetition of short phrases and single chords' that characterized the whole allegro.

26 [Charlton:] *Sätze*: Hoffmann could mean a unit as small as a phrase or as large as a complete movement.

27 [Charlton:] A common phrase of the period: see, e.g., the superscription to Beethoven's *Missa Solemnis*: 'Von Herzen – Möge es wieder – zu Herzen gehen!'. See 'Casual Reflections on the Appearance of this Journal', *E. T. A. Hoffmann's Musical Writings*, p. 428.

28 [Charlton:] The duet arrangement was by Friedrich Schneider, and appeared in July 1809, according to G. Kinsky and H. Halm, *Das Werk Beethovens: thematisch-bibliographisches Verzeichnis . . .* (Munich: Henle, 1955), p. 160.

of arrangements, but it cannot be denied that the solitary enjoyment in one's own room of a masterpiece one has heard played by the full orchestra often excites the imagination in the same way as before and conjures forth the same impressions in the mind. The piano reproduces a great work as a sketch reproduces a great painting, and the imagination brings it to life with the colours of the original. At any rate the symphony has been adapted for the piano with skill and insight, and proper regard has been paid to the requirements of the instrument without obscuring the distinctive qualities of the original.

Robert Schumann (1810–1856)

'[Review of Berlioz: *Fantastic* Symphony]' (1835)

'To attempt a closer analysis of [the *Fantastic* Symphony of Berlioz], to dissect the underlying ideas, thoroughly poetic as they are, and the final articulated form in all its perfection – truly this would be as vain a pursuit as to analyse the "Eroica" Symphony of Beethoven'. This remark, printed in Robert Schumann's *Neue Zeitschrift für Musik* on 22 December 1834,[1] is full of contradictions and ironies.

For a start, the first person to publish a close analysis of the 'Eroica', only three years later, was none other than Hector Berlioz;[2] and the first to do likewise for the *Fantastic* Symphony a year later was Schumann. Moreover, the term *Zergliederung* ('dissect' here is *Zergliederung geben*), is the very word that Schumann himself was to use with such ironic effect in his own review by allusion to Berlioz's earlier studies in anatomy when a medical student (see the Introduction to Part I of vol. I for an extended discussion of terms related to dissection as components of music-analytic language).

To take this remark at face value, however, would be unwise since it is a translation from French: the original was an unsigned concert report in the *Gazette musicale de Paris* of 9 November 1834. To compare the French with the German is to show how languages reflect their own cultural values as much as they do any common body of meaning. Thus our 'to dissect' should really be 'to examine analytically' (*faire un examen analytique*); and our 'would be as vain a pursuit as' (*wäre eben so vergebliche Sache als*) is a conflation of 'would be superfluous' and 'is as impossible as' (*serait superflu . . . est une chose aussi impossible que*). That is to say, the German subtly distorts the original, forcing it into Germanic terms, and making it materially less precise. How interesting, too, especially in the light of our earlier discussion of 'grandiosity' (vol. I, Introduction to Analysis 14), that where the French speaks of Berlioz's instrumentation as 'new, original and grandiose', the German, blind to the third attribute, calls it 'new and original'!

But we must not dwell on this linguistic sideshow, fascinating as it is. In one sense, the tiny, 300-word notice from 1834 in its *Neue Zeitschrift* form is a microcosm of Schumann's monumental critique of 1835 – the analysis given below. Both use a play of personae: a sober, judicious voice answering an ardent hothead. In the critique it is the voice of Schumann (Part II) answering that of Florestan (Part I). In the notice it is a 'calm German' ('Much of this "fantasy" looks rather

---

1 (1834), no. 76 (22 December), 306 (unsigned); reprinted from 'Concert de M Berlioz', *Gazette musicale de Paris*, I (1834), no. 45 (9 November), 368–9 (unsigned), esp. 369.
2 [*Revue et*] *gazette musicale de Paris*, 4 (1837), no. 15 (9 April), 121–3; *A travers chants* (Paris: Lévy, 1862), pp. 20–26.

confused, a bit like a puzzle that the listeners are incapable of guessing; but often the composer is comprehensible, even delectably so'), answering an 'enthusiastic review[er]' ('Anyone who wants to hear a sublime, truly poetic composition, full of originality [. . .] had better hurry along to hear this symphony').

Schumann's review of 1835, then, comprises Part I signed 'Florestan' (one of Schumann's critical *noms de plume*), and Part II signed 'R. Schumann'. Part II was issued in five instalments (thus there were six in all). At the same time, Part II falls systematically into four sections that partly cut across its five instalments; and these four sections comprise Schumann's fourfold 'agenda' for examination of the work (on analytical agendas, see vol. I, General Introduction §3): (1) form, (2) techniques of composition, (3) idea and (4) governing spirit. At the end of the fifth instalment – and the end of 'item' (2) – Schumann reviews this agenda and reflects on his progress before moving on to (3) and (4). In the translation given below, not only have the instalment breaks been preserved, but also editorial headings have been provided so as to emphasize the internal structure of the review, and also to show the interplay between outer structure (which is partly a product of publishing convenience, but has a logic of its own) and inner structure.

The review is too widely known to warrant detailed introduction here, and excellent discussions by Plantinga and Cone are available.[3] Suffice to say that Schumann was struck by the 'contradiction' between Fétis's disparaging review of Liszt's piano transcription of the *Fantastic* Symphony, published in Paris on 1 February 1835,[4] and an enthusiastic report 'On Berlioz and his Music' sent to him from Paris by Heinrich Panofka (a regular writer for the *Gazette musicale*) only twelve days later. Schumann published the latter on 27 February and 3 March in the *Neue Zeitschrift*, and then a translation of the former on 19 and 23 June. In the meanwhile, he wrote to Paris for a copy of the Liszt transcription, so that he could assess it for himself. He was so impressed by Liszt's translation of orchestral sonority into piano terms that he promised a discussion of it in its own right at a later date.[5]

The original Berlioz work itself called forth in him a veritable starburst of a response. It was in part a ricochet from Fétis's disparagement. Thus Schumann set up the whole of 'item' (2) of his agenda (techniques of composition) as an illustrated rebuttal of Fétis's comment 'I saw that he completely lacked melodic and harmonic ideas', which Schumann considered 'sheer blindness, a complete lack of feeling for this kind of music'. On the contrary, contended Schumann, Berlioz's harmony has a certain simplicity, and those chords that are odd or vague can be reduced analytically to normal ones; his irregular phrases are the exception not the rule;

3 Leon B. Plantinga, *Schumann as Critic* (New Haven and London: Yale University Press, 1967), pp. 235–50; *Berlioz: Fantastic Symphony* . . ., Norton Critical Score, ed. Edward T. Cone (New York and London: Norton, 1971), pp. 220–48 (with excellent translation), pp. 249–77 ('Schumann Amplified: An Analysis').

4 A translation of Fétis's review is given in *Berlioz: Fantastic Symphony* . . ., ed. Cone, pp. 215–20. The original appeared in *Revue musicale*, 9 (1835), no. 5 (1 February), 33–5.

5 These assertions appeared in the first column of the translation of Fétis's review, NZM, 2 (1835), no. 49 (19 June), 197–8; no. 50 (23 June), 201–02; the translation of Panofka's article in ibid, no. 17 (27 February), 67–9, and no. 18 (3 March), 71–2.

his melodies exhibit 'stylish and intricate craftsmanship', 'finesse', they are 'idiomatic and true to nature', they are like folksongs in that they lose their bloom when set to harmonies; his contrapuntal treatment is 'masterly', his double fugue is 'of orthodox design and clear construction'.

But Schumann did not give himself up to the *Fantastic* Symphony open-heartedly, as he had done to Chopin's *Là ci darem la mano* Variations Op. 2 in his famous youthful review of 1831. His opinion was already in 1836 a more mediated and conditional one. He admitted that at one point the accompaniment of the *Dies irae* is 'as crass and frivolous as could be', and that 'the only word for the final pages is "bad"'. Remarkably few of his adverse statements, however, are given as outright condemnations: almost all are either immediately justified (Berlioz's phrase structure is not immediately clear, *but* it eventually makes sense; consequent seldom matches antecedent, *but* both have a primitive, incorrigible rightness), or offered strategically as minor concessions before he launches a ringing counterattack.

Schumann found himself in the odd position of defending a very French composer against a French-speaking Belgian critic (Fétis) and yet at the same time judging that composer by German standards. His justifications thus were: that Berlioz is the natural symphonic heir to Beethoven; that he conforms to the standards established by Goethe and Mozart; but that his genius permits contravention of those standards; and that he is returning to a desirably more primitive state of art. And yet, if his opinion in 1836 was already conditional, then less than twenty years later, when Schumann came to edit this analysis for his collected writings, he made extensive modifications to his review, all of which distance him further from the work in subtle ways.

These modifications have (with the exception of minor and orthographical alterations such as *Sinfonie* for *Symphonie* and *kontrapunktiert* for *contrapunctirt*) been systematically traced in the footnotes. They are in themselves material for a fascinating critical study. Schumann softened some of the Germanness, for example, by excising altogether his paean to Goethe and Mozart and 'godlike effortlessness', and by changing a reference to the 'youth of Germany' to the 'artist of Germany'.

He seems to have felt that much of the original review was extravagant. He therefore excised the whole of Part I and the first three paragraphs of Part II. The wonderful reference to Scottish castles in the first instalment of Part II was removed, as was the cautionary tale from Odillon de Barrot near the end; and he seems to have thought the reference to 'a Bacchanalian night spent carousing in the company of handsome youths' tasteless.

But most tellingly, he tempered such enthusiasm as he had expressed over Berlioz, leaving the analysis much more reserved. Thus the way in which Berlioz counterpoints the *idée fixe* in the fourth movement is no longer 'like a master' (*wie ein Meister*), but merely 'very beautiful' (*sehr schön*). Thus in 'one cannot help admiring the spiritual coherence' of the work as a whole, 'admiring' is damped down to 'acknowledging'. Above all, he moderated his attack on Fétis of the passage:

> Let [Fétis] deny Berlioz everything, as he has done: creative imagination, power of invention, originality. But wealth of melody and harmony? – *Berlioz surely has nothing to answer for in those departments!*

The italicized clause (my italics) is excised, thus leaving the entire rebuttal equivocal. A paragraph later, Schumann quotes a waggish *bon mot* about Berlioz, then counters it with a quotation from D'Ortigue. For the collected writings he excised all reference to D'Ortigue, leaving the waggish remark hanging in the air, and giving a completely different thrust to the sentence that follows. Again, where Fétis asserts that the second movement theme is common and trivial, Schumann relegated his own sarcastic rebuttal (that ordinary people fail to see the great artist towering high above them in the clouds) to a footnote. Earlier, where Schumann had originally quoted Ernst Wagner at great length predicting a new era in which music was to be freed from the tyranny of beat, and capped the quotation with: 'Could it be Berlioz's Symphony that ushers this moment in?' (the final punch line of the second instalment), he cut all but the last few words of the quotation, and excised altogether the (admittedly non-committal) rhetorical question.

The reader may enjoy pursuing these modifications through the footnotes. They are presented here for the first time in an accessible way, as too is another component of Schumann's review that has been neglected hitherto. The banner of each *Neue Zeitschrift* issue sported a short quotation. That it was often related to the lead article can be shown from those above the Panofka report:

> There I got to know a young musician: his
> name is Berlioz, and he looks like a genius.
>   Börne.[6]

and the Fétis review:

> The has-been took to hating
> All new brooms aggravatious,
> The latter to deprecating
> All sweepers antiquatious.
>   *West-östlicher Divan*.[7]

The quotations for the six instalments of Schumann's review clearly relate to the content of that review: Goethe's paean to *Phantasie*, St Paul's ringing affirmation of the passing of the old and the coming of the new, Schiller's celebration of the exceptional man, Thibaut's defence of surface roughness in art of genius – in itself a wonderful counter to Fétis –, Heinse on the freedom of action of the genius, and Beethoven on Nature and art. (All of these were automatically excluded from the collected writings.)

Consider only the fourth instalment. Not by chance do Thibaut's words stand at the head of Schumann's intricate argument concerning Berlioz's harmonies. Schumann feints, parries, then delivers occasional stinging blows. He concedes certain irregularities, only to argue an essential simplicity and aphoristic harmonic quality, and an underlying logic to tonal structure. Pursuing Fétis's charge that Berlioz's 'harmony, composed of piling up tones into heaps that were often monstrous,

---

6 Ludwig Börne (1786–1837), German critic, feuilletonist and political writer: *Börnes Werke in zwei Bänden* (Berlin and Weimar: Aufbau-Verlag, 1964), where the quotation has so far eluded me.

7 *West-östlicher Divan* (1819), by Goethe, is a collection of exquisite poems that aim to bring together the characters of Oriental (particularly Persian) and Western poetry. I hope the reader will forgive my tongue-in-cheek rendering: 'Das Gewes'ne wollte hassen / Solche rüstige neue Besen, / Diese dann nicht gelten lassen, / Was sonst Besen war gewesen.'

was nevertheless flat and monotonous', he first admits crudenesses, concedes faults 'forbidden by the old rules', 'tortured, distorted' sounds; furnishes long lists of offending passages that seem to play Fétis's learned game and build an impregnable case; then appears to capitulate – 'May the time never come when such passages as these are sanctioned as beautiful' – only brilliantly to turn the argument round on itself: try altering his harmonies to fit the rules, he says with some sarcasm, and they immediately lose their lustre, become insipid. Then, echoing Thibaut, he delivers the coup-de-grâce: 'Somewhat coarse though it may still be in its outward expression, it is the more powerful in its effect the less we seek to tame it with critical carpings'.

Schumann's musical citations are all to page, system and bar number in Liszt's piano transcription (what an extraordinary phenomenon: a review of an orchestral work through the medium of a piano transcription!). In the translation below these have been converted into bar numbers of the Norton Critical Score. However, the Liszt citations have been preserved alongside them for anyone who wishes to read the analysis against its authentic musical object: thus 'bb. 280–92/p. 14, s. 4, bb. 6–18' means 'bars 280–92 of the orchestral score, or page 14, system 4, bars 6–18 of the Liszt transcription, first edition'. (Be warned, the references do not work for the second edition!)

One liberty has been taken with the original text. Schumann made extensive use of footnotes, some with music examples. In order to avoid sinking these among a welter of editorial footnotes, and in the interests of practicability, all of the footnotes in the *Neue Zeitschrift* review have been brought into the main text, complete with their examples. For identification, they are surrounded by angle brackets.

Are Schumann's extensive use of footnotes and his deployment of what we earlier called an 'analytical agenda' deliberate contrivances? They certainly give the critique an extravagant, almost manneristic appearance. Was he, with both of these devices, adopting a weighty apparatus to suit what he anticipated as a Herculean task? Or was he poking gentle fun at self-important commentators by sporting the garb of the learned scholar? – Was he especially, with his footnotes, silently enjoying the typographical irony of pages of his journal with more below the line, in small type, highly abbreviated and with music examples, than above? So many-layered is his thought in this review, so clearly tinged is it with self-deprecation, so full of irony, that it is hard to tell.

[Review of Berlioz: *Fantastic* Symphony]

Source:
Robert Schumann: [Review of Berlioz: *Fantastic* Symphony], NZM, 3 (1835), no. 1
(3 July), 1–2, no. 9 (31 July), 33–5, no. 10 (4 August), 37–8, no. 11 (7 August),
41–4, no. 12 (11 August), 45–8, no. 13 (14 August), 49–51.

> {1} To which of the immortals
> Shall the highest praise be given?
> I will quarrel with no one.–
> But I would give it
> To the ever-changing,
> Eternally-new,
> Wondrous daughter of Jove,
> To his best-beloved offspring,
> To *fantasy.*
>
> Goethe[8]

{1a}'From the Life of an Artist': Fantastic Symphony in Five Movements,[9] by
Hector Berlioz

I[10]

Let us enter the battle not with savage cry, as did our ancient German forebears,
but with the merry sound of flutes ringing in our ears, as did the Spartans. In all
truth, he to whom these lines are dedicated needs no shield bearer, and we hope to
see him become the reverse of Homerian Hector, and finally drag the ravaged city
of Troy from ancient times victoriously behind as his prisoner[11] – but if his art is
the flaming sword, then let this word be its trusty scabbard.

A wondrous feeling came over me as I cast my first glance at the Symphony. As
a child, I had often laid pieces of music upside down on my desk so as to delight
myself (as later I did with the palaces of Venice, inverted in the water) with the
strangely intricate structures formed by the note shapes. This Symphony, when
viewed upright, looks rather like such upside-down music. Thereupon other scenes
from his earliest childhood came crowding in upon the writer of these lines: for

---

8 Each of the six quotations which stand at the head of the six parts of this review is actually the
   last element of the banner for the issue of the journal containing that part. Since each part of the
   review is the lead article of its issue, and since the quotations seem to have been selected (presumably by Schumann) as appropriate to the lead article, all six have been included in this translation.
   The first quotation is stanza 1 of the ten-stanza poem *Meine Göttin*, from the 'Vermischte
   Gedichte'. The orthography does not precisely correspond with any of the editions that I have consulted. Most significantly, the emphasizing of *Phantasie* appears to be Schumann's own. See *Goethes
   poetische Werke: Vollständige Ausgabe*, vol. I, *Gedichte* (Stuttgart: Cotta, n.d.), pp. 305–08.
9 Schumann uses *Abtheilungen*, not *Sätze*, in all cases except one (noted in the text).
10 [Schumann:] A second critique will appear shortly (Editor). [Bent:] Schumann excised section I
   entire, and the first three paragraphs (of translation) of section II, from the text of this analysis,
   when preparing his *Gesammelte Schriften* [henceforth: GS] in 1852–3. The subsequent editor of
   the latter, F. Gustav Jansen, restored the missing material, but to an appendix rather than to the
   body of the review: see *Gesammelte Schriften über Musik und Musiker von Robert Schumann*,
   ed. Martin Kreisig (Leipzig: B&H, 5/1949), vol. II, pp. 212–16.
11 Homer's Hector was killed by Achilles before the walls of Troy, and dragged behind the Greek
   horses for days before being returned to King Priam for burial: *The Iliad*, books 22–4.

example, as when once, in the wee small hours, while the household lay fast asleep, he sleep-walked with eyes shut to his old, now broken-down piano {1b} and struck chords, weeping mightily over them. When he was told of this the following morning he remembered only a dream with curious sounds, and many strange things that he heard and saw, and he could make out clearly three mighty names, one to the south, one to the east and the last to the west – Paganini, Chopin, Berlioz.

The first two of these made their way with the strength and swiftness of an eagle. Their task was easier, for in their personalities both combined poet and actor. With Berlioz, the virtuoso of the orchestra, the task will be more difficult, the fight more rugged; and yet the rewards of victory may perhaps be the fuller. Let us hasten the moment of decision! Times are ever turbulent with strife; to future generations be left the judgment as to whether they advance or retreat, whether for good or evil. No one has yet been able to predict the latter for me from our present vantage point with any certainty.

Having gone through Berlioz's Symphony time and time again, at first in perplexity, then in shock, and finally with astonishment and admiration, I will attempt to rough it out for my reader in rapid brush strokes. I will depict the composer as I have come to be acquainted with him, his weaknesses along with his virtues, in uncouth as in high-minded moments, in violent, destructive rage as well as in tenderness. For I know that what he has given us cannot be called a work of art, any more than can the world of nature without the refining power of the human hand, or {2a} passion without the restraining force of loftier moral principle.

If character and talent, religion and art ennobled each other mutually in the aged Haydn; if in Mozart, the prototypical artist's nature evolved autonomously alongside the sensual being; where in the case of other poetically minded spirits, external pattern of behaviour and artistic creativity proceeded in diametrically opposed directions (as was the case with, for example, the dissolute poet Heydenreich, who could write the most heart-rending poem against debauchery);[12] then Berlioz belongs more with those Beethovenian characters whose artistic development conforms exactly to the course of their lives, such that for each fresh impetus in the former a corresponding new phase is initiated in the latter, to die in due course. Like Laocoön's snake,[13] music has entwined herself around Berlioz's feet. Without her he cannot take a single step. Thus he wrestles with her in the dust; thus she drinks with him from the sun. Even were he to throw her off he would

---

12 Karl Heinrich Heydenreich (1764–1801), a Professor Ordinary of Philosophy at Leipzig University whose voluntary retirement was perhaps connected with his addiction to opium and possibly also alcohol, and who died at the age of thirty-eight (K. G. Schelle, *Karl Heinrich Heydenreichs Charakteristik als Menschen und Schriftsteller* (Leipzig: Martini, 1802), p. 101; *Gedichte von Karl Heinrich Heydenreich*, vol. II, ed. A. H. Heydenreich (Leipzig: Baumgartner, 1802), p. xxii). The poem against debauchery is *Die Wollust* (ibid, p. 126); in the course of twenty-two stanzas, he shows first a young stripling, and then the father of a family destroyed by insidious lust, and concludes with a vision of the diseased human race in decay, mocked at by apes and 'pygmies'. See excerpt from his *System der Aesthetik* (1790) in le Huray/Day, 230–33.

13 The Laocoön Group: Hellenistic statue (first-century AD copy, Vatican Museum) depicting the Trojan priest Laocoön and his two sons in death agonies, two sea serpents coiled around their limbs (Virgil, *Aeneid*, book 2, vs 199ff). This was considered by the German Hellenists of the late eighteenth century as the greatest sculpture of classical Greece, and was the focus of aesthetic debate, discussed in long essays by Winckelmann and Lessing, also by Herder, Goethe, Schiller, Heinse, Hegel and others.

still have to express that act in musical terms, and were he to die his spirit would perhaps dissolve into that kind of music that we often hear drifting on the distant horizon at that quiet hour when the God Pan sleeps – the noontide hour.[14]

Such a musical being as this, barely nineteen years of age, of French blood, bursting with energy, and what's more locked in battle with the future and perhaps also with violent emotions of other sorts, is seized for the first time by the God of Love. But this is no bashful stirring of emotion, the sort that is happiest confiding to the moon; rather, it is that dark glow seen erupting from Mount Etna at night. . . . *That is where he sets eyes on her.* I imagine this feminine creature, like the principal idea of the entire Symphony, to be pale, slender as a lily, veiled, silent, almost cold; –but words are lifeless things, whereas his notes have a searing effect upon us, – you can see it written in the Symphony itself: how he rushes towards her and tries to embrace her with all his heart, how he shrinks back, his breath taken away by the iciness of that British woman;[15] and how he submissively once again goes to carry the hem of her train and kiss it, and then proudly straightens up and *demands* love – loves her so monstrously; – see it written: all of this is written in drops of blood in the first movement.

It's true that first love can render the most cowardly of men intrepid, but, on the other hand, Jean Paul tells us that 'a heroine steals the limelight from a hero'.[16] Sooner or later, passionate young men, when their love remains unrequited, cast aside their platonic guise and make countless sacrifices at epicurean altars. But there is none of the Don Juan in Berlioz's nature. He sits, eyes glazed, among his wild companions; at every pop of the champagne cork a string snaps within him! As if overcome by fever, he sees the dear familiar figure loom up before him from the wall and sink down suffocatingly upon his breast. He thrusts her away, and {2b} with shrill laughter a harlot throws herself on to his lap asking him what is lacking.

O spirit of art, you come to the rescue of your favourite, and he well understands the smile that quivers on your lips. What music the third movement contains! What intimacy, what contrition, what warmth! The image of Nature recovering her composure after the onslaught of a storm is an oft-used one, but I know of none more fitting nor more beautiful. The whole of creation still trembles from heaven's embrace, and weeps as from more than a thousand eyes; and the bashful flowers whisper together about the strange visitor who casts his gaze thunderously about him from time to time.

At this point anyone seeking the right to bear the name 'artist' would have called it a day and celebrated the triumph of art over life. But *you*, but *you*![17] Tasso finished

14   'that . . . noontide hour': *Pans- oder Mittagsstunde*: 'Die Stunde des Pans', referring to Pan's habit of sleeping at noon, occurs in German literature from the eighteenth century (K.Spalding, *An Historical Dictionary of German Figurative Usage*, fascs 31–40 (Oxford: Blackwell, 1934), pp. 1825–6).
15   *Brittin*: the reference is presumably to Harriet Smithson, the Shakespearean actress whom Berlioz first encountered in 1827, pursued and ultimately married, and the infatuation for whom he expressed in the *Fantastic* Symphony. [Jansen/Kreisig:] Berlioz's beloved was the English actress Harriet Smitson [*sic*].
16   Jean Paul Friedrich Richter (1763–1825), German poet and novelist, author of *Titan* (1800–03), and *Flegeljahre* (1804–05) and many other works. I have been unable to locate Schumann's quotation.
17   'Aber *Sie*, aber *Sie*!': GS has 'Aber *sie*, aber *sie*!' ('But *she*, [or: *it*; or: *they*] . . .').

up in the madhouse for it.[18] But in Berlioz, the old destructive rage wells up with redoubled force, and he strikes at everything in sight with the veritable fists of the Titans; and as he deludes himself that he possesses his beloved and warmly grasps the automaton-like figure,[19] the music also encloses his dreams and his attempted suicide in an embrace hateful and crude. The bells toll for that, and skeletons at the organ strike up the wedding dance. . . . At this point, the spirit [of art] turns away from him weeping.

Yet, at times it was as if I could hear in this same movement reminiscences, terribly soft ones, of that poem of Franz von Sonnenberg,[20] whose underlying tenor this entire Symphony shares:

> *Thou art!* – and art the ardently yearned-for heart,
> So fervently yearned-for at the silent midnight hour
> . . . . . .
> *'Tis thou* who once with sweet shudders, lying on my bosom
> In deep lingering silence, with tremulous
> Broken sighs, in confusion, whispered
> To my heart with lovely maidenly blushes:
> 'I am the sigh that ever cruelly constricted
> Thy heart and raised it once more to the world'
> . . . . . .
> 'Thy very first cry unknowingly summoned me:
> In that wild, blazing glow of devotion,
> Within thee, 'twas I whose hands
> Thou enfolded . . . .
> In every *I*, whereafter thou in life only
> Thrust the arms asunder with high breast.'
> . . . . . .
> Thou wert, thou art, the great unnameable,
> After whom in the twilight hour my heart heaves,
> Heaves, oh how voluptuously I tremble
> To press the whole of mankind to me.
> . . . . . .
> To seize one another – second immortality!
> The thrill of delight of all nature in me!
> The moment, Herkla, when
> Quivering and silent we at last embrace one another!
>
> Florestan

(to be continued)

---

18 Torquato Tasso (1544–95) was tormented by the criticisms of his epic poem *Gerusalemme liberata* (1575), in which he had striven to achieve a balance between historical truth and artistic invention, and was as a result incarcerated in the hospital of S. Anna between 1579 and 1586.

19 *Automatenfigur*: in the early nineteenth century this would presumably designate a mechanical doll or figure (see *Allgemeines Englisch-Deutsches und Deutsch-Englisches Wörterbuch*, vol. II (Brunswick: Westermann, 4/1891), p. 159: 'automaton figures'); but Schumann is perhaps referring to the musical figure, the *idée fixe*.

20 Freiherr Franz Anton von Sonnenberg (–1805), German poet and writer, author of *Das Welt-Ende* (Vienna: Heubner, 1801), *Deutschlands Auferstehungstag* (Göttingen: Schneider, 1804) and other works: see *Gedichte*, ed. J. G. Gruber (Rudolstadt: Hofbuchhandlung, 1808). I have been unable to locate the poem quoted by Schumann. [Jansen/Kreisig:] As Dean Emil Flechsig, the youthful friend of R. Schumann, mentions, Schumann had in his youth a high regard for this poet.

{33a} Old things are passed away;
behold, all things are become new.
II Corinthians 5.17

Hector Berlioz, Episode de la vie d'un artiste. Grande Symphonie Fantastique. Œuv. 4. Partition de piano par F. Liszt. Propr. de l'Auteur. Pr. net. 20 Fr. Paris, M. Schlesinger.[21]

II[22]

I have read with care what Florestan wrote about the Symphony, and have read the music through myself, or rather studied it in the very greatest detail. I am in almost wholesale agreement with that initial verdict. Nevertheless, I cannot help thinking that this psychological mode of critical treatment, when applied to the work of a composer who is little more than a name to most people, a composer concerning whom, to make matters worse, the most widely differing opinions have been bandied about, cannot do full justice; and that Florestan's verdict, favourable as it is to Berlioz, could easily be upset by all sorts of suspicions to which the thorough investigation of the specific techniques of composition might give rise.

I now recognize that it takes more than just a poetic mentality to find so early in the day the proper place for this remarkable work in the history of art – it takes someone who is not only a musician with philosophical grounding but also a connoisseur well versed in the history of the other arts, someone who has reflected upon the significance of and connection between individual products and also upon the underlying meaning of their broad succession. At the same time, the opinion of a {33b} musician ought also to be sought: someone who, even if standing alone, keeps track of the direction that the younger generation is taking, championing stoutly all that is good in it; someone who will not hesitate to break the rod over his protégé's head in full view of the world, however much he might prefer to pardon him in private. Fortunately, on this occasion there are many more laurel wreaths than rods to be broken.

So diverse is the material with which this Symphony confronts us, that in what follows the threads could all too easily become entangled. For this reason, I have chosen to make my way through it aspect by aspect [*in einzelnen Theilen durchzugehen*], dependent though one aspect must often be upon another for its explication. These aspects are the four perspectives from which a piece of music may be viewed: namely, from the viewpoint of *form* (at the level of the whole, of its separate parts, of the period, of the phrase), of *techniques of composition* [*musikalische Composition*] (harmony, melody, counterpoint, working out, style), of whatever *idea* [*Idee*] the composer was striving to convey, and of the *spirit* [*Geist*] which governs form, material and idea.

21 The original titlepage reads: Episode de la vie d'un Artiste | Grande Symphonie Fantastique | PAR | HECTOR BERLIOZ | ŒUV:4me. | Partition de Piano | PAR | F. Liszt. | Prop^e. de l'Editeur. Prix net:20:^f. | Paris, Chez MAURICE SCHLESINGER Rue Richelieu 97 | M.S. 1982 ||. The work is now designated Op. 14.

22 [Schumann:] See no. 1 of this volume. Cf. nos 17, 18, 49 and 50 of the previous volume. ['17, 18' = pp. 67–9, 71–2, 'Ueber Berlioz und seine Compositionen', signed 'Panofka'; '49 and 50' = pp. 197–8, 201–02, 'Fétis über Hector Berlioz und dessen Symphonie: Grande Symphonie fantastique . . .'] [Bent:] Of section II, Schumann excised the first three (translated) paragraphs from his collected writings. See note 10, above.

[I Form]

Form is the vessel of the spirit. The greater its capacity, the greater the spirit needed to fill it. The word 'symphony' designates the largest proportions so far achieved in the realm of instrumental music.

We are used to making initial[23] inferences about a thing from the name that it bears. We have one set of expectations of a 'fantasy', another of a 'sonata'.

We are satisfied if a second-rate talent shows that he has mastered the traditional range of forms, whereas with a first-rate talent we allow that he expand that range. Only a genius may reign[24] freely.

After *Beethoven*'s Ninth Symphony, greatest of all instrumental works in external proportions, {34a} form and intention seemed to have been exhausted. The monumental idea demanded monumental embodiment; the god demanded his own world in which to work his wonders. But art does have its limits. The Apollo of the Belvedere a few feet taller would be an offence to the eye.[25] Later symphonic composers sensed this, and some of them even took refuge in the comfortable forms of Haydn and Mozart.[26]

In addition,[27] I might cite here: *Ferdinand Ries*, whose distinctive originality was overshadowed only by that of Beethoven; *Franz Schubert*, the fantastical[28] painter whose brush was steeped as much in the gentle rays of the moon as in the blazing light of the sun, and who after Beethoven's nine muses might have born us a tenth;[29] *Spohr*, whose soft accents failed to resonate strongly enough in the great vault of the symphony where he sought to speak; *Onslow*, who besides undeniable talent for instrumentation was not sufficiently skilled in concealing the roots of his four principal voices;[30] *Kalliwoda*, that serene and harmonious fellow whose later symphonies, for all the thoroughness of their workmanship, lack the lofty imaginative quality of his early ones. From among the more recent composers, we know and have high regard for <L.> *Maurer*, *Fr[iedrich] Schneider*, <I.> *Moscheles*, *C<h>. G. Müller*, <A.> *Hesse*, <F.> *Lachner* and *Mendelssohn*, whose name we have intentionally kept to last.[31]

---

23 'initial' (*vorweg*) excised in *GS*, and a grammatical error corrected: *den* for *die* ('that').

24 'reign' (*schalten*) changed to 'deport itself' (*gebaren*) in *GS*.

25 The Apollo of the Belvedere: Hellenistic statue (Roman copy, Vatican Museum) regarded as the quintessence of classical Greek art by late eighteenth-century German Hellenists. Winckelmann gave this view a widely influential formulation in his *Geschichte der Kunst des Alterthums* (1764), where he stated: 'The statue of Apollo is the highest ideal of art among all the works of antiquity that have escaped destruction' (*J. J. Winckelmanns Werke*, ed. A. Dorner (Hannover: Sponholtz, 1924), p. 334). Hogarth said it was 'all the more wonderful because when one examines it, the disproportionate in it is obvious even to the common eye [. . .] in particular that the feet and legs in relation to the upper part are too long and too broad' (*Analysis of Beauty* (London: Reeves, 1753; Ger. trans. Berlin, 1754)).

26 'The monumental idea . . . Haydn and Mozart' excised from *GS*, and restored in editorial footnote, vol. II, p. 378.

27 'In addition,' (*ausserdem*) excised from *GS* because of excision from previous paragraph.

28 *phantastisch* changed to *phantasiereich* in *GS*.

29 [Schumann, in *GS*:] The Symphony in C had not at that time appeared.

30 'Onslow . . . voices;' excised in *GS*, and restored in editorial footnote, vol. II, p. 378.

31 Initials in <> are supplied by Schumann in *GS*. Ferdinand Ries (1784–1838) wrote eight symphonies; Louis Spohr (1784–1859) ten; Georges Onslow (1784–1853) four; Johann Wenzel Kalliwoda (1801–66) seven; Ludwig Maurer (1789–1878) one, two sinfonie concertante; Friedrich Schneider (1786–1853) twenty-three; Ignaz Moscheles (1794–1870) one; Christian Gottlieb Müller (1800–

None of the above, all of whom save Franz Schubert are still living, had ventured to make any significant modifications to the old forms – if we leave aside isolated attempts such as the most recent symphony of Spohr.[32] Mendelssohn, a composer as great[33] in profundity of thought as in productivity, could see that nothing was to be gained by pursuing this and so struck out on a new path – a path that had perhaps been pioneered by the first *Leonore* Overture.[34] With his concert overtures, which presented the idea of the symphony in microcosm, he established himself head and shoulders above the other instrumental composers of his day. There was now a real fear that the name of the symphony might become a thing of the past.

All was silent on this front abroad. Cherubini laboured long years over a symphonic work; but is said to have confessed, perhaps too soon and too modestly, his unfitness to the task. The rest of France and Italy busied itself writing operas.

Meanwhile, in an obscure corner of northern coastal France, a young medical student is brooding over something new. Four movements are too few for him; as if writing a play, he opts instead for five.

At first I took the Symphony of Berlioz for a successor to Beethoven's Ninth (not, of course, on grounds of the number of movements, for Beethoven's Ninth has four, but rather on other grounds). However, it was played at the Paris Conservatoire as early as *1820*, and Beethoven's symphony was not published until after this date, so there can be no question of imitation.[35] And now, courage! And so to the Symphony itself!

{34b} If we view the five movements as a whole, we find that they observe the customary sequence of events right through to the final two movements, but that these, being two scenes of a dream, appear to form an entity in themselves. The first movement begins with an adagio[36] which is followed by an allegro, the second does duty as a scherzo, the third as a central adagio, and the last two together make up the final allegro. They are coherent, too, as regards key structure, the opening largo being in C minor, the allegro in C major, the scherzo in A major, the adagio in F major, and the last two movements in G minor and C major. So far all is plain sailing.[37] As I accompany my reader through this outlandish building, traips-

63) at least four?; Adolf Friedrich Hesse (1809–63) six; Franz Paul Lachner (1803–90) eight. See Schumann's *GS* for reviews of many of these symphonies.

32 [Jansen/Kreisig:] 'Weihe der Töne' [Symphony No. 4 in F (1832), first performed on 11 December 1834; see Schumann's review, *GS*, vol. I, pp. 65–6].

33 'as great' changed to 'significant' (*bedeutend*) by Schumann in *GS*.

34 'a path . . . Overture' changed by Schumann in *GS* to: 'for which Beethoven had, it is true, cleared the way in his great *Leonore* Overture', the original being restored in editorial footnote, vol. II, p. 378.

35 Schumann's chronology is false: the Symphony was composed primarily between January and April 1830, and received its first performance at the Salle du Conservatoire in Paris on 5 December 1830. Beethoven's Ninth Symphony was published in 1826, and Berlioz had seen the score by 1830, but not heard the work performed. He had probably heard all of the symphonies except the Eighth and Ninth.

36 Liszt's arrangement has 'largo' (the score, too), as Schumann was aware. His use of 'adagio' here refers to the genre of introductory slow section to first symphonic allegro: Schumann is normalizing Berlioz's sequence of movements.

37 Schumann had first come to hear of the *Fantastic* Symphony from an 1835 notice in *Revue musicale* by Heinrich Panofka, reprinted in *NZM*, 2 (1835), no. 17 (27 February), 67–9, and no. 18 (3 March), 71–2 (see Introduction, above, for further details). This passage, and the diagramming of form below, were perhaps aimed at redressing Panofka's statement (p. 71): 'As regards form, [the *idée fixe*] surely deviates very greatly from the symphonies of the great composers; it gives rise to a tone painting in five frames, and can be called a symphony only insofar as *symphonia* means nothing more than "sounding-together"'.

ing up and down endless flights of steps, I might even succeed in giving him some impression of its individual chambers. We have read often of those ancient Scottish castles that English writers portray so vividly, our imaginations caught by the higgledy-piggledy windows and precariously perching towers. Our symphony is something like this. Join me in a tour of its fantastically winding passageways!³⁸

The slow introduction to the opening allegro differs only slightly from those of other symphonies – I speak here solely in terms of form. Its ordering of materials is perhaps not immediately clear, but after much juggling back and forth of the larger periods this dawns on one. What we actually have here are two variations on a theme, with free *intermezzi*: the principal theme extending up to b. 16/p. 2, b. 2;³⁹ [first] episode from there to b. 27/p. 3, b. 5; first variation to b. 41/p. 5, b. 6; [second] episode to b. 50/p. 6, b. 8; second variation, over the long-held pedal note in the bass (at any rate, I detect the intervals of the theme, albeit by implication, in the obbligato horn part) to b. 58/p. 7, b. 1; drive toward the allegro; preparatory chords; we step from the ante-chamber into the inner hall – allegro. Anyone who dallies on the way to look at details will fall behind and get lost.

Just let your eye skim across the page from the initial theme to the first *animato* [= *a tempo con fuoco*⁴⁰], b. 111/p. 9. Three ideas have been packed in tightly together: the first, which Berlioz calls the *double idée fixe* (for reasons which will be explained later) extends to the *sempre dolce e ardamente* [b. 87]; the second, which derives from the adagio, extends to the first sf, b. 103/p. 9; and at that point the third idea joins in, extending to the *animato* [b. 111]. What follows should be taken together up to the *rinforzando* of the basses in b. 149/p. 10, not overlooking the passage from the *ritenuto il tempo* [bb. 119–20] to the *animato* in b. 125/p. 9. With the *rinforzando* [b. 150] we reach a strangely lit clearing – the second theme proper – from which we can steal a quiet glance backwards at what has gone by. Section I draws to a close and is repeated. From then on, it seems as though the periods should follow each other more coherently, but as the music presses forward they become now shorter, now longer, from the beginning of section II to the {35a} *con fuoco* in b. 200/p. 12, from there to the *sec.* in b. 230/p. 13: general pause; a horn in the far distance; something familiar sounds up to the first *pp* in b. 280/p. 14; now the track gets harder to follow and more mysterious; two ideas, one of four bars, then one of nine; passages of two bars each; free phrases and turns; the second theme, in ever more compressed form, appears subsequently in its full glory up to the *pp* in b. 331/p. 16; third idea of the first theme stated in deeper and deeper registers; darkness; little by little, the silhouettes come to life and take form, reaching *disperato* at b. 371/p. 17; principal theme in its first guise in precipitous arpeggios as far as b. 408/p. 19; now the whole first theme in

---

38 'We have read . . . passageways!' excised by Schumann in *GS*, and restored in editorial footnote, vol. II, p. 378.

39 Schumann's references are to bar, system and page number of the first edition of Liszt's transcription. These have been preserved here, but preceded by movement number and bar numbers of the Norton Critical Score and /.

40 Cited markings are those that appear in Liszt's arrangement, and by no means correspond with the markings in the orchestral score. They are in Italian rather than Berlioz's French, reflect Liszt's taste by being more extreme, and are pianistic in intent.

gigantic splendour up to the *animato* in b. 441/p. 20; utterly fantastic forms, each emerging only once, as if fragmented, reminiscent of older ones; all disappears.

{37a} The exceptional man needs exceptional trust;
Give him scope and he will determine his own objective.

Wallenstein[41]

Surely Berlioz never dissected the head of some handsome murderer with greater distress[42] than that which I felt as I dissected his first movement. And did the surgery do my reader the slightest bit of good? What I was trying to achieve by it was threefold: first, to show those who are completely unfamiliar with the Symphony just how little enlightenment is to be gained about music from such a dismembering critique [*zergliedernde Kritik*];[43] [second,] to point out to those who have glanced casually through it, and perhaps laid it aside because they could not make head or tail of it, a few of the more salient points; and finally, to demonstrate to those who are acquainted with it but have not come to appreciate it that despite the apparent formlessness of this body as regards its major proportions it possesses a wonderfully[44] symmetrical disposition – to say nothing of its inner coherence. But the unfortunate misunderstanding is in part bound up with the unaccustomed elements in this new form, and in its novel mode of expression. Too many people at first or second {37b} hearing pay attention too much to incidentals. It is rather like deciphering a difficult handwriting, where one reader might get stuck on every single word and finish up using far more time than another who first skims through the whole document to get the general sense and intent of it. What's more, as I have already indicated, nothing so easily vexes people and gets their backs up as a new form under an old name. If, for example, someone wanted to call something in 5/4-time a 'March', or something in twelve short movements a 'Symphony', he would encounter instant opposition. Yet we ought always to look at a thing on its own terms. The stranger and more ingenious a thing outwardly appears, the more carefully ought we to judge it. And is not our experience with Beethoven a lesson for us? Were not his works, particularly his later works, at first unintelligible to us, with all the odd features of construction and the strange forms in which he was so inexhaustibly inventive, even as regards the spiritual content [*Geist*], though no

---

41 Schiller, *Die Piccolomini*, Act I Scene 4, lines 144–5, spoken by Max: *Friedrich Schiller: Gesammelte Werken in fünf Bänden*, ed. Reinhold Netolitzky (Gütersloh: Mohn, n.d.), vol. II, p. 64. 'He' is emphasized in all editions that I have consulted, but not by Schumann.

42 'distress' (*Schmerz*) changed to 'aversion' (*Widerwillen*) by Schumann in *GS*, and the German for 'dissected' changed (*seziert* for *auseinander genommen*) without altering the meaning.

43 For discussion of the history of the term *Zergliederung*, including Schumann's use of it, see vol. I, Introduction to Part I. Panofka had portrayed Berlioz as 'the music anatomist' at his grisly student occupation (*NZM*, 2 (1835), no. 17 (27 February), 68):

> Not infrequently, he would shatter the peace of the dissecting room with passionate outpourings of what he had been hearing in the theatre, and would accompany the rhythm of the saw and hammer that he used to open up skulls with melodies from [Spontini's] *La Vestale* [1807] and *Fernando Cortez* [1809].

In employing *Zergliederung* in this review, Schumann harnesses the inherent duality of the term (musically, thematic transformation by motivic proliferation; anatomically, dissection of a corpse; between which the sense of music analysis mediates) with ironic effect.

44 'wonderfully' changed to 'exactly' (*richtig*) by Schumann in *GS*.

one could surely deny the existence of that. If we now grasp the first allegro movement as a whole, without letting ourselves be bothered by its frequent rough edges,
small but jagged though they be, the following form emerges clearly:[45]

		First Theme (G major)		
	Middle Section with a second theme		Middle Section with a second theme	
	First Theme (C major)		First Theme (C major)	
Opening (C minor)				Close (C major)
	(G major, E minor)		(E minor, G major)	

against which we can set the earlier norm for comparison:

	Middle Section (A minor) (working out of the two themes)		
	Second Theme (G major)		First Theme (C major)
First Theme (C major)			Second Theme (C major)

{38a} We are at a loss to see how in terms of variety and uniformity the latter could
be preferred to the former. We only wish we possessed a truly colossal imagination
and could then pursue it wherever it goes.

It remains for us to comment upon structure at the level of the individual phrase.
Surely in no work of recent times are symmetrical and asymmetrical groupings of
bars and subphrases [*Rhythmen*] so freely mingled as in this. Scarcely ever does
consequent phrase conform to antecedent phrase, answer to question. It is to this
peculiar aspect of Berlioz, so akin to his southern character and so alien to us
nordic types, that the initial sense of unease, and the complaints of obscurity, can
perhaps be attributed and accounted for. The sheer audacity with which all of
this is accomplished has to be seen and heard to be believed: not the slightest thing
could be added or taken away without detracting from the impression of piercing
urgency, or driving[46] energy, that it leaves in the mind. Though the age of Goethe
and Mozart may justifiably be rated the highest in the realm of art, an age in which
the creative imagination wore with godlike effortlessness the shackles of rhythmic
periodicity[47] as if they were garlands of flowers,[48] music appears to be gravitating
back to its primeval origins, as yet still unoppressed by the rule of the strong beat,
and striving to attain the condition of prosody, to a higher poetic phraseology (such
as is found in the Greek choruses, in the language of the Bible, and in the prose
writings of Jean Paul).

45 The key of the 'Opening' is erroneously given as 'C major' in both versions of the text. See
   Cone's discussion of this and the key of the recapitulated second theme in Norton Critical Score,
   pp. 231, 251–2.
46 'driving' excised by Schumann in GS.
47 'rhythmic periodicity': *Rhythmus*.
48 'Though the age . . . flowers,' excised by Schumann in GS, and restored in editorial footnote,
   vol. II, p. 378; what follows begins a new sentence.

Let us not pursue this train of thought further, for it stirs rebellion within me.[49] To end this section of our critique, let us recall words written many years ago by that childlike poetic spirit Ernst Wagner[50] – prophetic words, yet spoken with innocence as if all the world knew it. Wagner says somewhere or other:[51]

> Even the nightingale's song has a momentum – one might almost say a melodic rhythm – to it. But what it lacks is some consistent character amidst all its rapid outbursts and retardations, some drawing-together of all its moments of freedom and motion under one presiding rule – that is, an underlying rhythm. The presence of a beat must in earlier times have imparted a very comforting feel. Indeed, we ourselves sometimes feel its comforting power. In fugues, in certain kinds of dissonances, and wherever tensions arise that cannot easily be followed, what most often gives us reassurance is the presence of beat, that serene and ever-unvarying measurement of time.
>
> Elsewhere, in slow melodies, sweet, melting ones, its encouraging beat draws us on from one beat to another, leading us irresistibly on toward the end. On the other hand, the presence of beat grievously subverts the music of our time; and under its present tyranny, music can no longer elevate itself to the state of a fine art (to the level of free consciousness, as some would put it), since whilst it would (perhaps) be able to present an idea that was almost beautiful, it would do so without the semblance of freedom. If music is to be a living form to our ears, then it must operate as freely as does poetry on our capacity to conceptualize. This the presence of beat does not allow so long as it restricts itself only to the measurement of time, and does not extend itself to the measurement of syllables; or, greater still, encompass within itself such latitude and freedom of action as are associated at least with the complete stanza in poetry. Metrical freedom in music is very great; but time depends on the strictest rules. We cannot think of a single movement that is marked *ad libitum* throughout. The performer really has no more than the liberty to start and stop; for between the acts of beginning and ending, tyrannical beat takes over (in itself no more than a human invention, mechanically acquired), forcing composers and listeners alike to obey its blatantly imperious command. All attempts to resist beat serve only to make its oppressive grip even tighter.[52] Whoever is entrusted with the task of completely hiding the tyranny of beat in music, and making us insensible of it, will give this art at least the semblance of *freedom*. Whoever then bestows *consciousness* upon it will empower it to present a beautiful idea. From that very moment on, music will be the *first* of the fine arts.

Could it be Berlioz's Symphony that ushers this moment in?[53]

---

49 'for it stirs rebellion within me' excised by Schumann in *GS*.
50 Johann Ernst Wagner (1769–1812), German writer influenced by Goethe and Jean Paul Richter, author of *Willibalds Ansichten des Lebens* (1809), *Isidora* (1812) and other works. He corresponded extensively with Richter on musical and literary subjects. In a letter of 3 January 1802, he stated: 'I am indeed most musical, although I play no musical instrument' (A. L. Corin, 'Hundert Briefe von Johann Ernst Wagner an Jean Paul Fr. Richter und August von Studnitz' (diss.: University of Liège, 1942)). I have been unable to locate Schumann's quotation.
51 'yet spoken with innocence as if all the world knew it. Wagner says somewhere or other' excised by Schumann in *GS*.
52 'Even the nightingale's song . . . even tighter' excised by Schumann in *GS*.
53 Sentence excised by Schumann in *GS*, and restored in editorial footnote, vol. II, p. 378.

{41a} Increased artistic training can certainly bring about improvements in surface polish. But what is commonly called the sap of life surges up always from the rich soil of genius, and vitality manifests itself most often where a certain lack of surface polish is in evidence and where there is a simple and sterling quality which artistic training, however complete, can never provide, indeed can all too easily stifle.

Thibaut[54]

As we have already remarked, it would take too long and serve no purpose if we were to dissect [*zergliedern*] the other movements in the way that we did the first. The second pursues a winding, gyrating course, just like the dance that it depicts. The third, surely the loveliest [of the five], swings ethereally pendulum-like up and down. The last two have no centre of focus whatsoever and surge unceasingly towards the end. For all its outward formlessness, one cannot help admiring[55] the spiritual coherence; the famous, albeit false, adage about Jean Paul comes to mind, whom someone dubbed a bad logician and a great philosopher.

So far, we have dealt only with the garment itself; now we come to the cloth out of which it is made: to *techniques of composition*.

[II Techniques of composition]

I should make the point right away that I have only the piano arrangement from which to judge; however, instrumentation is labelled there at crucial points. Even without that, everything strikes me as conceived from the outset so purely in the spirit of the orchestra,[56] every instrument sounding so right, its intrinsic tone quality so perfectly deployed, that any good musician could reconstruct a passable score – apart, of course, from the new combinations and orchestral effects that Berlioz so creatively, so unerringly[57] achieves. But more of this later.[58]

{41b} If ever I found a thing incomprehensible,[59] it is the brusque verdict of M Fétis in these words: *Je vis, qu'il manquait d'idées mélodiques et harmoniques* [I saw that he completely lacked melodic and harmonic ideas].[60] Let him deny Berlioz everything, as he has done: creative imagination, power of invention, originality. But wealth of melody and harmony? – Berlioz surely has nothing to answer for in those departments![61] I have not the slightest intention of polemicizing against this otherwise brilliantly and learnedly written review, for I see nothing of a personal nature in it, nothing unjust – only sheer blindness, a complete lack of

---

54 Anton Friedrich Justus Thibaut (1772–1840), *Über Reinheit der Tonkunst* (Heidelberg: Mohr, 2/1826), p. 70.

55 'admiring' changed to 'acknowledging' (*anerkennen*) by Schumann in GS, and restored in editorial footnote, vol. II, p. 378.

56 'in the spirit of the orchestra' changed to 'in the character of the orchestra' (*Orchestergeist* to *Orchestercharakter*) by Schumann in GS.

57 'so unerringly' excised by Schumann in GS.

58 'But . . .later.' excised by Schumann in GS.

59 'thing incomprehensible' changed to 'verdict unjust' by Schumann in GS, then continues 'it is the brusque one . . . .

60 See notes 4 and 5 above for citations. The complete relevant passage is:

> I perceived that he had no feeling for melody, nor scarcely any concept of rhythm; that his harmony, composed mostly of monstrous clumps of notes, was nonetheless commonplace and monotonous. In a word, I saw that he completely lacked melodic and harmonic ideas; and it was my judgment that his barbaric style would never be tamed.

61 'Berlioz . . . departments!' excised (significantly!) by Schumann in GS.

feeling for this kind of music. Nor am I asking the reader to take my word for it in anything that he cannot see for himself! Although music examples, torn from context, can often do as much harm as good, I shall nonetheless attempt with this aid to make each detail more vivid.

[i Harmony]

When we evaluate the Symphony from the point of view of *harmony*, we cannot but see how the awkward eighteen-year-old[62] composer, not given to beating about the bush, makes straight for his chosen objective. If, for example, he wants to go from G to D♭, he goes directly there, without so much as the time of day (as can be seen in Example 1[63]). What a way to go about it – we may well shake our heads!

Example 1

But discerning and musical folk who heard the Symphony in Paris assured us there was no other way the passage could be: somebody let drop that immortal *bon mot* about Berlioz's music: *que cela est fort beau, quoique ce ne soit pas de la musique* [It may not be music, but it certainly is lovely],[64] to which one French critic, J. d'Ortigue,[65] remarked: *s'il en est ainsi, M Berlioz est sans contredit le génie le plus étonnant qui ait paru sur la terre, car il* {42a} *s'en suit forcement qu'il a inventé un art nouveau, un art inconnu, et pourtant un bel art* [If that is the case, then M Berlioz must without question be the most astounding genius ever to appear on earth, for it follows logically that he has invented a new art, an unknown art, as well as an art of great beauty].[66] Pretentious repartee though

---

62 Berlioz was in fact twenty-seven.
63 Fourth movement, bb. 154–6; Example 1 appears at the foot of p. 42, beneath both columns of text.
64 I do not know the source of this remark.
65 Joseph d'Ortigue (1802–66), critic and close friend of Berlioz. I have been unable to locate the remark.
66 'to which one French critic . . . *un bel art*' excised by Schumann in *GS*.

this may have been, it contains more than a grain of truth. Such irregular passages [as this] are in any case very much the exception: <cf., however, fourth movement, bb. 129–30/p. 61, bb. 1–2>.[67] I might go so far as to say that, despite the variety of spacings and inversions[68] which he derives from such limited material, his harmony exhibits a certain simplicity, and at the same time a succinct, aphoristic quality of the sort that one meets with, albeit more[69] fully developed, in Beethoven. Or does he perhaps stray too far away from the tonic? We don't have to look any further than the first movement: section I[70] is plainly in C minor <bb. 1–27/ pp. 1–3, b. 5>, after which he reproduces the intervals of the first idea [*Gedanke*] completely unchanged in E♭ <bb. 28[–39]/p. 3, b. 6>; then he dwells at length on A♭ <bb. 46[–59]/p. 6, b. 4>, and so finds his way easily to C major. The outline that I gave in the previous issue[71] showed the allegro to be constructed in the simplest possible way from C major, G major and E minor. It is the same through- out the entire work. The second movement is pervaded by the bright key of A major, the third by the idyllic key of F major with its sister-keys of C and B♭ major, the fourth by G minor with B♭ and E♭ major. Only in the final movement are we, despite the prevailing C, thrown into colourful confusion, as befits an infernal wedding celebration. But we frequently stumble over harmonies that are crude and common-sounding: <first movement, bb. 20–21/p. 2, bb. 6–7; bb. 43–5/p. 6, bb. 1–3; bb. 64–71/p. 8, bb. 1–8; bb. 488–91/p. 21, last s., bb. 1–4; second move- ment, bb. 302–19/p. 35, s. 5, bb. 1–18>; harmonies that are faulty, or at least forbidden by the old rules: <immediately, first movement, b. 1/p. 1, b. 1, the B♮ (evidently an engraver's error[72]); bb. 24–6/p. 3, bb. 2–4; bb. 108–09, 115–19/p. 9, bb. 8–9, 15–19; bb. 142–5/p. 10, bb. 11–14; bb. 441–51/p. 20, bb. 8–18; second movement, bb. 348–51, 365–6/p. 37, bb. 11–14, 28–9; third movement, bb. 129–30/ p. 48, s. 5, bb. 2–3; fourth movement, b. 76/p. 57, s. 5, b. 3; bb. 154–9/p. 62, bb. 9–14; fifth movement, bb. 307–09/p. 78, s. 5, bb. 1–3 and all that follows; bb. 388–9/p. 82, s. 4, bb. 1–2 and all that follows; bb. 408–12/p. 83, bb. 13–17; bb. 464–6/p. 86, bb. 11–13; bb. 483–4/p. 87, bb. 5–6; let me repeat that I am dependent upon the piano arrangement – many things may look quite different in the score> – though in truth some of them sound quite splendid; harmonies that are vague and indistinct: <first movement, b. 433/p. 20, b. 3; perhaps the harmonies are really:

67 Passages surrounded by < and > appear in the original as lettered footnotes, where they supply only the page, system and bar numbers of the first edition of the piano arrangement. These num- bers have been preserved, but are preceded by bar numbers to the movement as a whole, and /, thereby facilitating reference to the score.
68 'spacings and inversions': *Combinationen*: Schumann generally applies this term to timbral combinations.
69 Changed to 'much more' by Schumann in GS.
70 'Section': *Satz*.
71 Changed to 'above' by Schumann in GS.
72 The leading-note B♮ is doubled in left and right hands (= 1st bassoon and 1st clarinet), then moves in double octaves to the tonic, the first infringement entailing the second. Schumann thought the change from treble to bass clef in the left hand should have been placed at the barline rather than before the final triplet quaver of b. 1, making that note (second line up) g' rather than B♮. His diagnosis is not borne out by the score.
73 *Becken*: there are no cymbals at this point, only a bassdrum roll (as noted in the Liszt transcription at b. 9) played by two players with sponge-headed sticks. Liszt's b. 11 corresponds with the score.

$$\begin{array}{llll}
6\text{--}7 & 6\ \ 6\sharp & 6\flat\ \ 6\natural & 6\text{--}6\sharp \\
3\sharp\ \text{---} & 3\ \text{---} & 3\flat\ \text{---} & 3\ \text{---}\ \text{etc.;} \\
D\sharp & E & F & F\sharp
\end{array}$$

fourth movement, bb. 158–9/p. 62, s. 5, bb. 1–2; fifth movement, b. 11/p. 65, s. 4, b. 3, which is apparently a joke on Liszt's part in an attempt to simulate the dying away of the cymbals;[73] bb. 317–19/p. 79, bb. 8–10; bb. 348ff/p. 81, bb. 6ff; bb. 491–3/p. 88, bb. 1–3; and many others>; {42b} harmonies that sound badly, that are tortured, distorted: <first movement, bb. 21–2/p. 2, s. 4; b. 36/p. 5, b. 1; bb. 115–19/p. 9, bb. 15–19; bb. 371ff/p. 17, from b. 7 onwards for some distance; second movement, bb. 160–61/p. 30, s. 4, bb. 6–7; fifth movement, bb. 387–94/ p. 82, b. 12–19; bb. 491–3/p. 88, bb. 1–3, and many others>. May the time never come when such passages as these are sanctioned as beautiful, any more than the century in which hunchbacks and lunatics are held to be Apollos and Kants with respect to beauty and reason.[74] With Berlioz, however, it is quite another matter. One has only to try adjusting things here and there, improving them a little – as is child's play for anyone well versed in harmony! – to discover instead how lack-lustre and insipid[75] the result! Immanent in these first outbursts of a sturdy youth-ful temperament is a wholly distinctive and indomitable spirit. Somewhat coarse though it may still be in its outward expression, it is the more powerful in its effect the less we seek to tame it with critical carpings. Any attempt to refine it by artistic means, or to confine it forcibly within certain limits, is doomed to failure, until such time as it has learned to wield its own resources more elegantly and attained for itself a purpose and sense of direction. Berlioz has no pretension to being pretty or elegant. All that he hates he grabs wrathfully by the scruff of its neck, all that he loves he crushes[76] in his ardour – subtle nuances are of secondary importance to an impetuous youth who cannot be judged by conventional stan-dards.[77] Better for us instead to search out the many tender and exquisitely original things in him, that make up for the coarse and bizarre elements. Thus the harmonic construction of the entire first melody <first movement, bb. 3ff/p. 1, b. 3 on> is pure and noble[78] throughout, as too is its repeat in E♭ <bb. 28ff/p. 3, b. 6>. The A♭ in the [cellos and] basses, held for all of *fourteen* bars <bb. 46[–59]/p. 6, b. 4>, is tremendously effective, and so is the pedal point that occurs in the middle parts <bb. 168–78/p. 11, b. 10>. The chromatic sixth chords, rising and falling steeply <bb. 200–225/p. 12, b. 13>, though meaningless in themselves, must be mighty impressive in context. It is impossible to judge from the piano arrangement those stretches in which gruesome octaves and false relations constantly occur, while

74 This sentence recalls Fétis's: 'In a recently published article, M Berlioz assures us that the day will come when people will no longer berate him for the way he applies his ideas, or for the means he employs to put his thoughts into practice' (*NZM*, 2, no. 50, 202a); 'any more than the century . . . reason' was excised by Schumann in *GS*, and restored in editorial footnote, vol. II, p. 380.

75 'and insipid' excised by Schumann in *GS*.

76 'crushes' changed to 'would like to crush' by Schumann in *GS*.

77 *den man nicht nach Loth und Zoll taxiren kann* (lit.: 'that cannot be assessed by weight and measure'): changed to *den man nicht nach der Krämerelle messen kann* (perhaps 'that cannot be sized up with a standard measuring rod') by Schumann in *GS*.

78 'pure and noble' excised (or omitted in error?) by Schumann in *GS*, forcing the sentence now to read: 'Thus the harmonic construction of the first melody throughout, as too is its repeat in E♭.'

imitations are going on between bass (or tenor) and soprano: <first movement, b. 371/p. 17, b. 7>. [Even] if the octaves are well covered, it must strike us to the depths of our being.

With few exceptions, the underlying harmony of the second movement is simple and less complex. For {43a} pure harmonic content, the third movement can rank alongside any masterpiece:[79] every note is alive. The fourth is packed with interest, and is in the most taut and concentrated style. The fifth threshes and convulses itself into a hopeless tangle. With the exception of one or two novel passages <fifth movement, bb. 269ff/p. 76 from s. 4 onwards; bb. 329–57/p. 80, where the E♭ in the inner parts remains static for twenty-nine bars; bb. 363ff/p. 81, b. 20 [*recte* 21], the pedal point on the dominant; bb. 386ff/p. 82, b. 11, where I tried in vain to eradicate the consecutive fifths in bb. 388–9/s. 4, bb. 1–2>, it is ugly, strident and repulsive.

[ii Melody, Counterpoint, etc.]

However neglectful Berlioz may be in matters of detail, however much he may sacrifice particulars to total effect, he is certainly[80] a master of *stylish and intricate craftsmanship*. But he does not squeeze the last drop out of his themes; nor does he stifle a good idea under tedious thematic development, as others so often do. Instead, he gives signs that he could have worked out his ideas in much stricter fashion if he had wanted to and felt it appropriate – sketches in the ingenious, epigrammatic manner of Beethoven. Some of his most delightful ideas[81] he presents only once, as if they were asides: <first movement, b. 24/p. 3, b. 2; bb. 280–92/p. 14, s. 4, bb. 6–18; bb. 361–8/p. 16, s. 6, bb. 1–8; bb. 429–43/p. 19, s. 5, bb. 12–15; third movement, bb. 49–64/p. 40, s. 4, bb. 1–16> (see Example 2[82]).

The principal motif of the Symphony (Example 3[83]) – neither beautiful[84] in its own right nor well suited to contrapuntal treatment – gains increasingly in stature with its later restatements. From the very beginning {43b} of section II [b. 167], its interest becomes more immediate, and this continues (see Example 2): <b. 363/p. 16, s. 6, b. 3> until it squirms its way through shrieking chords into C major: <b. 411/p. 19, b. 7>. In the second movement, he adapts it literally note-for-note to a new rhythm and gives it new harmonies, to form the trio: <bb. 120[–60]/p. 29, b. 1>. Just before the end he brings it back once more, this time subdued and hesitant: <bb. 302–19/p. 35, s. 5>. In the third movement, it emerges as a recitative, interrupted by the orchestra: <bb. 90[–100]/p. 43, last bar>, and is illuminated by the most fearful passion as it rises to the high piercing A♭ [bb. 100–102], at which point it seems to collapse in a swoon [bb. 110–11]. Later <bb. 150[–54], 160[–63]/p. 49, bb. 3, 13>, it appears calm and serene, supported by the principal theme [in violin I]. In the *Marche du supplice*, it tries to raise its voice once more, only to be cut off by the *coup fatale*: <bb. 164[–9]/p. 63, b. 4>. In the 'Vision' [*Songe d'une*

---

79 'any' changed to 'any other symphonic' by Schumann in GS.
80 *auch*; *doch* in GS.   81 *Gefühle*; *Gedanken* in GS.
82 First movement, bb. 361–8.   83 First movement, bb. 71–9.
84 'beautiful' changed to 'significant' (*bedeutend*) by Schumann in GS.

Example 2

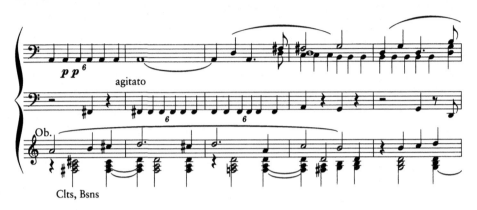

Example 3

nuit du Sabbat], it makes its appearance, shrunken, emaciated and degenerate, in the yelping tones of C and E♭ clarinets:[85] <bb. 21[-8]/p. 67, b. 1; bb. 40[-64]/ p. 68, b. 1> – vividly exploited by Berlioz.

The second theme of the first movement flows as if directly out of the first theme: <b. 150/p. 10, s. 5, b. 3>. So intimately interwoven are they that the beginning and end of the period cannot be detected with certainty until the point is finally reached at which the new idea detaches itself (Example 4[86]), to reappear soon, almost {44a} imperceptibly, in the basses:

85 *NZM* has 'E and E♭ clarinets'; corrected in *GS*.
86 First movement, bb. 157–60.

Example 4

<b. 163/p. 11, b. 5; b. 194/p. 12, b. 7>. Later he takes it up once again, sketching it out most ingeniously (Example 5[87]). In this last example, Berlioz's way of developing material is most clearly apparent. With equal finesse at a later point, he

Example 5

deploys in complete form an idea that seemed to have been totally forgotten: <bb. 119 [–25]/p. 9, b. 19; bb. 331 [–9]/p. 16, b. 3>.

87 First movement, bb. 313–25.

The motifs of the second movement are less artfully woven together, though the theme in the basses is a notable exception to this: <bb. 176[–91]/p. 31, b. 10; bb. 338[–60]/p. 37, b. 1> – with what dexterity he plucks out one bar from that same theme and develops it: <bb. 106[–17]/p. 28, b. 10>!

In the third movement, he brings back the solo principal idea in enchanting guises: <b. 20/p. 39, b. 4; b. 69/p. 42, b. 1; b. 131/p. 47, b. 1>. Beethoven himself could scarcely have worked it out more meticulously. The whole movement [*Satz*] is full of subtle inter-relationships. Once he leaps from C to the major seventh below; later he puts this insignificant stroke to good use (Example 6[88]).

Example 6

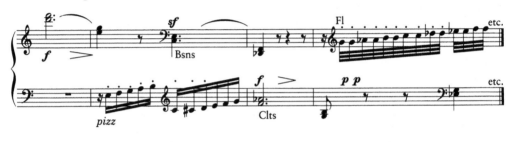

{45a} Every genius must be studied according only to what he himself wishes.

Heinse[89]

In the fourth movement, his contrapuntal treatment of the principal theme (Example 7[90]) is masterly.[91] The systematic way in which he transposes it into

Example 7

Eb major (Example 8[92]) and then G minor (Example 9[93]) is further evidence of his technical prowess: <bb. 33ff/p. 55, b. 15; bb. 49ff/p. 57 [*recte* 56], b. 12;

88 Third movement, bb. 155–8.
89 Wilhelm Heinse (1746–1803), novelist and critic. See *Sämtliche Schriften*, 10 vols (Leipzig: Insel, 1903–25). The most likely source is his *Musikalische Dialogen* (vol. I, pp. 205–332), which includes a dialogue on genius. I have searched for this quotation in vain.
90 Fourth movement, bb. 17–24.
91 'masterly' (*wie ein Meister*) changed to 'very beautiful' (*sehr schön*) by Schumann in *GS*, and restored in editorial footnote, vol. II, p. 380.
92 Fourth movement, bb. 33–7.   93   ibid, bb. 49–56.

Example 8

bb. 82ff/p. 58, b. 5; bb. 113, 122/p. 60, bb. 1, 10, and then the inversion in bb. 131ff/p. 61, b. 3>.

Example 9

{45b} In the final movement, he introduces the *Dies irae*, first in dotted minims, then in dotted crotchets, then in crotchets and quavers:[94] <b. 127/p. 71, s. 4, b. 7; b. 147/p. 72, b. 6; b. 157/ibid, b. 16>. Bells sound out tonic and dominant at regular intervals. The double fugue that follows (Example 10[95]), which he modestly calls a

Example 10

Fugato[96], while not exactly a Bach fugue, is of orthodox design and clear construction. The *Dies irae* and the *Ronde du Sabbat* are skilfully {46a} interwoven with one another (Example 11[97]), although the latter theme is maintained for only part of the way, and the new accompaniment is as crass and frivolous as could

Example 11

possibly be, made up as it is of a stream of ascending and descending parallel thirds.[98] With the third page from the end [i.e. from b. 479] everything goes head

94 *in ganzen, dann in halben, dann in Achtel-Noten*: lit. 'in semibreves, then in minims, then in quavers'. Strictly speaking, 'p. 71, s. 4, b. 7' does not exist in the orchestral score: Liszt allows an extra bar of sustained G on bells before bassoon and tubas enter with *Dies irae*.
95 Fifth movement, bb. 240–48.
96 The score contains no such designation: 'Fugato' is Liszt's nomenclature.
97 Fifth movement, bb. 414–16.
98 This is true of the piano arrangement but not of the score, which proceeds in compound tenths mixed with contrary motion, all widely spaced; all of this is compressed by Liszt into the right hand of the piano, in parallel octaves and thirds.

over heels, as remarked several times previously. The *Dies irae* begins once more
pp: <b. 486/p. 87, b. 8>. Without the orchestral score[99] the only word for the
final pages is 'bad'.

M Fétis contends that not even Berlioz's dearest friends would dare to defend
him on the question of *melody*.[100] If this be so, then I plainly belong to the enemy
camp. But let us not think in terms of Italian melody – the sort that we know
perfectly[101] even before it starts.

True enough, the principal melody running through the entire Symphony, which
we have repeatedly mentioned, does have something commonplace about it, and
Berlioz waxes {46b} perhaps a little too lyrical in the programme when he attributes
to it a 'noble and reticent character' [*un certain caractère passioné, mais noble et
timide*[102]]. We should remember, though: he did not set out to create a musical
thought [*Gedanke*] of great magnitude, but rather a haunting, irksome idea [*Idee*] –
the sort of thing that we often cannot get out of our heads for days on end. Indeed,
there is no better portrayal of the humdrum, the deranged.[103]

Likewise, Fétis, in that review, said that in the second movement the principal
melody is common and trivial.[104] Berlioz's intention (not unlike that of Beethoven
in the last movement of his A major Symphony) is to whisk us away to the ballroom – nothing more, nothing less. Sadly, that is how it is: it only takes a great
man to come trustingly down to the common level in life for people to say: 'There,
just see what he is capable of!' But they fail to see his head, for he towers high
above them in the clouds.[105] A similar situation arises with the opening melody of
the third {47a} movement (Example 12[106]), which I believe M Fétis dubbed gloomy
and devoid of taste.[107] One has only to go roving in the Alps or any other pastoral

Example 12

99 The full orchestral score was issued in 1845.
100 'His dearest friends dare not defend him on account of his weakness in melodic invention, and
     confess that it is grievously lacking in his music.' (*NZM*, 2, no. 50, 201b)
101 'perfectly' excised by Schumann in *GS*.
102 Berlioz's original programme, first movement.
103 It is now known that the first two phrases of the *Idée fixe* were originally composed for the lyric
     scene *Herminie*, which Berlioz entered for the Prix de Rome competition in 1828 and which
     gained him second prize: see *Symphonie fantastique*, ed. Nicholas Temperley, *Hector Berlioz:
     New Edition of the Complete Works*, vol. XVI (Kassel: Bärenreiter, 1972), p. IX. See also H.
     Macdonald, 'Berlioz's Self-Borrowings', *Proceedings of the Royal Musical Association*, 92 (1965/
     66), 27–64, esp. 29–30.
104 'The whole [second movement] is a waltz based on a common motif; for be it noted that M
     Berlioz descends to triviality the moment he becomes clear.' (*NZM*, 2, no. 50, 201b).
105 'Sadly . . . clouds.' relegated to an on-page footnote in *GS*, prefaced by 'Earlier addition:'.
106 Third movement, bb. 1–2.
107 *NZM*, 2, no. 50, 201b:

> suffers so grievously from its gloominess of invention (*Gedanke*) and its joyless long-windedness
> that one could not possibly endure to hear it through to its end did not the happy effects of
> the instrumentation diminish somewhat the boredom. Here, as elsewhere, invention fails him,
> and contrast of effects is the sole means that Berlioz knows to save himself.

region and listen to the shawms or alphorns to realize that this is just how things sound. So it is with all the melodies in this Symphony: they are idiomatic and true to nature. And yet there are occasional episodes in which they shed this individualism totally and transcend themselves, merging into a cosmic higher order of beauty.

To take a case in point, what accusation can we level against the melody with which the Symphony opens? – does it perhaps exceed the bounds of the octave by more than one step? –does it not contain enough melancholy? What can we say against the anguished oboe melody in one of the preceding examples? – does it perhaps leap in an unseemly fashion? But who wants to point the accusing finger at every single thing? If one were searching for something with which to reproach Berlioz, it would be his neglect of the middle parts; even there, in his defence I see special conditions applying that I have observed in very few other composers. His melodies are distinguished by a peculiar intensity to virtually every single note. Not unlike many ancient folksongs, this makes them often unable to tolerate even the slightest harmonic accompaniment. When put in contact with such accompaniment they often lose all their tonal richness. Because of this, Berlioz harmonizes them for the most part either with a sustained pedal note, or with chords of the [tonic,] dominant and subdominant: <the first method, e.g. first movement, bb. 412 [–22]/p. 19, b. 7, third movement, b. 131[–8]/p. 47, b. 1; the second method, in the principal melody of the *Bal*, where the fundamental harmonies are actually A, D, E, A [bb. 36–46]; then in the *Marche*, bb. 62–77/p. 57, b. 5[108]>. To be sure, more than just the ears should be involved in listening to his melodies. They pass us by uncomprehended if we do not give outward voice to our inward singing of them – and I mean not merely under our breath but full-chested and free.[109] Then they will take on a meaning for us which seems to grow ever deeper the more often we repeat them.

[iii Orchestration]

Lest we overlook anything, I might find room at this point for a few remarks on the Symphony as an *orchestral work*, and on the *pianoforte arrangement* by *Liszt*.

As a born virtuoso of the orchestra, Berlioz certainly makes inordinate demands both on the individual executant and on the whole body of players – more than Beethoven, more that any other composer. But it is not ever-greater mechanical dexterity that he requires of his instrumentalists; what he seeks is fellow-interest, study, love. Individuality must take a back seat in the service of the whole, and this must in its turn submit to the will of those in command. Nothing will be achieved in three or four rehearsals. This Symphony perhaps occupies in the world of orchestral music what the Chopin concerto occupies[110] in the world of pianoforte playing – though I imply no further similarities.

---

108 'p. 47, b. 1': dittography.
109 'and free' excised by Schumann in *GS*.
110 No. 1 in E minor (1830) was already published (1833); No. 2 in F minor (1829–30) was not published until 1836. Schumann may be referring to No. 1 alone, or to both collectively.

Even his adversary, M Fétis, metes out full justice to Berlioz's instinctive feeling for instrumentation.[111] {47b} The point has already been made earlier that the main solo instruments can be divined from the piano arrangement alone. Yet it would be hard for the liveliest imagination to get a clear notion of the many different instrumental combinations, contrasts and effects. Assuredly, he rejects[112] nothing to which the name pitch, sonority, noise or resonance could be given – thus he employs muffled timpani, harps, muted horns, cor anglais, even bells. Florestan said 'he hoped very much that he (Berlioz) might one day let all the players pipe up together in the tutti, although he might just as well write rests, since they would hardly be able to keep straight faces long enough to control their lips and play[113] – moreover, he (Florestan) looked forward keenly in future scores to convincing nightingales and accidental thunderstorms'. Enough. These things must now be heard. The experience will tell us whether the composer was justified in making such demands, and whether the net result affords pleasure commensurate with the effort involved. Whether Berlioz is able to cope[114] when he has smaller forces at his disposal remains to be seen. Let us content ourselves with what he has given us.

[iv Pianoforte arrangement]

The *pianoforte arrangement* by *Franz Liszt* merits extended discussion in its own right. Here we shall be brief, and[115] shall reserve that discussion, as well as some views on the *symphonic* handling of the pianoforte, for a later date. Liszt has brought to bear on its preparation so much industry, so much inspiration and genius,[116] that it has to be regarded as an original work, as a *resumé* of his profound studies, and as a practical manual of instruction in keyboard score reading.[117] This art of execution, so very different from the intricacies of the virtuosic style, the great variety of types of touch that it requires, the effective use of the pedal, the clear differentiation of voices as they interweave, the marshalling of the sonorities – in short, having command of the wherewithal, being privy to the many secrets enshrined in the pianoforte – this art is suited only for a master and a genius of

111 *NZM*, 2, no. 49, 198a.

It was plain to me [. . .] that M Berlioz was not at home in things that belong more to the rudiments of music. However, influenced by isolated extremely piquant and dazzling orchestral effects, I persuaded myself that something must stick in the head of someone who could contrive such effects. [. . .] I recognized in him an instinctive feeling for instrumentation, and recommended that he cultivate his talent for instrumental combinations so that others might then put them to better use than he.

112 'rejects' (*verschonen*) changed to 'disdains' (*verschmähen*) by Schumann in *GS*.
113 The passage is reminiscent of Fétis (*NZM*, 2, no. 49, 198a):

The orchestra [in a rehearsal at the Paris Conservatoire] wanted to burst out laughing. With each repetition of a passage some instrument was silent because the players one by one dropped out.

114 'cope' (*ausreichen*) changed to 'adjust' (*ausrichten*) by Schumann in *GS*.
115 'shall be brief, and' excised by Schumann in *GS*.
116 'so much inspiration and genius' changed to 'and so much inspiration' by Schumann in *GS*; the German of 'brought to bear' also modified (*gearbeitet* from *ausgearbeitet*).
117 *als praktische Clavierschule in Partiturspiel*: one contemporary manual in score reading was F.-J. Fétis, *Traité de l'accompagnement de la partition sur le piano ou l'orgue* (Paris: Pleyel, 1829).

performance, such as Liszt is considered by all to be. With such an artist, the pianoforte arrangement can be heard in its own right without undue modesty along-side orchestral performance. Liszt himself played it as an introduction to a later symphony of Berlioz, *Mélologue*, the continuation of the *Fantastique*, which was given its *début* in Paris a short time ago.[118] This pianoforte work must be recognized for its uniqueness, and drawn to the attention of all who would become familiar with the rare art of 'symphonic' execution. We ourselves feel impelled to pay heart-felt tribute to the credit that Liszt has brought upon himself by this work.

Passing mention must also be made of the careless engraving of the pianoforte arrangement.[119] The sharp-tongued critic ferrets out everything he can as weaponry against the unusual. So it is in this case. It is not easy to get the better of a lion with needles; the least that is likely to happen is that he will become aroused.

{48a} Let us spend a moment glancing back at the path that we have so far traversed. According to our original plan, it was our intention to deal in separate paragraphs with form, techniques of composition, idea and spirit. First we saw how little the form of the whole diverged from established form, how the individual movements mostly took on novel shapes, how periods and phrases were differentiated by unusual relationships of duration. Under techniques of composition, we paid great attention to harmonic style, to the ingenuity of the intricate crafts-manship, and of the sense of direction and the deliberate digressions that he creates, to the special character of his melodies, and subsequently to his instrumentation and to the pianoforte arrangement. We close now with a few words on the idea and spirit of the work.

(to be concluded)

---

118 *Le retour à la vie, mélologue en six parties* was the original title of what became at the revision in 1855 *Lélio, ou Le retour à la vie, monodrame lyrique*, Op. 14bis, the sequel to the *Fantastic Symphony*, which Berlioz wrote in 1831–2. It was first performed on 9 December 1832 at the Salle du Conservatoire, the *Fantastic* Symphony being the preceding item on the programme. 'This pianoforte work ... will become aroused.' excised by Schumann in *GS*, and restored in editorial footnote, vol. II, p. 381.

119 'engraving': *Orthographie*: the work was completely re-engraved at its second edition. See note 21 above for publication details.

120 i.e. *Ludwig van Beethovens Studien im Generalbass, Contrapunkt und in der Compositionslehre*, ed. Ignaz von Seyfried (Vienna: Haslinger, 1832, 2/1853; reprint edn Hildesheim: Olms, 1967), p. 88 ('art' reads 'true art').

121 *in einem Programme*: see N. Temperley, 'The *Symphonie Fantastique* and its Program', *The Musical Quarterly*, 57 (1971), 593–608.

122 Schumann's reading is based on a printed programme in leaflet form (version 8 of the fourteen known versions) that is not later than 1834, was probably produced for the first edition of the Liszt piano transcription, and has been found bound in one copy of that transcription.

{49a} Nature knows no cessation. Hand in hand with her
walks art, against whose pseudo-sister, artificiality,
may the heavens preserve us.

Beethoven (in his *Studies*)[120]

[III Idea]

Berlioz himself has set down in a programme[121] what he would like his audience to have in mind as they listen to his Symphony. We offer an abridged form of it below.[122]

The composer has sought to portray in musical terms some incidents from the life of an artist. The plan of an instrumental drama evidently needs verbal elucidation in advance. The programme that follows should be viewed rather like the spoken dialogue that leads into musical numbers in opera.

First movement: *Reveries, Passions*. The composer visualizes a young musician, afflicted with a certain moral sickness for which one famous writer[123] coined the phrase *le vague des passions*. This young man catches sight for the first time of a creature who is his very embodiment of idealized womanhood, the palpable incarnation of his imaginings. Through an odd caprice of fortune, the beloved image comes to him inseparably linked with a musical idea [*Gedanke*] in which he recognizes a certain passionate character, noble and reticent – the character of the very girl herself. Melody and image together pursue him unremittingly as a double *idée fixe*. Dreamy melancholy, interrupted only by occasional gentle tones of joy, and eventually leading to a climax of frenzied love; pain, jealousy, glowing ardour, tears – these symptoms of first love are the elements that make up the content of the first movement.

Second movement: *A Ball*. The artist stands amid the hurly-burly of festivities, rapt in {49b} contemplation of the beauties of Nature; but wherever he goes, in town or countryside, the image of his loved one pursues him, disturbing his peace of mind.

Third movement:[124] *Scene in the Country*. One evening, he hears two shepherds echoing one another as they pipe a round-dance. This dialogue, the place, the gentle rustling of the leaves, a glimmer of hope of requited love – all of these conspire to induce in him an unaccustomed calm, and cause his thoughts to turn to more cheerful things. He ponders how he will soon no longer be alone . . . But what if she were deceiving him! The adagio gives expression to these swings of mood, from hope to despair, from light to darkness. At the close, one shepherd pipes out once again his round-dance, but the other no longer answers. Thunder rolls in the distance . . . Solitude – rapt silence.

Fourth movement:[125] *The March to the Scaffold*.[126] The artist is now convinced that his love will never be returned, and so poisons himself with opium. The drug,

---

123 Presumably François-Auguste-René Chateaubriand (1768–1848), Romantic writer and diplomat, who discussed the term in his *Génie du Christianisme ou beautés de la religion chrétienne* (Paris: Migneret, 1802) (first authorized edn; two earlier incomplete edns pubd London 1799–1800 and Paris 1800–1801): see *Symphonie fantastique*, ed. Temperley, p. X.

124 'movement' in *GS* only.

125 'movement' in *GS* only.

126 Schumann adds the title in French parenthetically: *marche du supplice*. This is the form of title that he has used throughout his review, rather than Berlioz's later *Marche au supplice*; and yet he renders the German as 'March *to* the Scaffold' rather than 'Execution March'.

too weak to kill him, causes him to sink into a sleep filled with horrifying visions. He dreams that he has murdered her, has been condemned to death, and is now witnessing his own execution. The procession moves off. March music accompanies it, sometimes sombre and fierce, sometimes brilliant and triumphant, mingled with the thudding of the steps and the roar of the crowds. At the end of the march, the *idée fixe* is heard once again, as if the thought of his beloved were entering his mind for the last time, only to be cut off halfway through by the fall of the axe.

Fifth movement: *Dreams of a Sabbath Night*. He sees himself surrounded by gruesome ghouls, hags, freakish creatures of all kinds, assembled for his burial. Eery wailing, howls, brutish laughter, cries of agony. The beloved melody sounds out once more, but as a cheap, tawdry {50a} dance tune: *it is she*, arriving on the scene. Bellows of jubilation at her advent. Devilish orgies. Funeral knell. Travesty of *Dies irae*.

So much for the programme. He can keep it, so far as we Germans are concerned! Such handy guides always have something of the charlatan about them,[127] something degrading. At any rate, the titles standing at the head of the five movements would have sufficed on their own. The circumstantial details, bound as they are to be of interest to us since they tell us about the personality of the composer who lived through the Symphony, would have been passed on safely by word of mouth. In short, the Germans, with their sensitive feelings and their aversion to the invasion of privacy, prefer not to have their thoughts led by the nose in this crude way. They were affronted even by Beethoven, when he showed himself unable to trust them to discern the character of the Pastoral Symphony without being prompted. Man feels a certain squeamishness about the privacy of the genius's workshop. He prefers not to know about the origins, the ways and means, the trade secrets of creation. Nature does something similar, in fastidiously covering her roots with earth. So let the artist keep his travails to himself. If we could see the process whereby every work comes into being, and trace it to its very origin, we would meet with some appalling things.

Berlioz, however, was writing primarily for his fellow Frenchmen, who are not given to being much impressed by displays of delicate modesty. I can picture them sitting reading along with the music, slip of paper in hand, and applauding their countryman for portraying everything exactly *comme il faut*. The music in its own right means nothing at all to them. What I who had read the programme before hearing the work find impossible to judge is whether the music will suggest to someone ignorant of the composer's intentions the kind of images he had in mind. Once the eye has been directed to something, the ear loses its capacity for independent judgment. On the other hand, if anyone questions whether music can really fulfil what Berlioz asks of it in his Symphony, then the onus rests on him to demonstrate that other images, even quite diametrically opposite ones, fit just as well. Even I found at first that the programme robbed me of all pleasure and deprived me of independent response. But as it receded gradually into the background, and my own imagination came alive again, not only could I see it all present in the music, but what is more it was almost invariably clothed in vibrant living sound.

<hr/>

127 'have about them': German changed (*haben* from *behalten*) by Schumann in *GS*.

Many people get far too worked up over this thorny question of how far instru-mental music ought to go in representing thoughts and events. They do indeed delude themselves if they imagine that composers take up paper and pen with no more worthy intent than of expressing or depicting or portraying something or other. All the same, let us not belittle the effect of random external influences and impressions. Often when the musical imagination is at work, an idea [*Idee*] acts upon it unbeknowns. Often the ear is influenced by the eye – and that ever-alert organ, amidst the world of noises and musical sounds,[128] holds constant certain visual profiles which {50b} can transform themselves and develop into audible contours as the music takes shape. The more that elements related to music embody ideas or images manifested in the notes, the more poetic or graphic[129] will the com-position be; – and the more imaginatively and acutely the composer can observe all that goes on around him, the more sublime and exalted will his work be. Why should not the thought of immortality steal into the mind of an artist like Beethoven in the midst of his creative imaginings? Why should not the remembrance of a great hero fallen in battle give him the inspiration for a work? And for some other artist, why not the memory of a Bacchanalian night spent carousing in the company of handsome youths?[130] Or do we wish to be ungrateful to Shakespeare for having kindled a work worthy of himself in a young composer's heart?[131] – ungrateful to Nature in all her wonderment by denying that we arrogate to our works the beauty and sublimity which is hers? Italy, the Alps, the sight of the sea, a Spring twilight – could we really say that music has never evoked all of these things in our minds?

Not only these, but also smaller, more specific images can bring to music a sharp-ness of character which is a delight to behold, an incisiveness whose power to delineate individual features is quite astonishing. Thus, for example, one composer recounted to me how, while he was getting a piece down on paper, the image of a butterfly on a leaf drifting along in a stream constantly obtruded upon his mind. This brought the brief piece a delicacy and simplicity such as only the image in its living form could possess. Franz Schubert in particular was a master of this fine genre painting, and I cannot resist quoting from my personal experience how while once playing one of the Schubert marches the friend with whom I was playing duet responded when I asked him whether he did not associate specific images with the music: 'Oh yes, indeed, I am transported to Seville – the Seville not of today but of more than a hundred years ago, amidst Dons and Duennas[132] strolling up and down, wearing dresses with trains, pointed shoes, tapering swords and so on.' Our visions coincided to an amazing degree – even to the very same city. I hope my gentle[133] readers will not object to so trifling an example!

128 *mitten unter den Klängen und Tönen: Klängen und Tönen* could be rendered as 'sonorities and notes', or even as 'chords and notes'; but I have chosen to treat *Klängen* as an element in the 'ran-dom external impressions' to which reference has just been made, and therefore as the raw sounds of the external world.
129 *plastisch*: 'taking material shape; formed, or in process of forming . . .': J. and W. Grimm, *Deutsches Wörterbuch*, vol. XIII (Leipzig: Hirtzel, 1889), col. 1900.
130 'Bacchanalian night . . . youths' changed to 'time spent in happiness' by Schumann in *GS*.
131 Jansen/Kreisig and Cone suggest an allusion here to Mendelssohn's Overture *Ein Sommernacht-straum* (1826), written after Shakespeare's *A Midsummer Night's Dream*.
132 *Donnonen*, corrected (?) by Schumann to *Donnen* in *GS*.
133 'gentle' excised by Schumann in *GS*.

[IV Spirit]

Let us leave aside whether the programme to Berlioz's Symphony contains many poetic elements. The central question remains whether the music stands on its own when shorn of its accompanying narrative and elucidation; and particularly whether its spirit is immanent. I believe I have had something demonstrative to say on the former. Surely no one can deny the latter, even in those places where Berlioz plainly shows his weaknesses.

Anybody who chooses to run counter to the general drift of an age that can tolerate a *Dies irae* as a burlesque is going to have to re-enact what was said and written many long years ago against Byron, Heine, Victor Hugo, Grabbe and their ilk. At certain moments in eternity, poetry has {51a} donned[134] the mask of irony so as to conceal its pain-racked face from public gaze. Maybe a friendly hand[135] will one day untie the mask and remove it; and maybe by then the tumultuous tears will have turned into pearls.[136]

Very recently, Odillon Barrot has uttered words that have shaken the youth of our country to the core.[137] What he said was: *dans nôtre epoque, je ne sais, qui s'est imaginé, que tout ce qui est dans la nature est beau, qu'il y a une certaine poesie dans la crime* [I do not know who in our age could possibly have imagined that all that is in our nature is beautiful, that crime has a certain poetry about it], which might be translated in the mildest of terms as: 'Be careful, youthful ones, not to let yourselves be swept off into crime by your nature and passion; follow the bidding of your nature; declare as tenderly as you can how you love and whom you spurn! But protect your innocence, which alone makes your nature worthy of love; it may indeed sometimes be wanting, but it does not sin; it brings delight, but does not consume.'

We could go on all day debating good and evil in this way, but for now we must break off!

If these lines can do anything to encourage Berlioz once and for all to control his inspiration, so that the unpredictability of his spirit no longer needs justification on grounds of genius[138] – such that his Symphony has to be understood not as the work of art of a master, but rather as unlike anything that has gone before it by virtue of its inner strength and[139] originality –; and if finally my words can spur into renewed activity the youth of Germany[140] to whom he extends a strong supporting hand in league against talentless mediocrity, then my purpose will have been well and truly achieved.[141]

---

134 'donned' changed to 'tied on' (*vorgebunden*) by Schumann in *GS*.
135 'a friendly hand' changed to 'the friendly hand of a genius' by Schumann in *GS*.
136 'and maybe by then . . . but does not consume".' excised by Schumann in *GS*.
137 Odillon (or Odilon) Barrot (1791–1873), French public official and constitutional monarchist who served as minister of justice under Napoleon.
138 'unpredictability of his spirit . . . genius' changed to 'eccentricity of his present path may gradually tone down' by Schumann in *GS*.
139 'inner strength and' excised by Schumann in *GS*.
140 'youth of Germany' changed to 'German artist' by Schumann in *GS*.
141 'been well and truly achieved' changed to 'achieved its promulgation' by Schumann in *GS*.

Abramo Basevi (1818–1885)
Studio sulle opere di Giuseppe Verdi (1859)

As can be seen in the first volume of the present work, Baini set forth his classification of Palestrina's music in ten 'manners' or styles in 1828 (vol. I, Analysis
14); and Fétis, von Lenz and Ulïbïshev aired their classifications of Beethoven's
music in three 'manners' between 1837 and 1857 (vol. I, Analyses 16b–d). It was
in 1859 that the Florentine music critic Abramo Basevi published his own classification of Verdi's operas (up to but not including *A Masked Ball*) in four 'manners',
and in doing so showed himself well acquainted with the work of all four of these
earlier writers.[1] On Baini he remarked: 'The *Memorie storico-critiche* [. . .] is a work
of much greater value. [. . .] But [. . .] its critical side is too general'.[2] Citing Baini's
discussion of the seventh-manner Mass *Papae Marcelli* he observed: 'precisely
because the music is so remote from us, it cries out for a minute analysis demonstrating clearly its distinctive features and its particular qualities'. Of von Lenz
(Analysis 3, above, and vol. I, Analysis 16c), Basevi says that he offers here and
there some judicious analysis, 'but much of it is nothing more than poetic –
sometimes to the point of eccentricity and freakishness'.[3]

In Basevi's view, when Ulïbïshev, in his *New Biography of Mozart* of 1843
(see vol. I, Analysis 15) discusses 'music and words together, he may create some
confusion in the mind of anyone who wishes to fathom the organic part of music'.
Basevi was hardly an 'organicist' in the spirit of the German natural philosophers;
but neither did *organica* mean for him merely 'instrumental' (as it did for Baini):
rather, with *organismo* he seems to have had in mind autonomous musical process –
that is, harmonic syntax and form-building. Thus, where Ulïbïshev examines instrumental compositions, Basevi says he neglects 'how the particular forms come about',
providing instead 'fanciful descriptions (a near-universal fault among critics in
musical matters)'.[4] For Basevi, different aesthetic precepts governed instrumental
as against vocal music. Instrumental music admitted occasional use of what he
called *imitazione* – i.e. the depiction in music of physical objects or effects. Vocal
music, on the other hand, admitted no such thing. *Imitazione* was, however, always

1 Roger Parker first suggested this chapter for inclusion in the present volume. I am greatly indebted
to Harold S. Powers for his advice on many aspects of the analysis. Karen Painter made helpful
suggestions on the translation.
2 *Studio sulle opere di Giuseppe Verdi* (Florence: Tipografia Tofani, 1859), pp. VII–VIII. Basevi is
comparing the work with *Le Haydine ovvero Lettere su la vita e le opere del celebre maestro
Giuseppe Haydn* (Milan: Buccinello, 1812, 2/1823) of Giuseppe Carpani (1752–1825), the first
edition of which was heavily plagiarized by Stendhal in his *Lettres écrites de Vienne, en Autriche,
sur le célèbre compositeur Joseph Haydn . . .* (Paris: Didot, 1814, 2/1817).
3 *Studio*, p. VIII.
4 ibid, p. VIII.

an artifice; even in instrumental music its role was subsidiary: it should be used not as an end in itself but to ensure the efficacy of music's own language, which is 'indeterminate, universal and spiritual'. Basevi was a formalist at heart. He stressed the distinction that he perceived between 'imitation' and 'expression'. As an example he took up Ulïbïshev's contention (see vol. I, p. 288) that the full orchestra *fortissimo* C major chord at the words 'Fiat lux' in Haydn's *Creation* is a 'dazzling representation of light universal'. The music at this point, countered Basevi, 'seeks not to *imitate* light' but rather 'to excite in the soul that sense of satisfaction, or of surprise, which accompanies the impression that an unexpected blaze of light makes upon us'.[5] It was thus right, in opera, for notes to conspire with declamation to express the meaning of the words; but it must be the '*internal meaning* of the soul, not [. . .] the *material* impression conveyed to the senses'. Deploring the use of *imitazione* by Grétry in *Sylvain* to delineate a circular chain, and by Rossini in *William Tell* to depict a mountain, as leading only to a 'ridiculous exaggeration' or 'freakishness' that he dubbed *musicografia*, he meted out sharp criticism for the mimicry of sea breezes and waves in Simon Boccanegra's Act III monologue.

In his *A Study of the Operas of Giuseppe Verdi* (1859), the contents of which were published first as disconnected articles in the Florentine journal of which he was editor, *L'Armonia* (1856–9), Basevi termed his method of discussing a score 'analytic criticism' (*critica analitica*). Whereas poetic description (like that of Ulïbïshev) was aimed at the non-musician, his book was directed towards trained musicians (*maestri*), and his analytic criticism was 'necessary above all else, because, as the nearest equivalent to anatomical examination, it alone can lead to the study of the physiology of music'.[6] At the same time, he seems to have believed that the holistic view of musical form had only limited application in the world of opera: 'Objection can be made that when I examine an opera, as I do, by analytical means, many of its merits and shortcomings may pass unnoticed, indeed its most essential features, concerning the *totality* of the work. However, I do believe that the synthetic method [*il metodo sintetico*] cannot be adopted in music criticism on account of the small amount of development that opera displays overall in its music.'[7] What he intends by 'the synthetic method' is left unexplained, but clearly implied is an antithesis between 'analysis', dealing with detail (including the 'distinctive features and particular qualities' quoted earlier), and 'synthesis', dealing with the whole. – It is this remark that leads to his celebrated discussion of 'the colour or general hue' (*il colorito, o la tinta generale*) with which a composer of genius may imbue a whole opera.[8]

Basevi's division of Verdi's output into four style periods or 'manners' encompasses, of course, only the years 1839–57, for the final six operas, from *A Masked Ball* to *Falstaff*, did not yet exist. In works such as *Nabucco* (1842) and *Macbeth*

---

5   ibid, pp. 64–5; A. Ulïbïshev, *Nouvelle biographie de Mozart* (Moscow: August Semen, 1843), vol. III, p. 6.
6   *Studio*, p. IX.
7   ibid, 114.
8   Harold S. Powers aptly expresses this as 'a supervening musical patina that emerges from the agglomeration of diverse techniques, conventions, and novelties in several domains' ('"La solita forma" and "The Uses of Convention"', *Acta musicologica*, 59 (1987), 65–90, esp. 67).

(1847) Basevi saw Verdi's first 'manner', characterized by a grandiosity of style and impersonality of characterization that begin to diminish in *Luisa Miller* (1849), giving way to a simpler, catchier melodic style, suppler rhythm, and a more individualized character portrayal that constitutes the second manner, closer to the style of Donizetti. (On the 'grandiose style', and for extended discussion of 'manner' in music and art, see the Introduction to Part III of volume I.) The third manner, inaugurated with *La traviata* (1853), 'transported chamber music to the stage'. Strings dominate the orchestra, *parlanti* overtake recitative and aria as the main vocal medium, and the music is packed with a voluptuous passion that is without trace of exaggeration.[9] The fourth manner – the central topic of the analysis given below – shows Verdi supposedly under the influence of Wagner, with harmony predominant over melody and exhibiting a *recherché* character, music enslaved to the libretto and functioning as a 'translator' of images into sound (Basevi's aesthetic views are touched upon in the Introduction to Part II, above), and form becoming amorphous.

As to form, *Boccanegra*'s prime transgression according to Basevi was its disregard of structural convention – or, in terms of the listener, its lack of formal clarity. Never was this more conspicuous than in the duet between Simon and Fiesco in the prologue. Where Basevi looked for an essentially quadripartite scheme moving from dramatic (recitative: *tempo d'attacco*) to lyrical (*adagio*), to dramatic again (recitative or *parlante*: *tempo di mezzo*) and finally lyrical (fast: *cabaletta*),[10] he found instead a disconcerting fluidity of textures, fluctuation of tempo and metre, and blurring of demarcations: expectations set up only to be left unfulfilled, or fulfilled only to be betrayed moments later; and sections with no textural definition. To his foreshortened historical perspective, this was surrender to the Wagnerian 'system' as he knew it from *Tannhäuser* (1845); and it was compounded by Verdi's reluctance to let the two characters sing simultaneously, and by what in his eyes was a general overuse of *parlante*, a neglect of recitative, and restrictive use of *bel canto*. The *Boccanegra* discussion, given out of context as it is here, may appear only to exploit analysis in the service of a larger, more doctrinaire 'agenda'; it should, however, be seen as the penultimate one of twenty chapters, each eschewing all irrelevant biographical and circumstantial information and devoted to close examination of a single opera.

Simon Boccanegra, with libretto largely by Piave, was based on a play by the Spanish romantic playwright García Guttiérrez, whose work had already supplied the source for the highly successful *Il trovatore*. The first performance in Venice in 1857 was 'a fiasco', in Verdi's own words. Better received in Reggio Emilia, Naples and Rome, it was again a disaster at La Scala, Milan in 1859, and was openly ridiculed in the Florence performance to which Basevi refers. Verdi made sweeping revisions in 1880–81 with the aid of Boito, and the revised version was well received at its first performance in 1881.[11] It is the 1857 version that Basevi describes here,

---

9   See *Studio*, pp. 158–9, 230–31 for second and third manners. On *parlanti*, see note 35 below.
10 See Powers, '"La solita forma"', p. 69.
11 For reviews of the 1881 version by Filippo Filippi and Eduard Hanslick, see *Verdi's 'Otello' and 'Simon Boccanegra' (Revised Version) in Letters and Documents*, ed. and trans. H. Busch (Oxford: Clarendon, 1988), vol. II, pp. 666–78.

and the bar numbers editorially supplied in the text refer to the vocal score of that version in the Paris edition published by Escudier (see note 26).

In Basevi's text, many words and phrases appear in italic typeface. Most of these have been rendered non-italic in the translation, without the fact being noted. Basevi's *motivo* has normally been translated 'tune', *melodia* 'melody', and *canto* 'vocal line'.

Abramo Basevi was born in Livorno (Leghorn) in 1818 of Jewish parents. He took a degree in medicine at Pisa University, but then threw himself into music composition. Among his works were two operas, *Romilda ed Ezzelino* (1840) and *Enrico Howard* (1847), both unsuccessful on the stage. Abandoning composition in the late 1840s, he embarked on a career as a writer, theorist and entrepreneur in music in which he was to emerge as 'one of the most lively personalities of nineteenth-century Italian musical culture'.[12] As a critic, he came to wield considerable influence not only in Florentine circles but nationally. He was an advocate of the music of Beethoven, and of purely instrumental music, as is demonstrated by his book *Beethoven's Op. 18 with Analyses of the Six Quartets* (1874),[13] and by his founding in 1859 of the Mattinate Beethoveniane, which gave morning concerts of Beethoven's music, and in 1861 of the Società del Quartetto, which performed German chamber music in an effort to foster Italian instrumental composition on that model. He edited the latter's journal, *Il Boccherini*, from 1862, which effectively took over from the short-lived *L'armonia*, self-styled as 'the organ of musical reform in Italy', that he had founded in 1856.[14]

As well as promoting the music of Beethoven, he was an early campaigner for the works of Wagner – Wagner called him and his associates the 'Florentine reformers'.[15] As can be detected in the analysis given below, however, his advocacy of Wagner was not unalloyed: he several times lashes out at Wagnerian harmony and vocal style, tempering his view only in the final paragraphs. Ultimately for him the ideal contemporary figure was Meyerbeer, who combined German learning with Italian melody. At the same time, Basevi strove to raise Italy's consciousness of its own musical traditions, not only through his study of Verdi's operas (1859), but also by organizing 'melo-dramatic concerts' of music by Sacchini, Cimarosa, Paer and other neglected Italian composers, and by collaborating with the publisher Giovanni Gualberto Guidi in the production of pocket scores of such works as Peri's *Euridice*, Spontini's *The Vestal Virgin*, Rossini's *William Tell* and much instrumental music, as well as Meyerbeer's *Robert the Devil* and *The Huguenots*. As a theorist, Basevi produced two treatises on harmony, the first a historical account with an original final chapter, *Introduction to a New System of Harmony* (1862), the second, *Studies in Harmony* (1865), dealing with melodic construction as well as chordal progression, using music examples largely by Meyerbeer, Bellini and

---

12   Leonardo Pinzauti in *NGDM*, 'Florence', §3.
13   *Beethoven op. 18 con analisi dei sei quartetti* (Florence, 1874). I have been unable to consult a copy of this work.
14   See Bea Friedland, 'Italy's Ottocento: Notes from the Musical Underground', *The Musical Quarterly*, 56 (1970), 37–53.
15   Letter from Wagner 30 March 1856 (Zurich): *Richard Wagner: Sämtliche Briefe*, vol. VII, ed. H. -J. Bauer and J. Forner (Leipzig: VEB Deutscher Verlag, 1988), pp. 368–9.

Rossini, and rejecting the notion of 'dissonance' in favour of *meloarmonia*, whereby notes in a chord generate tension (*ansietà*) by being imbued with melodic character.[16] Basevi also wrote a *Brief History of Music* (1865). Towards the end of his life, he turned to writing philosophy.

16 *Introduzione ad un nuovo sistema d'armonia* (Florence: Tipografia Tofani, 1862); *Studi sull'armonia* (Florence: G. G. Guidi, 1865).

'Simon Boccanegra'
A *Study of the Operas of Giuseppe Verdi*

> Source:
> 'Simone Boccanegra', *Studio sulle opere di Giuseppe Verdi* (Florence: Tipografia Tofani, 1859), chap. 19, pp. 259–80.

translated by Walter Grauberg

I had to read Piave's libretto[17] no fewer than *six times* carefully before I could make head or tail of it – or thought that I could. I will try to reduce to a detailed synopsis this monstrous melodramatic mess [*pasticcio*], on which the composer had pinned so many hopes.

This libretto is divided into a prologue and three acts. Twenty-five[18] years pass between the prologue and Act I. The action takes place in and near Genoa, in the first half of the fourteenth century.

Prologue. SCENE 1. *A square in Genoa.* Pietro and Paolo, the latter a Genoese gold spinner, the former a citizen,[19] are in conversation. Paolo promises gold and possessions to Pietro, if the latter will agree to seconding the nomination of Simon, a privateer in the service of the Genoese Republic, for the post of Doge.

SCENE 2. Paolo, alone, inveighs against the patricians.

{260} SCENE 3. Simon Boccanegra enters in haste. Paolo tells him that he has arranged everything for his nomination as Doge. Simon is at first unwilling, but then agrees, in the hope that he will be able to marry Maria, who is being kept prisoner in the palace of the Fieschi family. The reader of the libretto needs to know that Simon's love was reciprocated by Maria, daughter of Jacopo Fiesco, that a daughter was born to her, and that Fiesco refused ever to recognize this union.

SCENE 4. On stage are Pietro, Paolo, artisans and citizens. They unanimously elect Simon Boccanegra. (*All leave.*)

SCENE 5. Fiesco comes out, *leaving his key in the keyhole* (!!!). He mourns the death of his daughter Maria. Women in mourning and servants come out of the palace, cross the stage and disappear.

SCENE 6. Simon meets Fiesco, and asks for his forgiveness, but the latter refuses. Simon persists, and Fiesco declares himself willing to grant it on one condition only, namely that Simon should hand over the 'poor innocent girl who was born from illicit love'. But Simon cannot do this, because he has lost her, and has long been searching for her in vain. Fiesco then leaves without forgiving him. Simon enters the Fieschi palace, to find in it only his Maria, dead. He returns to the stage, grief-stricken.

---

17   Francesco Mario Piave (1810–76), librettist, who wrote for Verdi the libretti of *I due Foscari* (1844), *Macbeth* (1847), *Il corsaro* (1848), *Stiffelio* (1850), *Rigoletto* (1851), *La traviata* (1853), *Simon Boccanegra* (1857 version), *Aroldo* (1857) and *La forza del destino* (1862). I have suppressed the italicization of this, and of many other proper names, throughout.

18   *alcuni lustri.*

19   'latter . . . former' reversed. The characters are correctly described in the original libretto.

SCENE 7. The people acclaim Simon Boccanegra.

Act I. SCENE 1. *The Grimaldi palace outside Genoa.* Maria Boccanegra, daughter of Simon, under the name of Amelia, is sad, and is expecting her lover.

SCENE 2. Gabriele Adorno, a gentleman from Genoa, arrives. The two express their love for each other.

{261} SCENE 3. News arrives that the Doge, on his return from the hunt, wishes to visit the palace.

SCENE 4. Amelia tells Gabriele that the Doge is coming to ask her to marry one of his favourites and therefore asks him to hasten the wedding.

SCENE 5. Gabriele, on leaving, meets Jacopo Fiesco, who has assumed the name of Andrea. Gabriele asks him for Amelia's hand. Andrea replies that she is an adopted orphan, to whom he has given the false name of Grimaldi so as to prevent the new Doge from seizing the wealth of exiled citizens. Ardently, Gabriele presses his request, and Andrea agrees. (*They leave.*)

SCENE 6. The Doge goes by with his retinue etc.

SCENE 7. The Doge remains with Amelia. Simon discovers that Amelia is his daughter, whom he believed lost.

SCENE 8. Simon tells Paolo, now a favourite of his and in love with Amelia, to give her up.

SCENE 9. Paolo, annoyed, tells Pietro, another favourite of the Doge, that he wants to abduct Amelia.

SCENE 10. *Vast square in Genoa. In front, the harbour, with ships beflagged.* The anniversary of Simon's elevation to Doge is being celebrated.

SCENE 11. Suddenly cries of 'Treachery!' are heard. Gabriele enters with his dagger drawn and advances against Simon, whom he believes to be responsible for the abduction of Amelia.

SCENE 12. Amelia, who has succeeded in freeing herself, enters, saying that the Doge is innocent. All cry 'Anathema!' on the head of the traitor.

Act II. SCENE 1. *Ducal palace in Genoa.* Paolo tells Pietro to have the two prisoners brought in.

{262} SCENE 2. Paolo complains of the Doge's ingratitude.

SCENE 3. Andrea and Gabriele come forward as prisoners. Paolo accuses Andrea, now known to be Fiesco, of betraying the Doge, and suggests that he kill the Doge in his sleep. Fiesco refuses.

SCENE 4. Paolo makes the same suggestion to Gabriele, to whom he says, in order to arouse his jealousy, that Amelia is with the Doge 'dedicated to infamous pleasure'. Gabriele too refuses.

SCENE 5. Only Gabriele remains on stage, a prey to jealousy.

SCENE 6. Amelia arrives and is accused of unfaithfulness by Gabriele. Amelia does not wish to disclose to him that the Doge is her father. The Doge arrives and Gabriele is hidden on the balcony.

SCENE 7. Amelia asks her father for permission to marry Gabriele. The Doge, though hostile to Gabriele, agrees. Amelia leaves, regretting that she cannot extricate the hidden Gabriele.[20]

20 Basevi misreads the libretto at this point: the reference should be to the Doge: 'Gran Dio! come salvarlo?'

SCENE 8. The Doge, left alone, falls asleep. Gabriele seizes the opportunity and brandishes a dagger to kill him.

SCENE 9. Amelia enters, and restrains Gabriele from killing the Doge. The latter awakens and inveighs against Gabriele, who, having discovered that Amelia is the daughter of the Doge, asks for forgiveness, which is granted. From offstage a clamour is heard against the Doge. Gabriele offers his [sword-]arm to Simon to defend him.

Act III. SCENE 1. *Scene as in Act II, with curtains drawn back to reveal the balconies at the rear of the stage.* The people and the senators congratulate the Doge on his victory. The Doge invites Gabriele to the church. Pietro tells Paolo that he has arranged everything to avenge himself on the Doge.

{263} SCENE 2. A chorus is heard announcing the marriage of Amelia to Gabriele. Paolo vents his fury. He opens a door and ushers in Fiesco, to whom he reveals that Simon has been poisoned.

SCENE 3. Fiesco is horrified at so great a crime, and says that he will find in death a way of escaping suspicion of having committed such an evil deed.

SCENE 4. The Doge enters with Pietro. He is beginning to feel the effects of the poison.

SCENE 5. Fiesco steps forward towards the Doge, who has remained alone, and makes himself known to him. The Doge recalls that Fiesco once offered him forgiveness, if he granted him the orphan girl whom he was mourning as lost, and now he tells him that this orphan girl is alive under the name of Amelia Grimaldi. Fiesco is greatly surprised, weeps and discloses that a traitor has poisoned him.

LAST SCENE. Maria,[21] Gabriele, etc., enter. The Doge presents Fiesco to Maria, as the father of her mother. The Doge blesses Maria and Gabriele, and then dies. Gabriele Adorno is proclaimed Doge.

I do not know how much the reader will have understood from this detailed synopsis, but I can assure him that he would have understood less by reading Piave's libretto.

I will say nothing about the historical aspect, which has not been so much altered as distorted: after all, as I see it, history is not learned in a libretto. I will forgive Piave the historical licence, provided he creates a story – or fable, if you will – in which something may be found deserving of our attention.

The characters are vague, cold, often {264} false and devoid of all dramatic effect. The situations, all contrived, old-fashioned, unclear and often lacking in verisimilitude, follow one another without logical order. The audience does not know where to direct its principal attention, since there is no centre of focus for its interest. The events, barely sketched in, are too fleeting, haphazard, without common sense, in short, of such a nature as to leave no trace in the mind of the spectator. Shall I speak of the verses? Piave's ability as a versifier is by now well known. As for the distribution of the musical items, whether it be good or bad, it is the composer who is responsible when the composer is none other than Verdi.

Great were the public's expectations of this, Verdi's latest music. All sorts of rumours were circulating as to which *manner* the famous composer would adopt.

21   Basevi resumes Amelia's true name, Maria.

Some thought that after the huge success of *La traviata* he would continue on the same path; others believed that he would pursue the approach that he had taken in *Giovanna di Guzman*.[22]

The great moment came. On the evening of 12 March 1856 the Fenice Theatre in Venice rang with the melodies of *Simon Boccanegra*. The reception of this opera was not a happy one. In other theatres, wherever it was performed, with the exception of Naples, the public was unremittingly severe. The fact is that with this opera, in devising somewhat *recherché* new forms to suit the dramatic expression, in giving greater importance to recitatives, and in giving decreased attention to melody, Verdi *attempted* a *fourth manner*, simulating somewhat German music. I would say that it is almost as if he wished, at least on the basis of this prologue, to follow – albeit distantly, but follow nonetheless – in the footsteps of the famous Wagner, {265} the subverter of current music. Wagner, it is well known, aims as far as possible to make of music an exact language – a veritable shadow of poetry.

Wagner's system [*sistema*] found, and still finds, many opponents in Germany, although that is a country which does not seem to find harmonic abstruseness as alien as does Italy, nor is it so readily attracted to simple melodies. Wagner's *Tannhäuser* is performed in Germany, but it does not attract crowds except for the novelty of the experiment,[23] nor does it prevent yawns, except when some melody, or *cantabile* or ensemble occurs, things which are indeed to be found, though contrary to the system and only in small quantities. If therefore Germany does not want this reform, there is all the more reason why Italy should detest it. It is *possible*, I grant, that the Wagnerian reform may represent the *music of the future*,[24] but I deny absolutely that it is the *music of the present*. And if there is one art that must seek to evoke immediate pleasure, then it is doubtless music, and opera [*musica teatrale*] in particular.

In the music of *Simon Boccanegra* there is certainly no abundance of *bel canto*, and the little that we do meet strikes us as a very old acquaintance which, given the discomfort of the listener, often turns out to be not unpleasing. Even so the vocal lines [*canto*] of this opera have in general the merit of not being exaggerated, thanks to the intrinsic vigour of Verdi's genius, hence they resemble the third *manner*, which in this respect marks significant progress. The orchestral accompaniment [*istrumentazione*] presents not so much ingenuity as abstruseness {266} in its harmonies, in the use of pedal points, and in certain ornaments, so that singing is often left to play a minor role. The recitatives, so numerous in this opera, do not stand out; the tunes [*motivi*] of the *parlanti*[25] are often without relation to the words.

22   *Giovanna di Guzman*: the Italian title under which Verdi's *Les vêpres siciliennes* (opera in five acts, first performed Rome 1855) was produced in Milan in 1856. As explained above in the Introduction, Basevi discerned four 'manners' (*maniere*) in Verdi's output. *La traviata* (1853) represented the third, whereas in *Les vêpres* all three manners were discernible along with even earlier styles, and yet a hint of a new manner in the making (pp. 256–7).

23   For evidence to the contrary, see E. Newman, *The Life of Richard Wagner* (London: Cassell, 1933–47), vol. II, pp. 101–02, 216–17, 303–12, 400, 411–13.

24   *musica dell'avvenire*: allusion to Wagner's prose work *Das Kunstwerk der Zukunft* (1849). Basevi italicizes each allusion, whether the whole phrase or merely *dell'avvenire* or *avvenire*, as he does its antithesis, *musica del presente*, almost with satirical effect.

25   *parlanti*: see note 35 below.

[Prelude and Prologue]

The prelude begins [p. 1][26] by referring, through *staccato* chords, to the Hymn to the Doge of Act I [p. 98]: a fairly traditional tune, and one which recalls an ancient and popular turn of phrase [*cadenza*] found in many church melodies;[27] yet Verdi gave it much weight, for he made it one of the dominating musical ideas [*frasi*] of the opera, and the one that accompanies like a shadow the person of the Doge. Then diminished seventh chords are heard resolving on to 6/5 chords [bb. 32–5, 38–41], [a progression] that will be used offstage by the chorus in Scene 5 of the prologue for the cry 'È morta, è morta' [She's dead, she's dead, p. 22]. Soon [allegro moderato] there appears the tune from the allegro of the duet between the Doge and his daughter in Act I Scene 7 [p. 86]. This tune acquires a certain importance in being later repeated by the orchestra during the Doge's dream in Act II Scene 8 [pp. 185f.]. The melody is far from new; on the contrary its rhythm is familiar, indeed commonplace; it is in this rhythm that Bellini wrote 'Suoni la tromba intrepido' [Sound the trumpet, and bravely I will fight].[28] There follows [p. 2: allegro agitato] the tune of the offstage chorus 'All'armi' [To Arms] of the finale of Act II [p. 198]: this device too is commonplace, indeed popular. A short phrase [*frasetta*] of four bars from the duet between the Doge and Fiesco of Act III Scene 5 [p. 228] is taken up at this point [p. 4], and with a brief cadence the prelude ends.

The three scenes of recitative with which the opera opens are not as significant as they should be when the audience's attention is drawn to them in this way. Verdi on the whole has rather neglected recitative in his operas; and {267} yet in recitative it is easier for the composer to display his genius for musical expression, as he is not bound by the need to observe certain symmetries and other regularities. Recitative is the very source of opera. It was in Florence that it was created for the first time towards the end of the sixteenth century. Vincenzo Galilei, father of the famous Galileo, was the first to write in an expressive manner for one voice only, setting to music those verses of Dante which relate to Count Ugolino.[29] Giulio Caccini followed his example, and so did Jacopo Peri and others. The success of these monodies inspired a learned and illustrious group that used to meet in the house of Jacopo Corsi with the idea of setting to music an entire drama in recitative style. Ottavio Rinuccini wrote the words, Peri and Caccini the music. Thus *Dafne* was the first opera with music, or rather the first attempt at an opera.[30]

---

26   Page numbers are cited from the following vocal score of the 1857 version: [All in double rule-frame:] SIMON | BOCCANEGRA | Dramma Lirico | in Gualtro [?] parti di | F. M. Piave | Musica di | G. VERDI | – | Prezzo 12ᶠ net | PARIS | Editeur LÉON ESCUDIER, 21 Rue Choiseul. [Below frame:] Cet Ouvrage étant déposé selon les Lois et Traités tout Contrefacteur sera poursuivi||

27   *di molti canti da chiesa* is unlikely to refer to plainchant; it is hard to know to what the *antica e volgare cadenza* refers.

28   Bellini, *I Puritani*, Act II finale, duet between Sir George Walton and Sir Richard Forth.

29   This is a reference to Galilei's setting of the lament of Count Ugolino in Dante's *Inferno*, which he performed in Bardi's Camerata in 1582, and which does not survive.

30   Jacopo Corsi (1561–1602), patron and composer; Ottavio Rinuccini (1562–1621), librettist and poet; Jacopo Peri (1561–1633), composer. *Dafne*, the result of a musical collaboration between Corsi and Peri on Rinuccini's libretto, was reportedly planned as early as 1594, its first attested performance taking place during the carnival of 1598. The claim of the composer Giulio Caccini (c.1534–1618), first made in 1614, to have contributed music to Peri's *Dafne* is doubtful.

Little by little, recitative improved. Vinci contributed greatly to this improvement, particularly in much of the last act of his *Didone*, so much so that according to Algarotti 'It is likely that Virgil himself would have been pleased by it, such is the feeling of animation and awe that it inspires.'[31] The celebrated Tartini recalls that in 1714 he heard in the theatre of Ancona 'a line of recitative accompanied by no other instrument than the bass, with the effect that in us musicians, as in the listeners, such emotion was aroused that all looked at each other for the changes in colour that were manifestly taking place in our faces. Thirteen times the drama was performed, and each time the same effect ensued in all.'[32] In the *History of Music* by Burney one reads, as if it were something extraordinary, {268} about the encoring every evening of a recitative in Jomelli's *Attilio*, as sung by Serafini.[33] Benedetto Marcello, Porpora, Pergolesi and others distinguished themselves with recitative. But the man who carried it almost to perfection was the famous Gluck.[34]

One can distinguish two kinds of recitative, i.e. simple recitative in which all the expression is in the singing part, and *obbligato* recitative, in which the orchestra too is important. In simple recitative the music sometimes strives to express the emotions contained in the verses, at other times it simply serves as a vehicle for the words without any further thought. This latter case occurs particularly in *opera buffa*, where I would prefer simple spoken dialogue, as in French *opéra comique*. *Obbligato* recitative is sometimes so melodically embellished by the orchestra that it almost approaches a *parlante*. Thus one could envisage a kind of scale between the various levels of vocal music, leading from simple recitative to *obbligato* recitative, to harmonic *parlante*, to melodic *parlante*,[35] and finally to aria.

Returning to the recitatives by Verdi discussed above, we will comment on one of the devices most favoured by Verdi, and which I consider often to be inappropriately used. I refer to the device of recitative on a monotone with the harmony changing, or the bass moving [against it], thereby simulating a [vocal] pedal point. All this cannot but indicate repose, gravity, and similar states; but no strong emotion. The words of Paolo, 'Il prode, che da'nostri mari cacciava l'affrican pirata, e al ligure vessillo . . . .' [The warrior who chased the African pirate out of our seas and to the Ligurian ships . . ., p. 5] are set to twenty-three successive Cs.

31 Leonardo Vinci (c.1690–1730), *Didone abbandonata* (first performed Rome 1726); Francesco Algarotti (1712–64) made these remarks in his *Saggio sopra l'opera in musica* ([n.p.], 1755) (see O. Strunk, *Source Readings in Music History from Classical Antiquity through the Romantic Era* (New York: Norton, 1950), p. 667).

32 Giuseppe Tartini (1692–1770), composer, violinist and theorist, *Trattato di musica secondo la vera scienza dell'armonia* (Padua: Giovanni Manfrè, 1754), p. 135.

33 Charles Burney (1726–1814), *A General History of Music from the Earliest Ages to the Present Period* (London: Author, 1776–89), ed. F. Mercer (New York: Harcourt, Brace, 1935), vol. II, p. 852 footnote; Nicolò Jomelli (1714–74), *Attilio Regolo* (opera seria, first performed Rome 1753).

34 Benedetto Marcello (1686–1739); Nicola Porpora (1686–1768); Giovanni Battista Pergolesi (1710–36); Christoph Willibald Gluck (1714–87).

35 Basevi has defined *parlante* earlier – 'In *parlante*, the theme [*motivo*] lies in the orchestra rather than in the voice' (p. 30) – and distinguishes three species: (1) *parlante melodico* ('while the principal tune [*motivo*] unfolds in its entirety in the orchestra, the voice doubles this tune at the unison or third or sixth for a certain stretch at a time (and not always so short a stretch, at that)', pp. 30–31); (2) *parlante armonico* (in which 'the voice does not have genuine melody [*melodia*] of its own, but creates a sort of counterpoint to the tune [*motivo*] in the accompaniment', p. 31) and (3) *parlante misto* ('the union of the other two', p. 32).

In his *Alcestis*, Gluck used this kind {269} of *cantabile* pedal point very knowingly for the chorus of the infernal gods, at the words 'E vuoi morire . . .' [And you wish to die . . .], with thirty-eight successive Ds in thirteen bars.[36] Rousseau considered this piece to be of sublime simplicity. The same technique was used by Mozart for the words of the Commendatore's statue in *Don Giovanni*, and by Rossini in Act I of the new *Mosè*, for the mysterious voice offstage.[37] It is in my view a mistake to use the technique similarly when the recitative expresses commonplace emotions. Clear evidence that recitative can still be effective today is provided by Act II Scene 6 of *La traviata*, which is for the most part in *obbligato* recitative.[38] Italians have a duty to honour recitative, if only because they have the most musical language in the world. The passage between Paolo and the chorus that follows [pp. 9ff] is ineffective and almost shapeless. The allegro 'L'Atra magion vedete?' [Do you see the gloomy mansion?, pp. 14ff] is a series of unrelated phrases. The vocal line often proceeds on one and the same note, a kind of pedal point much favoured by Verdi throughout the opera. Some variety of orchestral texture is to be found in this passage, which testifies to the care shown by the composer, but which hardly contributes to expression.

Fiesco's romanza 'Il lacerato spirito' [The wounded spirit, pp. 23ff] begins in the minor with a common enough rhythm; and after eight bars the *cantabile* solo part is interrupted by cries from offstage, 'È morta, è morta' [She's dead, she's dead]. It then changes to the major with a new musical idea, which, continuing simultaneously with the chorus, ends very effectively, thanks to its simplicity. The funeral march that follows [pp. 26f.] is poor stuff.

The duet between the Doge and Fiesco [pp. 28–36] strikes us as unusual in its form. After a recitative of a few bars {270}, it embarks on a kind of melodic *parlante* at the words 'Qual cieco fato' [What blind fate]; then Simon, at the words 'Sublimarmi a lei' [To devote myself to her], has a true *cantabile* that lasts only eight bars, giving way to a *parlante* the orchestral material of which involves some abstruse progressions along with some downright commonplace passages. All this in twenty-nine bars, after which Fiesco has a *cantabile* lasting six bars that gives way to an *obbligato* recitative of twelve bars. Simon then enters with a new *cantabile*, andantino 3/8, pastoral in character, at the words 'Del mar sul lido' [On the shores of the sea], which lasts no more than sixteen bars; then the music shifts from A♭ to the key of E major, and the vocal line proceeds for eight bars all on the same note, over the simplest of accompaniments, whereupon the next nine bars, the pitches [of the vocal line] varying only slightly, lead us back to A♭; and with a mixture of recitative, *parlante* and occasional hints of a tune the piece comes to an

---

36 Gluck, *Alceste*, tragedy in three acts (first performed Vienna 1767), Act II Scene 1: Coro de Numi Infernali non veduto (Vienna: Giovanni Tomaso, 1769), p. 95; Jean-Jacques Rousseau (1712–78) made the remarks in the following sentence in his *Lettre à M. Burney sur la musique, avec des fragmens d'observations sur l'Alceste italien de M. le chevalier Gluck* (c.1777), see *Projet concernant de nouveaux signes pour la musique* . . . (Geneva: Sanson, 1782), pp. 292–3.

37 Mozart, *Don Giovanni* (first performed Prague 1787), Act II; Rossini, *Mosè in Egitto* (first performed Naples 1818), in its second version, *Moïse et Pharaon, ou Le passage de la Mer Rouge* (first performed Paris 1827), end of Act I: 'Moïse, approche-toi . . .'.

38 i.e. the scene, following the duet with Germont, in which Violetta writes the letter to Alfredo, who then enters.

end after thirty-six bars. The form of this duet is undeniably novel, but not all novelties are beautiful, and we will not be so fond of novelties as not to prefer the old if it is finer. Wagner would have approved of this piece; indeed it is one of the most perfect models of a duet according to the followers of the *music of the future*: and it belongs so much *to the future* that Wagner himself would hardly dare to go so far. Indeed, in Act I Scene 2 of *Tannhäuser* there is a duet between Venus and Tannhäuser in which these characters not only sing several times together, but also repeat the same melody [*motivo*] three times, a melody that is fairly long and well developed.

If music were to aim for the goal toward which Wagner {271} and other innovators would have it go, and toward which Verdi in the above duet seems to be trying somewhat to lead it, then the future of music would be a return to recitative, and a solemn denial of historical fact.

But this false direction in which music has been pushed springs from a failure to keep carefully in mind the true and principal connections between music and poetry.

These connections may be viewed on two levels: on one as recitative; on the other as aria.

Recitative is here understood not only in the broader sense, but also in an extended mode that signifies *musical expression*, such as follows timidly and slavishly, step by step, the words and sentences that make up the text. Nor does it exclude those short melodies that interrupt the declamation and then vanish without any relation to others. Such was the case in the duet cited above, between Simon and Fiesco. Recitative is the first step in the musico-dramatic art.

Aria, too, is considered in a more extended mode, so as to include even the largest-scale ensemble pieces. With aria, music has achieved a certain independence, and has acquired a greater dignity, creating a species of 'musical paintings' [*quadri musicali*] which have a body of their own, even without the poetry. These musical paintings are vague pictures, but not without an influence on our mind. The poetry that is associated with them is like an interpretation, particularizing and delimiting the universal significance of these musical paintings. Thus in such instances the poetry stands to the music as arithmetic stands to algebra: {272} music is a formula, which the poetry applies to a special case. If the finale to Act IV of Meyerbeer's *The Prophet* were to be performed without words, beginning with the march,[39] this passage, which is a clear example of musical painting, could not but move the listener, even if in an indeterminate manner. Let the poetry be added, and the listener will then understand the reason for the emotion he was feeling. Now, the poetry does not add effectiveness to the passage because it is poetry – i.e. by virtue of its own art – but rather as an interpretation of the music.

For these reasons it becomes clear why the composer does not ask of the poet a piece of work which is perfect in itself, but rather a skeleton; which, when covered by the flesh that conceals it, does not lose its own form, but rather passes it on to the flesh.

---

39 Meyerbeer, *Le prophète* (first performed Paris 1849); reference here is to the coronation scene.

I consider it certain that the future of music lies in the improvement and development of the musical paintings just referred to. The past is my guarantee for the future. In instrumental music this progression is even more evident than in vocal music; one need only compare a symphony by Lully with one by Beethoven. As for vocal music one notes that composers, after creating little by little arias, duets and trios, sought to bring together a greater number of scenes into one musical painting, from which emerged the invention of the finale, attributed to Logroscino towards the middle of the last century.[40] When those arias, duets, etc. are compared with similar pieces from among the best of the modern ones, it will be seen that in these latter there are better links, greater unity and finer expression. In general, among the ancients, musical discourse dissolved into many digressions, or {273} was composed of too many repetitions; whereas among the best modern composers, if the musical discourse deviates to some extent, it does so in order to create episodes that could render the discourse itself more pleasing, and give it greater strength and vitality. Just as a recitative does not lose its character because traces of cantilena are found in it, so an aria does not cease to be an aria when it contains some elements of recitative.

In musical drama, recitative is as necessary as aria; and it is up to the ingenuity of the composer to decide on the time and place for it; but the composer must never forget that aria is of greater dignity than recitative.

Having cleared up these matters, we will proceed on our way.

The finale of the prologue [pp. 37–45], after a lengthy recitative, has an allegro assai vivo in which the chorus sings acclamations [to Boccanegra] and which comes as a relief after the monotony and flabbiness of the preceding music. The tune of this allegro is of the kind that is heard in Donizetti's *Parisina*, over the words of the chorus 'Alle giostre ai tornei che prepara . . .' [To the joustings, to the tournaments for which he is preparing . . .].[41] And the effect that it produces at this point is proof of the influence exercised by earlier pieces on those that follow.

[Act I]

Act I begins with Amelia's cavatina [pp. 46ff]. It is an adagio in 9/8, the vocal line has little expression; its only noteworthy feature is a very light accompaniment by stringed instruments, with chords widely spaced so that they extend beyond the [range of the] vocal line. After twelve bars, a 6/8 of eleven bars is reached that has little relation to the *cantabile* preceding it, and does not prepare very well for the rhythm of the *cantabile* when the latter is repeated above a different accompaniment. A short offstage *canzone* {274} by Gabriele [p. 51], in the *tempo di mezzo*, is a very slight thing. The cabaletta of the cavatina [allegro, pp. 52ff] is full of life, and takes us back to the Verdi of earlier operas. It stands out all the more, for it is a veritable flower of melody in the desert. Here Verdi forgot Wagner and all the *futuristic*

---

40 Nicola Bonifacio Logroscino (1698–?1765/7), composer of comic operas. His importance in the development of the finale has yet to be verified.

41 Donizetti, *Parisina*, opera seria in three acts (first performed Rome 1833): Act I, cavatina 'Forse un destin' with chorus of cavalieri.

composers, and gave to his allegro a form that, though older, is of surer effect, if perhaps a little popular in tone. The [andante] mossa of this cabaletta is a common closing device [*passo commune di cadenza*].

In the duet between Gabriele and Amelia [pp. 57–69], Verdi has followed the more usual form. The attention devoted by the composer to the accompaniment of the andantino in 3/8, 'Vieni a mirar la cerula' [Come and look at the sky blue sea] made him forget the vocal line, so that for eight bars Amelia sings on the same note. In the *Sicilian Vespers*, where at the words 'Presso alla tomba ch'apresi' [Near the tomb that opened] he used the same rhythm and vocal line, although at a different tempo, he employed one line of verse only, and not two as in these pieces.[42] I indicated earlier how much care has to be used with these *cantabile* pedal points, and in which special cases they are helpful. After a few, rather badly linked phrases, the period [*periodo*] 'Ripara i tuoi pensieri' [Direct your thoughts, pp. 60ff] is reached, which is repeated three times in the course of the piece. This period offers a vocal line of beauty, but in the last four bars it reminds us of the cavatina sung by Adina in *L'elisir d'amore*.[43] The allegro 'Sì sì dell'ara il[44] giubbilo' [Yes, yes, the joy of the altar, pp. 65ff] is written in imitation, with phrase answering phrase – an antiquated device [*sistema antichissimo*], in fact one of the first employed for the composition of duets. (Just consider the duets by Stefani, Durante, Scarlatti, Pergolesi, etc. etc.[45]) It is a device that I would certainly not want to see banned, but it needs to be employed appropriately, because its effect is not always pleasing – on the contrary, it is rarely so since, because of the brevity of the phrases and their frequent interruptions, it prevents {275} the transference of dramatic power into music.

Verdi made another attempt to achieve novelty of form in the duet between Fiesco and Gabriele [pp. 70–75]. A long recitative prepares the way for an andante mosso in which a melody [*motivo*] four bars long appears at the words 'Paventa o perfido' [Fear, O traitor], a rather unattractive melody, sung first by Gabriele with a pedal in the form of a timpani [roll], and then repeated by Fiesco a fourth below, with another pedal in the timpani. After that the parts proceed together for twenty-four bars, where I was not able to discern any overall musical conception. Besides, the dramatic situation is of little importance; and the music does not improve on it by repeating so many times 'Paventa' [Fear], addressed to someone not on stage to hear it: once would have been sufficient. This is the shoddiest piece in the whole opera.

In the duet between the Doge and Amelia [pp. 76–91] we encounter a form that is half novel, half conventional. The novel part extends as far as the cabaletta, which itself follows the old, indeed antique custom for cabalettas in duets of being almost obligatorily stated three times [pp. 86ff]. On the other hand, in the first part of the duet, after a recitative there comes a long *parlante* [pp. 77–9], which leads to the narrative 'Orfanella il tetto umile' [As a little orphan girl, the humble

---

42 *Les vêpres siciliennes*, Act II: scena and duet (Elena and Arrigo).
43 Donizetti, *L'elisir d'amore*, comic opera (first performed Milan 1832): Act 1 Scene 1: 'Benedette queste carte!'.
44 *al.*
45 Agostino Stefani (1654–1728), composer of operas and sacred works famed for his chamber duets; Francesco Durante (1684–1755), composer of sacred dramas and church music; Alessandro Scarlatti (1660–1725), composer of operas, oratorios and other genres.

roof] of pastoral character, but too long and disjointed. The Doge then sings an uncharacteristic eight-bar phrase, and then the two parts continue for nine bars in a kind of cadenza that finishes with a huge and ill-fitting flourish for the two singers together [*comune*]. Is it not time to get rid of these flourishes? Are they not nonsense? Are they really necessary? Is there no other way for the singer {276} to show his skill? Let composers think about it, and then banish these anti-artistic flourishes. In the *tempo di mezzo*, a *parlante* takes us to the cabaletta 'Figlia a tal nome palpito' [Daughter, at this name I tremble], which is the tune already observed in the prelude.

We will pass over without comment a brief duet, all in *parlante*, between Paolo and Pietro [pp. 92f], and come to the festive chorus, which is lively, perhaps all the more so in contrast to the music that has gone before [pp. 94–7]. The barcarolle that follows the festive chorus [p. 97] is the least attractive written so far by Verdi, who nevertheless used the same tune in the *Ballabile* which follows immediately afterwards [pp. 101–06]. The hymn 'Viva Simon' [Long live Simon, pp. 98–100] has already been observed in the prelude.

The sextet [pp. 107–28] sounds quite unlike Verdi. In Florence the opening bars gave rise to laughter in the audience, and even among the singers (something unheard of), in particular because of the repetition of the words 'Ella è salva' [She is safe] in several parts, so many times, and at [such] short intervals. The narrative by Amelia that follows [pp. 129–36] is almost bereft of melody. Its accompaniment tries to imitate, almost to translate, the words – a procedure that is far from the dignity and aim of music as an art. Next the stretta is an interweaving of voices which produces veritable chaos, rather than order. The unexpected sound of the harps continued over sixteen bars to accompany the word 'giustizia' [justice] is in my view bizarre.

[Act II]

In Act II we shall proceed directly to the aria by Gabriele [pp. 167–71]. Here too there is an element of novelty, namely the allegro before the adagio. The allegro 'Sento avvampar nell'anima' [I feel my heart burn] has an accompaniment in semiquavers, rising and falling in semitones, that does not work well with the voice. {277} After eighteen bars the vocal line more or less disintegrates, and turns into a short *obbligato* recitative. The largo, which is the last part of the aria, offers nothing else noteworthy except that it begins with the same rhythm as the romanza ['Il lacerato spirito'] sung by the bass [Fiesco] in the prologue: as for the rest, it proceeds in too uniform a manner.

The duet between Amelia and Gabriele that follows [pp. 172–8] also deviates in some respects from conventional forms. The andante is not very attractive. The means of expressing the tenor's words 'Dammi la vita, o il feretro' [Give me life or the coffin, pp. 174f.] through a falling chromatic progression is devoid of the spontaneity without which all expression lacks true worth. In the più mosso section there is no shortage of passion, and the passage in which Gabriele sings in falling semitones 'Si compia il fato egli morrà' [Let fate be fulfilled: he will die, p. 178] is well conceived and well contrasted with Amelia's role.

The orchestral part in the Doge's dream [pp. 179–86] is not very effective; there is, however, good justification for the repetition, beneath an accompaniment in the highest register, of the tune of the allegro ['Figla a tal nome palpito'] from the duet between the Doge and Amelia in Act I.

The trio which concludes the act [pp. 187–203] offers some lovely musical ideas [*frasi*], especially Gabriele's 'Dammi la morte, il ciglio' [Kill me, my eye I dare not raise, pp. 192ff]. The piece ends with an offstage chorus 'All'armi . . .' [To arms . . .], during which Verdi makes the three characters who are on stage sing in recitative: this too is a novelty, but how effective is it?

[Act III]

We will pass in silence over the choruses with which Act III opens, and jump straight to Scene 5, where the Doge seeks the cool of the sea breeze [pp. 216ff]. In this piece, too, Verdi misused musical imitation [*musica imitativa*], both for the breeze and for the sea, the waves of which he tried to imitate. {278} These imitations, accompanying as they do words that already express the same thing and do so to better effect, resemble translations, as I said earlier.[46] And it is certainly not the function of music to translate, since music is not a particular or exact language.[47]

The duet between the Doge and Fiesco [pp. 218–31] offers us in the largo over the words 'Delle faci festanti al barlume' [By the glimmer of the festive lights] a tune in which the *cantilena* is forced, far from spontaneous and lacking in expression. There follows an allegro [assai], which is neither pleasing nor moving, to the words 'Come fantasma . . .' [Like a ghost . . .]. We then meet, towards the end, a succession of minor ninths that continues over many bars without any real preparation and resolution, and that was intended to imitate weeping and grief! In this passage Verdi made skilful use of the differences in volume and musical accent among the dissonant parts. Finally we reach the largo 'Piango perchè mi parla' [I weep because there speaks], in which we find passion rather than a cold combination of notes: and not before time!

The final quartet [pp. 232ff] is the best piece in the opera. Verdi most skilfully clothed with music this dramatic situation, which is the finest in the libretto, and the only one that does not contradict common sense. For each of the four parts, he ingeniously crafted a vocal line that is distinctive and exactly appropriate. Particularly effective is the ensemble at the words 'Ah! . . . non morrai' [You will not die, pp. 238ff], Amelia singing a syncopated descending chromatic scale that excellently fits the despair of someone in tears. An abrupt break towards the end

---

46   i.e. p. 64:

> it is contrary to every sound precept of art, and to common sense, and indeed to effect, to translate into sound the words that are being sung, as if to suggest that the meaning of the words can never hope to be as clear as a group of notes.

and also twice in the present chapter.

47   cf. p. 64:

> Material imitations, in which music approaches common and particular language, dislocate it from that indeterminate, universal and spiritual language that constitutes its greatest value.

also the discussion of Wagner earlier in this chapter.

of this ensemble [p. 241], to make way for a lengthy recitative, diminishes the effect. This piece constitutes an example of one {279} of those musical paintings that were discussed earlier. It is not a huge painting, but it is nevertheless a lively and fine musical picture; where it becomes independent of the words, it does not disintegrate, but continues to be effective and expressive, true to the capabilities of music.

This opera must be considered an attempt on Verdi's part to emulate German music, where harmony takes precedence over melody. But our composer lacked the main thing: a suitable libretto. It has been said that 'Music sharpens the arrows which the poet has aimed at the heart',[48] but, if these arrows are brittle and weak, what is the point of sharpening them? Indeed, where the libretto does not provide the composer with material for dramatic and passionate music, all that is left is at least to make the music pleasing to the ear. But Verdi did not do this; he seems on the contrary to have taken great pains to create melodies that are unattractive, badly developed, disjointed in their periodic construction, utterly lifeless, totally unrelated to one another, and leading to clashes rather than mutual benefit.

I do not wish to condemn German music; on the contrary, I would like to see much more attention paid to it in Italy; but that does not make me approve the precedence given to certain harmonic abstrusenesses over expressive or passionate singing.

Let musical doctrine be put on the stage by all means; it can be done, indeed it should be done; and our Mercadante is specially praiseworthy on this account;[49] but let it be done as it is done by Meyerbeer, as it was done by Mozart and others, who used it, as it were, as a driving force to impel the art of music speedily {280} forward towards its proper goal.

For this reason I esteem musical classicism, and praise the very few who honour it in Italy and lovingly cherish it. Among these I am glad to recall T. Mabellini, C. A. Gambini, G. Maglione, F. Giorgetti (famous pioneer of the violin), S. Pappalardo and R. Manna.[50] And if I do not mention others, it is not that I want to do an injustice to their qualities. If greater encouragement and esteem were given in Italy to the study of the classics, we would not see composers go to the two extremes, either writing music that is feeble and almost consumptive, or losing themselves in abstruse creations resembling musical puzzles and charades.

---

48   This is not a well-known remark; it may perhaps have been made by another Florentine writer of Basevi's time.
49   Saverio Mercadante (c.1795–1870), composer of operas and other music.
50   Teodulo Mabellini (1817–97), composer of operas, cantatas and sacred music; Carlo Andrea Gambini (1819–65), pianist, composer of operas, piano works, masses, etc.; Giovacchino Maglione (1814–88), pianist, composer of piano works, a sacred drama and operas; Ferdinando Giorgetti (1796–1867), violinist, composer of chamber and sacred music, advocate of the German classics; Salvatore Pappalardo (1817–84), composer of operas, chamber music, etc.; Ruggiero Manna (1808–64), composer of operas and sacred works.

Adolf Bernhard Marx (1795?–1866)
Ludwig van Beethoven: Leben und Schaffen (1859)

Marx's published thoughts on the Ninth Symphony span thirty-three years, and form a majestic double arch, the pillars of which comprise his three major essays on the work – dating from 1826, 1847 and 1859 respectively. The first of these, a review of the score and parts, opens with a declaration: 'Beethoven has twice, assuredly, [yet] unaware of what he was doing, elevated his artistic individuality to be the content of a work.' Marx was referring not, as we might expect today, to works such as the intensely personal late F major String Quartet Op. 135, or the A♭ Piano Sonata Op. 110, but to the Fantasy for piano, chorus and orchestra, Op. 80, dating from 1808, and the Ninth Symphony.[1]

Different though these two works are in stature by present-day valuation, they had highly significant interconnections for Marx. Both works had overall forms that defied all previous standards: a long, purely instrumental component that was almost a composition in its own right, followed by a substantial choral component. Neither work could be viewed as either an instrumental composition with choral appendage or a choral work with instrumental prelude. Each was a fusion of forms. But that was by no means all: both effected a partial transfer of sonic medium from instrument to human voice; both entailed a shift from abstract music to a combination of music and language, or better, a shift in language from the purely musical to the human.

In the case of the Fantasy, a solo pianist stamps his identity upon the performance by playing at the very outset that paradigm of personal expression, the free improvised prelude – a prelude during which orchestra and chorus must sit silent and observe before embarking on their set of orchestral variations followed by a choral variation that forms the final section. The work was, then, an extended metaphor for the dominion of individual artistic personality over collective instrumental and vocal forces. Moreover, since at the first performance it was Beethoven himself who had improvised the prelude, the metaphor had been sharpened *ab initio* to manifest the composer as master of his own forces, and more than that: as the subject matter of his own composition.

The dynamic of the Ninth Symphony was different. There, voices represented the human world, and instruments the non-human. At its beginning (so Marx asserted in 1826), the work presented a Beethoven wholly absorbed in the instrumental realm and cut off from the vocal – this artistic circumstance mirroring

---

1   *Berliner AmZ*, 3 (1826), no. 47 (22 November), 373–8. Marx had reviewed the Fantasy in ibid, 2 (1825), no. 45 (9 November), 364–6. Marx does not refer to the similarity between the theme of the Choral Fantasy's variations and the main theme of the final movement of the Ninth Symphony.

the circumstances of his personal life, with its shunning of social contact and avoidance of personal communication. The fourth movement therefore emerges as a metaphor for the passage from this to the contrary circumstance: for the subjugation of the instrumental to the vocal; the besieging of the protean (the instrumentarium) by the singular (vocal melody), the victory of the simple and innocent over the multifarious and magical. All of these warlike processes act out Beethoven's longed-for psychological journey from isolation to companionship, from deafness to communication. It is in this sense that, like the Choral Fantasy, and despite the very different dynamics of the two works, the Ninth Symphony embodied Beethoven's individuality.

Despite his view of the Ninth Symphony as a process, Marx clings to the notion that the work is made up of two major forms, a symphony and a cantata, and that these are mediated by a recitative that is at first instrumental and then vocal. Indeed, this mediation is the crux not only of the work but of the realization of content. For the transference of the recitative from cellos and basses to baritone solo marks not only the initial penetration of human voice into what has hitherto been the instrumental realm, but also the moment at which the two planes of meaning – the semiotic, comprising patterns of musical sound, and the psychological, comprising Beethoven's aspirations – come into contact.

The second of Marx's essays was written in 1847, after completion of the first edition of his *Manual of Musical Composition in Theory and Practice*.[2] It was a much more searching examination of the separate natures and functions of vocal and instrumental music. Marx now carried much further his earlier rejection of one part as prelude or the other as appendage. Thinking still in two equally valid formal categories, symphony and cantata, Marx speculated as to how a work's content could be coherent and internally unified and yet at the same time 'be split between two essentially different media into disparate if not heterogeneous parts'. The answer: it is *intrinsic* to the work that 'the content of the cantata will differ completely from that of the symphony, that *the two halves of the work are to contrast with* [Gegensatz treten] *one another*' (italics mine). As before, the recitative is crucial, but this time the fulcrum of the work is no longer the transfer from tones to words, but the import of those words themselves: 'O friends, no more of these tones! But let us sing something more cheerful, and more full of gladness!' It looks back at the old content and forward to the new; it invokes the new content. Beethoven does not make the mistake of trying to implant the same musical idea in the two parts. Quite the opposite: he maximizes the difference between the two parts; he assigns to each medium the material appropriate to it, and develops that material comprehensively.

Between the essays of 1826 and 1847 a subtle shift of view had taken place. The earlier essay portrayed a journey from symphony to cantata that was part of the compositional process; Marx there viewed the work teleologically. The second

---

2 Indeed, the third edition of vol. I and second of vol. II had also been issued by then: 'Ueber die Form der Symphonie-Cantate: auf Anlass von Beethoven's neunter Symphonie', *AmZ*, 49 (1847), no. 29 (21 July), cols. 489–98; no. 30 (28 July), cols. 505–11. I am indebted to James Day for access to his unpublished translation, from which the quotations given below, cols. 495 and 505–06, draw.

presented an antithesis that was inborn in the initial conception, hence was pre-conceived, and ultimately static. The antithesis was itself the original insight. Only at the last moment before the change did Marx declare that 'the phrase "not these sounds" *is already taking shape* in [Beethoven's] soul. He is still imprisoned in this magic world. But whatever is taking shape here originates in and strives towards the expression of the spirit of man and human life' (italics mine). However, this last-minute premonition serves only to underline the static relationship between the two contrasting parts.

The 1859 essay, given in full below, reverts to the teleological view of 1826 – indeed, adopts a radical teleology that far exceeds the earlier view. The essay is a product of its context: Marx's full-length study *Ludwig van Beethoven*, which is subtitled literally 'Life and *Creativity*' (*Schaffen*) – not 'and *Works*' (*Werke*). (I have compromised somewhat below by rendering it 'Life and Creative Output'.) An earlier chapter of this two-volume, 750-page book accounts for the overall multi-movement form of sonata-type works as a single entity and psychological process. The account goes as follows: to compose a first movement is a spiritual birth-giving; its product is a self-image; composer and composition form a 'duality' (*Zweiheit*); duality prompts self-contemplation, a kind of sabbath-day rest from exertions that constitutes a second-movement adagio, during which the composer asks: 'Who am I?'; restored and refreshed, the composer then returns to activity – the final move-ment. The result is 'tripartiteness' (*Dreitheiligkeit*).[3] However, Marx says, during the adagio the composer may look back out at the world, and see it 'dancing its old round-dance':[4]

> Cheerful in the well-being of restored strength, whimsical to the point of high spirits or wildness [as he is], the intimate duality – not a hostile confrontation – reasserts itself: adagio and scherzo stand one to the other like heart and world. In the finale, life streams or storms on. The duality is conquered or forgotten. This is how we would try to account for 'quadripartiteness' (*Viertheiligkeit*) – the binding together of four movements into a whole.

Marx now alleged that Beethoven had had no intention of setting Schiller's *Ode to Joy* when he first embarked on the symphony. As initially visualized, the work was wholly instrumental. The necessity of enlisting the human voice was to assert itself only later, as a gradually dawning realization. Marx charted the progress of this realization as a series of decisive steps in the compositional process, equatable with a series of crucial moments in the score. Creation imagery is strong through-out. In Marx's explanation of tripartiteness we saw the slow movement invested with sabbath-day status – God resting from his six-day labours. The first movement is now associated with the words 'Let there be light!'; and in the first three move-

---

3 This discussion is prompted by the minuet of the Piano Sonata in F minor, Op. 2 no. 1: vol. I, pp. 123–7, in the four movements of which Marx notes 'unity and compulsive logic'. But the discus-sion is itself impelled by the scherzo of the Piano Trio Op. 1 no. 1, which raises the issue: 'What meaning has the existence of three or four movements?', vol. I, p. 114.

4 vol. I, p. 124. Round-dance (*Ringelreigen*) is a recurrent image: 1826 refers to the scherzo of the Ninth Symphony as 'a joyful, inexhaustible new round-dance (*Reigen*)' (p. 376); 1847 refers presumably to the scherzo as 'a whirling round-dance' (col. 508); 1859 refers to a 'stately round-dance' in the first movement, and to the 'gleeful, furtive round-dance' (and 'jugglers' dance [*Gaukeltanz*]') comprising the scherzo.

ments together, Beethoven fashions instruments as God, in the first chapter of *Genesis*, fashioned man in his own likeness. Overall, the four movements are seen to map on to the six days of creation in a non-specific manner, but with man as the specific final stage in the process. Other biblical allusions (notably to *St Matthew*, and the *Acts of the Apostles*), and the adoption at times of a biblical tone, all reinforce this suggestion.

Those crucial moments are: (1) the transmutation of the opening of the first movement into a *fortissimo* cry at the beginning of the recapitulation (b. 301), which he calls 'the moment of decision'; (2) an intimation, towards the end of the first movement, of a 'parting of the ways' from the purely instrumental realm, at which point the final chorus became an 'inner necessity'; (3) the closing bars of the scherzo, at which the farthest point of the instrumental journey is reached, and 'the die is cast'; (4) the onset of the adagio, which is Beethoven's leave-taking from the symphonic world, this leading to (5) the embracing of man in the finale. The recitative for cellos and basses is now seen in a quite opposite way from that of the 1826 essay. It is no longer the first step in the transference from instrument to voice; it now looks backwards, not forwards; it stands for the first three movements, and serves to expose the inarticulateness of instruments.

Underlying all three of Marx's essays on the Ninth Symphony is a form of aesthetic idealism. In the mind of every artist, Marx holds, there is a 'play of formations [*Spiel des Gestaltens*]', in itself purposeless, which generates 'raw material [*Stoff*]' from which works of art take shape. Marx speaks of a 'play of tones [*Spiel der Töne*]' that goes on in the composer's mind, and that he also calls 'primeval music [*Urmusik*]'. The composer's imagination tracks this aimless stream of sound for something reflective of his inner world of feeling, and upon finding it engages it, so imbuing it with purpose. This engagement of raw material with the composer's spirit [*Geist*], this fusion of external with internal, yields the 'Idea' [*Idee*], which is initially largely subsconscious. The process of composition is the 'liberating' of this Idea, it is its disclosure to public gaze. Marx's view clearly comes out of the metaphysical idealism of the Neo-Platonists whereby the artist intuits a vision of ultimate reality, universal Idea, and imitates this reality in art. In particular, it borrows from that version of metaphysical idealism developed around the turn of the nineteenth century by Schelling and Hegel, while being indentifiable directly with neither.[5] Marx's principal discussion of content in the musical work of art, to be found in his *The Music of the Nineteenth Century and its Cultivation* (1855), is in fact saturated with Hegelian language.

The genesis and evolution of the Ninth Symphony, presented in the essay below as a dawning realization, can be seen as precisely this 'liberating' of an Idea – an

5   My summary of Marx's formulation is derived partly from *Ludwig van Beethoven*, vol. I, pp. 275–8, partly from *Die Musik des neunzehnten Jahrhunderts und ihre Pflege: Methode der Musik* (Leipzig: B&H, 1855), pp. 44–55. On metaphysical idealism, see Harold Osborne's excellent *Aesthetics and Art Theory: An Historical Introduction* (London: Longmans, 1968), pp. 54–61. For an investigation of Marx's concept of *Idee*, see Scott Burnham, 'Criticism, Faith, and the *Idee*: A. B. Marx's Early Reception of Beethoven', *19th-Century Music*, 12 (1989/90), 183–92, which argues that Marx's *Idee* is not intrinsically Hegelian, but only a 'quasi-philosophical' reaction to Beethoven's forms, 'a concept imported from Idealist aesthetics but employed as a symbol of the critic's intuition about the wholeness and spiritual elevation of the musical work'.

Idea at first barely suspected, that unfolds implacably with each conscious decision. The Ninth is, we might say, an ideal example of the process by which all great works of art take shape. Moreover, Marx's view of the genesis of an Idea casts further light on the decisive vocal recitative at the beginning of the finale. If, as we have said, the composer's mind tracks the 'play of tones' for patterns reflective of his inner sentient life, then the words of the recitative (Beethoven's own words) 'O friends, no more of these tones!' signals a rejection of the raw material that has so far been used (and that has just been symbolically reviewed by the orchestra), and a call for wholly new material. Marx had emphasized the primacy of this wholesale change in his 1847 essay, by comparison with Mendelssohn's Second Symphony, the *Hymn of Praise*, in which the opposite happens. But there he was concerned with propriety of material to medium (orchestral or vocal) and form (symphony or cantata). Now, in 1859, all talk of 'cantata' is discarded, and in its place there is concern with the 'simplicity' and 'folk-like strain' of vocal melody: 'We are left in no doubt here how utterly committed Beethoven was to the idea of the simple folksong.'

Marx's *Ludwig van Beethoven: Life and Creative Output* is one of the pioneering composer-biographies of the nineteenth century. It is more ambitious than its predecessors in its charting of the life of the mind and spirit. While discussing many of Beethoven's works, it treats a limited set of compositions as diagnostic indicators of spiritual development – the nine symphonies, *Fidelio*, the *Missa solemnis* and the string quartets Opp. 59, 132 (see Analysis 13, below) and 135, among which the 'Eroica' Symphony and *Fidelio* occupy the greatest attention. Adolf Bernhard Marx became, after a short period as a lawyer, the founding editor of the *Berliner Allgemeine musikalische Zeitung*, a journal of major importance despite its having survived only seven volumes (1824–30). In 1830 he was appointed professor of music at the University of Berlin. Between 1837 and 1847 he produced the first edition of his four-volume *Manual of Musical Composition in Theory and Practice*, the first multi-purpose musical textbook, designed primarily for the lecture hall, but contrived also for self- and private instruction, and arguably the most influential theoretical work of its century. In the early 1840s he engaged in polemics against Dehn and Fink (see the Introduction to Part I, above, p. 20), and in 1855 he wrote his *The Music of the Nineteenth Century and its Cultivation: Method in Music*, which attempts a thorough-going mid-century assessment of music and a prognostication of the nourishment and educational policies that were needed for its future ('Progress is our watchword!'). In 1850, he founded what later became the Stern'sches Konservatorium in Berlin. His abiding interest in the music of Beethoven and Gluck resulted, late in life, in the production not only of the Beethoven biography and its offshoot, a short but fascinating *Introduction to the Performance of Beethoven's Piano Works* (1863), but also of his *Gluck and Opera* (1863).

'[Beethoven:] The Final Symphony'

Ludwig van Beethoven: Life and Creative Output

Source:
A. B. Marx, *Ludwig van Beethoven: Leben und Schaffen* (Berlin: Otto Janke, 1859),
vol. II, pp. 264–88.

Of all the plans and resolutions [that Beethoven had in mind during the period
from summer 1822 to late 1823, the Ninth and Tenth Symphonies, the opera pro-
posals on *Melusine*[6] and *The Diver*,[7] the oratorio *The Triumph of the Cross*,[8] the
proposed *Faust*[9]], only one was to come to fruition: the Idea [*Idee*][10] of the Ninth
Symphony. Should Beethoven stoop from his *Leonore*, idealized image [*Ideal*] in
music of the German wife, to the sorceress Melusine? Or should he join forces
with Weigl[11] [. . .] to collaborate on a wedding opera by Biedenfeld? Or should he
pursue the misconception, oft-repeated long after his time, that *Faust* was the
'highest goal' for music, since it was the greatest work of German poetry?

6   *Melusine*: a figure in French folklore. The legend was first recorded in literary form in 1378 by
Jean d'Arras, and in the fifteenth century in verse by Couldrette. Beethoven approached the Austrian
poet Franz Grillparzer (1791–1872) for a libretto. The latter agreed, and selected the Melusine
legend as its subject matter. Although Beethoven described the opera to Grillparzer as 'complete',
there was no trace of it among his sketch material at his death ('Meine Erinnerungen an Beethoven',
in *Franz Grillparzer: sämtliche Werke*, ed. A. Sauer, vol. I/16 (Vienna, 1925), pp. 29–37). Grillparzer subsequently wrote the funeral oration for Beethoven. The completed libretto, *Melusina:
Romantische Oper in drei Aufzügen* (ibid, vol. I/4, pp. 1–63 (text), pp. 213–28 (commentary)),
was eventually set to music by Conradin Kreutzer (1780–1849) in 1833.
7   *Der Taucher*: according to Marx (vol. I, p. 379), the Italian impresario Domenico Barbaia
(?1778–1841), who included the Kärntnertor-Theater and the Theater an der Wien among the
many major opera houses and theatres under his management at that time, proposed a three-act
opera on Schiller's *Die Bürgschaft*, already adapted by Ferdinand Freiherr von Biedenfeld (1788–
1862), theatre director variously in Berlin, Magdeburg and Breslau, author of tales, plays and
melodramas. Schindler says: 'All this is invention, though hardly of Marx's making', but McArdle
tells us that Biedenfeld vouches for it (Anton Schindler, *Biographie von Ludwig van Beethoven*
(Münster: Aschendorff, 1840, 2/1845, 3/1860), ed. D. W. McArdle as *Beethoven as I Knew Him*
(New York: Norton, 1966), pp. 260, 384).
8   *Der Sieg des Kreuzes*: oratorio commissioned from Beethoven by the Gesellschaft der Musikfreunde
in 1815, libretto by Joseph Karl Bernard (1780–1850), for which Beethoven had received an
advance payment in 1819, but on which he never set to work, although the project dragged on
until late in 1824.
9   Friedrich Rochlitz (1769–1842), the editor of the Leipzig *AmZ*, had in 1822 conveyed to Beethoven
Härtel's proposal for a work based on Goethe's *Faust*, along the lines of his *Egmont* music.
Rochlitz reports Beethoven's response: 'Ha! That would be a piece of work! That might be worth
doing!' (Marx, vol. I, p. 263; Schindler, Eng. trans. 1966, p. 455). Thayer believed that Härtel's
proposal was for an opera, and was independent of Rochlitz's (*Thayer's Life of Beethoven*, ed.
E. Forbes (Princeton: Princeton University Press, 1964, 2/1967), vol. II, pp. 801ff).
10 'Idea', with capitalized initial, is used throughout this essay to designate the German *Idee*, the
special Hegelian concept of transcendent vision, product of the spirit. Capitalization here creates
an artificial distinction between *Idee* and *Gedanke*: for the latter the uncapitalized form 'idea' has
been adopted, usually preceded by 'musical'. Whereas the latter appears in both singular and plural,
the former does so exclusively in the singular. Near the end, however, *Gedanke*, there translated
'thought', comes close to being identified with *Idee*; in the final two paragraphs, *Grundgedanke*,
'fundamental idea', fuses with *Idee*.
11 Presumably Joseph Weigl (1766–1846), composer of operas, ballets and choral works, pupil of
Albrechtsberger and Salieri, and Kapellmeister at the Kärntnertor-Theater.

However, the Idea of the Ninth Symphony cried out to be tackled. If his life and creative output were to be rounded out to harmonious perfection and brought to a close, then it was a necessity for him. And it was every bit as much a necessity for the development of the art of music. It *had* to be written. And the other works *should not* be written, for they would have been mere repetitions of what had already been achieved – albeit in magnified form. To Beethoven, however, the creator of the Idea within the world of instrumental music, it seemed fitting to determine his own boundaries in the fulfilment of his calling.

It was thus out of a spirit of necessity that he created his final symphony, which was published as his 125th work by Schott of Mainz, under the title: *Symphony with Final Chorus*[12] on Schiller's Ode 'To Joy', for Full Orchestra, Solo Voices and Four Choral Parts.[13] He was himself not yet clearly {265} aware of the true destiny of the work, for he had been carrying out preparatory work on a tenth symphony.[14]

In all probability, his very first intention was simply to write a further symphony (or rather, two), larger and more compelling than all the preceding ones. It may have occurred to him at a later stage to crown it, as the title still indicates, with a final chorus on Schiller's poem. The title should not necessarily be taken to mean literally that the symphony reflected Schiller's ode, or even just its underlying sentiment, right from inception. At least, we have no means of detecting such a thing. The first words to link the ode to the symphony are to be found in the sketchbooks:[15] 'Let us sing the song of the immortal Schiller!'[16] This inscription points to nothing more than a purely external link – for as Schindler bears out,[17] not even the double-bass recitative was in Beethoven's mind at this stage; and [it] quite clearly [implies] the linking of a new and foreign element to the symphony as it was already growing in his imagination. To tack a cantata on to the end of a symphony – a true symphony –, to attach the Hymn of Joy to a predominantly elegiac instrumental work: we must grasp that this was new and foreign, indeed without precedent for its time.

Finally, what was fated to occur did indeed occur. The keystone was set in the miraculous edifice of the Beethoven symphonies. That he was planning a tenth symphony tells us that he did not see the work in this light. Whether or not, despite this, he had dark premonitions of the end of the road – who can know? What is certain is that we can detect a particular elemental quality of sound reverberating within the work – one so mighty, so gigantically forceful, and yet so tender and full of sorrow.

12 *Sinfonie mit Schlusschor*: bold type.
13 The title page of this score, dating from early August 1826, reads: Sinfonie | mit Schluß-chor über Schillers Ode: "An die Freude" | für großes Orchester, 4 Solo- und 4 Chor-Stimmen, | componirt und | SEINER MAJESTAET dem KÖNIG von PREUSSEN | [coat of arms] | FRIEDRICH WILHELM III. | in tiefster Ehrfurcht zugeeignet | von | Ludwig van Beethoven. | 125tes. Werk. | [–] Eigenthum der Verleger. [–] | Mainz und Paris, | bey B. Schotts Söhnen. Antwerpen, bey A. Schott. ‖
14 Marx believed that Beethoven had begun work on a tenth symphony, and presented what purported to be sketches for it in *Beethoven*, vol. II, pp. 289–90.
15 [Marx:] See Appendix B. [Marx reproduces this entry in facsimile as Appendix B from Autograph 8, Bundle I, now in the Biblioteka Jagiellońska, Kraków. The facsimile had appeared in Schindler's *Biographie von Ludwig van Beethoven* (1840), Beilage II, after p. 296.]
16 'Lasst uns . . . singen!': spaced type.
17 Schindler, Eng. trans. 1966, pp. 296–70.

> A Shape like angels
> Yet of a sterner and a sadder aspect
> O spiritual essence.[18]

{266} He had already produced so much, created out of the marrow of his being. So many things could have wearied him. Perhaps more than anything else, what gnawed at him in the midst of the noisy, cheerful world was his isolation, the breathless silence that held him prisoner whilst all around him people exchanged happy greetings, gave each other friendship and trust. As to him, he laboured on. He created worlds full of faces and memories to surround his lonely spirit, and yet he remained in isolation. For such was the curse of deafness that he shunned even his closest friends in mistrust,[19] for lack of that tender word which is half taken for granted among good folk, which says all, resolves all.

One further curious thread within the work itself leads to those premonitions of the ultimate which may have worked and conspired together to form the final symphony. It is constructed quite differently from all earlier works, from all other orchestral works. The musical ideas [Gedanken], especially the subsidiary ones, are more fully developed than ever before, as if to exhaust their possibilities in all directions. This is not a matter of simply carrying the development further, by comparison with his earlier methods of working. Rather, it is a broadening out, and the impetus to this clearly does not lie in the musical ideas themselves. Granted that this is foreign to the composer's established way of working, it becomes even more striking as one becomes gradually more and more persuaded that this vast expansion of resource betrays no hint of strain or over-reaching, no trace of a slackening of concentrated energy. On the contrary, the only thing to emerge is the single-minded desire to say everything from every angle. The self-communing nature of this concentration can be likened to the minute attention and loving providence bestowed upon the drawing-up of his last will and testament.

This very same thing can be seen in his handling of the orchestra. If hitherto Beethoven's works have alternated clear marshalling of blocks of sound (as occurs in the *Battle Symphony* [Op. 91 (1813)]) on the one hand and dramatic individualization on the other, then in the Ninth Symphony the orchestra, so to speak, dissolves into its single voices, each wishing to express itself independently, by which means alone everything can be said from every angle, each one pursuing {267} its own path as if that path were intended for it alone. They move freely in and out of each other with the greatest feeling of individuality, as was never before (or after) dared or felt necessary. The student of style might say that Beethoven had at this point come close to quartet style as he had developed it in the late string quartets. That is not to say that this manner is ubiquitous; but it dominates particularly the first movement, which established the character of the work as a whole, so decisively that it infiltrates even the most massively developed outpourings (e.g. bb. 301–18).[20]

18 [Marx:] Byron, 'Cain' [Act I, lines 80–82, given here in the original: the German is subtly different: '. . . Yet with the dark and melancholy spirit of a noble spiritual mind'].
19 Stories of Beethoven's surliness, unsociability and reclusive tendencies were widely circulated: for interpretations of his deafness and eccentricity, see Maynard Solomon, *Beethoven* (New York: Schirmer, 1977), pp. 121–5, 256–9.

Whatever else may have been taking shape in his innermost mind, the final symphony had to be. And it had to be the final one because, as anyone who understands composition will recognize, and as the fragmentary materials for the Tenth Symphony perfectly bear out, it was impossible (artistically speaking – technically anything is possible) to go any further in the direction of elaboration and diversification of material.

'Once more unto the breach: the final symphony', the master called to his forces – the instruments [of the orchestra]. 'Once more from the raw element of sound we shall see emerge a world of inspired, vital beings who sing the eternal song of battle and lamentation which is called *Life*; beings who find one sole source of comfort: to love one another as little children of St John.'[21]

[First movement]

Arising out of the indeterminate – the fifth [Example 1] which quivers in the second violins and cellos, swelled by the faintest whisper from French horns –, out of the trembling, parturient night, {268} the lightning flashes of creation flicker and plunge into the depths [bb. 1–14]. Amidst the gradual emergence, gathering

Example 1

momentum with ever-increasing dread, there looms up a mighty, sombre shape [Example 2] – more a creation of commanding Will[22] than of rising spirit. For the Will now speaks through rhythm; it fashions this immutably sombre D–F–A so that *now!* it hammers with raging strength, *now!* it strikes downward, *now!* it pauses and roots itself even more firmly.

20 'p. 25' [=bb. 307–319]. Marx cites passages by reference to page numbers (and occasionally bar numbers within a page) of the original Schott score, of which details are given above, note 13. These references have been converted into bar numbers of the Eulenburg miniature score, with the original reference and its exact equivalence given in a footnote. It is not always easy to determine (as in this case) precisely which bars Marx has in mind.

21 These passages are not enclosed in quotation marks in the original. This rendering gives free rein to the Shakespearean overtones of *Noch einmal . . . Noch einmal* (*King Henry V*, Act III, Scene 1), and to the biblical reference of *sich untereinander zu lieben, wie Kindlein . . .* (*St John* 13.34: 'Little children . . . A new commandment I give unto you, That ye love one another . . .' (*Liebe Kindlein . . . Ein neu Gebot gebe ich euch, dass ihr euch untereinander liebet . . .*); also *St John* 15.12; *Romans* 13.8; *I Peter* 1.22).

22 'Will', with capitalized initial, has been used to denote the concept, derived from Schopenhauer, of *Wille* ('Music is thus in no sense, like the other arts, the image of ideas, but the image of the *Will itself* [. . .] and for this very reason the effect of music is far more powerful and penetrates far more deeply than that of the other arts': A. Schopenhauer, *Die Welt als Wille und Vorstellung*, vol. III (1819), in le Huray/Day, 325).

Example 2

This shaping of the main subject [*Hauptsatz*] – at heart profoundly simple, in outward form expressive of mighty, irresistible Will – is of the highest significance for the work as a whole. First and foremost, it eliminates any thought that the spirit of the symphony bears any relationship to the spirit of the Schiller ode. The symphony has embarked unguided upon its gloomy course with this starkly powerful unison of all its instrumental parts.

The subdominant, with that same stamp of overmastering Will (b. 2 [of Example 3]) {269} is introduced to establish this image still more firmly, as, amid

Example 3

the sound of trumpets and drums, it proclaims its lamentation far and wide and plunges back into the darkness with defiant wilfulness [Example 4]. This unyielding obduracy, unable, however, to restrain its twofold cry of lament (bb. 28–32);[23] this dwelling on the syncopated 6/4 chord (bb. 4–5 of Example [4]) which turns

Example 4

---

23   'bb. 1–3, p. 3 of the score'.

itself directly into the cadence chord with total disregard for the cadentially required dominant chord; this downward sweep in the violins, which breaks loose in disregard of all laws – all of this gives warning of titanic gestures, of supernatural powers.

But *is* not Beethoven the creator with supernatural powers, the lord of the world of instruments, which for the last time now hears his command? [24]

Once more, this time more firmly rooted on the tonic, the depths quiver as before, the stuttering figures of the violins and double basses [bb. 36–48] flicker and quickly die, they oscillate nervously and uneasily as before in the violins and violas [bb. 49–50]; and that same mighty shape looms out of the night for a second time, bright and more secure in B♭ major, {270} only to revert quickly to the gloom of D minor. This leads straight into a massive altercation – massive because of its rhythm, at first contemplative and then hard-hitting [Example 5], massive from the juxtaposing of great blocks of sound, with the full wind chorus against the full

Example 5

chorus of strings. Then the orchestra as a whole, pressing forward, deftly takes up the semiquaver motif [bb. 61–2]. From this, as if providing a coda (coda to the main subject), a plaintive melody arises in the first violin (with second violin, viola, [cello and] bass in full spate) [bb. 63–7], which is repeated by the bassoons in octaves coupled with violas, [cellos and] basses [bb. 67–71] and then imitatively a bar later by the flutes, oboes and clarinets [bb. 68–72] in double octaves.

In a swift and decisive modulation, the dominant of B♭ major (the key of the second subject [*Seitensatz*]) is introduced [b. 73], and is maintained amid the elegiac melodic exchanges of the bassoons, clarinets and flute [bb. 74–6, 78–80] against oboes and horns [bb. 76–8] right up to the entry of the second subject [Example 6]. {271} This is again an interchange of melodic materials between clarinet and bassoon (a) and flute and oboe (b), together with a counter-melody in the string section underpinned by double basses. The separate strands surge on from here, flowing virtually unchecked for more than an instant by two resolute blows [bb. 102–03, 106–07] into B major, modulating back to B♭ [bb. 115/116], plunging from semiquavers into double-speed movement [bb. 132–7], and at last, in

---

24   Is there perhaps a hint of Faust in this paragraph, or of Prospero in *The Tempest* (Act V, Scene 1
     '. . . and when I have requir'd Some heavenly music, – which even now I do, – To work mine end
     upon their senses that This airy charm is for, I'll break my staff . . .')?

Example 6

bb. 150–60,[25] fashioning a coda boldly and firmly in B♭ out of the unchanging kernel of the main subject. All the impetus so far stems at a deeper level from the elegiac lament [i.e. Example 4], which sets the prevailing tone of the movement as a whole, and after which even the most spirited coda now fails to make a joyful impression. The polarization of melodic lines, with the violins leading, the orchestra following, can be traced back to it as well, or at least to its opening; not until the fourth bar does the mighty unison passage come together in complete unanimity, rhythmically as well as tonally.

A single step from B♭ to A, and the opening ([Example 1]) stands before us once again [b. 160]. However, it is not a repetition of section I, but rather an introduction to section II. The A minor chord turns into the unstable 6/3 chord F♯–D–A, and this in turn moves to the subdominant [b. 178]. This key (G minor), by its special character, shows up softer and more plaintive than, but not so sinister as, the tonic. Moreover, both harmonic progressions take place at the midpoint of the bar. This premature lurch, so often encountered throughout the movement, this emphasis on the subordinate part of the bar instead of the main, is significant for the elegiac cast which overshadows the entire movement.

Now in G minor, the opening idea of the movement fans out into imitating lines. Against a background of sustained horns, flutes, clarinets and oboe, and amid the quivering notes of the second violins and cellos, the first violins (doubled by viola) {272} take the lead [Example 7]. The bassoon, then flute, oboe and clarinet together, follow, the double bass entering briefly. Out of these elements the coda

Example 7

25 'on the twenty-fifth line [i.e. the upper system of p. 13]' [=bb. 151–6].

again emerges powerfully, but accompanied by the painful chord C–F♯–A–E♭, which brings in its wake a further plaintive phrase, derived from the semiquaver motif of the dark but potent main subject. The two phrases alternate once more, undergoing expansion [bb. 197–210, 210–14]. The plaintive phrase is extended in a further development (bb. 3–4 of the main subject make up its kernel) first in the [cellos,] double basses [and bassoons] [b. 218], then in the first violin [b. 224], the second violin [b. 232], the wind [b. 236]. – It is downright impossible to give a true account of the chopping and changing of these melodic lines, sorrowful and yet at the same time so powerful, often so tender (bb. 257–68),[26] then again as agitated as if flailing about in delirium (violins bb. 237–51, cellos bb. 259–67, 287–97).[27] The moment of decision in any case approaches.

This moment of decision (b. 301)[28] is none other than that [initial] great cry, that first blazing-forth, which returns now as the opening of section III – i.e. recapitulation of section I – having already provided the dominating musical idea [*herrschender Gedanke*] of section II, and the underlying idea [*Grundgedanke*] of section I, for which it furnished the main subject and coda. Now the victorious power of the idea is decided. It is given out full blast by all the violins and violas, amidst the ringing cries of the full wind chorus, amidst the incessant thundering of {273} drums [Example 8A], amidst the shuddering of [cellos and] double basses [Example 8B] as they range across three octaves for twelve whole bars [bb. 301–12]. This idea

Example 8

stands, like a phantom of horror, like the Earth Spirit standing suffused in reddish flame before Faust who had summoned it up but could not endure the sight of it,[29] immovable on F♯–A–D, only to shift over to E♭ major in the twelfth bar [b. 312] – again at the weak point on the fourth quaver-beat – and finally to shift back to the home key of D minor three bars later [b. 315], completing the main subject in that key. But completion is something that the cheerless giant spirit will not allow. The very chord on which the main subject is re-introduced (F♯–A–D) cannot be heard purely as D major, either in the context of the whole or at the moment of occurrence: it leans towards G minor, the subdominant, as if it were actually D–F♯–A–C. It now pivots back around the tonic of the home key (D–F–A becomes C–D–F♯–A [bb. 322–4]) driven by the raging of the storm until an inviting stretch of blue sky shines down from between the storm clouds sixteen bars later. It is the second subject that wafts consolingly by, bringing solace without concealing the accents of its melancholy.

26 'p. 21'.   27 'violin pp. 19, 20 [=bb. 233–56], cello pp. 21, 23 [=bb. 257–68, 281–92]'.
28 'p. 24' [=bb. 293–306].
29 Goethe's *Faust*, Part I, lines 460–521, esp. lines 480–85; Marx actually says 'suffused in dismal (*trübflammend*) flame'.

Thus does the first movement of the final symphony draw to its close. We do not have space to follow the development, in all its vast power and superabundance, down to the last detail, and so must deny ourselves the gathering together of these many features which knit tightly to one another, and every one of which has its significance for our understanding. Richer and yet bleaker than any movement that has appeared in any work before it, these mighty waves roll on like the dark river of the underworld. Where Beethoven normally likes in the final coda [*Anhang*] to give vent to his most robust and cheerful powers, here the colossal sombre image reaches its appointed end looming higher than ever before in its dark dominion.

After the imperious coda material [Example 9], {274} the harmonic movement settles on to the closing chord [b. 427]. The first violin, shadowed by the bassoon

Example 9

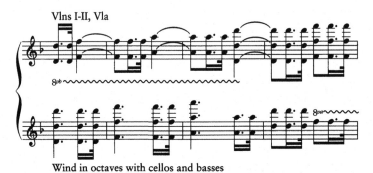

Vlns I-II, Vla

8vb

Wind in octaves with cellos and basses

far below (we must pass over the importance of the subordinate lines), takes up once more the initial idea [Example 10], and now for the first time lays bare unmistakably the sorrow-laden heart that beats in this mighty breast, unable to find

Example 10

espressivo

p

release from this profoundly felt lament. After this, the flute intervenes with its innocence-laden tones admonishing in fantasia-like freedom [bb. 432–52]. Once again, as in section I [cf. bb. 92–101], the instrumental lines pass and re-pass one another in their stately round-dance [bb. 453–62]. Once again, that figure which is derived from bb. 3–4 of the main subject [. . .] recurs, this time however in the consoling tones of the natural horn [bb. 469–77], as if resounding from afar, the second horn providing the dark-toned drone beneath it [Example 11]. What began so gloomily in C minor on [cellos and] double basses in section II [bb. 218–23], continued {275} so sorrowfully in G minor [bb. 224–] and showed no signs of ever brightening up, sounds so gracefully reassuring here in D major in these stalwart

Example 11

lines. Even here it quickly takes on a dismal cast as it is repeated in D minor [bb. 477–] in the heavy-hearted *piano* unison with all strings *including* double basses and leads back once again to the bare keynote [b. 513].

At this point [b. 513], a new idea rises up as if out of the realm of the shades. Violas, cellos, double basses and bassoons begin their unearthly trudging line extremely softly (violas and cellos tremolando). The second violins, and then the firsts after them, take up the tremolando of the others. Against the lamenting cries of the wind, this deep-running stream [Example 12] stirs up in incessant quivering

Example 12

its shadowy river bed, running far beneath all existence. It broadens out across all registers and surges out of its hidden depths with thundering power. With outstretched arms it gropes about, and it resounds back like the urgent tolling of bells summoning rescue.

This living world of musical instruments harbours awful secrets within its bosom. What must their creator have had to endure in his fateful solitariness, imprisoned in eternal silence within his own breast! To unlock the enigma of his own interior existence there was only the enigmatic language of music – one mystery as solution to another! But he stood unbowed though profoundly shaken. What control and self-possession does this total freedom of all parts, among other things, bear witness to, each line appearing to exist in its own right alone, while {276} yet he holds them all on course and steers them with a tight rein! What sure foundation does this perfectly stable and lucidly formed structure evince in the depth and richness of its musical ideas! If the form-breakers of modern times should wish to enlighten themselves instead of bedazzling themselves and their devotees, this final, great work offers them the most reliable model.

The first movement of each of the symphonies is decisive for the idea [*Gedanke*] of the work. In the Ninth it is more so than ever. What does it convey to us? This ceaseless complaint of eternal discontent from which he is no longer able to free himself in his kingdom of musical instruments – he who has imbued and inspired this kingdom with his creative spirit. Even though the voices of those instruments can conjure up the whole of nature, even though they can encircle us in angelic whisperings, even though they can – as he sought to do in the 'Benedictus' of his second Mass[30] – descend from the sky like a cherubic greeting to the children of man; man is always closest to man; man's voice is the most familiar, the most sympathetic, the most intelligible. That is a general truth – a truth which came to Beethoven in the midst of this world that he had populated so richly, and now entered his consciousness.

Here lay the parting of the ways. If some intimation of approaching death, unknowable to us, should have reached his noble spirit, then that would have awakened this realization in him and would have been identified with it in his mind. Was he not solitary in the noisy world of men? How lonely must he have been in the world of his instrumental voices and faces? And how his heart – open as it was, capable of love, guileless to its innermost depths – craved for the beloved comradeship of men! How this feeling for brotherliness, this love of humans, pervaded his entire life, his work, his letters! How it shows up as a deep longing for confidence and trust itself even in all his suspecting outbursts, all his unjust words, which led ultimately to reconciliation.

It was here that the outward plan to give the symphony a new shape by incorporating a final chorus must have {277} become an inner necessity. What was a general truth, what was an experience peculiar to Beethoven, became now the Idea of the Ninth Symphony.

The first movement has shown no sign of fulfilment; but more, unlike the [Fifth] Symphony in C minor, it has offered no prospect of such a thing. The first movement of the C minor Symphony may not actually have delivered a verdict of conquest, but it harnessed together and precipitated the powers that guarantee conquest. The first movement of the Ninth Symphony accumulates power to titanic proportions, but its heart is full of sorrow.

[Second movement]

Once more we hear the stroke of the magician's staff, stirring life in us mightily [Example 13],[31] and immediately the sprites of music, ever-obedient to the signal of their master, begin their gleeful, furtive round-dance. The second violin leads, the viola follows [Example 14], then the cello, after that the first violin, then the double bass. All is hushed and furtive. It all trips along in haste, restless, exactly in step (with the exception that the initial notes of every bar are picked out by solo wind instruments in unison with the instruments presenting the lines, e.g. [in Example 14], the violin is reinforced by the oboe, then that and the viola by oboe

---

30   The *Missa solemnis*: Beethoven wrote his Mass in C, Op. 86, in 1807, and the Mass in D (*Missa solemnis*), Op. 123, in 1819–23; the latter shared its (incomplete) first performance with that of the Ninth Symphony on 7 May 1824 at the Kärtnertor.

31   [Marx: note to Ex. 13:] The timpani, as in the Eighth Symphony, play F–f.

Example 13

Example 14

and clarinet), all in breathless, interminable gyration. It is not the melody which counts here, nor the individual voices, for they swirl in among each other in bewildering rhythmic indistinguishability, just as they did at the {278} beginning. Its significance lies in its superabundance of vitality and in its ghostly, unrelenting activity: 'ghostly', since no human round-dance[32] would be equal to such regularity of movement, at so hurried and unrestrained a tempo. These whirlwinds of dance build up from furtive beginnings to wild, howling merriment (bb. 41–60),[33] with the timpani entering audaciously [b. 57] and playing in syncopation [on the weak bars] at will. The figures, without abating in sheer activity, slip away after the dinning triumph of their jugglers' dance [Example 15], and a momentary doubt

Example 15

seems to flit by. Then the phrase rekindles vigorously, this time with a noteworthy modification [Example 16A] (b. 1 is derived from [Example 14] b. 2, and deserves study), and asserts itself amidst the defiant hammering of all the strings in all octaves (Example 16B). They strike sixteen times before the final stroke – and that furtive idea returns without fail.

---

32   *Regen* should read *Reigen*.

33   'p. 47 of the score'.

Example 16

Now at long last, at the end of the repeated section I, the giddy dance comes to a standstill for a first time, then a second, only to begin again even more dizzily at the outset {279} of section II. At this harmonic progression [Example 17: bb. 159–65], the choruses of strings and brass take turns bar-by-bar at the hammering motif. Then the main subject scuttles past softly in precipitate haste, the four-bar pulse giving way to a three-bar pulse.

Example 17

It is an interminably gyrating, breathless attrition of life, intensely furtive, its essential regularity of measure bombarded with thunderbolts of genius, torn into fragments, a vitality, superabundant and – unfulfilled. It has no aim within itself, and betokens nothing outside itself. Even the most exciting trick of this troupe of jugglers, whose members crouch hidden among the instruments and then come flashing out like elves in peals of laughter, even this does not fulfil the ultimate longing of the soul, the longing of man for man.

At this point, everything presses forward impetuously [bb. 404–11], in twofold quadruple time (3/4 becomes 4/4)[34] [b. 412]. A new image of life takes instant shape as if by magic, a new world of being opens up wholly unsuspected from all that has gone before and beckons the dizzy confusion benignly into its tranquil circle. As intimate as a childhood memory, as balmy as the breath of the pastures and woods, guileless in its charm of rustic innocence, this melodic strain, {280} played by oboes and clarinets blending together and bassoons, speaks to you in a glow of satisfied, complacent well-being [Example 18]. The second part of the strain gives just

Example 18

---

34 Marx seems to take the metronome marking at b. 412 as being semibreve = 116, as it erroneously appeared in the Schott 8vo score and later B&H critical edition, and not as minim = 116.

a hint of solemnity, as if of rustic prayers offered in the peace of the evening after an honest day's toil. The picture is painted with lingering rapture, long-drawn-out, extended with all the skill and all the feeling at the composer's command. All must draw near and receive balm from the tranquil presence. The horns, with their soft, echoing tones [bb. 438–54], accompanied by the fine-spun tones of the violin high above (whereas before it was the bassoon far below) give out the melody anew, whereupon the bassoons take it over [bb. 454–75] with the crisp tone of the oboe accompanying. All must draw nigh, even finally the trombones [bb. 475–529] (who were kept silent throughout the gigantic first movement), with their horn-like sound ten times more powerful – such is the effect that they make here. It is ever the same image that smiles the same smile down upon you, its form and colour seeming constantly to change. It is a world of pure magic.

Does the *second movement* achieve satisfaction at this point? No, for the simple reason that it bears no spiritual relationship whatsoever to what has gone before, or to the first movement, even despite the connection between b. 3 of the melody [b. 416: Example 18, b. 3] and that discussed [in Example 16][35] above. And that is how Beethoven felt it. The picture fades, the earlier round-dance tries to start itself anew and then disappears, the melody lingers a moment longer – then a wave of the hand and everything scatters.

Now the die *is* cast. This world of instrumental music, richly animated though it is, a thousand-faceted, intoxicating to the mind, transporting the imagination far beyond the limits of man's capacity in a way that no other art can, [this world] cannot of itself vouchsafe satisfaction in full measure. He who has opened up its riches to the conscious mind; he to whom it has shown itself obedient and thankful with its abundance of possibilities; he has arrived at its farthest bourn, he will take his leave of it now because he can find no gratification for his ultimate longing. This is no conjecture, no deduction from some assumption or another. – *He himself* will testify to it *in words* of his own expressing. If we can accept this for the moment as true, then {281} the course of the work's Idea can at last be grasped in all its fullness, as we have sought to grasp it up to now. The force of each individual movement becomes clear. The absence of relationship, of interconnection, from one movement to another makes sense. We need only add that what has been said in this respect about the first two movements applies equally well to the adagio that follows.

Relationship and interconnection are not lacking among these movements. It is simply that they are not to be discovered in the individual movements themselves: they reveal themselves only after the third movement.

[Third movement]

This *third movement*, in B♭ major, inscribed *adagio molto e cantabile*, is the parting word. Steeped in love, rapt in profound thought, and filled with inexhaustible melancholy, just as a person of great and indomitable character takes leave of this life, his mind overflowing with ceaseless memories.

35 'on p. 278'.

Two choruses – one of woodwind, the other of strings – alternate with one another, their sorrowful strains mingling. Two musical ideas – one of the present with its valedictory words, the other of the past with its memories, with its smile through tears – follow one another by turns: outwardly they are clearly differentiated, as befitted Beethoven's transfigured gaze, inwardly they are one, two aspects of the same countenance.

The woodwind usher in the movement with gently sighing accents, supported after a moment by the lower strings. Then the strings, without double basses, introduce the song of farewell, steeped in tender melancholy and devotion [Example 19]. The woodwind (clarinets, bassoons and horns) {282} echo the cadence, and in this way the second strophe succeeds the first, and then the third and fourth follow, all

Example 19

with an air of ceremonious moderation, all with deep, heartfelt emotion. At first the woodwind repeat just the cadence, but later – with the sensuous liquid sound of the clarinet at the top of the chorus – they repeat the whole of the final strophe, which soars as if beyond the power of the human breast to contain it.

The strings join this, with the double basses adding their enriching sonority for the first time [b. 19], and [violins and violas] play little flights of arpeggio grace notes which resemble the sound of a harp. As the volume of sound dies, the harmony contracts from F–A–C–E♭ to F♯–A–D, the latter standing for D major, and then the second melodic strain enters [Example 20], different in every respect from

Example 20

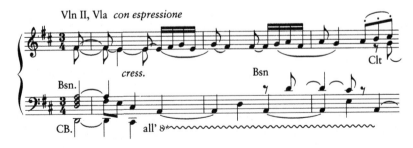

the first strain although related in mood. The attribution of 'memories' to this strain earlier was no arbitrary thought. Some sort of resonance from happy, peaceful hours is being re-lived in the melody as well as in the bass line [. . .], only here tinged with melancholy through the coupling of the veiled sound of the viola on the melody line with the second violin, through the lingering line of the double basses, through the brooding low A held by cellos (which it was not possible to reproduce above [in Example 20]), through the penetrating sighs that are interjected by first bassoon, clarinet, then oboe, then flute.

We cannot pursue the movement further. In a word, it adopts variation form in order to engrave its content ever {283} more deeply upon our heart. Toward the end (bb. 120–22, 130–32),[36] the composer's Will soars high and with inexorable strength, even though his eyes are dim with tears. However, the song ends in the spirit in which it was begun. –

And here, following the well established laws of symphonic structure [. . .], the *fourth movement* would properly have begun. In that way, the Ninth Symphony would have been completed and perfected in the image of the preceding eight. But something totally different was sealed fast in the destiny, in the creative genius of the composer.

He stood now at the farthest limit of his symphonic realm. Fate had separated him from other men. He had founded this realm, had lived his life among this world of instruments, filling it with his vitality and spirit, opening it up with magic power to the invasion of the Idea. The inhabitants of this world, which appear to others as mere implements of wood and metal, he fashioned *after our own likeness*, in the image of man,[37] imbuing them with the spirit of mankind, so that one often feels: Now, now, the mouth must surely open to utter the word, the human word!

All of that – yet it was not man, not his equal, not satisfaction for his heart, laden as it was with love, pining for affection, often erring, often deceived, always yearning for love. *Humanity!* He needed fellow-beings, the trusty companionship that he once hankered after in his will[38] and longed for at all times: brotherly comradeship. That trusty companionship would have been more than all the magic of that estranged world from which fate had pitilessly excluded him.

This he now embraces.

[Fourth movement]

Just where the finale of the symphony should have begun, a wild outcry from the orchestra rends the atmosphere of harmony, breaks in on the peace of this world as if by some shattering magic bolt. Then follows a {284} mighty recitative for [cellos and] double basses,[39] highly emphasized – *are the instruments intended to speak?* Once more the rebellious orchestra enters, and the [cellos and] double basses speak again in incomprehensible words. And now there flit by, like shadows of drifting clouds, the dream images of life gone by: the 'Let there be'[40] of the first

36 'pp. 89 and 91 of the score' [=bb. 118–23, 129–33].
37 cf. *Genesis* 1.26 'And God said, Let us make man in our image, after our likeness.'
38 [Marx:] see vol. I, pp. 246 [–9] [reference is to the Heiligenstadt Testament of 6 and 10 October 1802].
39 [Marx:] In the score, p. 96 [=bb. 1–14] the double basses are marked: 'Selon le caractère d'un Recitative mais in Tempo.'
40 *Werde!*: cf. *Genesis* 1.3 'And God said, Let there be light: and there was light.' (*Und Gott sprach: Es werde Licht! und es ward Licht*).

movement against the milder oratory of the [cellos and] basses, the jugglers' dance of existence against the more insistent oratory – the silent, prayerful farewell – and these orators, the first from among the world of instruments to be awakened to the word, give voice to the strains of that[41]

> Spark from the fire that Gods have fed –
> Joy – thou Elysian Child divine,

not in the tones of the lofty hymn, which goes on to say:

> Fire-drunk, our airy footsteps tread,
> O Holy One! thy holy shrine,

but in the *popular manner*.[42] Fellow-men! If only there were fellow-men, in brotherly union, simple and unpretentious, with whom to wander thither arm in arm! That is now his sole desire, so weary is he of presiding in state over his isolation, far from human beings!

The melodic strain sets out in such shyly secretive and confiding calm in the hollow tones of [cellos and] basses [Example 21], like memories of youth long-buried and suppressed. It is like a half-forgotten song that one pieces together again

Example 21

piano

by conscious effort. Then, when the song has been tried out and we are satisfied with our recollection of each phrase in the double basses (with cellos), and is repeated on cellos blending with violas at a higher octave, a second line appears as if by accident, ambling comfortably alongside, and then another [Example 22].

Example 22

{285} It is truly the wise intuition of the artist's spirit, so unerring in its judgment, to introduce this innocent, artless strain of folk melody amidst the highest flight of imagination, amidst the most tumultuous emotions and the tenderest feelings. It says all that there is to say! It confirms all that we ventured previously to puzzle out and to construe, with the incontrovertible force of a child's faith. If there be any who cannot find a sympathetic place in their heart for this, to them must be

41   The translation of Schiller's ode used here is that by Sir Edward Bulwer Lytton.
42   *im Volkston*: in the manner (and tempo) of a *volkstümliches Lied*, i.e. a popular song of the late eighteenth century in simple style, thought to have the qualities of folksong.

said what the holy teacher said to his disciples: 'Except ye be converted, and become as little children, ye shall not enter into the kingdom of heaven!'[43]

For the first time, we can now see the full meaning of that image of life which was presented to us in the second movement [. . .]; that new world which brought us such intimate tranquillity; which opened up before our eyes so radiantly, so delightfully; as to the long-absent traveller the beloved homeland appears stretching out unexpectedly beneath him under the evening sun as he overtops the last peak and gazes down with moist eye. '*That* is what we have come so far for, that is what we have striven for, and it beckons us *thither*!' For this is the miraculous unity of the work. It is a product not of man's handiwork but of his experience.

Little by little, additional lines enter the texture, and the folk-like strain blossoms and waxes into joyous triumph. After this, following on from all the jubilation, a moment of tender emotion (bb. 203–05,[44] at *poco ritenente*) draws us back into the past. We have always found Beethoven to be purely human in his exaltation, never abstract or contrived.

For the third time, the cry of the rebellious orchestra shatters the calm.

{286} But this time the basses [and cellos] are transmuted into the human voice. The instrumental recitative has become the spoken word, has become human recitative.

> *O friends, no more of these tones! But let us sing something more cheerful, and more full of gladness!*

cries Beethoven, his heart full of yearning. This is the deciding word. The composer has discovered it for himself, and has uttered it. Let no cheap wiseacre find fault with the way the thought has been expressed. He who has been able to grasp it and has 'spoken with tongues',[45] as Beethoven has in this symphony, only he is vouchsafed to grasp the words just as the deeply felt, simple-at-heart spirit within him stumbled across them.

And now voices – human voices – call:

> *Joy! Joy!*

and it is human voices that strike up the Hymn of Joy:

> Spark from the fire that Gods have fed –
> Joy – thou Elysian Child divine,
> Fire-drunk, our airy footsteps tread,
> O Holy One! thy holy shrine,

and strike it up in that same strain of folk melody. For that which is the most profound, the greatest, always finds its ultimate consecration and affirmation in the hearts and minds of the people.

The remainder of the symphony does not require examination in detail. The folk-like strain is first sung by a solo voice (baritone), and then answered by the choir without sopranos as a refrain. Then at:

---

43 *St Matthew* 18.3.   44 'p. 109 of the score' [bb. 197–203].
45 *Acts of the Apostles* 2.4: 'And they were all filled with the Holy Ghost, and began to speak with other tongues'; ibid, 10.46: 'For they heard them speak with tongues'; also *St Mark* 16.17; *I Corinthians* 12.10, 28, 30.

> He who this lot from fate can grasp –
> Of one true friend the friend to be –

it is repeated by solo voices, and answered again as a refrain by choir, this time with all four voices. We are left in no doubt here how utterly committed Beethoven was to the idea of the simple folksong. The words:

> Yes, each who but one single heart
>   In all the earth can claim his own! –
> Let him who cannot, stand apart,
>   And weep beyond the pale, alone!

{287} are sung movingly to the same strain – and this by the solitary Beethoven. The following lines are sung by the solo voices, once again with answering refrain from the choir, to the same melody but this time varied (or ornamented). But the words:

> And on the Cherub, room by God!

bring a solemn turn of phrase to the song, modulating over to the dominant of B♭ major.

At this point, a passage in march rhythm – itself a variation on the selfsame strain – full of pomp and circumstance yet begun in hushed tones, leads to a broadening out as the lines:

> Joyous as Suns careering gay
>   Along their royal paths on high,
> March, Brothers, march your dauntless way,
>   As Chiefs to Victory!

are sung in heroic tones by the solo tenor with the male voices of the choir accompanying. The orchestra extends this triumphal pageant on its own, a long and glittering parade in fugato style, until (b. 213 of the *alla marcia*[46]), against rushing scales in all strings, and rhythmic cries from the woodwind and brass, the folk chorus strikes up the first line [of the poem] again with the [same] simple strain, sweeping it on in bacchanalian jubilation.

The male voices of the choir intone the:

> Embrace, ye millions!

with mighty solemnity – a chorus of beatific priests of the brotherhood of man, summoned forth. As the higher choral voices enter, and the full wind together with trombones are heard spread over many octaves, and the double basses [and cellos], along with the other strings, wend their stately way through the broad expanses of sublime harmonies, solemnly treading their dactylic rhythm; at this moment, one is moved as by the sound of organ and choir in a vast cathedral, still empty but flooded with sunlight through its high windows, peaceful and splendid in spirit.

{288} The final chorus crowns the whole work with a richly elaborated version of the original strain which forms a wild climactic Hymn of Joy.

---

46   'on the sixteenth page of the score' [presumably p. 160 of the score, which corresponds to bb. 208–15 of the *alla marcia*].

The heart of the matter lies not in these countless individual occurrences, nor in the wonders of the instrumentation, nor even in the marvels of the invention, which we are able to discuss in words. It resides in the fundamental idea [*Grundgedanke*], which reaches its ultimate realization in the transmutation of the instrumental and the symphonic into the music of man, into song, victory. To anyone who has trained himself to perceive ideas in music, this transmutation, this fusion of opposites – in which the instrument strives towards the word, and human oratory, recitative, remains unable to shake off entirely the instrumental guise – will appear as full of artistic genius as the transmutation of the shade of Helen of Troy into new corporeal form in *Faust,* or the journey of Dionysus to the underworld in Aristophanes' *The Frogs.*[47] One sees with one's very eyes the impossibility, and yet one believes. Therein lies the triumph of art.

The fundamental idea of this work has, however, a threefold significance. First, a biographical one: Beethoven's life-work in all its majesty and breadth; indisputably intertwined with the unfulfilled yearning of a lonely being, surrounded by the circle of humanity. Next to this an artistic significance: both halves of the world of musical art are weighed upon a just scale, and are united with equal rights for all, insofar as each does and may partake of them. Finally one of pure humanity: Man, as distinct from the world outside himself, exerts his highest claim upon his fellow-men. Proceeding beyond this point, things outside the domain of man, reconciled and alloyed with humanity, pass into his proper sphere. Neither nature, nor those things in the life of the spirit that exist outside or above us, can we comprehend with love or understanding, except by means of our humanity.

47 Helen of Troy (wife of Menelaus, whose flight to Troy with Paris was partly responsible for the Trojan War) features in Goethe's *Faust,* Part II (1831, but substantially complete by the 1800s), Act III, set in Menelaus's palace in Sparta. In Aristophanes' *Batrachoi* (The Frogs: 405 BC), Dionysus, disenchanted with modern tragedy, disguises himself as Hercules and goes to Hades to bring back Euripides, but returns with Aeschylus.

Theodor Helm (1843–1920)
Beethoven's Streichquartette (1885)

Helm claimed his *Beethoven's String Quartets* (1885) as the first full and coherent 'presentation and explication' of the composer's string quartets, its only partial precursor having been a 'comparative account' of the last five quartets published in 1868 in Oscar Paul's journal *Die Tonhalle*.[1] (Helm shows no awareness of Basevi's analytical study of the Op. 18 quartets, dating from 1874.) By that time, as he was aware, a good many studies of both the complete symphonies and the complete piano sonatas had been published.

The title page of Helm's volume foretells the tension that we find in this analysis, with its subtitle 'Essay in Technical Analysis of these Works in Relation to their Spiritual Content'; and it is perhaps worth noting that Helm was lecturer in both the history of music and music aesthetics at the Horak Conservatory of Music in Vienna from 1874 until late in his career. Explanation of the miraculous effect of Beethoven's quartets could be achieved 'only by means of the most fundamental technical analysis of the scores with reference to their poetic mood – insofar as that can be determined'. The balance of technical to interpretative treatment was clearly a matter of concern to Helm. Where he erred on the poetic side, he did so 'never in the spirit of a definitive "programme", but rather to stimulate the listener's imagination'.[2] Setting this balance meant for Helm putting a just distance between his own analyses and those of his illustrious predecessor Marx (see above, Analysis 12). The latter had included in his *Ludwig van Beethoven: Life and Creative Output* (1859) brief treatment of four of the Op. 18 quartets, and lengthier treatment of Op. 59 nos. 1 and 3, Op. 132 and Op. 135. In remarking on Marx's wholesale neglect of many of the quartets, the annoying tendency of his analyses to break off 'just at the most interesting stage of development', and above all his 'notorious over-effusiveness and flights of fancy', Helm set himself the task of writing an account of Beethoven's entire quartet output that did not neglect a single movement, and that was characterized by 'accuracy in word and musical example'.[3] In Helm we can detect a shift from the symphony to the string quartet as the prototypical form for absolute music. To Marx the string quartet was 'less ambitious than orchestral composition',[4] its parts 'more monochrome' than those of the orchestra, hence lacking

---

1 Helm, *Beethoven's Streichquartette: Versuch einer technischen Analyse dieser Werke im Zusammenhange mit ihrem geistigen Gehalt* (Leipzig: Fritzsch, 1885, 2/1910), p. 2; Oscar Paul (1836–98) was editor of *Die Tonhalle: Organ für Musikfreunde* (1868–73), and subsequently *Musikalisches Wochenblatt* (1870–).
2 Helm, pp. iii, iv.
3 ibid, iv–v.
4 Adolf Bernhard Marx, *Ludwig van Beethoven: Leben und Schaffen* (Berlin: Janke, 1859), vol. I, p. 202.

in character. Marx acknowledged that Beethoven came, later in life, to conceive of the four string players as 'ideal voices', no longer characterful in the orchestral sense, but rather 'similitudes of people, in whose veins runs [. . .] the Ciceronian *quasi-sanguis*, the simili-blood of the appearances that people seek to emulate'.[5]

For Helm, by contrast, it was in the very equality of forces embodied in the string quartet, 'strength pitted against strength on an individual basis', that Beethoven's highest genius revealed itself, dwarfing his contemporaries. The medium's asceticism, its voluntary limitation, eschewing all external colour, reaped its reward in its ability 'to open up [. . .] an infinite world'. Beethoven's quartets 'run the entire gamut of the tonal realm; there is not a mood that is missing, from the most scurrilous to the most sublime, from the commonest tongue to the loftiest mysticism'. The quartet's corporate sounds were no longer harmonies: they were 'spiritual combinations'. Helm's discussion is tinged with a sense of prophecy – not the oracular foretellings of the ancients, but the divine visions of the old testament prophets. The quartet was the chosen medium, in which Beethoven enshrined 'his most profound and most elevated thoughts, and bequeathed them to posterity'. In his late quartets, as an isolated figure, he was 'the voice crying in the wilderness'.[6]

In thus giving the quartet its due in Beethoven's output, he 'did not shrink from appropriating [Marx's] description, even the very turn of phrase, if it got to the heart of the matter'. Accordingly, of Marx's account of Op. 132 he retained all eight music examples and a little over a quarter of the 1,700-word text. Some of these examples he extended; he also added twenty-seven new examples, and more than 5,000 words of extra text. The outcome was a near-quadrupling of the size of Marx's original. In the text given below, an attempt has been made to throw light on the relationship between Marx's and Helm's texts by placing the material retained from Marx in italics. Not that this can be done with total rigour in a translation, which inevitably modifies the fabric of the original text; moreover, Helm sometimes adjusted Marx's wording to its new context, and I have refrained from detailing all these adjustments; finally, there is a grey area between borrowing and accidental parallelism. Imprecise though it is, this italicization serves not only to convey Helm's dependency upon Marx – earlier we saw a parallel situation with von Elterlein (Analysis 4) – but also to suggest that Marx was a 'source' for other late nineteenth-century writers on music.

In a sentence that Helm discarded, Marx remarked: 'It is possible to follow the musical structure with pathological-psychological specificity, and to trace each step throughout with justification.'[7] Of Marx's subjectively elucidatory material, in which he traced Beethoven's path from illness to recovery, Helm accepted only the more generalized remarks, reflecting states of mind but not attributing causes.

Helm's text can thus be seen (archaeologically, so to speak) as comprising two strata: a substratum of material retained from Marx, in almost every case signalled as quoted matter; and a surface stratum of material by Helm. But it is more helpful to interpret this analysis as comprising four elements, and as reflecting an intertextual

5 ibid, vol. II, pp. 45–6.
6 Helm, pp. 1, 323; cf. *Isaiah*, 403.
7 Marx, vol. II, p. 305.

relationship more typical of medieval than of modern texts. What we have by this interpretation on the one hand is a core of elucidatory material by Marx, surrounded by a 'gloss' of descriptive material by Helm that reflects a shift in aesthetic outlook; and on the other hand a core of sonata-form analysis by Marx, surrounded by a 'gloss' of motivic analysis by Helm that imposes a quasi-Wagnerian interpretation on the music. These two text-pairs are interwoven with one another.

Within each text-pair we have not merely an accretion of material upon material, but a dynamic relationship in which gloss is keyed to core by common vocabulary, and in which gloss comments upon core; and also in which the gloss builds up allusions to other works – the Ninth Symphony, the quartets Op. 59 no. 3, Op. 95 and Op. 127, and Piano Sonata Op. 101, also Wagner's *Faust* Overture and the *Tristan* Prelude – and cites other writers, Schumann and Ambros. All of these are strategies typical of the medieval glossator's art.

The relationship between Marx's elucidatory text and Helm's gloss is particularly complex, since the latter interacts not just with quoted matter from the former but with the whole of Marx's (three-quarters absent) text. Helm chooses carefully the manner in which he signals quotation so as to express whole-hearted acceptance, slight distaste or outright rejection ('Marx rightly says . . .'; 'in which Marx likes to find illustrated'; 'Marx incomprehensibly suggests . . .'; or merely a well-placed exclamation mark). All of this he 'sets up' by questioning Marx's premises at the very outset: to attribute concrete images to movements that do not bear a superscription by the composer is, he contends, unwarranted; only 'general expressivity' is to be seen, a 'consistent process of psychological evolution'. Helm's own characterizing epithets are meant to illuminate this rather than to have psycho-biographical reference. Only in the third movement, for which Beethoven provided a superscription, is this injunction lifted; elsewhere, notably in the second and fourth movements, Helm returns to the issue, so that the analysis as a whole gives the impression of being a critique of Marx's reading.

Theodor Helm was, according to Riemann, 'one of Vienna's best music critics'. He worked for a number of newspapers and journals, notably from 1884 to 1901 as correspondent for the Leipzig *Musikalisches Wochenblatt*, out of a series of essays in the columns of which the present book arose;[8] and for the *Neue Zeitschrift für Musik* after the two journals merged in 1906; and in particular as critic for the Viennese *Deutsche Zeitung* from 1870 to 1905, in which post he offered a countervailing voice to that of Eduard Hanslick in the *Neue Freie Presse*, its critic from 1855 to 1895.[9] He was an untiring champion of the music of Wagner and Bruckner, while at the same time greatly sympathetic with that of Brahms.

8   'Beethoven's Streichquartette', *Musikalisches Wochenblatt*, 4 (1873), 577–8, 601–02, 625–6, 649–51, 669–70, 698–701, 721–3; 5 (1874), 93–5, 117–20, 187–8, 209–12, 265–7, 289–92, 337–9, 401–03, 433–5, 449–51, 473–6, 509–11, 521–2, 549–50, 597–9, 609–11, 625–8, 637–9; 6 (1875), 89–91, 129–31, 209–11, 233–6, 269–72, 321–2, 380–82, 401–04, 589–90, 617–18; 12 (1880–81), 1–2, 13–14, 37–9, 101–02, 117–19, 129–31, 141–2, 155–6, 178–9, 253–5, 277–80, 289–90, 309–12, 416–17, 449–51, 529–31, 541–2, 553–5, 565–7, 577–9, 593–4, 609–11, 625–7; 13 (1881–2), 97–8, 109–11, 121–2, 133–4, 157–8, 173–4, 205–07, 241–3, 257–8, 405–07, 417–18, 429–31, 441–3, 453–6.
9   Hanslick was critic for *Presse* 1855–64, then for the break-away *Neue Freie Presse* 1864 to 1895. Riemann's evaluation of Helm appears in his *Musikalisches Lexikon*, 1/1882, and changed in later editions from 'best' to 'most distinguished'.

It is therefore not surprising that in the more technical of our pairs of text elements, Helm took over rather than eliminated Marx's sketchy traditional formal analyses, but constructed around them a motivic fabric that is largely – not quite entirely – absent from Marx's original discussion. For the first movement, Helm adopted and exploited Marx's *Hauptsatz* and *Seitensatz*. He even reinforced Marx's tripartite sonata-form framework and made it more concrete by naming sections II and III development and recapitulation. At the same time as adopting them, he neutralized them: Beethoven had followed sonata form 'instinctively'; thus the elements of sonata form, though present, were now only vestigial. In place of the 'thematic working [*Arbeit*]' that sonata form applied to its 'subjects', a new principle now held sway: 'melodic discourse [*melodische Rede*]', spontaneous mutual association of 'motifs' (cf. the somewhat parallel comparison of *thematische Arbeit* and *motivische Gestaltung* struck by Spitta in Analysis 5 above, and its introduction). Helm adduced seven motivic elements (*a*, a, b, c, d, e, f), and to them he assigned vaguely Wolzogenish affective or descriptive tags: 'scurrying semiquaver figure *a*', 'heroic figure *d*', and so forth. These do not, however, conflict with the sonata-form analysis. The two systems cohabit, fusing at two points: the first subject, which Marx had called 'a song of soft lament [*in leisem Klagesinge*]', and which becomes the 'lament motif a [*Klagemotiv* a]'; and the second subject, 'full of consolation [*trostvoll*]', which becomes the 'consoling second subject f [*tröstende zweite Hauptsatz* f]'. By this interpretation, Beethoven is shown to have rendered inert the formerly dynamic principle of sonata form, and to have raised it to the new and higher dynamic principle of motivic association; thus in the analysis the terminology of sonata form is sublimated into that of motivic analysis.

At the level of the whole work, Marx, with his normative concept of the four-movement unit (described in the Introduction to Analysis 12, above), was troubled by the number of movements not only in Op. 132 but also in others of the late Beethoven quartets. Unable to reduce Op. 132 to fewer that five movements, Marx conceded that 'in this case, everything occurs with an inner compulsion due to the Idea of the overall tonal conception [*Tongedicht*]'.[10] Clearly the work held no such problem for Helm, who stressed a 'newness, freedom and spiritualization of form' in the late works, that 'nevertheless remains plastically comprehensible and strictly logical', and said of Beethoven that 'even in his freest, boldest conception he never discarded technical-formal logic'.[11]

10   Marx, vol. II, p. 311.
11   Helm, pp. 233, 322.

'[Beethoven:] String Quartet in A minor, Op. 132'

Beethoven's String Quartets: Essay in Technical Analysis of these Works in Relation to their Spiritual Content

> Source:
> 'Quartett in A-Moll Op. 132', *Beethoven's Streichquartette: Versuch einer technischen Analyse dieser Werke im Zusammenhange mit ihrem geistigen Gehalt* (Leipzig: Fritzsch, 1885, 2/1910), pp. 267–95.

It was in the Spring of 1825, just after recovery from an illness, that Beethoven completed this work, conceiving and executing its adagio expressly as 'Holy Song of Thanksgiving by a Convalescent to the Divinity'.[12] The direct and indisputable connection of this celebrated 'Canzona di ringraziamente' to Beethoven the man, the link to a personal experience on the part of the composer which immediately {268} preceded his conception of the Quartet, have induced the zealous biographer and interpreter of Beethoven, Professor A. B. Marx,[13] to read into the work the psychological portrayal of this experience – the chronic infirmity and eventual restoration to health of Beethoven himself. *'The scene of action of the entire composition was to be the sickbed; the keynote was to be the nervous condition, the feverish excitability and pathological state; stringed instruments, with the abrasive sound of their bowing, were to be the sole and specific medium for the work'.*[14]

While subscribing wholeheartedly to the last part of Marx's proposition, and with reservation to the second, we believe that in the first part of what he asserts the distinguished professor has gone much too far. For a start, the portrayal of physical suffering is scarcely an aesthetic object for pure instrumental music, indeed for art of any sort; but quite apart from that, if the listener were intended to hear this in every detail of the A minor Quartet, as Professor Marx maintains, Beethoven would surely have had to designate each movement, above all the first movement, as specifically 'programmatic'. If the first movement had actually been headed 'The Illness', we would have joined Professor Marx in discovering for ourselves without difficulty a whole host of fine and relevant detail – it is perfectly possible that Beethoven in some measure did intend to indulge in representational devices of this sort, aimed at expressing in notes his memories of that 'illness' at certain specific points. But since he has not, as we have already remarked, directed our imagination towards that concrete realm of feeling by means of a 'programme', we are not empowered to take those movements of the A minor Quartet that bear no superscription in

---

12 [Helm:] The A minor String Quartet was first played by the Schuppanzigh Quartet on 9 [and 11] September 1825 at a private performance in the tavern 'Zum wilden Mann' on the Prater, in Vienna. The first public performance took place, however, at the instigation of the cellist of the Schuppanzigh Quartet Society, Joseph Linke, in a concert organized under his auspices on 6 November 1825 in what was then the Music Room 'Unter den Tuchlauben'.

13 'A. B. Marx': spaced type.

14 Marx, vol. II, p. 304 (see also Analysis 12, above). Passages placed here in italics are those that Helm took over from Marx. See the introduction, above, for discussion of the interrelationships of the two texts.

terms of anything other than the general musical expressivity that they undeniably display. What this tells us is strictly limited: we are dealing with a profoundly individual and miraculously unified work in which a consistent process of psychological evolution is unmistakably at work, the passionate, agonizingly slow striving of a great soul, mortally stricken by fate, and from the very outset languishing beneath a burden of fearsome oppressiveness, and yet borne by an equanimity and a fervent, undying devotion towards a higher power.

[First movement: Assai sostenuto – Allegro]

The very first movement of the A minor Quartet brings to a head our interpretation. It is a heart-wrenching depiction of night, wrapped in nameless darkness despite isolated flashes of light and moments of renewed vigour, with all the fevered over-wroughtness of a sick man. But this is a sick man in mind only. We cannot think in terms of those *'protracted agonies'*,[15] in the sense of purely physical suffering, that Marx will have us see right away in the introduction.

{269} Yet every listener will instinctively sense the strangely unearthly feeling, the almost spectral quality of these minims, slipping and sliding around mysteriously on the [diminished] seventh chords of A minor and E minor [Example 1: bb. 1–7]. *'All of this throws the contour of each individual line, especially that of the viola, into sharp relief.'*

Example 1

'The first violin now breaks in at the onset of the first movement[16] *(allegro) with feverish haste [Example 2: bb. 9–21].* {270} *It then hovers in tense anxiety, turns to a song of soft lament, then rises again,*[17] *finding the strength where it thought none was left.'*[18] (Marx's description – absolutely right so long as it is applied at the purely spiritual rather than pathological level.)

We have quoted the first twelve bars of the allegro in their entirety because within them are encapsulated the most salient elements of the thematic development of this whole wondrously expressive movement. For easier reference, we shall denote

15 ibid, 305.
16 'first movement': spaced type.
17 Helm suppresses Marx's '(first subject)' after 'rises again', probably to avoid appearing to refer solely to the first violin figure in bb. 14–18.
18 Marx, vol. II, p. 304, including Ex. 1 but not Ex. 2.

Example 2

the scurrying semiquaver-figure at the beginning as *a*, the motif of lament as a, the unison figure descending to the lower register as b, and the chromatically modulating block chords in crotchets in the following bar as c.

What is distinctive about the formal shaping of this movement is that Beethoven instinctively adheres to sonata form. Clearly recognizable are first subject and second subject [*Haupt- und Seitenthema*] – or really several subsidiary ideas [*Nebenge-danken*] –, and equally clear are a development section {271} and a section III [*Durchführungs- und dritter Teil*] as in the customary scheme. On the other hand,

Beethoven has thrown all of that into flux by causing the various themes to take over turns of phrase from one another in spontaneous fashion; and what used to be called 'thematic working' [*Arbeit*] disappears without trace, giving way wholly to 'melodic discourse' [*melodische Rede*].

We can see in the last example the way in which, after first being presented with infinite sorrow by the cello in its high register, the principal motif a lodges itself more firmly with the first violin, which exchanges melodic phrases with its fellow-instruments, so that – as so often occurs in these late quartets! – the parts seem to be conversing with one another. The lament now swells mightily, but is cut off abruptly by the descending figure b and the crotchet chords c, stands fast as if broken off at the adagio bar, after which the semiquaver figure *a* ushers back the lament, and this time the movement is at last set properly in motion. The unison figure b [b. 29] drives it towards F minor, at which point the motif a begins again, each instrumental part in turn more ardent, more pressing than the last, until the consuming ardour cools for the moment, the melody resolves in first violin on to F major,[19] and the topmost line inwardly muses with such sweetness and tenderness for just four bars, accompanied in the other parts only by soft offbeat tenuto chords [Example 3: bb. 34–6]. After this the three upper instruments come together

Example 3

(violins in octaves, viola a third below the second violin), over staccato quavers in the cello, in an energetic figure that we shall denote d [Example 4: bb. 38–42] – {272} a figure that recalls the heroic power of the third Rasumovsky Quartet (Op. 59 [no. 3] in C major).[20] However, figure d breaks off sharply in the third bar, making way for a curious little canon (e), itself also only four bars long; whereupon the

Example 4

19   Marx: 'D major'.

20   Helm states that 'Austrian musicians have given the work [Op. 59 no. 3] the name "Heroic Quartet" [*Helden-Quartett*], thus assigning it the same position among the quartets that the "Eroica" occupies among the symphonies' (p. 102). Helm himself uses 'heroic' [*Heroisches*] of a passage in the finale of that quartet.

first violin, based on figure b, with the inner voices in contrary rhythm, surges power-fully upwards. These last twelve bars ([bb. 36–47][21]) answer perfectly to Marx's epithet, quoted earlier, of *'rising again, gathering strength'*.[22]

This latter upward motion of b leads to a pleasant but fleeting cadence on F major, and at this point the *second subject [Seitensatz]*[23] (the second principal idea [*Hauptgedanke*], or song-melody of sonata form) enters in the second violin [Example 5: bb. 48–52]. {273} This is – as Marx once again rightly says – *full of consolation and yet* (because of the independent patterning of the lower parts!) *disquieted and disjointed.*[24] The modulation of the second subject (f) to C major

Example 5

seems to bring a freshness with it, but this is promptly undermined by its consequent phrase [bb. 52–6], in which the first violin, described by Marx as *'strenuously high in register'*[25] ([Example 6] – though use of this high writing for violins is a feature common to all the late quartets), modulates by way of B♭ major back to F – *back to the pathologically nervous condition.*[26]

Example 6

21   Helm: 'p. 45 of the Peters score'.
22   Marx, vol. II, p. 304.
23   'second subject': spaced type.
24   Marx, vol. II, p. 304, also the first two-and-a-half bars of Ex. 5.
25   ibid, 305, including Ex. 6.
26   ibid.

Nevertheless, at this very point ([bb. 60–64])[27] a robust spirit sets in: energetic contrary motion among all the parts on a semiquaver figure beloved by Beethoven, after which motif b in agitated form, is played *ff* and in the minor, first in descent then in ascent [bb. 67, 69], each time followed by a sweet sigh in soft minims, reconciliation coming in the form of a quasi-formal close to section I of the movement on the dominant of F major ([bb. 70–72]:[28] ritardando).

Short, stabbing quavers, related to the staccato figure c, furnish the transition from section I to section II of the sonata form, with F major harmony, that appears to drive towards Bb by way of an Eb in the second violin. Then the mysterious minims of the introduction creep in again surreptitiously in the cello, now augmented to semibreves so as to adjust to the allegro tempo [bb. 75–8], as if to introduce a sort of fixed countermelody (a cantus firmus, in an improper sense of the term) to the principal melody, the lament, a [bb. 79ff]. By dint of an F♯ in those mysterious cello semibreves, the tonality has shifted from Bb to G minor, and now the lament, a, burrows ever deeper into the various instrumental parts, modulating to C minor [b. 84], accompanied inexorably by the semibreve motif of the introduction, sometimes emerging prominently, sometimes deeply submerged. If any part of Marx's image of 'illness' fits the music precisely it would be this, which we have called the development section. As if the confused imagination of the unhappy sufferer can no longer endure such a {274} painful *idée fixe* (those selfsame semibreves of the introduction), the passage is precipitously broken off [b. 91] by a restatement of the staccato figure c, now hammered out wildly. The first time, the abrupt cessation on the dominant of C minor is followed by an apparently brand new episode, though motivically derived from a [Example 7: bb. 91–4], playing on ambiguities between C major and A minor in a unison which speaks almost in recitative. This quickly

Example 7

and urgently spreads through the upper instruments [bb. 94–6] in imitative fashion and brings all four parts together [b. 97] in a somewhat modified version of figure b, as if a more cheerful image had momentarily entered the sufferer's soul, as a smile may shine through tears. Thereupon, however, the motif of the introduction in the three upper parts brings back the cello lament [bb. 99–101]. And after the staccato figure c [b. 102] (in E minor), which with its wild hammering now causes the melody to break off, the introduction motif re-enters with truly fearful

27   Helm: 'p. 46 of the score'.
28   Helm: 'last three bars of p. 46 of the score'.

violence [b. 103], all four parts in *ff* unison [*recte*: octaves]. It is as if warring demons had just achieved some mighty victory, or as if some terrible nightmare had invaded the composer's mind and built up to annihilating proportions. But still there remains for the tormented heart the deliverance of the lament [bb. 107–10], before which the appalling tonal apparition of those inexorable semibreves diminishes bit by bit, finally dwindling to nothing. By now, the sufferer (if we want to extend Marx's interpretation), after the searing bars that have just passed, appears to want finally to 'settle down to sleep' at the wondrously soothing modulation ([bb. 116–17][29]), but the dark powers will not permit the sufferer the peace for which he longs, ah so much! Far from it – the staccatos of c, which enter again {275} as harshly as possible, bring back the feverish semiquaver-figure *a* [bb. 119–20] (with which the allegro opened) on E minor and thrust us at the same time into section III of the sonata form.

It is truly remarkable and admirable to see how Beethoven, in the midst of this most spontaneous, most individual outpouring of the soul – as we surely must call the first movement of the A minor Quartet – upholds the strictest, most consistent musical logic; and yet how this in no way impairs or stifles the warm, glowing breath of the feeling. So we sense in this – and we say this as a result of frequent listening and reading of the score – the introduction of section III of the movement (that is, of the recapitulation [*Reprise*], modified in innumerable ways, of section I) not as an act of formalism that stultifies the process of psychological evolution, but as something borne of inner necessity, as something even intensifying through clarity the musical expression of ideas, as a certain symmetry of ordering with respect to the return of the motifs inseparable from the essence of pure instrumental music (one need think only of the artistically freest, most spiritualized pieces of music, such as Richard Wagner's *Faust* Overture or *Tristan* Prelude!).

However, we do not need to follow the passage [from b. 119 to b. 187],[30] for formally speaking its elements are essentially those of the corresponding passage in section I. Once figure *a* has opened [the new section] in E minor,[31] the lament melody logically begins in the same key, and the whole modulatory process proceeds as before. The heroic figure d [bb. 149–50] and its curious attendant canon e [bb. 151–4], and the consoling second subject f appear in C major [bb. 159ff], in which key essentially the refreshing transitional development of [bb. 168ff][32] also occurs.

The cadence (or rather, the half-cadence) of section III likewise falls in C major [b. 187]. Now ensues a wonderfully expressive coda, the spirit of the composer battling with ever-increasing vigour and fortitude, ultimately in truly heroic vein, after which Marx's portrayal of illness is no longer really tenable. True, at the beginning of the coda ([bb. 193ff][33]) the forces of adversity – personified by the semibreves of the introduction – regain the upper hand, tormenting the composer so sorely that the motif of lament a swells forth powerfully, and finally appears to cry perplexedly for help {276} [Example 8: bb. 209–12].

29   Helm: 'p. 48 of the Peters score, bb. 6–10'.
30   Helm: 'from p. 48 to half way down p. 51 of the score'.
31   Marx: 'C minor'.
32   Helm: 'p. 50'.
33   Helm: 'p. 51 of the score'.

Example 8

(NB Play the middle voices with the left hand, at the piano, and play the cello notes after.)

The composer immediately takes up the busy little canon e [bb. 214ff], following it, as in section I, with the spirited intensification of motif b [bb. 219–22], leading again to the second subject f [bb. 223–31] – now in the bright refreshing key of A major. Yet this consoling melody loses its brightness as it moves into the minor [b. 231] and gives way to the lament theme of the first subject a, as if the two melodies were a single[34] interrelated musical period.

What we said at the beginning of our analysis of this movement as to the constant improvisatory interchange of motifs and melodies applies here more than ever. So, as the first subject a is reintroduced, it is combined with the heroic figure d thus [Example 9: bb. 236–9] – only to give way two bars later again to the second subject

Example 9

Vln 1

f as the melodic continuation of that combination [Example 10: bb. 240–45] – {277} which takes on the character of a lofty song of defiance, then of resignation, then of renewed bold defiance. So vivid has the expression become that the psychological phases can be traced bar by bar in the varying dynamic levels and the phrase markings.

Example 10

cres - cen - do

34   'single': spaced type.

The final crescendo does lead – for one final time! – into the hostile semibreves of the introduction. These, as they enter in a screeching *ff* [bb. 247–8], are counterpointed by the lament motif a, played in matching energetic fashion *ff*, after which the lament dies away, dissolving into wonderfully dwindling chordal suspensions ([bb. 249–53][35]). Then the lower parts are set aquiver with a curiously dissonant contrary motion [Example 11: b. 254], first hushed, then growing

Example 11

stronger as the violins enter [bb. 256–7]. The semibreves from the introduction, motivically overtopped by these surging semiquavers, now give way, and the second violin gives out a truly monumental closing melody [bb. 258ff; Example 12: bb. 258–9] of unyielding, rock-hard octaves in crotchets against the passionate, strenuous semiquaver figure of the first violin.

Example 12

{278} In the compelling, unremitting rhythmic character of this final figure, the motivic kernel of which even so are the first three notes of the lament theme, one might think to see – just as in the presto of the finale of the F minor Sonata Op. 57 (a brief, stormy march movement) – the composer himself, and to hear him as he cries out: 'I will not bend, I will not submit.'[36]

The movement now reaches its conclusion with unbounded energy, no trace of illness sapping its mighty force, and yet the sombre character of the minor mode is etched most sharply. – This whole coda with its strongly organic condensation of all the principal motifs and the overpowering cumulative effect of the final pages of score (whose inner parts simply cannot, alas, be playably transcribed for piano) has few pieces to equal it in the quartet literature. There was a precedent indeed in

35 Helm: 'p. 54, bb. 5–10'.
36 [Helm:] This interpretation – which we intend only figuratively – is by no means wholly accurate. The close of the first movement of the A minor Quartet could be construed persuasively as the victory of the hostile, evil principle. In truth, the Danaïdes, condemned eternally to fill a sieve with water, or Sisyphus fruitlessly rolling a stone uphill, could not be more expressively portrayed in music than by the first violin with that semiquaver figure mentioned above. The monumental theme in the second violin resounds along with it as a mighty utterance: 'For ever lost!' An apotheosis of despair such as Liszt depicted, al fresco, in the *Inferno* of his *Dante* Symphony.

the orchestral literature: the riveting, demoniacal effect of the closing stages of the first movement of the Ninth Symphony bears a close kinship. Here, too, as there, a sense of terrifying joylessness culminates.

[Second movement: Allegro ma non tanto]

What follows this first movement, as its sounds recede in awesome, melancholy splendour, is a sort of intermezzo,[37] allegro ma non tanto, A major, 3/4, in which Marx – committed as he is to the representation of the stages of an illness – likes to find illustrated *'the first pleasant sensations of improvement in the convalescence, although still in short, gasping breaths, now irregular, now more steady; though it is still not in stable condition – section II is destined particularly to depict that'*.[38]

Unquestionably, coming after the pronouncedly minor character and the fevered strivings of the first movement, with constant rhythmic changes, the first four bars of the intermezzo, with their A major tonality (unison in all four parts), and with their gently moving, dance-like 3/4 rhythm, suggest to the listener a picture of spiritual re-awakening and renewed vigour, a musical feeling that is confirmed when the true principal theme enters in b. 5: {279} [Example 13] (we give just the two violin parts, which are sufficient to convey an overall idea).

Example 13

(All four instruments in unison)

Quite apart from the very general way in which it effects a contrast between the first two movements, we are able to discern in the intermezzo a subtle – in a truly Beethovenian sense – restless interplay of tonalities, which at times appears more inwardly animated (as, for example, at the turn to C major in section II, where the two violins play together in thirds [bb. 28–31], which to Marx incomprehensibly suggests a *'shiver'*[39]), at times takes on an appearance of whimsical humour, as, for example, where the first violin in [bb. 42–4][40] elaborates on and extends the principal motif as follows [Example 14: bb. 42–5].

Example 14

37 'intermezzo': spaced type.
38 Marx, vol. II, p. 305; in the last clause Helm uses present subjunctive where Marx used indicative mood: 'it is still not in stable condition – section II particularly depicts that'.
39 Marx (ibid) as an adverb (*fröstelnd*), where he is actually referring to the diminished fourth in b. 35, making no reference to the thirds, as 'After the close of section I in E♭, [section II] emerges in C major, moves via F major with a shiver into G minor, . . .'
40 Helm: 'the opening bars of p. 56 of the score'.

In general, this movement is graphically clear in its design. With only a little attentiveness on the part of the listener, it needs no commentary. It offers a succinct example of the way in which Beethoven in his late works pursues certain favourite ideas with an almost obsessive single-mindedness. It is almost as if he were insatiable in his desire to hear them played. In this respect, our A major intermezzo is a kindred piece to the scherzo of the Eb major Quartet Op. 127, though the latter – as Marx so rightly says – at every stage of the composer's evolving musical imagination opens up new paths hitherto unperceived, constantly enlarging the musical horizon,[41] whereas the second movement of the A minor Quartet, midst all the incessant activity with which the motivic elements (unison upward-stepping figure, a; the principal theme seen either as a whole or in its two component parts, b and c, partly on their own, partly in combination, c particularly in masterfully light canonic imitations) are developed, so to speak fails to make any headway.

This last point is even truer of the intermezzo's {280} surprising contrasting middle section [*Alternativ*], also in A major, which now begins; but it is true only of its principal melody. This is really an exquisite musette rendered into high art, in which the improved condition of the composer shines through, indeed at one point [bb. 201–12?] throwing out completely the formal balance of the movement.

Very tellingly, Marx comments: '*After the short-breathed phrases that have occurred so far, each two bars long, the breadth of the new strain comes as a surprise* [Example 15: bb. 125–32]; *it is eleven bars long and repeats immediately for a second eleven bars (with viola and cello entering and sustaining an octave A–a as the second violin did first time round), hence twice eleven bars*'. But the distinguished Beethoven biographer goes too far by adding: '*As the refreshing section II unfurls*

Example 15

41   This quotation appears in later editions of Marx: see 6/1908, vol. II, p. 437.

its long phrases, it makes us faintly recall how the quartet began (illness, the adagio of the first movement)'.[42] Such musical reminiscence seems to us far-fetched, for Marx is clearly referring to the passage in which Beethoven with reckless high spirits overthrows the rhythm of his contrasting middle section – a passage [bb. 212–27] to which we shall come in a moment.

Directly after the twice eleven = twenty-two bars described above, the viola introduces a new idea, the first violin then imitating, though with modified ending {281} [Example 16: bb. 147–9], a quaver figure (cf. [bb. 144–205][43]) which in turn engenders a passage brimming over with the freshest, merriest vitality. See how

Example 16

(Accompaniment staccato throughout)
(Quavers as clear as possible)

beautifully, for example, the new quaver motif transforms itself in [bb. 157–65],[44] the melody rising and falling in genial fashion in the viola across the two primary triads of E major [Example 17: bb. 163–7], while the other instruments accompany

Example 17

it with bouncing equal-accented staccato crotchets whose exhilarating gyration (the pronounced dance-like character might suggest a waltz) later becomes more animated after the first violin takes over the melody [bb. 179ff]. The composer's musical style is distinctly popular at this point, certain turns of phrase perhaps surprising us by recalling Haydn and the peasant dances that have turned into minuets in his symphonies; but there is something spiritual about it, something in which we hear the great Beethoven, something which says to us: it is not all meant innocently, it is really knowingly done, introspective, it conveys an image. This contrasting middle section has had the same effect upon us as the famous scherzo of the Pastoral Symphony, 'Jolly Gathering of Villagers'. Even if we did accept Beethoven's illness and recuperation as the underlying concept of this quartet, can we be convinced now by an interpretation which goes on: 'The convalescent

---

42   Marx, vol. II, p. 306, not including the music example.
43   Helm: 'pp. 58 and 59 of the score'.
44   Helm: 'the last few bars of p. 58, leading to the top of p. 59, of the score'.

ventures outdoors, draws the pure air deeply and with relish into his lungs, catches the strains of a burlesque scene of dancing which so entrances him that he joins the merry throng and finally throws himself {282} heartily into the leaping and dancing, whooping loudly'?[45] Or are these sixteen episodic bars, which lurch all of a sudden into dance rhythm with the delicious alla breve [Example 18: bb. 212–27], really something other than the crazed 'leapings' of the boldest of musical tem-

Example 18

peraments?! And Marx reads into this light-hearted, frolicsome passage (we ought to add that there is something slightly startling about the C♯ minor harmony, {283} but startling in a droll and hobgoblinish sort of way) a link to the concept of illness from the first movement, on the basis of the long notes and conjunct melodic steps! But how utterly different is the rhythmic formation and hence the musical meaning of this passage, as it forges ahead without so much as a glance back at what has gone before!

45   The source of this quotation eludes me.

At all events, the effect of the intermezzo's contrasting middle section at first hearing in the original medium is electrifying, astonishing. We have seen it happen more than once that, given the right temperament for the performance of the movement (Hellmesberger[46] in Vienna was, among others, the right interpreter for it), a whole audience was swept up with the composer in a sort of Bacchanalian frenzy.

There is no denying that the literal repeat of section I which follows brings with it a slight cooling off of the intensity that has been powerfully built up, and we might feel a twinge of regret that Beethoven does not return again briefly to the contrasting middle section at the end, as he does in the scherzo of the E♭ major Quartet Op. 127, but leaves us with one of those musical surprises that make the closing stages of his movements almost always stand out from those of the other great classical composers.

[Third movement: Molto adagio]

The third movement[47] of the A minor Quartet is the celebrated 'Canzona di ringraziamento offerta alla divinità da un guarito, in modo lidico', which lies at the very heart of this composition and serves unquestionably as its psychological centre of gravity and turning point. This piece has a quality of sublime reverence and inner contemplation[48] that attests more to Beethoven's religious beliefs, his trust in a higher power and his reliance on a *personal god* than could be told in lengthy dissertations on the subject. It is a baring of the soul so unfathomably profound and so intensely personal that, as Ambros so aptly put it in his *Cultural-Historical Pictures*, it seems strangely out of keeping whenever <this adagio> played in a hall aglow with candles before a glittering assembly of people is followed by applause or <worse>, as is said to have happened <in earlier years>, by hissing.[49]

In the original manuscript,[50] which passed into the possession of the quartet's dedicatee, *the Prince Galitsin, the superscription, written in Beethoven's own hand,* reads in German:[51] 'Heiliger Dankgesang eines Genesenen an die Gottheit, in der lydischen Tonart' [Holy Song of Thanksgiving by a Convalescent to the Divinity, in the Lydian Mode]. The Italian wording found its way only later – with or without the composer's sanction – into the score.

In his desire to imbue this, his invocation of the Most High, with a character right from the very first notes of utmost solemnity, of renunciation of all that is worldly, {284} Beethoven adopts instinctively one of the old church modes for the

---

46   'Hellmesberger': spaced type. The Hellmesberger String Quartet, founded by Joseph Hellmesberger in 1849 and regarded as the leading quartet of its day in Vienna, featured the late Beethoven quartets prominently in its repertory (*NGDM*).
47   'third movement': spaced type.
48   Ambros: see below, note 49.
49   'This piece . . . contemplation', 'it seems . . . hissing.' (A. W. Ambros, *Culturhistorische Bilder aus dem Musikleben der Gegenwart* (Leipzig: Matthes, 1860), p. 25). This description occurs in an essay (pp. 7–32), 'Das ethische und religiöse Moment in Beethoven', in which Ambros places this third movement, along with the Ninth Symphony, in the first of three categories of works: 'those in which thought of God, Immortality, virtue and reward are presented, in the sense of so-called natural religion' (p. 21). Angle-brackets indicate Helm's interpolations into Ambros's text.
50   Berlin, Staatsbibliothek Preussischer Kulturbesitz, Mend.-Stift 11. The German superscription is entered in Beethoven's hand, the Italian evidently later and in another hand.
51   'in German': spaced type.

main section of the adagio. The claim that it had to be the Lydian rather than any other because that mode was assigned to the expression of pathological (?) weakness long ago by the Greeks, and that Beethoven wished thereby to recall the illness that he had surmounted, seems to us again a case of Professor Marx 'reading too much into it'.[52] This is the more so when we consider that by the Greek modal nomenclature this must have been called not the Lydian but the Hypolydian mode. Beethoven selected the Lydian mode simply as representative of the old church modes in general, as something distinctively liturgical and religious in feeling – nothing more than that.[53]

The form of the adagio, as already indicated, is of a (twice repeated) main section with a (once repeated) contrasting middle section.

The main section is the *'Song of Thanksgiving' itself, a sort of chorale with imitative prelude and interludes* [Example 19], in which *the Lydian mode* takes the

Example 19

form effectively of our F major with *strict avoidance of B♭ (which would cause the tonality in terms of the church mode system to turn into the Ionian genus molle)*,[54] and the chorale is expanded over three and two half bars, [Example 20], the

Example 20

52 Marx's statement (vol. II, p. 306) is:
> And that this [superscription] is no mere afterthought can be seen not only from the very content of the piece but also from the adoption of the old Lydian mode, itself pathologically weak in character.

This is then cross-referred to his *Die Lehre von der musikalischen Komposition*, vol. I (Leipzig: B&H, 1837), where (p. 368) he states:
> the inner dissatisfaction, the constant yearning to the brighter sounding original, imparted to the Lydian mode a still deeper expression of soft, longing, wistful desire. A more recent composer, the deeply reflective Beethoven, has exploited this quality in a masterly new way when in his Quartet Op. 132 he intones the Lydian strain for his prayer of thanksgiving . . .

53 Marx (ibid, 368–9) makes the point that:
> The profundity of the ancient system is unmistakable, and we must allow that in many points it embodies finer distinctions and more exactly appropriate characteristics than our present-day system [. . .] but] if a composer [. . .] wishes to adopt to some extent the concept of the ancient modes, he must use it in his own way.

For a recent discussion of these issues, and of Beethoven's knowledge of the theoretical literature on the modes, see S. Brandenburg, 'Beethoven's A-minor Quartet Op. 132', *Beethoven Studies*, vol. III, ed A. Tyson (Cambridge: CUP, 1982), pp. 161–91.

interludes (including the prelude) on the other hand over one and two half bars, [Example 21], both elements stated five times in regular succession, such that the *Cantus lydicus*[55] at its first appearance occupies thirty bars.

Example 21

{285} A transitional bar (on the dominant of D minor) leads into the *contrasting middle section*,[56] andante, D major, 3/8, which in the original manuscript bears the superscription 'Neue Kraft fühlend' [Feeling renewed strength], whereas in the first engraved score[57] it reads 'Sentendo nuova forza'. The motif formation of the passage is curiously wayward, and yet thoroughly Beethovenian[58] [Example 22:

Example 22

bb. 32–5], and this is intensified by the carefully marked alternation of staccato and tenuto notes, of strong and light accents. This is expressive music of a most idealized kind.

'*Strangely, there are signs here*' – we can safely leave Professor Marx to describe it this time, since a misunderstanding of Beethoven's prescribed 'programme' is unlikely – thus: '*Strangely, there are signs here in this andante of a regaining of spiritual strength. It is not the greater compactness of the material, but the nerve, the bolder outlook though still with lingering nervous excitability.' The first violin takes up the melody in conjunction with the second violin (yes, at times ingeniously intertwined with one another: in bb. 10 and 12 from the beginning of the andante [i.e. bb. 41, 43]) carrying it through to its close with incomparable sweetness, indeed with the rapture of a rejuvenated life force which trembles through every fibre,* [Example 23: bb. 61–4], {286} *though not without trace still of the*

54 Marx, *Beethoven*, vol. II, p. 307, including the music example. 'Ionian genus molle', i.e. the major scale in a one-flat key signature.
55 'Cantus lydicus': in spaced type.
56 'contrasting middle section': spaced type.
57 *Quatuor pour 2 Violons Alto Violoncelle . . . par Louis van Beethoven . . . Oeuv.132* (Berlin: Schlesinger, [1827]), p. 26.
58 Music example in Marx, vol. II, p. 307, but laid out there on three staves.
59 Marx/Helm: '*p. 63 of the* Peters *score*'. In Ex. 23, Helm has displaced the second violin's pairs of demisemiquavers backwards by one semiquaver. I have preserved this, since Helm's examples are piano transcriptions rather than score reductions.
60 Marx, vol. II, p. 308, including the music example.

Example 23

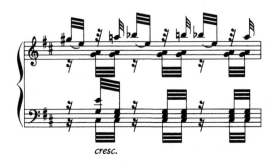

Example 24

*dark shadows of past sufferings now overcome. Now the last change of mood is
headed 'cantabile espressivo' ([b. 68ff]*[59]*). For its significance in our* (i.e. Marx's)
interpretation, the cello part should be noted:[60] [Example 24: bb. 68–72]. For the
present writer, {287} on the other hand, this last passage recalls something from
the D major Mass – one could set words of fervent, pious thanks to the melody of
the uppermost line. The way in which this concluding part of the D major Andante
(note particularly [bb. 76–7]*[61]*) intensifies its expressiveness even more inwardly is
something which can be seen by reading the score.

*The passage dies away 'più piano', in D major. As if in an echo, the chord
E–G–C (rather than E–G–B♭–C) is sounded pianissimo, and then the* 'Song of
Thanksgiving' *returns, the chorale melody placed high in the first violin, giving it
an almost visionary quality, the introductory motif* (of the prelude and interludes)
*being developed as an elaborative motif against the chorale with syncopating
rhythmic modifications.*[62]

The succession of melodic events is just as at the beginning: the chorale and
interlude motif are each stated five times; and once again the passage comprises
thirty bars with one supplementary bar effecting the transition to D major.

At this point [b. 116], the contrasting middle section returns, but by comparison with the previous statement it is richly elaborated, animated and intensified in
rhythm and figuration to an exceptional extent that makes it – as Marx eloquently
puts it – *one of those Beethovenian variations 'in which a state of supreme intro-
spection transcends all ordinary contemplation'*,[63] such as we have come to recognize
in, among others, the miraculous variations in the adagio of Op. 127.

The chorale then returns [b. 169] 'Mit innigster Empfindung [With utmost
intimacy of feeling]', as Beethoven *inscribed* in the manuscript, or 'Con intissimo
sentimento',[64] as engraved in the score.

The elaborative motif from the first repeat, primarily in quaver motion, *is now
more actively developed*, with quavers mostly subdivided into semiquavers, *working
in imitation against the chorale melody, which is itself also treated imitatively in
all parts as a second figuration.*[65] The spiritual expressiveness of the movement
achieves an unbounded radiance, a rapture, lofting the rapt listener involuntarily
far far 'from all earthly toil', yet at the same time conveying an unshakeable trust
in God which comes through tangibly in monumental style in the C major bars
[bb. 190–94] marked with *sforzati*, especially the last three of these. (The *lofty
unconcern* for surface *harshness of harmonic effect* that Beethoven exhibits,[66]
swept up as he was with the melodic aspects of his musical ideas, should be noted
here, for example the pungent, bitter-sweet ninths sounding between the two violins
at the first two *sforzati*.)

---

61 Helm: 'bb. 4–5 after the last music example'.
62 Marx, vol. II, p. 308, with explanatory footnote on elaborative motif [*Figuralmotiv*]. In place of
    'Song of Thanksgiving', Marx has 'the *first idea*', in place of 'in . . . quality', 'with utmost intensity'
    (note Marx's rhetorical *hochliegend, hochgespannt*).
63 ibid, 309.
64 ibid.
65 ibid.
66 ibid, 310. This characteristic is attributed by Marx to Beethoven's style in general, and also to
    that of J. S. Bach.

{288} The section [*Satz*] as a whole draws to its close not with the *forte* or *fortissimo* of the near-apocalyptic level of inspiration[67] attained through those *sforzati*, but completely hushed, *pianissimo*. The chorale melody and its figuration fade gradually in one long constant *diminuendo* (the melody, with all its individual *crescendos*, being like calm, steady breathing), like some heavenly apparition. The bright C major of the *sforzato* bars makes almost no impression on this, and the adagio closes wholly in F major without Bb – the Lydian mode, though ultimately in the long-held final chord there is no way that this can be distinguished from our modern F major.

[Fourth movement: Alla marcia, assai vivace]

What follows this wonderfully exalted, this transfigured Song of Thanksgiving[68] [. . .] is a short march movement (alla marcia, assai vivace, A major, 4/4), in binary form with strictly regular eight-bar periodicity, section I beginning as in [Example 25],

Example 25

occupying eight bars, modulating to E major and closing in that key, the whole thing repeated. Section II, which opens with the first violin phrase {289} [Example 26: bb. 9–10], expands over sixteen bars, closing in the tonic key, A major, and is correspondingly repeated. The movement is energetic, fresh, invigorating, section II

Example 26

67 apocalyptic: *psalmistisch*.
68 [Helm:] Perhaps this chorale adagio is what Wagner had in mind when he spoke in general of the style of the late Beethoven string quartets in such a telling fashion: 'So intimate is it that we must count it the highest honour to be allowed even to hear its strains'.

recalling slightly the triumphal march from King Stephen, and the noble and sublime popular vein of the latter that is unique to Beethoven.[69]

Marx sees in this movement '*the confident stride of renewed vigour as the convalescent nears full recovery and secure good health; if not yet total recovery, then at any rate stalwart bearing*'.[70] In support of this construction he could cite the decisive *forte* outbursts which then instantly drop to *piano*.

However, Beethoven throughout his late works was fond of using this telling interplay of *forte* and *piano*, especially when writing in march form or in comparably tight rhythmic style. It comes of a certain artistic self-composure. We need think only of the second movement of the Piano Sonata Op. 101.

In the case of Op. 132, no sooner is section II of the march with its repetition complete than there follows on immediately a più allegro (4/4), based on the quavers of the previous example, which opens in A minor and leads via F to C major, in which key the first violin [bb. 27–39], over a tremolando in the lower instruments, gives out one of the most impassioned recitatives[71] in all instrumental music. The music throbs vibrantly, culminating in a swift, resolute close. The first violin, its recitative ended in D minor, plunges into a typically Beethovenian cadenza of running quavers (presto, A minor, alla breve), cascading rapidly down and up again, to resume its recitative, then to lead after a bar of fatigue and hesitation (poco adagio *smorzando*) directly (*attacca*) into the finale[72] (allegro appassionato, A minor, 3/4).

[Fifth movement: Allegro appassionato–Presto]

As Marx so eloquently puts it: This [finale] is '*a psychological culmination that rings wonderfully true*',[73] recalling the bygone struggles, elations, sorrows and consolations of this work. '*It ventures to new life and occupation. But it is no longer the fresh, undimmed life of youth. Illness is conquered, but the toll that it has taken is not to be forgotten; that initial, unbounded vitality has not returned.*'[74] We could extend Marx's interpretation: {290} at least not immediately[75] – not for as long as the music remains in the minor, questing, exploring. Right from the opening bars of the finale, *the minor modality, the sense of haste, the unresting tempo*,[76] bear out this reading (note particularly in the following example the gait of the lower parts): [Example 27]. But from b. 3 onwards we hear the voice of Beethoven's soul speaking[77] in the supremely tender melody of the upper line – a great soul unbroken yet wounded to the very core, longing to be understood, consumed with yearning for happiness. – Unable to tear himself away from this melody (surely one of the most touching that he ever invented), Beethoven comes back to it

69   Beethoven's incidental music to *König Stephan* (1811), third movement, 'Siegesmarsch', where the similarity is with the opening measures.
70   Marx, vol. II, p. 309.   71   'one . . . recitatives': spaced type.
72   'finale': spaced type.
73   Marx, vol. II, p. 309, which in fact says: 'It is once again a musical portrayal that rings wonderfully true'.
74   ibid.   75   'immediately': spaced type.
76   Marx, vol. II, p. 309, including the first five bars of the following music example.
77   'the voice of Beethoven's soul speaking': spaced type.

Example 27

throughout this finale again and again (splendidly lucid, abundantly endowed, crafted with vitality). In the eight bars that follow immediately on from the last example, the melody is repeated, now an octave higher, in first violin partly reinforced by viola, in its passionate drive from A minor to the relative major. Only then does the consequent phrase bring its closure of the melodic period: {291} [Example 28: bb. 19–26].

Example 28

(Accompaniment: analogous to the consequent, as shown in Ex. 27)

This is similarly repeated, whereupon the music takes on a doughty, defiant, energetic character as it combines the two cadential bars of the consequent with an intervening figure sharply accenting the weak beats of the bar. The piano reduction given here attempts to convey the effect: [Example 29: bb. 34–42]. Note the pungently shrill ninth produced by the two violins in the second and sixth bars (the held E of the second violin is really an octave lower).

These last eight bars, too, are repeated (extremely regular form and balanced phrasing predominate in this finale), yet in such a way that the three upper instruments now {292} carry the intervening figure with its mettlesome quavers high in the upper register [b. 42], while the cello takes over the melodic figure from the first subject. Then short, stabbing quaver chords (corresponding to the final bars of the

Example 29

last example) bring about a modulation to G major that in turn ushers in the second subject [bb. 50ff]. This, with its capricious construction, so contrasting in its characteristic trills and cheerful manner [Example 30: bb. 52–7], recalls the 'Sentendo nuova forza' of the adagio, though now with a more humorous disposition.

Example 30

Midst curiously fleeting accompaniment, the second subject modulates to E minor, making way for an episode which is intense and gripping ([bb. 59ff][78]). From the fifth bar of this it combines with a figure from the principal theme of the movement, sharply etched, marked *fortissimo* throughout, to be played high in the tenor register of the cello with tied chords in the upper instruments producing

78   Helm: 'p. 71, system 3 of the Peters score'.

scintillating harmonies – a portrayal of true Beethovenian resoluteness and unbending demeanour. Translated to the piano, this goes roughly as in {293} [Example 31:

Example 31

Vcl

bb. 62–6]. Attention then moves to the first violin (see [Example 32: bb. 67–70]) in what forms a striking contrast with the preceding monumental chords but is a

Example 32

no less emphatic phrase of 'supplication' or 'conciliation' – who can ever divine the master's intentions down to the very last detail?! The cello figure and tied chords as they resume in the succeeding four bars [bb. 71–5] take on a harder, more granite-like aspect, and while the [first violin] phrase just quoted speaks with greater urgency, the music then, over a dwindling *diminuendo* [bb. 82ff], and using those overlapping harmonies of which Beethoven (and after him Schumann) was so enamoured in the late works, becomes progressively calmer, until (at what is the last decisive modulation to A minor) the opening melody slips in almost unintentionally [b. 92] – as if it was the most natural thing in the world. The thirty-two bars which now follow ([bb. 92–123][79]) correspond in essence to the first statement of the first subject (antecedent and consequent phrases, with their repeats). [Bars 123ff],[80] however, set out – first in F major, with the basic motif of the first subject in first violin in modified form {294} [Example 33] – a fertile and

Example 33

highly wrought development sustained over forty bars, which in its *pianissimo* passages recalls the strangely humorous sound fabric of the scherzo of the F major

79   Helm: 'p. 72 of the score'.   80   Helm: 'p. 73 of the score'.

Quartet Op. 95, especially vibrant and fiery thereafter [bb. 164ff], as the cello takes over the main melodic argument. What ensues is an unremitting struggle, a constant labouring towards freedom and contentment of the soul – a travail which does not, however, achieve its aim immediately. Before that comes about, the whole of section I of the finale is restated [bb. 176–243] in accordance with sonata form, and after that there occurs a distinctively imaginative coda that is derived from the phrase of 'conciliation' (as we called it – see [Example 32]) by inversion of the cadence bars: [Example 34: bb. 243–8]. For twenty bars it pursues its

Example 34

(All molto legato)

whispering course, the parts entering softly in successive imitations, and continues on its way until the motif of this secretive development merges imperceptibly into that of the principal theme [bb. 263–4], which now presses on, passing from voice to voice, in an impassioned *accelerando* (marked by Beethoven in German with the words 'Immer geschwinder' [pressing forward constantly]), then storms forward, now is swept up ultimately into a *presto* ([b. 280][81]). Here the principal melody [bb. 280–94] (this time antecedent and consequent locked together without the repetitions of previous statements) sounding first in the cello playing in its highest range, then in cello and first violin in unison [*recte* compound octaves], in a robust, full-bodied sound, powerfully accompanied, almost drumlike, by the inner parts in double-stopped quavers, {295} achieves its most passionate, most fervid expressiveness.[82] The first violin sustains the dominant E *decrescendo* for five bars while the cello meanwhile frees the melody from the sombre realm of the minor and plunges joyfully into the A major so long awaited![83]

Only now, now at long last, is the composer restored to the full flood of his original strength and vigour (in denying the finale such restoration, Marx completely overlooks this A major coda[84]). Every sorrow, every spiritual or (if indeed it is intended) physical torment is surmounted and forgotten . . . We invite the reader to take a look at the score, or still better to listen to a really fine performance of this masterpiece, and see for himself whether the parts in this coda do not glide swiftly and delightfully by, joke, flirt and tease in private pleasure-making, and

81   Helm: 'p. 77 of the score'; 'presto': spaced type.
82   'achieves . . . expressiveness': spaced type.
83   'plunges . . . awaited': spaced type.
84   Marx, vol. II, p. 309: 'It embarks on new life and activity. But this is no life of youthful freshness and unrestraint. Lingering illness has been surmounted, but the debilitation cannot be overlooked and the unsullied strength of childhood has not reasserted itself. The minor mode and the music's scurrying restlessness tell us this right at the beginning in the main theme and throughout the movement in the clearest possible way.

then break out into loud jubilation, and whether all of this has not been conjured forth from that one principal theme, aroused with infinitely painful yearning from its minor-mode state!! We have, as it were, a foreshadowing of this triumph of Beethovenian rejoicing and good humour in the brief, incomparable fifth movement (allegro, F major) of the Quartet Op. 95. In the A minor Quartet, however, all is more richly endowed, more freely and fully developed: Beethoven cannot tear himself away from the sweet play of sportive high spirits. Once he has taken up a genuinely and strikingly humorous closing phrase [Example 35: bb. 347–50],

Example 35

(All parts in unison)

he begins the whole merry gyrating dance all over again (here and there it seems about to become an idealization, a spiritualization of the style of Haydn), builds it up, and then finally, reaching back again to his original cadential idea, with a few bold leaps 'stands before the door',[85] before we realize it. At any rate, Schumann's profound remark, coined as a description of the endings of the Scherzo of the Seventh Symphony and the Allegretto of the Eighth by Beethoven, applies no less fittingly to these supreme closing bars of the A minor Quartet: 'We can just picture a euphoric Beethoven flinging down his pen, which was probably by that stage fit for nothing'.[86]

85 *beim Tore draussen*: perhaps an inexact quotation of the first line of Goethe's poem 'Was hör ich draussen vor dem Thor', *Wilhelm Meisters Theatralische Sendung*, Book IV, chap. 12, or the biblical 'Petrus stand draussen vor der Tür', *St John* 18.16.
86 R. Schumann, *Gesammelte Schriften über Musik und Musiker*, ed. Martin Kreisig (Leipzig: B&H, 5/1914), vol. I, p. 114.

Afterword to volumes I and II

The analyses presented in these two volumes have been drawn from a wide variety of sources; they represent multifarious kinds of activity, conducted in dissimilar environments by men of differing status, and destined for a readership that was far from homogeneous.

To strike at the extremes, in the shadowy figure of Ernst von Elterlein (vol. II, Analysis 4) we have a musical amateur (a minor legal official), writing, in wholly non-technical language, for amateur music-lovers, and selling a large number of copies on the open market in the German- and English-speaking worlds; whereas in Jérôme-Joseph de Momigny (vol. I, Analysis 1; vol. II, Analysis 8) we have a musical professional (organist, composer and publisher) addressing himself to the exclusive membership of the French National Institute (as had Rameau before him), seeking official approval for his theory of music, and publishing in instalments by subscription to a very small circle of readers.

The writers represented in these volumes were variously composers (Berlioz, Schumann and Wagner in the first rank, Reicha and Hoffmann in the second – others, too, composed, some of them prolifically), performers, theorists, pedagogues, critics, historians, amateurs and popular spokesmen. Their analyses appeared in treatises, biographies, monographs, textbooks, concert programmes, dictionaries and periodicals – some in austere, quasi-philosophical discourse, some laden with technical jargon and bestrewed with musical graphs, others in flowery, quasi-literary language, others in homely everyday prose. In some cases, analysis was the sole purpose for writing, in others a partner in a dual activity, and in yet others a means to some other end such as critical evaluation, or compositional instruction.

Three particular markets facilitated the abundance of analytical writing in the nineteenth century. First and foremost, the establishment of music conservatories – in Paris in 1795, London in 1822, Leipzig in 1843, Munich in 1846, Berlin in 1850, Dresden in 1856 and so forth. With their new approach to music education these created a need for authoritative textbooks for use in the classroom and lecture hall: textbooks that were distinctly different from those intended for self-instruction and private tutoring, as represented in the present volumes by Momigny, Vogler and Weber. The books by Reicha, Marx and Lobe were designed to meet this new need, as the title pages of such works often proclaimed in formulations such as 'Treatise on Harmony . . . *adopted by the [Paris] Conservatoire as the basis for study at that institution*' (Catel, 1802), or 'Manual of Harmony: Practical Introduction, *designed primarily for the Royal Conservatory of Music, Leipzig*' (E. F. Richter, 1853), many seeking to maximize their sales by some such form of words as 'Manual of Musical

Composition in Theory and Practice, *for self-instruction, or as a companion book to private teaching or public lectures*' (Marx, 1837), or 'The Forms of Musical Compositions, *analysed, and arranged as a graded series of lessons for the practical studies of school pupils and for self-instruction*' (Jadassohn, 1883). Reissues through many editions, and translations into other languages bringing textbooks to the schools of Italy, Spain, England and America offered the prospect of a mass market. The second such market was met by the increasing number of music journals, of which Rochlitz's Leipzig *Allgemeine musikalische Zeitung* (1798/9–1882), Fétis's *Revue musicale* (1827–35) and Schumann's *Neue Zeitschrift für Musik* (1834–) were in their day arguably the most distinguished, and which were aimed at the music professional, the creative artist, and the well informed and widely read non-professional. The third market was that of the musical amateur, with modest ability at the piano, who perhaps enjoyed playing the duet arrangements of the symphonic literature that proliferated during the century, and who needed readable, non-technical guides to the orchestral and chamber repertory, oratorios and opera. Analyses answering all three of these needs are represented in these two volumes.

The relatively high number of analyses translated here out of German (nineteen, if Czerny is counted) reflects the influence of German Nature Philosophy and Idealism discussed in the General Introduction to volume I, and a more general Germanic interest in penetrating deep structure that goes back to Burmeister, and that is fed by the rising tide of German nationalism, and hence the belief in intrinsic German spirituality, from at least the 1840s on. What is surprising is that of the eleven analyses translated from French, only one is by a Frenchman – and a Frenchman at odds with the French musical establishment at that: Hector Berlioz. The other authors were Belgians (Fétis, Momigny), a Czech (Reicha) and Russians (Ulïbïshev, von Lenz). There are two analyses translated out of Italian.

The representation of composers as *subjects* of analysis here is a direct result of historical and social forces at work in the nineteenth century. The high proportion of Beethoven analyses was inevitable, given the centrality of his music in artistic culture during the decades following his death, and the extent to which in nineteenth-century eyes he typified the Romantic artist in his superhuman energy, his revolutionary outlook and solitary, heroic stance. Analysis of his music must have seemed to promise the ultimate reward: the unlocking of the mysteries of the compositional psyche. To Beethoven's nine analyses, Mozart receives four and Haydn one (part of another being included in the General Introduction to vol. II) as the other representatives of Viennese Classical perfection. Where the music being analysed is that of Berlioz, Meyerbeer and Wagner, music theory can be seen coming to terms (literally!) with more complex, chromatic idioms; where it is that of Palestrina and J. S. Bach (in at least two of the works featured here) we see the emergent revival of early music.

The editor has sought to make these two volumes a showcase for nineteenth-century analysis. They are the first volumes of their kind, and there was evident virtue in displaying diversity of analytical method and stylistic range of subject. Equally possible would have been to select a small number of compositions and to present several analyses of each. That would have produced a different kind of work, and one perhaps for a future editor to compile. To do that would have been almost entirely to exclude operatic subject matter, whereas it has proved possible here to include no fewer than five operatic analyses (vol. I, Analyses 8 and 13; vol. II, Analyses 1, 6 and 11), two of entire operas. In practice, a balance has been achieved by presenting analyses of six fugues, five symphonies, six chamber works, four keyboard works, five operas and one choral work, in a stylistic spectrum discontinuously spanning the 1550s to 1880.

To structure such a work was no easy task. The history of ideas does not move in uniform step on a European scale. Hence, a purely chronological ordering would have resulted in a confused tangle of threads. Presentation by country, or original language, would have been marginally more defensible, yet scarcely more helpful. I therefore looked for a thematic arrangement. In the end, I settled upon what is essentially a threefold scheme broadly classifying the material according to intention and method: (1) technical/formal, (2) stylistic and (3) hermeneutic. This had the virtue of separating out three largely distinct kinds of analysts: (1) theorists, (2) historians, (3) writers for popular and enlightened consumption. It also had a semblance of temporal logic about it: (1) 1805–90, (2) 1828–57, (3) 1805–98. I then modified this in two ways. Since there was a substantial body of fugal analyses that possessed some coherence, I divided the first category into two groups, fugue and non-fugue (vol. I, Parts I and II). Finally, and less excusably, I extracted six of the longest and most celebrated examples of analysis, examples that were less easily categorized than others, and that tended to straddle methodologies, but which broadly speaking fulfilled the ideal of hermeneutic analysis on a grand scale, and put them together in volume II, Part II. My reader will quibble with my allocation: the Vogler should have been treated as fugue in Part I of volume I, the Berlioz as form and style in Part II of volume I, or perhaps in Part II of volume II, it was perverse to place Spitta among popularizers rather than historians, and so on. I plead guilty to all charges. I was painfully aware of the problems myself. I hope, nonetheless, that with all its faults my final arrangement will have proven instructive and suggestive to those who have used these two volumes.

Bibliographical essay

Bibliographical essay

Introductions to the field of music analysis can be found in Ian Bent with William Drabkin, *Analysis* (London: Macmillan, 1987), and Hermann Beck, *Methoden der Werkanalyse in Musikgeschichte und Gegenwart* (Wilhelmshaven: Heinrichshofen, 1974), both with a strong historical orientation; also in Jonathan Dunsby and Arnold Whittall, *Music Analysis in Theory and Practice* (London: Faber, 1988), and Nicholas Cook, *A Guide to Musical Analysis* (London: Dent, 1987). Leo Treitler's '"To Worship that Celestial Sound": Motives for Analysis' (*Journal of Musicology*, 1 (1982), 153–70) is thought-provoking on the nature of analysis. In its coverage of the music theorists of the seventeenth, eighteenth and nineteenth centuries, but exclusive of critical writers and historians (men such as Spitta and von Lenz), *Music Theory from Zarlino to Schenker: A Bibliography and Guide*, ed. David Damschroder and David Russell Williams (Stuyvesant: Pendragon, 1990) is excellent, though far from exhaustive. Heavily biased, and now out of date, Hugo Riemann's *Geschichte der Musiktheorie im IX.–XIX. Jahrhundert* (Leipzig: Hesse, 1898), available in translation as *History of Music Theory, Books 1 and 2: Polyphonic Theory to the Sixteenth Century*, trans. Raymond H. Haggh, and *Hugo Riemann's Theory of Harmony, with a Translation of Riemann's 'History of Music Theory', Book 3*, trans. William C. Mickelsen (Lincoln: University of Nebraska Press, 1962, 1977) is still unreplaced. Its successor in German is the long-term project *Geschichte der Musiktheorie*, ed. Frieder Zaminer (Darmstadt: Wissenschaftliche Buchgesellschaft), planned in fifteen volumes, in which coverage of the nineteenth century has made a magisterial beginning with *Die Musiktheorie im 18. und 19. Jahrhundert* by Carl Dahlhaus, Part I: *Grundzüge einer Systematik* (vol. X, 1984) and Part II: *Historischer Teil I: Deutschland* (vol. XI, 1989, ed. Ruth E. Müller), with Part III: *Historischer Teil II* (vol. XII) to be issued. Vol. I, *Ideen zu einer Geschichte der Musiktheorie: Einleitung in das Gesamtwerk* (1985), is of general interest.

Many volumes of the series *Studien zur Musikgeschichte des 19. Jahrhunderts* (Regensburg: Bosse, 1965–) are relevant; for example vols. IV, *Beiträge zur Musiktheorie des 19. Jahrhunderts*, ed. Martin Vogel (1966); V, *Beiträge zur Geschichte der Musikkritik*, ed. Heinz Becker (1965); XII, *Musiktheoretisches Denken: Versuch einer Interpretation erkenntnistheoretischer Zeugnisse in der Musiktheorie*, ed. Peter Rummenhöller (1967); XIV, *Die Ausbreitung des Historismus über die Musik*, ed. Walter Wiora (1969); XVIII, *Das Zeitalter der thematischen Prozesse in der Geschichte der Musik*, ed. Karl Wörner (1969); XXV, *Hegels Musikästhetik*, ed. Adolf Nowak (1971); XXIX, *Wagner und Beethoven: Untersuchungen zur Beethoven-Rezeption Richard Wagners*, ed. Klaus Kropfinger (1975), Eng. trans. Peter Palmer as *Wagner and Beethoven: Richard Wagner's Reception of Beethoven* (Cambridge: CUP, 1991); XXXIII, *Anfänge institutioneller Musikerziehung in Deutschland (1800–1843): Pläne, Realisierung und zeitgenössische Kritik . . .*, ed. Georg Sowa (1973); XXXVIII, *Die Harmonielehren der ersten Hälfte des 19. Jahrhunderts*, ed. Manfred Wagner (1974); XLIII, *Beiträge zur musikalischen Hermeneutik*, ed. Carl Dahlhaus (1975); and XLIV, *Musikästhetik und Musikkritik bei Eduard Hanslick*, ed. Werner Abegg (1974).

Histories of, and monographs on, music of the nineteenth century are too numerous to list here. Of those in English, two classics are Gerald Abraham, *A Hundred Years of Music* (London: Duckworth, 1938), and Alfred Einstein, *Music in the Romantic Era* (New York: Norton, 1947). Excellent more recent products are Carl Dahlhaus, *19th-Century Music*, Eng. trans. J. Bradford Robinson (Berkeley: University of California Press, 1989; Ger. orig. 1980), and Leon Plantinga, *Romantic Music: A History of Musical Style in Nineteenth-Century Europe* (New York: Norton, 1984). An authoritative charting of historical concepts is Friedrich Blume, *Classic and Romantic Music: A Comprehensive Survey* (New York: Norton, 1970; London: Faber, 1972), which derives from articles in the encyclopedia *Die Musik in Geschichte und Gegenwart* (1949–69).

Comparable in nature to the present volume, but very different in content, are five other works: two companion volumes in the series Cambridge Readings in the Literature of Music (CUP), *Music and Aesthetics in the Eighteenth and Early-Nineteenth Centuries*, ed. Peter le Huray and James Day (1981), and *Music in European Thought 1851–1912*, ed. Bojan Bujić (1988) – to both of which the present volume refers frequently; also, in the series Aesthetics in Music (Stuyvesant: Pendragon), *Musical Aesthetics: A Historical Reader*, ed. Edward A. Lippman, vol. II: *The Nineteenth Century* (1988), and *Contemplating Music: Source Readings in Musical Aesthetics*, ed. Ruth Katz and Carl Dahlhaus (1987–); and finally the time-honoured *Source Readings in Music History from Classical Antiquity through the Romantic Era*, ed. Oliver Strunk (New York: Norton, 1950), Parts XVII 'Literary Forerunners of Musical Romanticism' and XVIII 'Composer-Critics of the Nineteenth Century' (available as a separate volume, 1965). In addition to these five readers, there are two excellent studies of aesthetics: Andrew Bowie: *Aesthetics and Subjectivity: from Kant to Nietzsche* (Manchester: Manchester University Press, 1990), and Edward A. Lippman, *A History of Western Musical Aesthetics* (Lincoln: University of Nebraska Press, 1992). For a delightful survey of music criticism in the eighteenth and nineteenth centuries, see Max Graf, *Composer and Critic: Two Hundred Years of Musical Criticism* (London: Chapman and Hall, 1947).

General Introduction

A useful historical introduction to hermeneutics is Richard E. Palmer, *Hermeneutics: Interpretation Theory in Schleiermacher, Dilthey, Heidegger, and Gadamer* (Evanston, IL: Northwestern University Press, 1969). A deeper study that includes a historical section is *Paul Ricoeur: Hermeneutics and the Human Sciences: Essays on Language, Action and Interpretation*, ed. and trans. John B. Thompson (Cambridge: CUP; Paris: Editions de la Maison des Sciences de l'Homme, 1981). For a selection of texts, see *The Hermeneutics Reader: Texts of the German Tradition from the Enlightenment to the Present*, ed. and trans. Kurt Mueller-Vollmer (New York: Continuum, 1992). A particularly good historical account of the nineteenth century is Carl Dahlhaus, *Grundlagen der Musikgeschichte* (Cologne: Gerig, 1967), Eng. trans. J. Bradford Robinson as *Foundations of Music History* (Cambridge: CUP, 1983), chap. 2 'Hermeneutics in History'. Lippman's concise discussions of hermeneutics and musical meaning in *A History of Western Musical Aesthetics*, pp. 353–9, 381–92, and Bowie's in *Aesthetics and Subjectivity*, pp. 146–75, are helpful.

The principal text by Ast is *Grundlinien der Grammatik, Hermeneutik und Kritik* (Landshut: Thomann, 1808), and that of Wolf is 'Darstellung der Alterthums-Wissenschaft nach Begriff, Umfang, Zweck und Werth', the manifesto article (on pp. 1–145) to the first volume of the periodical *Museum der Alterthums-Wissenschaft*, ed. Friedrich August Wolf and Philipp Buttmann (1807), of which only two volumes were issued. Schleiermacher did not publish his ideas on hermeneutics definitively. Best access is gained via Heinz Kimmerle's edition, *Hermeneutik* (Heidelberg: Winter, Universitätsverlag, 1959), Eng. trans. James Duke and H. Jackson Forstman as *Hermeneutics: the Handwritten Manuscripts*, American Academy of Religion Texts and Translation Series, vol. 1 (Missoula, MT: Scholars Press, 1977). This last contains not only Kimmerle's important introduction and his later afterword (1968) but also a fine introductory essay by James Duke.

On Schleiermacher's relation to the Romantic movement see Jack Forstman, *A Romantic Triangle: Schleiermacher and Early German Romanticism* (Missoula, MT: American Academy of Religion and Scholars Press, 1977), and Schleiermacher's own *On Religion: Speeches to its Cultured Despisers*, Eng. trans. Richard Crouter (Cambridge: CUP, 1988; Ger. orig. 1799), which has an excellent introduction on this topic and on the work itself, pp. 1–73. For the circle and ellipse as central symbols within Romantic thought, see Marshall Brown, *The Shape of German Romanticism* (Ithaca: Cornell University Press, 1979). For Wackenroder's writings, see *Wilhelm Heinrich Wackenroder's 'Confessions' and 'Fantasies'*, ed. and trans. Mary Hurst Schubert (University Park, PA: Pennsylvania State University Press, 1971); translated excerpts from the *Confessions* appear in Strunk, *Source Readings*, pp. 750–63, and in Lippman, *Nineteenth Century*, pp. 5–31. Schlegel's fragmentary novel *Lucinde* is available as *Friedrich Schlegel's 'Lucinde' and the Fragments*, ed. and trans. Peter Firchow (Minneapolis, MN: University of Minnesota Press, 1971).

Humboldt's writings are collected in *Gesammelte Schriften*, ed. A. Leitzmann and others (Berlin: Behr, 1903–16; reprint edn Berlin: de Gruyter, 1968), in seventeen volumes, and the major study of him in English is Paul R. Sweet, *Wilhelm von Humboldt: a Biography* (Columbus, OH: Ohio State University Press, 1978, 1980), in two volumes. A new edition of Droysen's works is underway (Stuttgart and Bad Cannstatt: Fromann-Holzboog, 1977–). A partial translation of his *Historik: Vorlesungen über Enzyklopädie und Methodologie der Geschichte* (1857) is available as *Outline of the Principles of History*, ed. and trans. E. Benjamin Andrews (Boston: Ginn, 1897). For Boeckh, see *On Interpretation and Criticism*, ed. and trans. John Paul Pritchard (Norman, OK: University of Oklahoma Press, 1968), which presents the relevant sections of the *Encyklopaedie und Methodologie der philologischen Wissenschaften* (1877; Berlin: Teubner 2/1886).

Dilthey's works, a large proportion surviving in manuscript bundles at his death, are collected in *Wilhelm Diltheys Gesammelte Schiften* (Leipzig and Berlin: Teubner, 1914–77), in eighteen volumes, of which vols V (1924) and VII (1927) contain material of particular relevance. A useful collection is *W. Dilthey: Selected Writings*, ed. and trans. H. P. Rickman (Cambridge: CUP, 1976). A key work is his *Introduction to the Human Sciences: An Attempt to Lay a Foundation for the Study of Society and History*, ed. and trans. Ramon J. Betanzos (Detroit: Wayne State University Press, 1988). Among the many studies of Dilthey's work are Michael Ermarth, *Wilhelm Dilthey: The Critique of Historical Reason* (Chicago: University of Chicago Press, 1978), H. A. Hodges, *The Philosophy of Wilhelm Dilthey* (London: Routledge & Kegan Paul, 1952), and H. P. Rickman, *Wilhelm Dilthey: Pioneer of the Human Studies* (Berkeley: University of California Press, 1979). Many of his musical writings are assembled in *Von deutscher Dichtung und Musik: Aus den Studien zur Geschichte des deutschen Geistes*, ed. Herman Nohl and Georg Misch (Leipzig and Berlin: Teubner, 1933; reprint edn Stuttgart: Teubner, 1957). The central essay 'Das musikalische Verstehen' is available in translation in Bujić, 370–74, together with an essay on Mozart, 375–8.

The setting up of the Leipzig *Allgemeine musikalische Zeitung*, its commercial and publishing practices and its philosophical outlook during the first ten years (1798–1808) are treated in Martha Bruckner-Bigenwald, *Die Anfänge der Leipziger Allgemeinen musikalis-chen Zeitung* (Sibiu-Hermannstadt, 1938; reprint edn Hilversum: Knuf, 1965). Its founding editor as writer, historian and aesthetician is the subject of Hans Ehinger, *Friedrich Rochlitz als Musikschriftsteller* (Leipzig: B&H, 1929). On Kanne and other writers on music between 1800 and about 1820, including even E. T. A. Hoffmann, see Hartmut Krones, 'Rhetorik und rhetorische Symbolik in der Musik um 1800: Vom Weiterleben eines Princips', *Musiktheorie*, 3 (1988), 117–40, which discusses the roots of such writing in the Baroque rhetorical doctrine through the agency of Johann Nikolaus Forkel's work, and in the pre-Romantic view of instrumental music as dependent on words. On Beethoven criticism in the composer's lifetime, see Robin Wallace, *Beethoven's Critics: Aesthetic Dilemmas and Resolutions during the Composer's Lifetime* (Cambridge: CUP, 1986).

On E. T. A. Hoffmann, the complete Eng. trans. with introductory materials is *E. T. A. Hoffmann's Musical Writings: 'Kreisleriana', 'The Poet and the Composer', Music Criticism*, ed. David Charlton, trans. Martyn Clarke (Cambridge: CUP, 1989), which has extensive bibliography; and see also Dahlhaus, *The Idea of Absolute Music*, trans. Roger Lustig (Chicago: University of Chicago Press, 1989; Ger. orig. 1978), pp. 42–6. On the sublime, see Edmund Burke, *A Philosophical Enquiry into the Origin of our Ideas of the Sublime and the Beautiful* (London: Dodsley, 1757), ed. J. T. Boulton (London: Routledge & Paul, 1958), and Immanuel Kant, *Kritik der Urteilskraft* (Berlin and Libau: Lagarde und Friederich, 1790), Eng. trans. Werner S. Pluhar as *Critique of Judgment* (Indianapolis: Hackett, 1987); see excerpts le Huray/Day, 69–74, 214–29.

Many of Karl Franz Brendel's writings are to be found in the *NZM*. See in particular 'Die Aesthetik der Tonkunst', *NZM*, 46 (1857), 185–6, Eng. trans. in Bujić, 129–31. See also his *Geschichte der Musik in Italien, Deutschland und Frankreich von den ersten christlichen Zeiten bis auf die Gegenwart* (Leipzig: Hinze, 1852; reprint edn Vaduz/Liechtenstein: Sändig, 1985) and his *Die Musik der Gegenwart und die Gesammtkunst der Zukunft* (Leipzig: Hinze, 1854). On Kretzschmar, see §7 below.

Heidegger's *Sein und Zeit* (1927) is available in an English translation by John Macquarrie and Edward Robinson as *Being and Time* (New York: Harper & Row, 1962), and see also Michael Gelven, *A Commentary on Heidegger's 'Being and Time'* (New York: Harper & Row, 1970). Of Bultmann's many works, see the early work *Jesus* (1926) in English translation by Louise Pettibone Smith and E. Huntress as *Jesus and the Word* (New York: Scribner, 1934), and his later *Jesus Christ and Mythology* (New York: Scribner, 1958). For the 'Bultmann school' see James M. Robinson and John B. Cobb, *The New Hermeneutic* (New York: Harper Row, 1964).

The central work by Gadamer is *Wahrheit und Methode: Grundzüge einer philosophischen Hermeneutik* (Tübingen: Mohr, 1960, 3/1972), trans. Garret Barden and William G. Doerpel as *Truth and Method* (New York: Seabury, 1975). *Philosophical Hermeneutics*, ed. and trans. David. E. Linge (Berkeley: University of California Press, 1976) comprises a selection of his theoretical writings from 1960–72. As examples of his hermeneutic writings see *Hegel's Dialectic: Five Hermeneutical Studies*, and *Dialogue and Dialectic: Eight Hermeneutical Studies on Plato*, both edited and translated by P. Christopher Smith (New Haven: Yale University Press, 1976 and 1980).

The relevant works by Schering are *Beethoven in neuer Deutung*, vol. I (Leipzig: Kahnt, 1934) and *Beethoven und die Dichtung, mit einer Einleitung zur Geschichte und Ästhetik der Beethovendeutung* (Berlin: Junker und Dünnhaupt, 1936). See also *Vom Wesen der Musik: ausgewählte Aufsätze von Arnold Schering*, ed. Karl Michael Komma (Stuttgart: Koehler, 1974), notably the essays 'Musikalische Symbolkunde', pp. 98–119, 'Geschichtliches zur "Ars Inveniendi" in der Musik', pp. 120–34 and 'Musikalische Analyse und Wertidee', pp. 183–200. For his other writings see *NGDM*, and see also Bent/Drabkin, pp. 38–9.

Tovey's programme notes appeared as *Essays in Music Analysis* (London: Oxford University Press/Milford, 1935–9, 1944; reprint edn 1972), vols I *Symphonies ([I])* (1935); II

Symphonies (II), *Variations and Orchestral Polyphony* (1935); III *Concertos* (1936); IV *Illustrative Music* (1936); V *Vocal Music* (1937); VI *Supplementary Essays, Glossary and Index* (1939); VII *Chamber Music* (1944). See also his *A Companion to Beethoven's Pianoforte Sonatas (Bar-to-Bar Analysis)* (London: Associated Board, 1931; reprint edn 1976), his *Musical Articles from the Encyclopaedia Britannica* (London: Oxford University Press/ Milford, 1944), and *Beethoven* (London: Oxford University Press, 1965). See Joseph Kerman, 'A Profile for Musicology', *JAMS*, 18 (1965), 61–9, and correspondence, 222, 426. See Peter Kivy, *The Corded Shell: Reflections on Musical Expression* (Princeton: Princeton University Press, 1980). For a survey of developments in musical hermeneutics in the 1960s and 1970s, see Anthony Newcomb, 'Sound and Feeling', *Critical Inquiry*, 10 (1984), 614–43. Lawrence Kramer's two books are *Music and Poetry: The Nineteenth Century and After* and *Music as Cultural Practice, 1800–1900* (Berkeley: University of California Press, 1984 and 1990). See, further, *Music and Text: Critical Inquiries*, ed. Steven Paul Scher (Cambridge: CUP, 1992), pertinent among its excellent essays being Thomas Grey, 'Metaphorical Modes in Nineteenth-century Music Criticism: Image, Narrative, and Idea' (pp. 93–117), Anthony Newcomb, 'Narrative Archetypes and Mahler's Ninth Symhony' (pp. 118–36), Lawrence Kramer, 'Music and Representation: The Instance of Haydn's *Creation*' (pp. 139–62), Edward T. Cone, 'Poet's Love or Composer's Love?' (pp. 177–92), Ruth A. Solie, 'Whose Life? The Gendered Self in Schumann's *Frauenliebe* Songs' (pp. 219–40) and Hayden White's commentary (pp. 288–319). Of particular interest is Carolyn Abbate's investigation of narrative 'voice' in *Unsung Voices: Opera and Musical Narrative in the Nineteenth Century* (Princeton: Princeton University Press, 1991).

Part I Elucidatory analysis

Two fascinating books by George Steiner are *After Babel: Aspects of Language and Translation* (London: Oxford University Press, 1975), concerned with the nature of meaning and interpretation, and *Real Presences* (Chicago: Chicago University Press, 1989), which explores the relationship between the creative mode and the critical mode.

The series of concert guides published by Schlesinger, Reclam and others are footnoted in the text. On Sir George Grove, see Percy M. Young, *George Grove 1820–1900: a Biography* (London: Macmillan, 1980), especially the astonishing list of writings, pp. 299–313, and in particular Grove's *Beethoven and his Nine Symphonies* (London: Novello, 1896, 2/1896, 3/1898; reprint edn 1962), and the first edition of *Grove's Dictionary of Music and Musicians* (London: Macmillan, 1878–89). There were ten editions of Hanslick's *Vom Musikalisch-Schönen* (Leipzig: Weigel, 1854) in his lifetime, featuring many revisions; there have been two principal translations: *Eduard Hanslick: The Beautiful in Music*, trans. Gustav Cohen, ed. Morris Weitz (New York: Liberal Arts Press, 1957), from the seventh edition (1885), and *Eduard Hanslick: On the Musically Beautiful: A Contribution towards the Revision of the Aesthetics of Music*, trans. Geoffrey Payzant (Indianapolis: Hackett, 1986), from the eighth edition (1891). A study of one late nineteenth-century Viennese annotator, Robert Hirschfeld, appears in Leon Botstein, 'Music and Its Public: Habits of Listening and the Crisis of Musical Modernism in Vienna, 1870–1914' (PhD diss.: Harvard University, 1985), pp. 926–87 (Reading About Music: Program Notes and Concert Guides). For hermeneutic trends at the outset of the twentieth century, see Lee A. Rothfarb, 'The "New Education" and Music Theory, 1900–1925', in *Music Theory and the Exploration of the Past*, ed. Christopher Hatch and David W. Bernstein (Chicago: Chicago University Press, 1993), pp. 449–71, and *Ernst Kurth as Theorist and Analyst* (Philadelphia: University of Pennsylvania Press, 1988).

On Hauptmann and Riemann, see vol. I, Bibliographical Essay §§3 and 6. On Brendel and Dilthey, see above. On Kretzschmar, see §7 below.

On nineteenth-century aesthetics, see August Steinkrüger, *Die Ästhetik der Musik bei Schelling und Hegel: ein Beitrag zur Musikästhetik der Romantik* . . . (Bonn: Verein Studentenwohl, 1927); Georg Wilhelm Friedrich Hegel, *Ästhetik*, ed. Georg Lukács (Frankfurt: Europäische Vertragsanstalt, 2/1965); and two English translations, T. M. Knox (Oxford: Clarendon, 1975) as *Aesthetics: Lectures on Fine Art*, and F. P. M. Osmaston (London: Bell, 1920; reprint edn New York: Hacker Art Books, 1975) as *The Philosophy of Fine Art*; *Hegels Musikästhetik*, ed. Adolf Nowak, Studien zur Musikgeschichte des 19. Jahrhunderts, vol. XXV (Regensburg: Bosse, 1971); Friedrich Theodor Vischer, *Aesthetik oder Wissenschaft des Schönen* (Reutlingen: Macken, 1846–57, 2/1922). See also Carl Dahlhaus, *The Idea of Absolute Music* (Chicago: University of Chicago Press, 1989; Ger. orig. 1978), and *Analysis and Value Judgment*, Eng. trans. Sigmund Levarie (New York: Pendragon, 1983; Ger. orig. 1970).

1 Berlioz/Meyerbeer

For an inventory of Berlioz's critical writings, see *Hector Berlioz: New Edition of the Complete Works*, vol. XXV, *Catalogue of the Works of Hector Berlioz*, ed. D. Kern Holoman (Kassel: Bärenreiter, 1987), pp. 435–88 'Feuilletons'. There is no complete edition of the critical writings. Selections may be found in *Les grotesques de la musique* (Paris: Bourdilliat, 1859; reprint edn 1969); *À travers chants: études musicales, adorations, boutades et critiques* (Paris: Lévy, 1862; reprint edn Farnborough: Gregg, 1971), translated by E. Evans variously as *A Critical Study of Beethoven's Nine Symphonies* (London: Reeves, 1913), *Gluck and His Opera* (1915) and *Mozart, Weber and Wagner, with Various Essays on Musical Subjects* (1918); *Les musiciens et la musique*, ed. André Hallays (Paris: Calmann-Lévy, 1903); *Cauchemars et passions*, ed. Gérard Condé (Paris: J. C. Lattès, 1981). Other literary works include *Les soirées de l'orchestre* (Paris: Lévy, 1852; reprint edn 1968), Eng. trans. Jacques Barzun as *Evenings with the Orchestra* (New York: Knopf, 1956; reprint edn 1973), Eng. trans. C. R. Fortescue, ed. David Cairns, as *Evenings in the Orchestra* (Harmondsworth: Penguin, 1963); *Mémoires de Hector Berlioz* (Paris: Lévy, 1870; reprint edn Farnborough: Gregg, 1969), Eng. trans. and ed. David Cairns as *The Memoirs of Hector Berlioz* (London: Gollancz, 1969).

On Berlioz and criticism, see David Cairns, 'Berlioz and Criticism: Some Surviving Dodos', *Musical Times*, 104 (1963), 548–51; Henry Pleasants, 'Berlioz as Critic', *Stereo Review*, 23 (1969), 89; Robert Cohen, 'Berlioz on the Opéra (1829–1849): A Study in Music Criticism' (PhD diss.: New York University, 1973), and 'Hector Berlioz critique musical: ses écrits sur l'Opéra de Paris de 1829 à 1849', *Revue de musicologie*, 63 (1977), 17–34; Katherine Kolb-Reeve, 'Hector Berlioz (1803–1869)', in *European Writers*, vol. VI *The Romantic Century* (New York: Scribner, 1985), pp. 771–812, and 'The Poetics of the Orchestra in the Writings of Hector Berlioz' (PhD diss.: Yale University, 1978). For a translation of Berlioz's review of Rossini's *Guillaume Tell* (1834), see Strunk, *Source Readings*, pp. 808–26.

On Berlioz and Meyerbeer, see Jacques Barzun, 'Did Berlioz Really Like Meyerbeer?', *Opera*, 3 (1952), 719–25; Patrick Besnier, 'Berlioz et Meyerbeer', *Revue de musicologie*, 63 (1977), 35–40.

On Berlioz in general, see the excellent D. Kern Holoman, *Berlioz* (Cambridge, MA: Harvard University Press, 1989). See also Jacques Barzun, *Berlioz and the Romantic Century* (Boston: Little, Brown, 1950; New York: Columbia University Press, 3/1969). *Revue de musicologie*, 63/1–2 (1977) is devoted to Berlioz. See also Eric Gräbner, 'Berlioz and French Operatic Tradition' (PhD diss.: University of York, 1967).

On Meyerbeer's *Les Huguenots*, see W. L. Crosten, *French Grand Opera: An Art and a Business* (New York: King's Crown Press, 1948).

2. Wagner/Beethoven

Wagner's prose writings were collected, under Wagner's supervision, in *Gesammelte Schriften und Dichtungen von Richard Wagner*, vols I–X (Leipzig: Fritzsch, 1871–3, 1883; 2/1887, reprint edn 1976). The fifth edition, ed. Hans von Wolzogen and Richard Sternfeld, had two volumes added in 1911, and was retitled *Sämtliche Schriften und Dichtungen von Richard Wagner: Volks-Ausgabe* (Leipzig: B&H). The sixth edition, 1914, had four further volumes added, making sixteen in all. The second edition, 1887, was translated into English by William Ashton Ellis as *Richard Wagner's Prose Works*, in eight volumes (London: Routledge, 1892–9; reprint edn New York: Broude, 1966; 2/1895, 1900, vols. I–II only). A good translation of some of Wagner's early writings is *Wagner Writes from Paris: Stories, Essays and Articles by the Young Composer*, ed. Robert Jacobs and Geoffrey Skelton (London: Allen & Unwin, 1973), and of the essays 'Music of the Future', 'On Conducting', and 'On Performing Beethoven's Ninth Symphony', *Three Wagner Essays*, trans. Robert Jacobs (London: Eulenberg, 1979).

On Wagner, see Ernest Newman, *The Life of Richard Wagner*, in four volumes (London: Cassell, 1933–47; reprint edn 1976); Curt von Westernhagen, *Wagner: A Biography*, Eng. trans. Mary Whittall (Cambridge: CUP, 1979; Ger. orig. 1968); Brian Magee, *Aspects of Wagner* (London: Ross, 1968, rev. 2/1972); Edward A. Lippmann, 'The Esthetic Theories of Richard Wagner', *The Musical Quarterly*, 44 (1958), 209–20; John Deathridge and Carl Dahlhaus, *The New Grove Wagner* (London: Macmillan, 1984). On Wagner and Beethoven, see Amanda Glauert, 'The Double Perspective in Beethoven's Opus 131', *19th-Century Music*, 4 (1980/81), 113–20; and *Wagner and Beethoven: Richard Wagner's Reception of Beethoven*, ed. Klaus Kropfinger (Cambridge: CUP, 1991; Ger. orig. 1975).

On the reception and criticism of Beethoven's Ninth Symphony there is a large literature. See in particular David B. Levy, 'Early Performances of Beethoven's Ninth Symphony: A Documentary Study of Five Cities' (PhD diss.: Eastman School of Music, 1980); Leo Treitler, 'History, Criticism, and Beethoven's Ninth Symphony', *19th-Century Music*, 3 (1979/80), 193–210, repr. in his *Music and the Historical Imagination* (Cambridge, MA: Harvard University Press, 1989), pp. 19–45; Leo Treitler, '"To Worship that Celestial Sound": Motives for Analysis', *Journal of Musicology*, 1 (1982), 153–70; Wallace, *Beethoven's Critics*, pp. 73–92; Maynard Solomon, 'Beethoven's Ninth Symphony: A Search for Order', *19th-Century Music*, 10 (1986/7), 3–23.

3. Von Lenz/Beethoven

See Joseph Kerman's fine Foreword to *Beethoven et ses trois styles*, new edn, ed. M. D. Calvocoressi (Paris: Legouix, 1909; reprint edn New York: Da Capo, 1980), pp. v–xiv; also Ernest Newman, 'Wilhelm von Lenz', *Music & Letters*, 8 (1927), 268–72; Joseph Kerman and Alan Tyson, 'Beethoven', §11 'The "Three Periods"', in *NGDM*, and *The New Grove Beethoven*, pp. 89–91. On the Romantic reception of Beethoven, see Arnold Schmitz, *Das romantische Beethovenbild* (Berlin and Bonn: Dümmler, 1927; reprint edn 1978); Jean Boyer, *Le "romantisme" de Beethoven* (Paris: Didier, 1938); Leo Schrade, *Beethoven in France: The Growth of an Idea* (New Haven: Yale University Press, 1942); William S. Newman, 'Some 19th-Century Consequences of Beethoven's "Hammerklavier" Sonata, Opus 106', *The Piano Quarterly*, no. 67 (Spring 1969), 12–18, no. 68 (Summer

1969), 12–16; Hans Heinrich Eggebrecht, *Zur Geschichte der Beethoven-Rezeption – Beethoven 1970* (Wiesbaden: Steiner, 1972); William S. Newman, 'The Beethoven Mystique in Romantic Art, Literature, and Music', *The Musical Quarterly*, 69 (1983), 354–87.

4. *Von Elterlein/Beethoven*

There is no literature on von Elterlein. See §§2 and 3 above on the Romantic reception of Beethoven. On the *Appassionata* Sonata, see Maximilian Hohenegger, *Beethovens Sonata appassionata op. 57 im Lichte verschiedener Analysemethoden* (Frankfurt: Peter Lang, 1992), which includes a bibliography of writings on the sonata, a history of hermeneutic and structural analyses and comparative study of different analytical methods.

5. *Spitta/Bach*

Spitta's *Johann Sebastian Bach*, in two volumes (Leipzig: B&H, 1873–80; reprint edn 1964), was translated into English by Clara Bell and J. A. Fuller Maitland, in three volumes (London: Novello, 1884–99; reprint edn 1951). Other important works by Spitta are *Ein Lebensbild Robert Schumanns* (Leipzig: B&H, 1882), *Zur Musik* (Berlin: Paetel, 1892; reprint edn 1975) and *Musikgeschichtliche Aufsätze* (Berlin: Paetel, 1894). He was editor of the organ works of Buxtehude, in two volumes (1876–7), and the complete works of Heinrich Schütz, in sixteen volumes (1885–94), and of Frederick of Prussia, in four volumes (1889), and co-editor of the complete works of Mozart, in twenty-four volumes (1877–87).

   On Spitta and his work, see H. Reimann, *Philipp Spitta und seine Bach-Biographie* (Berlin, 1900); Willibald Gurlitt, 'Der Musikhistoriker Philipp Spitta', *Musik und Kirche*, 14 (1942), 27ff; Friedrich Blume, *Johann Sebastian Bach im Wandel der Geschichte* (Kassel: Bärenreiter, 1947).

   On the Bach gamba sonatas, see Hanns Epstein, 'Über die Beziehungen zwischen Konzert und Sonate bei Johann Sebastian Bach', *Bach-Studien*, 6 (Leipzig: VEB, 1981), 87–93; Christoph Wolff, 'Bach's Leipzig Chamber Music', *Early Music*, 13 (1985), 165–75; Laurence Dreyfus, 'J. S. Bach and the Status of Genre: Problems of Style in the G-minor Sonata BWV 1029', *Journal of Musicology*, 5 (1987), 55–78. See also the edition (1984) and Critical Report (1989) by Hanns Epstein in the *Neue Bach-Ausgabe*; and the edition by Lucy Robinson, with report by John Butt (London: Faber, 1987).

6. *Von Wolzogen/Wagner*

Von Wolzogen's principal writings on Wagner are *Die Tragödie in Bayreuth und ihr Satyrspiel* (Leipzig: Schloemp, 1876); *Thematischer Leitfaden durch die Musik zu Richard Wagner's Festspiel 'Der Ring des Nibelungen'* (Leipzig: Schloemp, 1876), Eng. trans. N. H. Dole as *Guide to the Music of Richard Wagner's Tetralogy 'The Ring of the Nibelung': A Thematic Key* (New York: Schirmer, 1895); *Die Sprache in Wagners Dichtungen* (Leipzig: Reinboth, 1878); *Thematischer Leitfaden durch die Musik zu Richard Wagner's 'Tristan und Isolde'* (Leipzig: Schloemp, 1880), Eng. trans. as *Guide through the Musical Motives of Richard Wagner's 'Tristan and Isolde'* (New York: Schirmer, [1889]); *Thematischer Leitfaden durch die Musik zu Richard Wagner's 'Parsifal'* (Leipzig: Senf, 1882), Eng. trans. J. H. Cornell, as *Thematic Guide through the Music of 'Parsifal'* (New York: Schirmer, 1891); *Erinnerungen an Richard Wagner* (Vienna: Konegen, 1883); 'Leitmotive', *Bayreuther Blätter*, 20 (1897), 313–30.

   On Wagner's music dramas (see also §2 above), see Jack M. Stein, *Richard Wagner and the Synthesis of the Arts* (Detroit: Wayne University Press, 1960; reprint edn 1973);

Carl Dahlhaus, *Richard Wagners Musikdramen* (Velber: Friedrich Verlag, 1971), Eng. trans. Mary Whittall as *Richard Wagner's Music Dramas* (Cambridge: CUP, 1979); Carolyn Abbate, *Unsung Voices: Opera and Musical Narrative in the Nineteenth Century* (Princeton: Princeton University Press, 1991). On *Parsifal*, see Ernest Newman, *Wagner Nights* (London: Putnam, 1949; reprint edns 1961, 1977), pp. 670–764; *Kobbe's Complete Opera Book*, ed. and rev. The Earl of Harewood (London: Putnam, 9/1976), pp. 316–32; *Richard Wagner: Parsifal*, ed. Lucy Beckett (Cambridge: CUP, 1981); William Kinderman, 'Wagner's "Parsifal": Musical Form and the Drama of Redemption', *Journal of Musicology*, 4 (1986), 431–46.

7. Kretzschmar/Bruckner

Kretzschmar's essays are collectively available in *Gesammelte Aufsätze über Musik und Anderes* (Leipzig: C. F. Peters; reprint edn, 1973), vols. I *Gesammelte Aufsätze über Musik aus den Grenzboten* (1910); II *Gesammelte Aufsätze aus den Jahrbüchern der Musikbibliothek Peters* (1911); III *Gesammelte Aufsätze über Musik aus dem Verlag Breitkopf und Härtel* [never pubd?]. See in particular Bujić, 114–20. See also Werner Braun, 'Kretzschmars Hermeneutik' and Tibor Kneif, 'Musikalische Hermeneutik, musikalische Semiotik', in *Beiträge zur musikalischen Hermeneutik*, ed. Carl Dahlhaus (Regensburg: Bosse, 1975), pp. 33–9 and 63–71.

Kretzschmar's other writings include *Musikalische Zeitfragen* (Leipzig: Peters, 1903), *Geschichte des neuen deutschen Liedes* (Leipzig: B&H, 1911; reprint edn 1966), *Geschichte der Oper* (Leipzig: B&H, 1919; reprint edn 1970), *Einführung in die Musikgeschichte* (Leipzig: B&H, 1920; reprint edn 1970).

Insight into Kretzschmar's analytical strategies, and comparison (generally unfavourable) with the descriptive strategies of contemporary Robert Hirschfeld, appears in Leon Botstein, 'Music and Its Public', pp. 964–84.

Part II : Objective–subjective analysis

For Lobe, see vol. I Bibliographical essay §12. On hermeneutics and the hermeneutic circle, see the General Introduction of this Bibliographical Essay, above.

8. Momigny/Haydn

The authoritative work on Momigny is Albert Palm, *Jérôme-Joseph de Momigny: Leben und Werk: ein Beitrag zur Geschichte der Musiktheorie im 19. Jahrhundert* (Cologne: Volk, 1969). On Momigny's *Cours complet*, see Birgitte P. Moyer, 'Concepts of Musical Form in the Nineteenth Century with Special Reference to A. B. Marx and Sonata Form' (PhD diss.: Stanford University, 1969), pp. 30–35, 250–55; Renate Groth, *Die französische Kompositionslehre des 19. Jahrhunderts* (Wiesbaden: Steiner, 1983), pp. 88–90, 165–6, 192–6; Bent/ Drabkin, *Analysis*, pp. 20–25; Ian Bent, 'Momigny's "Type de la Musique" and a Treatise in the Making', in *Music Theory and the Exploration of the Past*, ed. Christopher Hatch and David W. Bernstein (Chicago: Chicago University Press, 1993), pp. 309–40).

On Momigny as analyst, see Palm, 'Mozart und Haydn in der Interpretation Momignys', in *Gesellschaft für Musikforschung: Kongressbericht: Kassel 1962* (1963), pp. 187–90, 'Mozarts Streichquartett D-moll, KV 421, in der Interpretation Momignys', *Mozart-Jahrbuch 1962/63* (1964), 256–79, and 'Unbekannte Haydn-Analysen', *Haydn-Jahrbuch*, 4 (1968), 169–94. On the present analysis see Malcolm S. Cole, 'Momigny's Analysis of Haydn's Symphony No. 103', *Music Review*, 30 (1969), 261–84; Mark Evan Bonds, *Wordless Rhetoric: Musical Form and the Metaphor of the Oration* (Cambridge, MA: Harvard University Press, 1991), pp. 134–8, 171–4.

9. Hoffmann/Beethoven

The authoritative English edition is *E. T. A. Hoffmann's Musical Writings: 'Kreisleriana',* *'The Poet and the Composer', Music Criticism*, ed. David Charlton, trans. Martyn Clarke (Cambridge: CUP, 1989). The standard German edition is *E. T. A. Hoffmann: Schriften zur Musik: Nachlese*, ed. Friedrich Schnapp (Munich: Winkler, 1963, 2/1978). For a selection of important essays on the Fifth Symphony, including that of Hoffmann, see *Ludwig van Beethoven: Symphony No. 5 in C Minor: An Authoritative Score, The Sketches, Historical Background, Analysis, Views and Comments*, Norton Critical Score, ed. Elliot Forbes (New York: Norton, 1971), pp. 143–200.

Two books of interest are Harvey W. Hewett-Thayer, *E. T. A. Hoffmann: Author of the Tales* (Princeton: Princeton University Press, 1948; reprint edn New York: Octagon Books, 1971), and R. Murray Schafer, *E. T. A. Hoffmann and Music* (Toronto: University of Toronto Press, 1975). See also Klaus Kropfinger, 'Der musikalische Strukturbegriff bei E. T. A. Hoffmann', in *Bericht über den internationalen musikwissenschaftlichen Kongress Bonn 1970* (Kassel: Bärenreiter, 1973), pp. 480–82; Eric Sams, 'E. T. A. Hoffmann, 1776–1822', *Musical Times*, 117 (1976), 29–32. *19th-Century Music*, 5, no. 3 (Spring 1982) is largely devoted to E. T. A. Hoffmann and music. Hoffmann's criticisms of Beethoven, and interaction with his contemporary critics, are excellently described in Wallace, *Beethoven's Critics*, pp. 20–35, 129–40. A penetrating study of language in Hoffmann's Beethoven criticism is Peter Schnaus, *E. T. A. Hoffmann als Beethoven-Rezensent der Allgemeinen musikalischen Zeitung* (Munich-Salzburg: Katzbichler, 1977). On Hoffmann's writing as rooted in Baroque rhetorical doctrine, see Hartmut Krones, 'Rhetorik und rhetorische Symbolik in der Musik um 1800: Vom Weiterleben eines Prinzips', *Musiktheorie*, 3 (1988), 117–40. See also Matthias Brzoska, 'Das "Anscheinende" der "Willkür": E. T. A. Hoffmanns Es-Dur-Symphonie und seine Beethoven-Deutung', ibid, 141–55. The Fifth Symphony analysis is examined as 'a hermeneutic model' in Carl Dahlhaus, *The Idea of Absolute Music*, trans. Roger Lustig (Chicago: University of Chicago Press, 1989; Ger. orig. 1978), pp. 42–6; see also Beck, *Methoden der Werkanalyse*, pp. 60–70.

10. Schumann/Berlioz

No complete English edition of Schumann's writings on music exists. Selections include *Robert Schumann on Music and Musicians*, trans. Fanny Ritter Raymond (London: Reeves, n.d.); *Robert Schumann on Music and Musicians*, trans. Paul Rosenfeld, ed. Konrad Wolff (London: Dobson, 1947); *The Musical World of Robert Schumann: A Selection from His Own Writings*, ed. Henry Pleasants (London: Camelot Press, 1965; reprint edn New York: Dover, 1988). The complete German edition, first compiled by Schumann himself in 1852–3, then edited by F. Gustav Jansen in 1891, and subsequently edited by Martin Kreisig, is the two-volume *Gesammelte Schriften über Musik und Musiker von Robert Schumann* (Leipzig: B&H, 5/1949). For a selection of important essays on the *Symphonie Fantastique*, including that of Schumann, see *Berlioz: Fantastic Symphony: An Authoritative Score, Historical Background, Analysis, Views and Comments*, Norton Critical Score, ed. Edward T. Cone (New York: Norton, 1971), pp. 215–301.

The authoritative study of Schumann's critical activity is Leon Plantinga, *Schumann as Critic* (New Haven: Yale University Press, 1967; reprint edn 1977). Relevant to his critical writings are Edward A. Lippman, 'Theory and Practice in Schumann's Aesthetics', *JAMS*, 17 (1964), 310–45; Leon Plantinga, 'Schumann's View of Romantic', *The Musical Quarterly*, 52 (1966), 221–32; Eric Sams, 'Why Florestan and Eusebius?', *Musical Times*, 108 (1967),

131–4; Thomas A. Brown, *The Aesthetics of Robert Schumann* (New York: Philosophical Library, 1968); Leon Plantinga, 'Schumann and the "Neue Zeitschrift für Musik"', and Henry Pleasants, 'Schumann the Critic', in *Robert Schumann: The Man and His Music*, ed. Alan Walker (London: Barrie & Jenkins, 1972, 2/1976), pp. 162–78, 179–87; Anthony Newcomb, 'Schumann and Late Eighteenth-Century Narrative Strategies', *19th-Century Music*, 11 (1987/8), 164–74. See also le Huray/Day, 489–91; Beck, *Methoden der Werkanalyse*, pp. 70–83.

11. Basevi/Verdi

Literature on Basevi is sparse. See Andrea Della Corte, *La critica musicale e i critici* (Turin: Unione tipographico, 1961), pp. 481–3; A. Pironti, 'Basevi, Abramo', in *Dizionario biografico degli italiani* (1960–), vol. VII (1965), pp. 67–8; Bea Friedland, 'Italy's Ottocento: Notes from the Musical Underground', *The Musical Quarterly*, 56 (1970), 37–53. Harold S. Powers deploys Basevi's statements of principle and analytical observations in his own structural analyses of Verdi's operas: 'By Design: The Architecture of "Simon Boccanegra"', *Opera News*, 49/7 (22 December 1984), 16–21, 42–3, '"La solita forma" and "The Uses of Convention"', *Acta musicologica*, 59 (1987), 65–90, and '"Simon Boccanegra" I.10–12: A Generic–Genetic Analysis of the Council Chamber Scene', *19th-Century Music*, 13 (1989/90), 101–128.

12. Marx/Beethoven

Marx's writings, influential long after his time as they were, do not figure in the anthologies of Strunk, le Huray/Day, Bujić or Lippman, or in Katz and Dahlhaus. Although almost universally alluded to by historians and theorists of history, he has rarely been discussed in depth, and a revaluation of his work is due. Moreover, few of his writings have been translated into English: only vol. I of *Die Lehre von der musikalischen Komposition* (by Saroni c.1851 and Wehrhan in 1852), his book of musical rudiments, *Allgemeine Musiklehre* (by Wehrhan in 1853 and Macirone, n.d.), his *Die Musik des neunzehnten Jarhhunderts* (by Wehrhan in 1855) and the *Anleitung zum Vortrag Beethovenscher Klavierwerke* (by Gwinner in 1895).

On Marx variously as theorist, critic and analyst, see Arnfried Edler, 'Zur Musikanschauung von Adolf Bernhard Marx', and Helmuth Kirchmeyer, 'Ein Kapitel Adolf Bernhard Marx: Über Sendungsbewusstsein und Bildungsstand der Berliner Musikkritik zwischen 1824 und 1830', in *Beiträge zur Geschichte der Musikanschauung im 19. Jahrhundert*, ed. W. Salmen (Regensburg: Bosse, 1965), pp. 103–112, 73–101; Kurt-Erich Eicke, *Der Streit zwischen A. B. Marx und G. W. Fink um die Kompositionslehre* (Regensburg: Bosse, 1966); Arno Forchert, 'Adolf Bernhard Marx und seine *Berliner Allgemeine musikalische Zeitung*', in *Studien zur Musikgeschichte Berlins im frühen 19. Jahrhundert*, ed. Carl Dahlhaus (Regensburg: Bosse, 1980), pp. 381–404; Wallace, *Beethoven's Critics*, pp. 45–64, 126–43; Scott Burnham, 'Aesthetics, Theory and History in the Works of Adolph Bernhard Marx' (PhD diss.: Brandeis University, 1988), and 'Criticism, Faith, and the *Idee*: A. B. Marx's Early Reception of Beethoven', *19th-Century Music*, 13 (1989/90), 183–92; Bonds, *Wordless Rhetoric*, pp. 154–6, 159–60. On the educational background in Germany, see *Anfänge institutioneller Musikerziehung in Deutschland (1800–1843): Pläne, Realisierung und zeitgenössische Kritik . . .*, ed. Georg Sowa, vol. XXXIII of Studien zur Musikgeschichte des 19. Jahrhunderts (Regensburg: Bosse, 1973).

On Marx's view of musical form, see Birgitte Moyer, 'Concepts of Musical Form'; Carl Dahlhaus, 'Formenlehre und Gattungstheorie bei A. B. Marx', in *Heinrich Sievers zum 70. Geburtstag*, ed. Richard Jakoby and Günter Katzenberger (Tutzing: Schneider, 1978), pp. 29–35, and 'Aesthetische Prämissen der "Sonatenform" bei Adolf Bernhard Marx', *Archiv für Musikwissenschaft*, 41 (1984), 73.

A reader containing translations of important passages from Marx's *Die alte Musiklehre*, his manual of composition, his Beethoven study and other material, is forthcoming as *Music and Spirit: Selected Writings of Adolf Bernhard Marx*, ed. Scott Burnham (Cambridge: CUP).

On the reception and criticism of Beethoven's Ninth Symphony see §2 above.

13. Helm/Beethoven

Theodor Helm is a neglected figure. See M. Ungar, 'Zwei Jubilare: Theodor Helm und Max Kalbeck', *Neue Zeitschrift für Musik*, 87 (1920), 2–4.

On Beethoven's String Quartet Op. 132, see Deryck Cooke, 'The Unity of Beethoven's Late Quartets', *Music Review*, 24 (1963), 30–49; Philip Radcliffe, *Beethoven's String Quartets* (London: Hutchinson, 1965; reprint edn 1978); Joseph Kerman, *The Beethoven Quartets* (New York: Knopf, 1967); Harold Truscott, *Beethoven's Late String Quartets* (London: Dobson, 1968); Sieghard Brandenburg, 'The Autograph of Beethoven's String Quartet in A minor, Opus 132', in *The Quartets of Haydn, Mozart, and Beethoven*, ed. Christoph Wolff (Cambridge, MA: Harvard University Press, 1980), pp. 278–301, and 'The Historical Background to the "Heiliger Dankgesang" in Beethoven's A-minor Quartet, op. 132', in *Beethoven Studies*, vol. III, ed. Alan Tyson (Cambridge: CUP, 1982), pp. 161–91; Robin Wallace, 'Background and Expression in the First Movement of Beethoven's Op. 132', *Journal of Musicology*, 7 (1989), 3–20.

Index to Volumes I and II

Lightning Source UK Ltd.
Milton Keynes UK
UKOW07f0438121016

285074UK00006B/236/P

9 780521 673471